Henry Crossley Irwin

The Garden of India; or, Chapters on Oudh History and Affairs

Henry Crossley Irwin

The Garden of India; or, Chapters on Oudh History and Affairs

ISBN/EAN: 9783337081935

Printed in Europe, USA, Canada, Australia, Japan

Cover: Foto ©ninafisch / pixelio.de

More available books at **www.hansebooks.com**

THE GARDEN OF INDIA.

THE

GARDEN OF INDIA;

OR

CHAPTERS ON OUDH HISTORY AND AFFAIRS.

BY

H. C. IRWIN, B.A. Oxon., B.C.S.

LONDON:
W. H. ALLEN & CO., 13 WATERLOO PLACE.
PUBLISHERS TO THE INDIA OFFICE.

1880.

(All rights reserved.)

LONDON:
PRINTED BY W. H. ALLEN AND CO., 13 WATERLOO PLACE, S.W.

TO
MY BROTHER OFFICERS OF THE OUDH COMMISSION
I BEG LEAVE
TO INSCRIBE THIS LITTLE BOOK
WITH A PROFOUND SENSE OF ITS MANY DEFICIENCIES
BUT IN THE HOPE THAT
HOWEVER WIDELY SOME OF THEM MAY DISSENT FROM
NOT A FEW OF THE OPINIONS I HAVE VENTURED TO EXPRESS
THEY WILL AT LEAST BELIEVE
THAT THESE ARE INSPIRED BY A SINCERE LOVE
OF THE PROVINCE AND THE PEOPLE
WHOSE WELFARE WE HAVE
ALL ALIKE AT HEART.

> "Garden of India! fading flower!
>   Withers thy bosom fair;
>   State, upstart, usurer devour
>   What frost, flood, famine spare."
>
> A. H. H.

> "Ce que [nous voulons] c'est que le pauvre, relevé de sa longue déchéance, cesse de trainer avec douleur ses chaines heréditaires, d'être un pur instrument de travail, une simple matière exploitable . . . . . . Tout effort qui ne produirait pas ce résultat serait stérile; toute réforme dans les choses présentes qui n'aboutirait point à cette réforme fondamentale serait dérisoire et vaine."
>
> *Lamennais.*

> "Malheur aux résignés d'anjourd'hui!"
>
> *George Sand.*

> "The dumb dread people that sat
>   All night without screen for the night,
>   All day without food for the day,
> They shall give not their harvest away,
> They shall eat of its fruit and wax fat:
>   They shall see the desire of their sight,
> Though the ways of the seasons be steep,
>   They shall climb with face to the light,
> Put in the sickles and reap."
>
> *A. C. Swinburne.*

CONTENTS.

	PAGE
CHAPTER I.—A Bird's-eye View	1
CHAPTER II.—A few Facts and Figures	16
CHAPTER III.—Early Oudh History and Legend	62
CHAPTER IV.—The Nawabi [1720-1856]	77
CHAPTER V.—Annexation	156
CHAPTER VI.—Fifteen Months of Zami'ndari' Policy [1856-1857]	178
CHAPTER VII.—Ten Years of Taluqda'ri' Policy [1858-1868]	191
CHAPTER VIII.—Conclusions	297

THE GARDEN OF INDIA.

CHAPTER I.

A BIRD'S-EYE VIEW.

If the reader were gifted with telescopic powers of vision, and could take his stand at sunrise some bright morning in early April on a certain wind-swept hill-side, almost exactly 82° E. longitude and 23° N. latitude, which is very vividly present before my mind's eye at this moment, he would see before him, sloping gently southward to the Ganges, the great plain of Oudh. Behind him would rise in green, tumbled masses the pine-clad hills of Naipál, shutting out the distant glories of the snowy range. At his feet, and stretching far away on either hand to east and west, he would see a broad belt of primæval forest—the shrunken remnant of that mighty wood, the great Gandharb Ban, which once covered the country north of the Sarjú river up to the hills—intersected by a gleaming line where the waters of the Rápti glisten brightly in the morning sunlight. Here only in Oudh may still be tasted, though in diminished measure, the indescribable charm, which no one who has once known it can ever forget, of the wild, free, irresponsible life of the forest.

Life has not many better things to offer in the way of purely natural pleasure than it bestows on a hard-working

Anglo-Indian who, having fairly earned a month of holiday by eleven months of honest toil in court-house or in tent, can resort to these happy hunting-grounds, and abandon himself for a season to the bliss of an existence such as Browning has sung of in " Saul " :—

> "Oh, the wild joys of living! the leaping from rock up to rock,
>   The strong rending of boughs from the fir tree, the cool silver shock
>   Of the plunge in a pool's living water, the hunt of the bear,
>   And the sultriness showing the [tiger] is couched in his lair."

Think of the awakening in the early twilight from such slumber as only a couch in the forest, after a long day in the howdah, can afford, to see the morning star growing pale in the green sky before the gathering flush of the dawn, and to taste in anticipation the coming bliss of a long, objective, irresponsible day! Think, next, of the exquisite plunge into the blue dancing ripples of the river, as it comes racing down from the hills over tree trunk and boulder! Hard to believe that it is the same stream whose steady murmur lulled us to sleep overnight, as we lay with half-closed eyes watching it shimmering past in the starlight. Strike out boldly, and lend yourself without fear to the cool fresh embrace of its mimic waves. No dread of crocodiles here to mar your rapture as you

> "Try the water with delighted limbs."

Lower down the stream the elephants are enjoying to the uttermost their morning bath, lying stretched out in uncouth *abandon*, and uttering subdued grunts and squeals of delight, while their mahouts clamber about their huge persons, and scrub their rugged hides. Then come the saunter through the camp, the inspection of the horses, and the *alfresco* breakfast, followed by the arrival of the wise old *shikári* who went out overnight, and has now returned with sure *khabar* of a tiger's whereabouts. Then the long slow march of elephants in line, winding their way to the distant cover, through deep forest glades where the spotted deer scurry away unscathed by random bullet, skirting noble streams wooded to the water's edge, crossing rugged ravines and sandy nullahs, over broad grassy plains with no sign of human presence save, at wide intervals, the gipsy camp, or the frail hut of the catechu gatherer, or the wandering herdsman with his buffaloes.

And when the great swamp is reached, and the beat has begun, and every howdah is swaying to and fro like a ship at sea, as the labouring elephant ploughs his oozy way through the tall crackling reeds, in whose cool wet depths the jungle king lies dreaming of that succulent young heifer, the remains of whose tell-tale carcase are still lying not three hundred yards off—why, then, you must indeed be *blasé* if your heart does not beat quickly and your blood tingle as you grasp your favourite old smooth-bore and lean forward, eager to catch the first glimpse of the black and tawny stripes. And when the mighty game is afoot, and the low wooded hills all round echo to the quick peals of volleying thunder, the smoke of which hangs heavily among the reed-tops, and after a mad charge among the elephants that scatters half of them to right and left like rabbits, the great cat sinks with a sullen roar, never to rise again, and when—but, ah, well! We must not linger too long over the pleasant memories of this "simple and violent" life, for it is with far other scenes, for the most part, and with other modes of being, that we have to deal in the pages that are to come. So let us transfer ourselves back to our perch on the breezy hill-side, and look forth again, resolutely dismissing all thought of the forest and its charms, or retaining them only as a cool green back-ground to the dusty, quivering heat and stress of the great panorama beyond.

There it lies, the great plain! with its dim myriad memories dating back from before the earliest dawn of history, ancient home of strange long-forgotten dynasties of aboriginal husbandmen, or Scythian nomads "ranging trackless fields," who here lived out their rude anarchic lives for many a slow far-off century, before the inroads of the Rájpút hordes from the north and west, followed hard by the pursuing armies of Islám, crushed their weaker organisations, and made them bondsmen and herdsmen and hewers of wood and drawers of water, unto this day. There it lies, the great plain! a land of narrow fields and wide rivers, of open barren tracts, and great single trees, and dense mango groves, of jungle patches, and shallow reedy lakes, and dry watercourses, and rugged ravines worn by the rushing rain-torrents.

And what sort of life is it, you may ask, that is led by the scantily clad, dusky dwellers in those groups of mud-built, thatch-roofed, creeper-covered houses that dot the country so thickly—the men who are irrigating their fields from tank and channel, the children herding cattle on the bare-looking grazing-grounds, the women with their water vessels clustering round the village well? And it must, I fear, be answered that theirs is, for the most part, a dim, slowly moving, and too often a poverty-stricken and hunger-bitten life, a life of small observances and petty superstitions, a narrow round of struggle with the rent-collector and the village usurer, enlivened only by the rare excitement of a marriage-feast, or a pilgrimage to some quasi-religious fair. They are a much-enduring, little-complaining race, these earth-tillers, "men to much misery and hardship born," who, blessed indeed in that they expect little, yet even of that little too often disappointed, wear away their lives from hand to mouth and year to year,

> "Muttering across the barley bread
> In daily toil and drearihead."

This is not a pleasant sketch of the condition of the rural masses of Oudh, but I do not think that it is, so far as it goes, an unfaithful one, or drawn in too sombre colours. "Tales of rustic happiness," as Coleridge has told us, are too often but

> "Pernicious tales, insidious strains,
> That steel the rich man's breast,
> And mock the lot unblest,
> The sordid vices and the abject pains,
> That evermore must be
> The doom of ignorance and penury."

That, however, the poorer, *i.e.* the great majority of the peasantry are, as a rule, consciously or acutely miserable, may be safely denied ; and this is, perhaps, the most consolatory reflection which a study of their condition can suggest. They are fortified against suffering by the most effective of all anæsthetics, that of never having known anything much better than their present lot. Were it not so, however, were they really as wretched as they apparently *ought* to be, the day of their deliverance might, perhaps, be more nearly at hand than it is. For it is a truth of very wide application that the main agent in the world's working is pain. In the history of every people, it has been said, there is a stage of transition between barbarism and civilisation, which always seems more bleakly miserable than either. This stage has not yet been fully entered on by the mass of the Oudh peasantry.

These masses, however, are by no means the whole of the rural population. In spite of their preponderating numbers, they are what in England would be called a *residuum*. There still exists in Oudh a peasant aristocracy, a class of yeomen, consisting of high-caste Hindús with a sprinkling of Musalmáns, many of the latter being converts from Hindúism, and retaining most of the characteristics of their ancient faith. These are further removed, as a rule, from actual want of food and clothing than the ordinary low-caste cultivators, and far less bovine and unconscious of their condition, far more keenly alive to its disadvantages, and less inclined to accept the situation as it is, capable of higher pleasures, and exposed to keener pains. With their fine physique, and still retaining much of their old high and turbulent spirit, passionately clinging to the remnants of their rights in the soil, at ceaseless war with the rent court and the rent-collector, these are the men to whom the task of administration owes much of its difficulty, and still more, perhaps, of its interest. If they are hard to govern, they are worth governing. And it may, perhaps, be not unfairly said that the interest which they have for us is their own, but that the difficulties which we find in governing them are mainly of our creation. For we have here no ardent aspirations for national independence, no enthusiastic hostility to contend against. The Oudh yeoman can hardly be said to have a political consciousness. What he does beyond all question care for, what he is often ready to give his own life, or take the lives of others, in order to retain, is his land, or the land which once was his. *Cæteris paribus*—a large assumption—he would, as an individual, doubtless prefer to be ruled by a government of his own race and creed. But the effective force of his preference is so slight, and his power of combination with any larger number of his fellows than are to be found in the immediate neighbourhood of his own village so small, that no government which secured him in the undisturbed possession of his fields at a light rent, and in most other respects left him to himself, would have anything whatever to fear from him.

His desires can hardly be called immoderate. They include a mud-walled house, roofed with tiles or thatch, such as might be built for Rs. 50 or 60; a couple of pounds of flour daily, with a modicum of oil and spices, for his own consumption, and for his wife and children in proportion, say 8 lbs. for an average household; a moderate wardrobe for himself and his family, of which the prime cost might be from Rs. 40 to 50; half-a-dozen brass waterpots and cooking dishes; two or three yoke of bullocks, worth from Rs. 20 to 50 a yoke; a milch buffalo, a few rude agricultural implements, a ploughman whom he feeds and clothes at a cost of Rs. 18 or 20 a year, and who is often a hereditary serf, and, perhaps, an ambling cow-hocked pony which would be dear at Rs. 10—such or something not very unlike it, is his notion of comfort. He wants, in fact, a stock of possessions worth from Rs. 300 to 400, and an income, after his rent is paid, of from Rs. 150 to 200 a year. An Oudh yeoman thus endowed would be considered well-to-do, or, as he himself would phrase it, *khúsh*. In addition to this, custom demands that he should be able to spend something like a year's income on the marriage of each of his daughters, a feat which he rarely accomplishes without getting into debt. This is, no doubt, reprehensible, but considering that it is the only extravagance of his life, and that it is enforced by a rigorous *dastúr*, of the stringency of which it is difficult for a non-

Asiatic mind to form an adequate conception, it may perhaps be forgiven him. Let the opinion of the Dakkhan Riots Commission be noted to the effect that "undue prominence has been given to the expenditure on marriage and other festivals as a cause of the ryot's indebtedness. The expenditure on such occasions may undoubtedly be called extravagant when compared with the ryot's means; but the occasions occur seldom, and probably in a course of years the total sum spent in this way by any ryot is not larger than a man in his position is justified in spending on social and domestic pleasures." This remark is as applicable to the north as it is to the south of the Jamna. Moreover, it should be remembered, though it is commonly forgotten, that the greater part of this outlay is not wasted, but consists of an actual transfer of hard cash, or cattle, or household furniture from the father of the bride to the father of the bridegroom, or *vice versâ*, according to the relative position of the parties. It is regarded as an investment for the benefit of the boy or girl, as the case may be, and differs but little in principle from the dowry and marriage settlements which are not absolutely unknown in lands further west. Altogether, the Oudh yeoman's scheme of expenditure, his standard of living, can scarcely be deemed extravagantly luxurious or in urgent need of reduction. What he requires to realise it is the undisturbed possession of, say, 25 to 30 acres of average land, at a rent varying according to the circumstances of the locality, from Rs. 2 to 3 an acre. Considering that agricultural produce is generally more than twice as cheap, the out-turn per acre seldom half as large, and the rate of interest from three to six times as high as in England, can this be called an immoderate demand?

Thus far concerning the Oudh cultivator and the Oudh yeoman. But a much more august personage, far more widely known to fame, remains to be delineated. Need it be said that that personage is the Oudh Taluqdár? The Taluqdárí body forms the most prominent, though not, of course, the most intrinsically important feature of the agricultural system of Oudh. It may be roughly divided into three classes.

1. *Feudal Chiefs.*—These are almost entirely Rájpúts—some few of whom have been converted to Islám—and are either heads of clans, entitled to be called Rája, or descended from leaders of offshoots of clans, and known by the honorific appellations of Bábú, Bhya, or Thákur. These had all undeniable rights in the soil at the time of annexation in 1856, which must have been recognised by any Government, whatever its speculative opinions as to the ideally best form of land tenure, so long as it admitted the existence of private property in the land at all. For all the feudal chiefs possessed a greater or smaller number of villages or portions of villages, in which their rights of ownership were undisputed. These formed the nucleus round which they had in troubled times accumulated—sometimes by force, sometimes by collusion with the officials of the native government, sometimes by purchase, sometimes by *boná fide* agreement with the zamíndárs,—a number of other and previously independent villages. It was over these latter, principally, that the land war raged so long and so fiercely in our settlement courts. But of this hereafter. Ancestral lands, it may be here observed, are commonly known as *bapans*; purchased land as *molans*; and land acquired by force or fraud as *dabans*. The latter term is nearly, if not quite, as common as the two former, though it has not, like them, found its way into Mr. Carnegy's latest publication; perhaps because it was not considered sufficiently "technical" to be recognised in a "kachahri."

2. "*Mushroom*" *Taluqdárs.*—These were generally either officials of the King of Oudh's Government, who made use of their uncertain but, while it lasted, practically unrestrained power to get together an estate for themselves; or capitalists, who acquired village after village by giving security for the embarrassed proprietors. When the latter failed to discharge the revenue demand, their lands were made over by the Názim or Chakladár to the sureties. A footing once gained in this way was very often maintained for many years previous to annexation, so that the application of our twelve years' law of limitation barred the claim of the original

zamíndárs. Taluqdárs of this class are generally either Musalmáns or Kayaths. But the largest and most conspicuous specimen of a "Mushroom" estate is at present in, or on, the hands of a Deputy Commissioner as manager on behalf of a Bráhman proprietor.

3. *Loyal Grantees, or Khairkhwáhs; literally, well-wishers.*—These are mainly Panjábis, who were given estates in reward for their services during the Mutiny. They are sometimes profanely styled "Carpet-baggers," and though not unfrequently good landlords, as Indian notions of a good landlord go, are still generally regarded by the people somewhat in the light in which American Southerners regard the Northern leeches who prey upon them, or as Irish peasants regard an English capitalist who manages his estate without much reference to Irish ideas. The grantees, however, as being mainly an exotic and not very numerous class, and being almost confined to two districts, Rai Bareli and Bahraich, need not here be discussed at any length.

Even this brief sketch suffices to show that the Taluqdárs are by no means a homogeneous body, and that they differ widely in race, birth, religion, and habits. There is, indeed, perhaps only one point common to them all without exception. They are all, as Hamlet puts it, "spacious in the possession of dirt," a peculiarity which they share with every other body of large landlords known to history. There is still, moreover, an undeniable difference, speaking generally, in the attitude of the people towards these three different classes. Yet these differences should not, I think, be recognised in any steps that may hereafter be taken towards modifying the system and its working. The practical ground for this opinion is that the differences themselves are yearly decreasing. Feudal sentiment, if nowhere actually dead, is certainly on the wane; and it seems highly probable that in no very long time the relations between each Taluqdár and the under-proprietors and tenants on his estate will depend almost entirely on the mode, beneficent or otherwise, in which he employs the great power over them which his position necessarily gives him, and not to any appreciable extent on the mode by which he attained that position, whether as the descendant of a long line of chieftains, or as the son or grandson of a lucky revenue farmer or speculative capitalist.

From an abstract point of view, again, the relation of all Taluqdárs alike to the British Government and their claims upon it are based solely and simply on their *sannads*, and on our acts and proclamations since the Mutiny, which abrogate any distinctions between them that previously existed, except such as are specially recognised by us in the *sannads* themselves or otherwise. We owe them all alike a faithful observance of our promises, so long as they observe their engagements, and we owe none of them a jot or tittle more than this. None of the existing Taluqdárs can well be said to have received less at our hands than he was entitled to, and if some have obtained more, that is no reason for now yielding anything more to those, if any such there be, who have received only what was their due. If I dwell on this point with what may seem needless prolixity, it is because there has been noticeable in some quarters a tendency to insist on the gulf that separates the "Chieftain" from the mere Taluqdár—(which is no doubt true and interesting as a historical fact)—without stating the supplementary fact that the distinction is one on which no practical action can now be advantageously taken. It is a sorrowful admission to have to make, that we have fallen into an irretrievable blunder, and have by our own act cut ourselves off from all hope of ever settling the land question of Oudh in an ideally satisfactory manner. But the done thing cannot be undone, and it only behoves us to accept as loyally and solve as wisely as we may the problem on the condition under which it has been handed down to us.

Now, however, before venturing any further into the mazy imbroglio of Oudh land controversy, let us try to form something like a concrete conception of the Oudh Taluqdár as he is in the flesh and outside the Blue Books. Come with me, and let me introduce you to my friend Bábú Sídhá Singh of Saráwanpur, chief of a cadet but long separately established branch of the great Bais clan. His ancestors emigrated northwards from Baiswára some four or five centuries ago, drove out the Bhars, or whoever the aborigines were, and mastered the country about Saráwanpur, which was then chiefly forest, with occasional patches of cultivation, but is now mostly under the plough, with insignificant strips of jungle interspersed. There is his house, that irregular, nondescript building, partly tile-roofed, partly thatched, surrounded by a high fence of thick bamboos, and with a weedy uneven approach, leading to a lofty square-topped gateway, the rough wooden doors of which are studded with iron nails, and are surmounted by a rude painting of a very scaly fish on each side. The fishes are the arms of the Muhammadan kingdom of Oudh, and correspond to our lion and unicorn. Our approach has been already announced to the master of the house, who hastens out to greet us, and escorts us into a good-sized courtyard. We take our seats in a verandah on the proffered cane stools, while our host sits down on his *takhta*, or large square wooden bench, and talks in his broad Doric patois of the crops, the new road that is being made from Saráwanpur to the head-quarters of the district at Banáoganj, the ravages of the wild pigs and *nilgai* in the neighbourhood, and other kindred topics, much as an English farmer would talk under similar circumstances. Meanwhile his servants, and a few neighbouring zamíndárs who had been smoking a morning hookah with him when we arrived, stand or sit around us, and contribute an occasional remark to the conversation.

He is still a fine-looking man, the Bábú, with his tall, well-set, stalwart frame, somewhat inclining to corpulence though it be, and his keen yet sturdy Aryan face, close shaven except for a large white moustache. Five and twenty years ago, in the stirring lawless times when every man's hands had to keep his head unbroken as best they might, he was a bold rider and a keen swordsman, and could drive his own elephant as well as any man on this side the Ganges. Then, too, he was adored by his clansmen, a body of four or five hundred sturdy Rájpúts, living here and there in the surrounding villages, who always rallied round him as their connecting link when there was a Názim to be passively, or a detachment of the king's troops to be actively resisted; and accepted as a not wholly unbeneficent law of nature by the low-caste cultivators in his own special group of some thirty or forty villages. Of these latter he was the undisputed proprietor, though the same tenants went on paying the same rents for the same land from generation to generation. With the internal affairs of the forty or fifty other villages held by his clansmen he had, in an ordinary way, little or nothing to do. They generally paid their revenue through him, and presented him with a yearly offering in cash and kind, varying according to the size of their village, in token of his lordship. In short, he was generally accepted by his clansmen as their *primus inter pares*, and by his tenants as their earthly providence, and all things worked smoothly enough, so long as the Government officials allowed them to do so. Things, however, have changed a good deal since then. But little real alteration was made in the *status quo* by the summary settlement which followed immediately on annexation. Sídhá Singh retained his own undisputed villages, and those of his clansmen were settled with them directly. He grumbled somewhat at this arrangement, but his harvest offerings were spontaneously continued to him by the now independent zamíndárs, and things were finding their level when the Mutiny broke out. Our friend the Bábú took no very active share in the disturbances which followed. He stayed at home, for the most part, and awaited the course of events. He would have done more wisely had he diligently searched the highways and hedges if haply he might find a fugitive Englishman to whom to give shelter and solace. It would have been the best investment of hospitality he ever made in his life, as not a few Taluqdárs are now in a position to testify. Not being far-sighted enough for this, however, he sat still, except when he indulged in the prosecution of a long-standing feud, which had been temporarily checked by annexation, with the neighbouring Rája of Sázishábád. He went into Lucknow in obedience to the proclamation of amnesty, and under the new policy of Lord Canning, who was "in the giving vein" that day, was recognised as proprietor of the whole eighty villages which now constitute the Saráwanpur taluqa, instead of some five and thirty only, as before. Of his clansmen, some have retained proprietary possession of their *sír* lands only, *i.e.* of the fields cultivated with their own ploughs, subject to payment of a rent fixed for a term of thirty years by the settlement courts. Others, more fortunate, have been decreed what is called a subsettlement of their villages, which means that they retain the management of the whole village in their own hands, but have to pay to the Taluqdár, in addition to a considerably enhanced Government revenue, a percentage of from 10 to 25 per cent. on that revenue, as his share of the profits, instead of their former nominal offerings. To this they markedly object; and as he, not unnaturally, insists on payment, and has even in some instances had resort to the rent courts to enforce it, a considerable coolness has arisen between him and many members of his brotherhood. Even where there has as yet been no actual breach, the relations between them are what diplomatists would call strained. Even the mere tenants are not quite as disposed as formerly to yield implicit obedience; and he, being a somewhat arbitrary old gentleman, with no notion of allowing any opposition to his wishes, is less inclined to a policy of conciliation and *parwarish*. All this may be a step towards a higher stage of civilisation, but its present tendency is undeniably towards increased friction. Unlimited freedom of contract, and unrestrained liberty to do what one wills with one's own, are excellent things, no doubt; especially where there is a certain degree of equality between the contracting parties, and where "one's own" is unencumbered by any rights or claims, legal or moral, of others. In the absence of these conditions, unphilosophic minds are sometimes tempted to question the good results of an unshackled assertion of individuality.

However, we have sat long enough by this time, and are getting near the bottom of our conversational fund. So let us take our leave of the worthy old Bábú, and ride on to Sázishábád, the abode of Rája Ghair Insáf Ali Bahádur, whose family has not been so long settled in Oudh as that of our friend Sídhá Singh. It is said, indeed, that the grandfather of the present Taluqdár came down from Delhi some time during the first quarter of the present century, and filled a not very exalted office in the household of one of the late kings of Oudh. He soon, however, obtained the favour of his royal master, took farming contracts of the land revenue, and was so fervent in business that in the course of a few years he put together the present Sázishábád Iláqa of some 300 villages. This he succeeded in doing by means so consonant with the feelings and customs of the country as to render himself universally beloved, and even to earn for himself the honourable soubriquet of the "Rája Manhús," which, being interpreted, signifies the auspicious or fortunate Rája, a title which has descended in due course to his grandson, through a father not unworthy either of the founder of the family or of its present representative.

It was owing, indeed, to the abilities of the second member of this noble line, displayed during the Mutiny, that much of its present prosperity is due. While the issues of the struggle were still uncertain, his judicious impartiality of mind enabled him to attain success in the difficult feat of running with the hare and hunting with the hounds. This happy flexibility of character earned him golden opinions from both parties, and ultimately led to a considerable increase of his estates. For a short period, it is true, after the capture of Lucknow, he was somewhat under a cloud, and was, indeed, for some little time in imminent danger of being hanged, owing to a mistake, which was fortunately rectified ere it was too late, on the part of Lord Clyde. His merits, however, were soon recognised; he was restored to liberty and augmented estates, and was one of the foremost members of that interesting assemblage of the landed aristocracy of Oudh with which Sir Bartle Frere, when he visited Lucknow in November 1861, was so favourably impressed. But his useful life was cut short by his unremitting toil for the good of the province, and he was succeeded by his son Ghair Insáf Ali. The latter resides in a large mansion of solid masonry which he has recently erected at great expense, and receives us in a drawing-room furnished in European fashion with lacquered chairs, ormolu clocks, representations of Her Imperial Majesty, and other symptoms of advanced civilisation. Behind his chair stands Ziyáda

Wusúl Khán, formerly a Tahsíldár on the estate, but recently promoted for long and faithful services to the important post of confidential manager and adviser to its master, or, as it pleases him to be called, Wazír of the Ráj. Ghair Insáf Ali speaks English not unfluently, wears patent leather shoes, offers us champagne and cigars—which, it being early in the day, we decline—discusses the last debate of the British Indian Association, the draft of the Oudh Revenue Bill, and the situation in Turkey, with equal depth and vivacity, and altogether deports himself in a manner becoming an intelligent young native nobleman. It is needless to add that he is a warm admirer of Lord Beaconsfield's Eastern policy, but deprecates the amalgamation of Oudh with the North-Western Provinces as likely to be injurious to the interests of his order. He has been sagacious enough to recognise the fact that he lives in a talking and a writing age. Therefore he takes a prominent part in the debates of the *Anjuman-i-Hind,* and judiciously works the *Laluckabad Chronicle.* These are qualities which an appreciative Government is not slow to honour, and its approbation has recently been signalised by the appointment of Ghair Insáf Ali to be an Honorary Assistant Commissioner.

> "So our virtues
> Lie in the interpretation of the time."

CHAPTER II.*

A FEW FACTS AND FIGURES.

THE districts which since the beginning of the present century have composed the province of Oudh form an irregular pentagon, bounded on four sides by the North-Western Provinces, and on the fifth or northern side by the territory of Naipál, which for about sixty miles, or rather more than a third of the line of contact, towards the east, is conterminous with the first range of the Sewálik hills, but towards the west includes a strip of the Tarai country at their base, varying in width from ten to thirty miles. The area of the province amounts, in round numbers, to 24,000 square miles, of which about 13,000, or, say, 55 per cent., containing 8,400,000 acres, are cultivated. Of the re-

---

* As this chapter is mainly a compilation from official or semi-official literature, I can, of course, claim but little originality for its contents. To obviate the necessity of a wearisomely frequent recourse to inverted commas, I may here note that I am indebted for most of my materials, to the "Oudh Census Report of 1869," by Mr. J. C. Williams; the "Oudh Gazeteer," by Mr. C. W. McMinn; and the "Introduction to the Oudh Gazeteer," by Mr. W. C. Benett, all members of the Bengal Civil Service.

mainder, 5,305 square miles, or 22 per cent., are culturable waste, and it may be said, roughly speaking, that—

Barren waste comprises	6	per cent.
Groves	4	,,
Lakes and rivers	$6\frac{1}{2}$	,,
Town and village sites	2	,,
Roads of all kinds	1	,,
Government forests	$3\frac{1}{2}$	,,

Oudh is for the most part a portion of the great Gangetic plain which slopes gradually down from the north-west to the south-east, and does not differ appreciably in physical characteristics from the surrounding districts of the North-Western Provinces in which it is embedded. It is the *terra media* of Hindústán, where the features of scenery, climate, and national character common to the lands both east and west of it may be found concentred. The greater part of the country consists of a wide cultivated tract broken up into tiny, hedgeless fields, divided by low, flat-topped, earthen banks, only a few inches in height, and from one to two feet broad. In rice lands, however, these partitions, or *merhs*, are higher and more substantial, much more copious irrigation being requisite than is needed for any other crop. The monotony of this level surface is relieved by numerous mango groves, occasional barren plains of what is called *úsar* soil, on which nothing will grow but a short coarse grass, and frequent *jhíls* or swamps, often covered with reeds, and most of which are only entitled to be called lakes during and shortly after the rainy season. Nine-tenths of the country may be described as pretty but monotonous, but the remaining tenth, or the strip of Tarai to the north of the three northern districts of Kheri, Bahraich, and Gonda, which includes nearly all the Government forests, has a character of its own, and can show scenery which for wild beauty it would be hard to surpass in any plain country in the world, set off by a background of precipitous, wooded hills, behind which tower in stainless, unapproachable grandeur the eternal snows of the Himálaya.

2

Population is sparse in this region, and large game comparatively abundant, though much scarcer by all accounts than it was twenty years ago. Tigers may still be found, and wild elephants occasionally heard of. The wild buffalo used to be not uncommon, but is now extinct. Sambhar and the barking and four-horned deer are rare; antelope and spotted deer are fairly plentiful; *nilgai* and pigs superabundant, and extremely mischievous to crops. The *gónd* or swamp-deer—a noble animal with large branching horns, a species of water-sambhar—and the hog-deer, or *párha*, are to be found among the vast sheets of high grass that cover the low ground along the Girwa and Koriála rivers which, issuing from the hills in a single stream, divide their waters and flow, the former to the east, the latter to the west, until they unite, some thirty miles lower down, to form the mighty river Ghághra. The principal forest tree is the *sál* (*shorea robusta*), but many other valuable species, such as the *khair* or catechu, the *mahua*, *shísham* or blackwood, and the *ábnús* or ebony, are abundant. The catechu tree yields a kind of resin which is collected by a peculiar caste, the Khairáhas (a subdivision of the Cháis), who live principally in the Gonda district, but migrate northwards about the beginning of January, and return with their spoils towards the end of April. The manufacture of catechu being no longer allowed in Government forests, the Khairáhas have mostly transferred their enterprise to those of Naipál. The climate of these northern districts is generally preferred by Europeans to that of southern Oudh, being somewhat cooler. Native officials, however, from other parts regard it as feverish, and especially consider sojourn north of the Ghághra, which divides Bahraich and Gonda from the rest of the province, as little better than banishment to a penal settlement. The climate of Oudh generally does not differ appreciably from that of the rest of Upper India. Suffice it to say that it is very hot and dry from early in April to the end of June; very hot and moist from July to the middle of October; and bright, clear, and pleasant during the remainder of the year. The general aspects of the scenery have been so well described by Mr. Benett that I cannot refrain from a brief quotation, premising that it is not applicable to the Tarai :—

"The scenery is, as might be expected, entirely devoid of any features of boldness or grandeur; everywhere there are four elements, and four only, to the picture. The sky, covered in the rains with masses of magnificent clouds, in the cold weather a level sheet of uninterrupted blue, and later on brazen and lurid with heat; the lakes, whose still surface reflects the colour above; the groves; and the brilliant expanse of crops. If there is scarcely any beauty of form beyond what grace is lent to small scenes by the grouping of trees and water, the colour at least, when the ripening harvests are seen in an atmosphere whose transparent clearness is saved from glare by a soft and almost imperceptible haze, is beyond all description lovely, and the never absent abundance of the richest foliage gives a sufficient variety to every landscape."

The chief rivers of Oudh are the Ganges, the Gumti, the Ghághra, and the Rápti. The first separates the province on the south-west from the regulation districts of Farukhábád, Cawnpore, Fattihpur, and Allahábád. It is crossed by a railway and passenger bridge at Cawnpore. The second flows past Lucknow and Sultánpur, and is four times bridged at the former, and once at the latter town. The third, entering at the north-west corner of Bahraich, divides that district from Kheri and Sítapur. It joins the Chauka at Bahrámghát, and passing Faizábád city separates the district of that name for some fifty miles of its course from Basti and Gorakhpur. It is spanned by bridges of boats at Bahrámghát and Faizábád in the cold and dry seasons, but in the rains can only be crossed by ferry, a process which usually takes from one to six hours, according to the height of the water and the direction and strength of the wind. In the middle of the rains it is not less than three miles in width from bank to bank. The Rápti, rising among the lower hills of Naipál, at first flows almost due west. It then takes a sudden turn, and issuing from the hills flows south-eastwards through Bahraich and Gonda, after which it enters the North-Western Provinces district of Basti. It is un-

2 *

bridged, and likely to remain so. The aggregate dry-weather discharge of these rivers is 18,800 cubic feet per second. If the smaller streams be added, the entire discharge will amount to 20,000 cubic feet, or half the quantity of the five rivers of the Panjáb. This would be a great economic power, were it not that the channels lie on an average from forty to fifty feet below the level of the country. The navigable length of the Oudh rivers amounts to 1,347 miles. They all follow the general slope of the country, from north-west to south-east.

The soil of Oudh may be briefly described as consisting two-thirds of loam or a mixture of clay and sand (which is expressed by its vernacular name of *domat* or *doras*), while of the remaining third, one half is a stiff clay (*matiyár*), and the other a light sand (*bhúr*). It is tilled with the most primitive ploughs drawn by small bullocks, and then carefully harrowed, or, more strictly speaking, the clods are crushed by a beam (*saráwan*), on which the driver stands to keep it down, while it is drawn backwards and forwards. The number of ploughings varies from two to twenty, according to the nature of the crop and the industry of the cultivator. The whole process amounts to little more than scratching up and minutely pulverising four or five inches of the surface soil. Attempts have been and are being made to introduce improved ploughs and deeper ploughing. The chief obstacle to their success is the weakness of the ordinary country cattle.

The principal crops are wheat, barley, rice, and maize of all kinds. The two former are *rabi* or spring crops, *i.e.* they are sown in October or early in November, after the rains, and cut in March, or early in April. The two latter are the staples of the *kharíf*, or autumn harvest, and are sown from just after the beginning of the rains to the end of July, and cut from about the middle of September to the end of November. Other spring crops are peas, gram (*chana*, Lat. *cicer arietinum*), *gujai* (a mixture of wheat, *gehún*, and barley, or *jáú*), tobacco, poppy, and all the garden growths, such as potatoes, carrots, onions, &c. Minor autumn crops are *kodo*, *kíkun*, *moth*, *másh*, and *masúr*. The *rabi* harvest depends principally on irrigation; the *kharif* on natural rainfall. Sugar-cane is planted in March and assiduously watered until the rains begin. It is cut in January and February. *Arhar* (*cytisus cajans*) from which the Revalenta Arabica is made, is planted in June, often together with *kodo*, and not cut until the following April. It is very sensitive to frost.

Few subjects are more disputed than the productiveness of the soil, but having neither space nor inclination to enter into the controversy here, I will only state my own belief that the out-turn of wheat on first-rate land, well manured and irrigated, and in a favourable season will very rarely be found to exceed 1,500 lbs., or 25 bushels per acre. The usual land-measure, it may here be noted, is the *bigha*. The standard, or *pakka*, *bigha* is five-eighths of an acre; the village, or *kachcha*, *bigha* varies locally from one-third to two-fifths of the standard *bigha*, but, generally speaking, may be taken as equivalent to one-fifth of an acre. There are similar variations in the dry measures. A standard maund (*man*) contains 40 *sirs*, of 2 lbs. each and a fraction over, but may be regarded as equal to 80 lbs. avoirdupois; while *kachcha* maunds and *sirs* are respectively two-fifths of the standard measures of the same name. Thus, for ordinary calculations it may be assumed that the *kachcha* maund is to the *kachcha bigha*, as the *pakka* maund to the *pakka bigha*.

To return from this digression to the question of out-turn, it must be remembered that a yield of 1,500 lbs. to the acre could only, as a rule, be obtained from the best land and under the most favourable circumstances. And the best land is but a small proportion, less, probably, than one-fourth of the whole; while favourable seasons, of late years at any rate, seem to have been rather the exception than the rule. It is probable, however, that the produce of wheat lands is seldom less than 500 lbs. to the acre, as it is seldom sown in any but good soil, while the poorest and most thriftless classes of cultivators rarely sow it at all, owing to the labour and expense which it requires. The yield of barley, rice, and maize differs but little from that of wheat, but of the inferior crops the out-turn per acre is probably not more than from one-half to two-thirds of it, while in really bad years the cultivator often reaps little more than enough to recoup him for his seed. Perhaps ten per cent. of the total area entered as cultivated lies fallow every year, while one-third bears two harvests, and garden lands lying immediately round the *ábádí*, or village site, often yield three. It is extremely difficult to make anything like an accurate estimate of the total average out-turn per acre. Any such attempt can be little more than a guess, and to treat it as a basis for practical measures would be most dangerous. If compelled, however, to hazard an estimate, I should not venture to assume the annual out-turn at more than 800 lbs. per cultivated acre. The cultivated area of the province is usually stated to be 8,400,000 acres. It is now probably nearer 9,000,000 acres, of which 8,000,000 may be taken as the area under food grains, and the remainder allowed for cotton, oil seeds, and other non-edible produce. The yield of 8,000,000 acres at 800 lbs per acre, would amount to the somewhat bewildering total of 6,400,000,000 lbs., or about 2,857,143 tons.

Now, how would such an out-turn answer to the requirements of the population, which, according to the census of 1869, is somewhat less than eleven millions and a quarter? Excluding from the calculation some 1,220,000, as representing infants in arms and young children who consume but very little grain food, we have ten millions left to be provided for. Let us say that, one with another, men, women, and children, they eat a pound and a half apiece of grain during the day, an estimate which those who know the province will probably consider to be rather over the mark than under. This would give a total daily consumption of 1,500,000 lbs., and an annual consumption of 5,475,000,000 lbs., equal to 2,444,196 tons, or 925,000,000 of pounds less than the assumed total yearly out-turn. The surplus of production over consumption would thus amount to a little more than 412,946 tons. The export of grain in 1869 was, according to not very trustworthy trade returns, somewhat less than 178,000 tons, but in subsequent years it seems to have considerably declined, and in 1872 is shown as but little over 50,000 tons. The import of grain, too, in some years, has fallen not very far short of the export.

A considerable amount of food grain is, of course, consumed by horses and cattle, wasted by damp and insects, and destroyed by fires; but it is impossible to make even an approximate guess at the quantity thus disposed of. Common country cattle and ponies get little or no grain, and live chiefly on grass, chaff, and chopped maize stalks. There is reason to fear that the estimate of a pound and a half of food grain daily per head of population is above the mark. Except in years of more than average plenty, many of the poorer classes, *i.e.* of the great majority of the people, hardly get a full meal once in three days during the five or six weeks immediately preceding each harvest, and feed, or rather graze, at such seasons on pounded mango stones, *gúlar* berries, watery squashes, and melons, and other miserable expedients for appeasing hunger, which never find their way into the returns of current prices. The consumption of meat is confined to too limited a class to need consideration here.

For nearly twenty-one years from the date of annexation in February 1856 Oudh was a separate Chief Commissionership, with an administration of the usual non-regulation pattern, the most distinguishing features of which, as opposed to the regulation system, are (1) that the district officers are styled Deputy, Assistant, and Extra-Assistant Commissioners, instead of Magistrates and Collectors, Joint and Assistant Magistrates and Collectors, and Deputy Collectors, respectively; and (2) that executive authority and judicial powers of all kinds, civil, criminal, and rent, are united in their hands, whereas in regulation provinces all civil judicial work is disposed of by a separate staff of Judges and Munsifs. The strong point of the non-regulation system is its comparative cheapness; its defect, if it be one, is its— well, let us call it, roughness. But in January 1877 Oudh was declared amalgamated with the North-Western Provinces, and the functions of Chief Commissioner have since been vested in the Lieutenant-Governor. The revenue divisions are four, each presided over by a Commissioner, who is also a Sessions Judge, and each containing three districts in charge of as many Deputy Commissioners.

The divisions and districts are as follows:—

1. Lucknow division, including			1. Lucknow district.	
			2. Bárabanki	,,
			3. Unáo	,,
2. Rai Bareli	,,	,,	4. Rai Bareli	,,
			5. Sultánpur	,,
			6. Pratábgarh	,,
3. Faizábád	,,	,,	7. Faizábád	,,
			8. Gonda	,,
			9. Bahraich	,,
4. Sítapur	,,	,,	10. Sítapur	,,
			11. Hardui	,,
			12. Kheri	,,

In July 1879 a long-incubated "judicial scheme" was introduced, by which all civil judicial work was taken out of the hands of Deputy Commissioners and their staff, and special courts created for its disposal. The total strength of the commission now amounts to forty judicial and sixty-seven executive officers. The judicial staff consists of a Judicial Commissioner, four divisional Judges, twelve district Sub-Judges, twenty-two Munsifs, and one Small Cause Court Judge of Lucknow. The executive branch includes four Commissioners and Sessions Judges, twelve Deputy Commissioners, twenty-four Assistant, and twenty-four Extra-Assistant Commissioners, one City Magistrate of Lucknow, and two Cantonment Magistrates, who are also Small Cause Court Judges. All the Munsifs, several of the Sub-Judges, and one Judge, are natives of India; while on the executive side, all but the great majority of the Extra-Assistants and one Assistant Commissioner are Europeans. Besides the above, there are in Oudh forty-three Tahsíldárs, each of whom is in charge of a tahsíl, or sub-division, of a district, and whose special duty is the collection of the revenue. They all, however, exercise criminal powers, and are competent to try suits under the Rent Act, and carry out all miscellaneous executive orders of the Deputy Commissioner. They are a very hard-worked and capable body of men, whose pay ranges from one hundred and fifty rupees to two hundred rupees a month, while the average area of their jurisdiction is five hundred and thirty-four square miles, and the amount of land revenue for the collection of which they are responsible exceeds, on an average, £32,000 yearly. Perhaps one of the most effective directions which administrative reform in Oudh could take would be that of increasing the number and salary of Tahsíldárs. Their present charges are so large that, though it is wonderful how well they do know them, it is almost impossible for them to know them thoroughly.

The steps in the administrative ladder, then, are the Tahsíldár, the Deputy Commissioner, the Commissioner, and the Chief Commissioner, with lateral supports in the shape of Assistants and Extra-Assistants. The Tahsíldár has also at his disposal the services of a peshkár or deputy, and of a kánúngo for each pargana or sub-division of a tahsíl. This latter official keeps up revenue records and registers, and supervises the village accountants, or patwáris, who, with the chaukídárs, or village watchmen, are the ultimate sources of the voluminous statistics and tabular statements which fill so many pages yearly in provincial reports and Imperial Blue Books.

The aggregate strength of the Oudh police in 1877 was 7,680 officers and men, of whom 5,887 were paid from provincial, and 1,793 from municipal, funds. Their total cost was slightly over £105,000. The proportion of policemen to population was as 1 to 1,560, and the cost per head was $2\frac{1}{4}$d.; while in the North-West Provinces the proportion was as 1 to 1,193, and the cost $2\frac{3}{4}$d. per head. On the other hand, the chaukídárs, or village police, in Oudh were as 1 to 321 of the population, against 1 to 453 in the North-West Provinces, and the cost considerably greater. If the Oudh chaukídárs were fewer in number, and regularly paid by Government, their efficiency would probably increase. As it is, they are paid partly by landholders in cash or rent-free grants, generally of inferior land, partly by cultivators in the shape of petty grain dues (*tihái*), in the realisation of which much of their time is apt to be spent; and thus their sense of responsibility to Government is naturally weakened.* The pay is very small, rarely more than Rs. 36 a year, yet, strange as it may seem, there is considerable competition for the post.

The military force of the province is divided between the three cantonments of Lucknow, Faizábád, and Sítapur, and consists of one regiment of European, and two regiments and one detachment of native, cavalry; five batteries of European artillery; and four regiments of European, and four of native, infantry. Its annual cost is somewhat in excess of £350,000. Orders have recently been issued for the abandonment of Sítapur as a military station.

There are eleven district jails in Oudh, and a central prison at Lucknow. The average daily population of these establishments is about 8,000, and their yearly cost about £30,000 or Rs. 38 per head.

There are more than 1,400 schools of different grades managed by the Educational Department, with nearly 70,000 pupils, the total cost of whose instruction amounts to more than £50,000. Nearly 5,000 of these study English; Urdu and Hindi are read by about 35,000 and 34,000 respectively; more than 10,000 learn Persian, but Sanskrit and Arabic seem to find few disciples. These latter languages, however, are taught privately by Pandits and Maulavis to pupils of the classes whom our schools do not attract.

The imperial taxes collected within the province amounted in 1877 to somewhat more than £1,670,000, of which somewhat less than £1,400,000 is derived from land revenue,† and from excise and stamp duties about £90,000 each. Other miscellaneous sources, the principal of which were the forests and the post office, yielded some £90,000 more. Disbursements within the province were less than £550,000, adding to which the military charges, or some £350,000, there

---

* It must be admitted, however, that there are peculiar difficulties in the way of anything like sweeping reform of the chaukídárí system of Oudh.

† The incidence of the land revenue is nearly Rs. 2 per cultivated acre, which is about one-fifth heavier than in the North-West Provinces, and nearly five times as heavy as in the Central Provinces.

remains a clear contribution to the resources of the empire of more than three-quarters of a million sterling. And this is exclusive of the income derived from the great opium and salt monopolies, which amount on an average to not less than £500,000 and £200,000 respectively. Thus, the total contribution of Oudh to the imperial treasury, after defraying the cost of the garrison and all local charges, is but little short of a million and a half sterling. Even if it be said, as it not unfairly may, that the income derived from opium, forests, and the post office, is not really taxation, and involves no drain on the country, it still remains true that considerably more than £900,000 sterling raised by taxation within the province is expended outside its limits.

"Alles das geht von des Bauern Felle,"

and it is obvious how severe must be the drain of such an outflow on the resources of a poor and overcrowded country. Depletion may be sometimes a salutary process, but if carried too far it is apt to result in death from inanition, and in any case the balance of opinion is not in favour of trying it upon a starving patient.

The population of Oudh is, perhaps, more dense than that of any other portion of equal extent of the earth's surface. It amounted at the census of 1869, in round numbers, to eleven millions and a quarter, or 474 to the square mile. During the ten years that have elapsed since then, it can hardly have failed to increase, though to what extent there are no means of knowing. The province, to quote an old Administration Report, is "a little smaller than Scotland, a little larger than Denmark, but with a population more than double that of both put together." It is not uninstructive to compare Oudh in this respect with a few other Indian provinces and European countries:

	Population per Square mile.	Date of Census.
Oudh	474	1869.
England and Wales	344	1861.
Belgium	400	1855.
Holland	254	1853.
France	178	1856.

	Population per Square mile.	Date of Census.
Saxony	354	1855.
Italy	268	
Bengal	269	1872.
North-West Provinces	361	1865.
Central Provinces	79	1866.

These figures suffice to show how much more densely crowded is the soil of Oudh than that of the most populous regions in Europe, or of other parts of India. And if some 4,800 square miles to the north of the province, including the Government forests, be excluded, the population of the remainder, some 19,600 square miles, or 84 per cent. of the whole area, is 514 to the mile; while on the cultivated and culturable area alone, or 77 per cent. of the whole, it is 550 to the mile.

And in no part of India, moreover, is the proportion of urban to rural population so small. Only 7·1 per cent. live in towns of more than 5,000 inhabitants. And of these so-called towns, many might be more correctly described as large, straggling country parishes. There is but one large city, Lucknow, with a population of 284,000, the largest in British India after the three Presidency towns, and the eighth in point of numbers in the British Empire. After Lucknow, *longo sed proximus intervallo*, comes Faizábád, with some 37,000 inhabitants, and then Bahraich, with 20,000. There are 15 other towns with from 10,000 to 20,000 inhabitants, and 39 with from 5,000 to 10,000.

"There is," writes Mr. McMinn, "only one town in Oudh, Tánda, which owes its size and prosperity to manufactures or trade. There are seventeen more with a population above 10,000; of them, three, Lucknow, Faizábád, and Nawábganj, rose from being grassy plains or small villages to the position of cities by being the residence of the Oudh Court. Nine others, Bahraich, Sháhábád, Khairábád, Sandíla, Radauli, Bilgrám, Jáis, Sándí, Zaidpur, were Musalmán military colonies in the middle of the Hindú population; the remaining five Balrámpur, Gonda, Laharpur, Purwa, and

Malláwan, were the residences of feudal barons, or of Government revenue officials."

At least 72 per cent. of the people of Oudh are agriculturists, *i.e.* are engaged in the cultivation of land, often conjointly with other occupations. This enormous rural population, excluding the insignificant proportion to be found living in towns and cultivating the surrounding lands, is scattered over some 24,000 villages and 54,000 hamlets, there being, on an average, one village and more than two hamlets to every square mile. The total number of clusters of houses in the country is thus nearly 78,000, with an average population of nearly 150 each. "Every rood" in the garden of India has certainly to "maintain its man"; that it *well* maintains him is not, perhaps, so certain.

Out of 2,500,000 houses, less than 20,000 are of brick, and most of these are relics of former Muhammadan prosperity. The enormous majority are mud-built. These are frequently tile-roofed, but the use of thatch is more common, especially in the northern districts where thatching-grass abounds. In the Tarai, whole villages may be found consisting entirely of grass matting. Of course houses built of such materials are terribly obnoxious to fires, both accidental and incendiary, and one of the favourite methods of annoying an unpopular neighbour is to insert a dry piece of lighted cow-dung in his roof on a dark night when the wind is blowing freshly. During the summer months, when everything is as dry as tinder, and hot winds prevail, fires are fearfully common, and it would hardly be an exaggeration to say that every thatched house in the country is burnt down once in ten years. The use of tiles would much diminish the risk of conflagrations, but the facilities for obtaining thatching-grass, and its cheapness, prevent recourse to the less dangerous but more costly material. Newly founded villages are often shadeless and bare-looking, but those of old foundation are nearly always overshadowed by lofty tamarind, *pípal*, or *banyan* trees. Under one of these, generally in front of the house of the most influential resident of the village, is to be found the *chaupál* or place of meeting, where such political life as the people possess exhibits itself in nightly discussions of their local affairs and transactions. Small bázárs are numerous all over the country. They are held once or twice a week, in the shade, generally, of the grove of some good-sized village, where petty traders and agriculturists congregate, and the exceedingly simple wants of the latter are supplied.

Manufactures are at a very low ebb. The three principal industries under native rule were cotton-weaving, salt-making, and spirit-distilling. Of these, the first has been crippled by Manchester competition; the second has been annihilated, so far as legislation can annihilate it, and the occupation of a numerous caste destroyed; while the third has been transformed into a department of administration, by the conversion of the private distiller into a paid *employé* of Government. "Formerly," states the Oudh Administration Report for 1876–77, "the weavers of Tánda used to produce the most delicate muslin, but now their looms are seldom used, except in the preparation of the coarsest cloths." Cotton-weavers and salt-makers have certainly no cause to bless our rule, which has taken the bread out of their mouths, indirectly as regards the former, directly and under criminal penalties as regards the latter. The salt manufacture having been crushed, £400,000 worth of salt is imported yearly. The makers of brass water and cooking vessels are perhaps the most flourishing class of artisans, these being among the few articles the use of which is universal. Their prices are determined by ordinary competition; while the village artisans, the carpenter, the blacksmith, and the leatherworker are paid by customary grain dues, after each harvest. "They are really," to quote Mr. Benett, "integral parts of that complete political system which has for its basis the grain heap on the threshing-floor at the end of the harvest, and take their place more correctly with the rája, the village proprietors, and the tillers of the soil than with the trading classes."

The correctness of the trade returns is open to suspicion, and the value of exports and imports is practically an unknown quantity. It may, however, be regarded as certain that imports are almost always considerably in excess of exports. The province has nothing to export save agricultural produce, timber, *ghí*, hides, and wool. Unless, indeed, we may say that it exports two commodities which do not figure in the returns, viz. land and men. Many of the large landholders' estates are heavily mortgaged to bankers and moneylenders outside the province; and great numbers of Oudh Rájpúts and Bráhmans are employed as soldiers and peons in Bengal and Central and Southern India, whose home-remittances doubtless cover some portion of the excess of imports over exports. So far as the returns may be trusted, the chief articles of import are cotton (raw or in thread), salt, and English piece-goods, with average annual values of £340,000 for the first, and £400,000 each for the two latter; while exports of edible grains, oil seeds, and sugar aggregate about a million sterling. There seems, on the whole, but too much reason to doubt the truth of the popular opinion concerning the capabilities of Oudh as the granary of India. Grain may, it is true, leave the province in large quantities on an emergency occurring elsewhere, but it can only do so because her own hungry masses have not the means wherewith to retain it when prices rise. In recent years the import of food grains has much increased, and in 1875-76—a year when grain was very cheap in Oudh—fell less than 17,000 tons short of the exports.

The land of Oudh, the cultivation of which affords their only means of subsistence to nearly three-fourths of the people, or some 8,000,000 souls, is owned by about 100,000 proprietors. Its distribution is extremely unequal. There are a few very large proprietors with estates of from 50,000 to 500,000 acres; some 300 who hold from 4,000 to 50,000 acres; 21,000 small zamindárs with properties, on an average, of about 150 acres each; and some 78,000 peasant proprietors holding 3,000,000 acres, or an average of about 38 acres a-piece. Something like two-thirds of the soil is owned by taluqdárs, *i.e.* by landholders whose names are entered in a list prepared by the Chief Commissioner under Act I. of 1869. A yearly payment of not less than Rs. 5,000 as revenue is understood to be a usual though not an indispensable qualification. There are 272 of these gentlemen, most of whom hold *sannads* or grants from the British Government, conferring on them an indefeasible hereditary and proprietary right in their estates.

The first district to come under the "regular" or thirty years settlement of the land revenue was Pratábgarh in 1862; the last to emerge from the ordeal was Kheri, in 1878. The theory on which it rests is that each village is assessed separately, and that the Government demand amounts to one-half of the gross rental, which again is generally estimated at from two-fifths to one-third of the gross produce. The other half of the gross rental belongs to the proprietor, but out of it he has to defray the expenses of chaukidárs and patwáris (the village police and village accountants), calculated at 12 per cent. on the revenue. Local cess and other rates absorb 7 per cent. more, so that his share of the gross rental, assuming it to be double the revenue, amounts to little more than two-fifths. Nor is this by any means all clear profit. Village expenses, including such items as revenue process fees, receipt stamps, stationery for patwárí, food of patwárí when required to leave his circle, and other miscellaneous charges, will hardly be defrayed under 5 per cent. of the gross rental. Cost of management will probably, in a large estate, absorb 5 per cent. more. So that even in an estate of which the gross rental is really as well as nominally double the assessment, the proprietor's income is by no means equal to the assessment. An example will put this in a clear light. Suppose the gross rental of a village to be Rs. 200, and its assessment Rs. 100. Then the payments which the zamíndár will have to make on account of it will stand as follows:—

1. Revenue	Rs. 100	0 0
2. Chaukidár	6	0 0
3. Patwárí	6	0 0
4. Local rates	4	8 0
5. Local cess	2	8 0
6. Village expenses	5	0 0
7. Cost of management	5	0 0
Total	Rs. 129	0 0

He thus derives from his village only Rs. 71 out of a gross rental of Rs. 200. The first five charges are inevitable, and the last two have been put at a very low figure. No allowance, moreover, has been made for unrealisable balances of rent, which, especially in bad seasons, are frequent enough. If a Taluqdár, he would have to pay an additional 1 per cent. as his subscription to Canning College and the British Indian Association of Taluqdárs. It is true, however, that the charges for chaukidárs and patwáris are not ordinarily collected with the revenue. Zamíndárs are left to make their own arrangements with these functionaries, and it is only in the event of failure to satisfy their demands that Collectors are authorised to realise their pay in cash, at a rate not exceeding 6 per cent. on the revenue. Landlords, especially in grain-rented villages, often realise considerably more from cultivators under the heads of pay of patwári and chaukidár, in addition to rent, than they actually disburse.

Again, over a considerable portion of some taluqas, and over some portion of almost all, there exists a double ownership. In some cases, whole villages are subsettled with under-proprietors, who pay their revenue through the Taluqdár, *plus* from 5 to 25 per cent., according to circumstances, of the assumed profits as a rent-charge. They are also liable for all the other charges above enumerated, and the share of profits which accrues to them is small exceedingly. Much more common than subsettlements of entire villages are smaller deductions from the rental in favour of persons who have been decreed the right to hold a certain quantity of land, called *sír* or *nánkár* or *daswant*, at a lighter rent than that ordinarily payable.

Estates or villages not included in any taluqa are called *zamíndárí* or *mufrid mahals*, and are sometimes the property of single individuals, but more frequently of coparcenary communities. In either case, the revenue is paid directly to Government. There are a few—a very few—tenants who have been decreed, under the Oudh Rent Act, a heritable but not a transferable right of occupancy in the whole or a portion of their holdings, at rents less by two

3

annas in the rupee, *i.e.* by one-eighth, than are payable by ordinary tenants of the same class for similar land, and which are liable to enhancement once in five years. And there are a great many—a very great many—tenants at will, the amount of whose rent is entirely a matter of agreement between them and their landlord, and for the determination of which no court in the country has at present any legal authority to interfere. Below these again are a great mass of day-labourers, some of whom cultivate small patches of land, while the rest have no land all.

We are now in a position to classify "the agricultural interest" of Oudh as follows :—

    1. Taluqdárs ;

    2. Zamíndárs, who hold no *sannads*, and whose property on their death is divided according to the usual law of inheritance ;

    3. Independent coparcenary communities ;

    4. Subsettled coparcenary communities ;

    5. Holders of *sír, nánkár, daswant*, and other minor rights, in subordination to a superior proprietor, generally a Taluqdár ;

    6. Holders of occupancy rights ;

    7. Tenants at will—the "will" in question not being, as a rule, so much their own as their landlords' ;

    8. Day-labourers, whose wages, *while they are employed,* range *from a shilling to eighteenpence, or, at most, two shillings a week,* if paid in cash, and from *four to six pounds a day of coarse grain,* if paid in kind.

The condition of Taluqdárs varies economically, much as that of landlords in other countries. Some are wealthy and unembarrassed, others quite the reverse. It may be said that, with good management and reasonable economy, they should nearly all be very well-to-do. There are, however, a few exceptions, where assessment has been heavy, and at the same time a large proportion of the profits is intercepted by under-proprietors, and in some such cases as these it must be admitted that the Taluqdár's embarrassments are not due to any fault of his own, save the original sin, which our policy invited, and indeed almost forced him to commit, of claiming the superior proprietorship in a number of villages to which he had, properly speaking, no real right. A number of the most embarrassed of these estates, assessed to an aggregate revenue of £200,000, were in 1871 brought under the management of six Encumbered Estates Courts, under the superintendence of special officers. The special agency was abolished in 1876, and most of the estates are now managed by Deputy Commissioners, in addition to their other duties. The experiment cannot be pronounced to have been a distinguished success. All that could be done by the superintendents was done, but the difficulties were in many cases almost insuperable, and are so still. Our rent law is perfectly effectual for recovering rents from ordinary cultivators. But it fails as against high-caste under-proprietors and ex-proprietors, mainly because these men believe themselves to have rights in the soil which our legislation and our courts have either ignored altogether, or have saddled with a rent which they consider unduly heavy, made payable to persons whose right to receive it they in many cases totally deny. No law or system which is in direct conflict with the notions of justice entertained by the people to whom it is intended to apply, will ever work happily or smoothly. The true remedy for the friction, to use a mild term, which now attends the recovery of rents from the high-caste peasantry of Oudh, is, not to increase the stringency of the Rent Act, or to disfigure the Statute Book by class legislation, but to remove the actual distress and sense of wrong under which that peasantry suffers. A great step to its removal might even now be taken by allowing, if not compelling, the sale of portions of these huge, disorganised estates, carefully selecting for the purpose those villages in which the antagonism between the Taluqdár and the under-proprietors is most bitter. A right of pre-emption on the part of Government might then be asserted, and direct engagements for the revenue be taken from the under-proprietors. Any sum that might be required could

3 *

easily be raised at 4 per cent., and the purchase-money might be made repayable by instalments spread over a period of twenty years, with interest at 6 per cent. The zamíndárs, thus made once more independent, would eagerly embrace such an offer, and the hypothecation of the village to Government would afford ample security for the recovery of the debt. We might thus "take up this mangled matter at the best," and make a long step towards reducing some of these overgrown estates to something like the dimensions to which they should originally have been confined, viz. the ancestral villages which form the nucleus of each taluqa, and to proprietary right in which no one but the Taluqdár has, or asserts, any claim. We might thus hope to see something like the end of the present hideous imbroglio of conflicting interests in the soil, though where, as in some "mushroom" estates, there is no such nucleus, the evil would, of course, be only diminished.

Single zamíndárs generally are, and always ought to be, well-to-do and comfortable. Their estates are not too large for them to manage themselves, without the intervention of agents, or *kárindas*, and they have, as a rule, very few sub-proprietors to intercept a portion of the profits. If they are in difficulties, these may fairly be ascribed to their own carelessness or bad management.

Independent coparcenary bodies are generally so numerous that each individual has but a small share of the profits. Their tenures are sometimes extremely complicated; one man may have an undivided share in half-a-dozen villages. Their condition is a function of several variables, such as their numbers, the severity or lightness of the assessment, the terms, good or bad, on which they live among each other, the honesty and competence of the *lambardár*, or headman, of their *patti*, or share, and their readiness to stick to him and follow his lead. The same remarks apply to subsettled coparcenaries, except that their position is worse by their loss of independence of the Taluqdár, and by their enjoying only a portion of the profits instead of the whole. It may be said generally that they are a good deal more poverty-stricken and discontented than independent communities.

Holders of *sír, nánkár*, and other minor rights are in a less difficult, if less dignified, position than those who have obtained the subsettlement of entire villages. Their standard of comfort is about the same, but the dangerous power which they possess of mortgaging their lands, and so raising money without immediate loss of possession, has brought many of them to ruin and heavily involved many more.

Holders of occupancy rights are so few that their position need hardly be discussed; indeed, but for considerations of symmetry, they might almost have been left out of the classification altogether.

Of the great mass of tenants at will—seven millions or more, including their wives and families—it seems almost enough to say that they *are* tenants at will, and that in eight out of the twelve districts of Oudh the proportion of cultivated acres to adult agricultural males is but as three to each man. Custom is everywhere in these southern districts giving way to competition, and unless something is very soon done to arrest the evil, the tenants will all be mere cottiers. It is too plainly apparent to be any longer doubted, that, with occasional exceptions, the tenure of all ordinary cultivators has already become, or is rapidly becoming, cottier tenure as defined by Mr. Mill at the beginning of chapter IX. of the second book of his Political Economy, *i e.* a tenure under which "the labourer makes his contract for land without the intervention of a capitalist farmer, and in which the conditions of the contract, and especially the amount of rent, are determined, not by custom, but by competition." It would doubtless be absurd to assert that custom has ceased to exercise any influence on rents. It still keeps, for instance, the rents of some castes lower than those of others. But there is no custom which prevents a landlord, large or small, from endeavouring—and generally succeeding in the endeavour—to raise rents whenever he thinks his tenants will stand another turn of the screw, or from ejecting them if he thinks he can make more by putting in another tenant, or by taking the land into his own cultivation. While this is so, it would be futile to assert that rent is not mainly determined by competition. If there is not always the competition of one tenant against another, there is always the competition of the landlord, as a potential cultivator, against his tenant. So long as rents are not fixed by either custom or law, it seems idle to hope that the condition of the cultivator will not go on from bad to worse.

And that it is bad now there can be no doubt. It is less depressed in the northern districts, where population is less dense, competition less keen, holdings larger, and rents lighter. But the gradual extension of the curse of competition and rack-renting to these hitherto comparatively fortunate regions can only be a question of time. Even now, taking the province as a whole, it is scarcely too much to say that a large proportion of cultivators have neither food sufficient to keep them in health, nor clothes sufficient to protect them from the weather; that their cattle are miserably thin and weak from under-feeding; that they are hardly ever out of debt for twelve months together, though in a good season they can pay off their debt within the year, while in a bad one it accumulates; and that, except in specially favourable seasons, they are dependent on the money-lender for their food for from two to six months in the year.

It may not be out of place here to give a few figures, the result of an inquiry which I once had occasion to make into the condition of ordinary cultivators in the Bahraich district. The 60 families whose circumstances I endeavoured to analyse consisted of 436 persons, of whom 169 were men and 134 women, over twelve years of age, while there were 71 boys and 62 girls under that age. They had 76 ploughs and 173 bullocks, and of cattle of all kinds, including goats, sheep, pigs, and ponies, they had 712. The average area of their holdings was a trifle over 8 acres, or a little more than $6\frac{1}{2}$ acres to each plough, or $1\frac{1}{7}$ of an acre per head. Thirty of these cultivating families paid rent in cash, and thirty in kind. Ascertaining as nearly as was practicable the amount of grain-rent paid by the latter during three years, (1283, 1284, and 1285 Fasli, *i.e.* from October 1875 to September 1878), and converting it into cash at the current prices of those years, the result was that the rent paid by the whole sixty families aggregated 2,116 rupees, or an average of a little over

35 rupees per family, nearly 28 rupees for each plough, and 4 rupees 3 annas 9 pies per acre. The cost of cultivation was almost 2 rupees 5 annas per acre, or an average of 19 rupees 4 annas for each family. The average amount of produce (probably somewhat, but not very much, below the mark) was 3,748 maunds of 82 lbs. each, or nearly 138 tons, the value of which, at average prices of the three years in question, was 5,352 rupees, or about 1 rupee 7 annas per maund. This allowed an average of $62\frac{1}{2}$ maunds for each family, worth about 89 rupees, and rather less than 50 maunds, worth about 71 rupees, per plough. The average produce per acre was 7 maunds 20 seers, worth, at average prices, 10 rupees 11 annas. The surplus remaining after rent and expenses of cultivation were defrayed, amounted to 2,083 rupees 4 annas, or 34 rupees 11 annas 6 pies for each family, 27 rupees 6 annas 6 pies per plough, and nearly 4 rupees 1 anna per acre. The value of the food consumed by the 436 individuals under examination, at the rate of 20 oz. per head per diem, at average prices, amounted to 4,466 rupees 4 annas, or a fraction over 6 maunds 33 seers, worth 10 rupees 3 annas 9 pies per head per annum. Their expenditure on clothes, salt, and sundries, aggregated 1,308 rupees, or exactly 3 rupees per head per annum. The combined cost of food and general expenditure, being 5,774 rupees 4 annas, was 3,691 rupees in excess of the value of the surplus of grain available after payment of rent and costs of cultivation, or, on an average, 61 rupees 8 annas per household. Only four families could show any surplus, and their total was under 40 rupees. The total amount of indebtedness was 1,620 rupees, of which 1,453 rupees were owed by 18 cash-rent paying cultivators, and 167 rupees by 8 grain payers. The other 34 were not in debt. The average indebtedness was 24 rupees per household. Of the thirty cash payers, only twelve were out of debt, while of the same number of grain payers, only eight were in debt. It may be laid down as a generally true proposition, that indebtedness is far more general and more heavy where cash-rents have been introduced than where grain-rents still prevail. Tenants paying cash-rents are, practically, almost obliged to resort to

the money-lender for payment of the demands upon them. In good years, when the harvest is plentiful and ripens early, they may avoid this necessity; but in a series of seasons there are sure to be several not answering to this description, and then a demand for cash payment almost inevitably drives cultivators who have no capital and live from hand to mouth to borrow from a mahájan on the security of their crops. The habit of borrowing, once contracted, establishes itself more and more strongly, and becomes more and more difficult to break through. Originally, in most instances, forced upon them to meet the demand for rent, it soon passes into a habit of borrowing for food, for clothes, for cattle, and every other contingency.

It is time, however, to return from this brief excursus, and to meet the inevitable question—How, then, do these people contrive to live, for if these figures are anything like correct, they ought all to have become bankrupt long ago? The seeming impossibility is to some extent explained by the fact that in nearly every case they eke out the scanty income which they derive from the soil by day-labour, weaving, sale of milk and *ghí*, or other extraneous sources. A further explanation is to be found in the fact that the out-turn is probably too low, being little over 600 lbs. per acre. It should be borne in mind, however, that the years in question were none of them years of specially good harvests, while in one the crops were notoriously deficient; and that, under the comparatively careless cultivation of the northern districts, the produce of the soil is less heavy than in central and southern Oudh. But it is to be feared that the most effectual explanation of all is that the food estimate, low as it is, is pitched too high, and that the Oudh tenantry and their families, men, women, and children together, do not, on an average, consume even so much as 20 oz. of food-grain per diem. Well-fed-looking men are certainly the exception among them rather than the rule, and it is notorious that the able-bodied adult convict nearly always increases in weight after a few months on a jail diet of 24 oz.

The condition of the Oudh cultivators might seem to be life reduced to its lowest terms. But there are hundreds of thousands all over the province compared with whom he, as Lear has it, is "sophisticated"; the landless village labourer is "the thing itself." Everywhere, in every hamlet, there is a residuum of half-clad starvelings who have no cattle and no means of livelihood, save, perhaps, a tiny patch of spade-tilled land, and their labour, remunerated at the rate of 4 lbs. of coarse grain, or of three-halfpence, or, at most, twopence farthing per diem. And even this wretched employment is not procurable all the year round. How, underfed and almost unclothed as they are, they contrive to live through the cold nights of winter, which they often spend in field-watching to keep off thieves, human and other, is a standing marvel. They are quite a distinct class from the coolies whom one sees employed on the roads and other public works, and who earn from threepence to fourpence halfpenny, or sometimes as much as sixpence, a day. The village drudge is seldom fit for hard work on the roads, being generally too weak for efficient spade labour.

The primary classification of the people of Oudh is, of course, as elsewhere in India, into Muhammadans and Hindús. The former may be subdivided into higher castes of Muhammadans, converts from the higher Hindú castes, and lower castes of Muhammadans. The latter also resolve themselves into higher and lower caste Hindús. To these must be added aboriginal tribes who have no distinct place in either the Hindú or the Muhammadan system, and religious sectaries and mendicants, who, though belonging to one or other faith, are above or beyond all caste distinctions.

High caste Musalmáns are of four classes, Syads, Mughals, Patháns, and Shaikhs. The Syads, who claim descent from Hasan and Husen, the sons of Ali, the fourth khalif, by Fátima, daughter of the Prophet, number about 50,000, of whom two-fifths are residents of Lucknow, and the rest are to be found in small colonies scattered throughout the province. Mughals number about 27,000, of whom more than half belong to Lucknow. The name originally denoted the Tartar invaders of Persia and India, but has long been applied to naturalised descendants of Persians as well as Turanians, and Mughals are now generally divided into Iráni and Turání. The ex-royal family of Oudh are of this race, as also a great many of their former dependants, most of whom now receive pensions from the British Government. Patháns are more than 190,000 in number, being the most numerous Musalmán tribe in Oudh, and are distributed pretty generally over the province. They are descended from the Afghán invaders of India, and are the only Musalmáns properly entitled to the appellation of Khán, though it is often assumed by others. They claim to be derived from the patriarch Jacob, and their chief subdivisions, according to Herklot, are Yúsúfzai, or offspring of Joseph, and Lodi, or offspring of Lot. Next to Patháns, the Shaikhs are most numerous. There are about 166,000 of them, of whom a third belong to Lucknow. The name primarily denoted descendants of the first four khalifs, and was afterwards extended to the posterity of all who were converted to the faith during their reigns. It is now often assumed wholesale by all sorts and conditions of new converts to Islám.

The only high-caste Hindús who have embraced Muhammadanism in any considerable numbers are Rájpúts. The motive was almost always the same, viz. the retention of ancestral lands, or the acquisition of fresh ones. Practically, however, such converts, or Khánzádas as they are usually termed, differ only from their unconverted brethren in being circumcised, wearing beards, praying in a mosque instead of in a temple, and calling themselves "Khán" instead of "Singh." Many of them still retain their clan names. Perhaps the most powerful of these converted Rájpúts are the Bhále Sultáns, or "lords of the spear," who are chiefly to be found in the Sultánpur district. Mr. Patrick Carnegy, late Commissioner of Rai Bareli, in his "Notes on the Races and Tribes inhabiting Oudh," thus describes the process of conversion:—

"The old Hindú houses seem to have deputed one member to become Muhammadan, and shelter their interests when necessary in a Muhammadan Court—just as in the Mutiny very many families sent one member to the rebel force and another to the British, to secure their possessions whichever side might win. If you ask a Bais how his kinsmen became Khánzádas, he will probably tell you there was once upon a time a terrible and tyrannical Súbahdár (the terror of whose name is such that it escapes his recollection). This ferocious gentleman sent for all your informant's ancestors, and, after shocking oaths by the beard of his prophet, demanded that one of them should forthwith become Musalmán, and then, amid the lamentations of the clan, one of the brethren was solemnly circumcised."

The total number of these high-caste converts to Islám is between twelve and thirteen thousand. They include fourteen Taluqdárs. Instances of a Bráhman becoming Musalmán are almost unknown; and even Rájpút conversions have during the last hundred years been few or none.

Lower classes of Musalmáns number about 660,000, and are divided in the Oudh *Census Report* into 35 castes, of which, however, several are extremely small, and 19 contain less than a thousand individuals each. The most numerous are Dhuniyas or cotton-cleaners, Darzis or tailors, Ghosis or milkmen, Juláhas or weavers, Kunjras or greengrocers, Kasáis or butchers, and Manihárs or glass bangle makers. These low-caste Musalmáns are, no doubt, descendants of low-caste Hindús who have embraced Islám at any time since the Muhammadan invasions of Oudh, beginning some eight centuries ago. Motives to conversion are obvious enough, such as expulsion from a Hindú brotherhood for breach of its rules, or desire to rise in the social scale, or to gain favour with the dominant class. Conviction of the truth of the adopted creed has probably been one of the rarest.

Alien to the true spirit of the Muhammadan faith as are all distinctions between man and man founded upon accidental differences of birth or position, there can be no doubt that these lower classes of Musalmáns constitute genuine *castes*, not mere professions. Or, perhaps, trades unions would be a more correct descriptive term for them. They have very little to do with religion, but a great deal to do with social conduct and social ceremonies, in which their members are even more strict and jealous than are Hindús. In these lower castes, writes Mr. McMinn, " Musalmán and

Hindú traditions unite to work out problems of social organization. In point of fact, the conquerors borrowed the caste system from the conquered, relieved it from its galling allegiance to the Hindú religion, relaxed slightly the restrictions upon intercourse between the different bodies, and, above all, rendered the system more elastic and durable by providing means of returning to the fold for backsliders who had been tempted to violate their laws. Musalmán castes, in short, are trades unions which anyone may enter on payment of a fee in the shape of a good dinner to the brotherhood. Nor are they meddlesome or tyrannical in their treatment of the business relations which may exist between individual members and employers. A tailor may work as many hours as he pleases, or for what wages; if he is maltreated, his union will support him in an appeal to the law. When he marries, it feasts at his expense; when he dies, at his widow's. If he is sick or out of work, the nearest mess of his brethren shares its meal with him. In return for these benefits, the only conditions are that he shall marry within the clan, that he shall not undertake work other than that proper to his trade, nor eat things unlawful"—nor with unlawful persons—"nor dishonour his fraternity by immoral conduct."

Of the inner life and rules of these trades unions, few Englishmen have any exact knowledge, and I cannot claim to be one of the enlightened minority. For the purposes of trades unions they are most effective, for they not only prevent outsiders from taking up the trade they have made their own, but also nearly always prevent those born inside the fraternity from adopting any other. Their marriage law may be described as a system of free love tempered by Panchayats, or caste meetings.

"It seems to be an invariable rule," writes Mr. Williams, "that in those professions which Muhammadans have adopted they form the great majority; and probably they do in time succeed in monopolizing every trade they adopt. By this I do not mean that they drive out the Hindús, for Muhammadans are not generally so industrious as Hindús; but that all the Hindús of any caste, the principal occupation of which has been invaded by Musalmáns, eventually become Musalmáns. The conversion is rendered easier when it does not involve the abandonment of an hereditary trade, which is the chief barrier opposed to the extension of Muhammadanism and Christianity among the lower classes of Hindús by the system of caste, and when this is not a necessary accompaniment of change of religion, the attractions of comparative freedom from caste rules (?), greater laxity in the choice of food, less subjection to priestly influence, and a certain rise in the social scale, all of which Muhammadanism offers to the new convert, become too great to be resisted."

Speaking generally, it may be said that all Oudh Musalmáns are more or less Hindúised, and have imbibed the caste feeling more or less strongly. The strength of this feeling among them varies inversely with elevation in the social scale, and with general intelligence. Most Muhammadan gentlemen, for instance, will not scruple to drink tea or soda-water with an Englishman, and from his cup or glass, though their attendants regard the act as rather a breach of orthodoxy. The Musalmáns of Oudh cannot, as a body, be accused of bigotry or intolerance. On the contrary, they are very tender, as a rule, of the prejudices of their Hindú neighbours, who, in their turn, often take part in the Muharram ceremonies, and carry about their *tázias*— or models of the tomb of Hasan and Husen, the procession and burial of which are the chief features of the festival— with as much zest as if to the manner born, which indeed, as a matter of fact, they are. It is common for wealthy Musalmán landlords to contribute to the expenses of Hindú festivals, and very rare for them to kill cattle or touch beef. This mutual tolerance and good feeling is one of the pleasantest features in the social aspects of the province, and is no doubt partly owing to British impartiality towards both the creeds. Among Muhammadans themselves, too, there is very little religious dissension, and Sunnis and Shias, who are at such deadly feud in many parts of Asia, including the Panjáb and Kashmir, have, in Oudh, always freely intermarried.

The chief peculiarities noticeable in the distribution of the

Oudh population according to race and caste are (1) the small number of Musalmáns, scarcely one-eleventh of the whole, which is a smaller proportion than prevails in any other part of Upper India; and (2) the great predominance of Bráhmans, who number 1,400,000, or nearly one-seventh of the Hindú, and one-eighth of the entire, population. Oudh is, as both these facts, and especially the latter, sufficiently testify, a stronghold of Hindúism, perhaps its most important centre. Nowhere in British India has the spirit of the Hindú system and polity emerged with more freshness and vitality from its long-sustained struggle with the repressive forces of a Musalmán dynasty.

Bráhmans are considerably more numerous than any other Hindú caste, high or low, being about 12 per cent. of the whole population. They are divided into innumerable divisions and subdivisions, the principal of which are the Kanaujias—a name derived from the once great Hindú city and kingdom of Kanauj—and the Sarwarias, a corruption of Sarjúpáras, meaning an inhabitant of the country beyond the Sarjú river, as the Ghághra is sometimes called. The latter, as their name would lead one to expect, are to be found principally in Gonda and Bahraich, and the former over all the rest of Oudh, though the Rai Bareli and Bárabanki districts form a border-land where both tribes are common. Bráhmans are to be found in all sorts and conditions of life, from the rája to the beggar. Their most frequent occupations are as cultivators, priests, soldiers, petty merchants, and pedlars, money-lenders, rent-farmers, and out-door servants or peons. Only ten of them are Taluqdárs, and of these one is a Kashmíri Pandit, and another, a loyal grantee, is a Bengáli; none of the ten are of old family. Caste prejudice forbids Bráhmans to hold the plough, and their share in the operations of agriculture consists for the most part in watching their ploughmen at work. Their priestly functions do not generally include the temple service of particular deities, for that, to quote Mr. Benett, "is usually left to the religious orders which are above caste, but the direction of the family life of the people down to the smallest acts—from the solemnisation of marriage and performance of funeral rites, to the selection of a favourable day for starting on a journey, or for cutting the ripened corn. No ceremony, no feast, is perfect unless conducted under their auspices, and commencing with their entertainment. The last sciences which survive are those bearing on the daily life of a people, and in the decay of Hindú learning, it is the Bráhman only who studies the old languages of the country, to make himself conversant with ceremonial and astrology." Almost every indigent Bráhman who can read and write sets up as a Pandit, and ekes out his income thereby. They are a handsome and athletic race, bad cultivators and rent-payers, but good soldiers; and one of the most numerous of their subdivisions gave the generic name of "Pándes" to the mutinous sepoys in 1857. They are held in bad repute by English district officers, being litigious and quarrelsome, and, in our courts, at any rate, guilty of perhaps more shameless mendacity than men of any other caste. They can hardly fail to dislike our rule, which endeavours, though not, perhaps, with very visible success, to diffuse information and ideas which, if generally accepted, could not but prove fatal to their priestly supremacy, while, though careful to avoid causing any needless offence to the prejudices of any caste, it necessarily treats the Bráhman, for all judicial and administrative purposes, as on a footing of absolute equality with the Chamár. Still, with all their faults, which are many and grave, the nation owes them much. Though they fought, of course, mainly for their own predominance, yet it has been chiefly their work that the spirit of Hindúism has been maintained through centuries of oppression in the vitality in which we now see it. And though their original function of conducting the worship of the gods has passed into the hands of Gosáyins and Bairágis and other casteless sectaries, whose claims to veneration are based, not on accident of birth, but on austerity of life— the voluntary principle having thus superseded the hereditary—yet the Bráhman still receives from the masses a reverence of which no depth of poverty, of crime, or of immorality can deprive him.

Less numerous, but still more important, from some

points of view, in modern Hindú life, are the Chhatris or Rájpúts, who amount to nearly 663,000, or 5·9 per cent. of the whole population. They are *par excellence* the zamíndárs or landholders of the province, and are divided into large clans, most of which have a part of the country which is especially their own, but they particularly predominate in the south and east. Their strength, influence, and possessions vary locally in pretty nearly inverse ratio to those of the Muhammadan landholders. The ancient Oudh dynasties and the popular heroes were all of this race, and a Rájpút king, acting under the spiritual and moral direction of a Bráhman adviser, is the Hindú ideal of government. Their occupations are of more limited range than those of Bráhmans, being, indeed, only three in number, viz. agriculture, both as landowners and as mere cultivators; military service in our army and with native princes; and private service, as peons, bailiffs, and personal retainers, with large landlords and bankers. They share the prejudice of Bráhmans against holding the plough, and like them are excellent soldiers. There are said to have been sixty thousand Oudh Rájpúts and Bráhmans, or between two and three, on an average, from every village in the province, in the service of the East India Company.

More than half of the land in the country is in their hands, and they number 155 Taluqdárs among their ranks; while 76 of that fortunate body, including the 14 Khánzádas, are Muhammadans. They own, roughly speaking, 14,000 out of 24,000 villages, though they are little more than one-twentieth of the population. With the exception of the Sikhs, they are the finest peasantry in India, and their character is of a type markedly distinct from that of any other caste. Brave, easy-going, large-natured, generous, but with a certain latent ferocity underlying their more attractive qualities, and possessed of a far greater power of cohesion than Bráhmans, they are looked up to by the Hindú masses in the secular, as are the latter in the spiritual, sphere. Yet though practically the most influential class of the population, and recognised by the people themselves as their leaders, as is evidenced by their common title of Thákur (the lord, the master), they have perhaps less officially recognised influence, except in their capacity as Taluqdárs and large landlords, than any other of the higher castes, and less capacity for adapting themselves to the requirements of English rule. Their habit of intermarrying with the Chhatris of the North-West Provinces, and of Rájpútána, gives them the *entrée* into a larger world and a more extended circle of interests than is possessed by any other equally numerous class of Hindús. But their present position, as a general rule, is much depressed. The two great fields of employment which were open to them under the kingdom of Oudh —viz. service in our sepoy army outside the province, and as armed retainers of local landowners within it—are now very much narrowed, and tens of thousands, who would formerly have been helping their families with remittances of their savings from abroad, are now driven back for subsistence on the overcrowded soil. The great reduction of the native army since the Mutiny, and the abolition of the Oudh local force, have been serious blows to their prosperity, while the establishment of the reign of law within the province has rendered the services of a large body of retainers no longer needful to the Taluqdárs. It may be said that such employment as this could not much increase the real wealth of the country, and that the application to the soil of the additional labour thus released from unproductive employments must cause such an increase. But it must be remembered that though an armed retainer or a soldier is not a directly productive agent, yet their pay was a very distinct and considerable addition to the resources of their stay-at-home brethren, and often more than equivalent to a rent-free holding. The labour, moreover, of a Bráhman or Rájpút is, as has been said, seldom of a highly productive character, and, in so densely populated and closely cultivated a country as Oudh, can seldom be held an equivalent to the cost of his own support.

Another principal cause of the depressed condition of Rájpúts, and, in a minor degree, of Bráhmans, is that they have been very generally engaged in litigation in our settlement courts to establish their rights; and, indeed, under our settlement rules, it was almost impossible for them to refrain from such litigation. The settlement officers, under the orders of Government, practically went out into the highways and hedges and compelled them to come in. Whether successful or not in getting decrees for the rights they claimed, they spent large sums, both legally in lawyer's fees and court expenses, and illegally in douceurs to native underlings, in making the attempt.

And while their means have thus been reduced, the revenue demand which they have, when landholders, to meet, has been largely increased. Instances are not uncommon in which the assessment of a coparcenary village has been raised at a stroke by 50 or even 100 per cent. It was hardly to be expected that, in a single year, the habits of the coparceners should undergo so complete a change as would enable them to pay so large and sudden an increase of demand. The revenue may have been unduly light before, but it was too often forgotten that what we have to assess is not only land, but also *men*. It is practically impossible for a village divided and subdivided, with infinite intricacies, among a numerous brotherhood, to pay a demand which might be met without difficulty if the village were in the hands of a single owner. A good deal has been done in the way of revision and reduction of assessments, but these remedial measures, it is to be feared, were in many cases too late.

Again, the relations between under-proprietors and the Taluqdárs to whom our policy has kept them in subordination, even when it has not itself placed them there, are, generally speaking, changed for the worse since annexation. Mr. Freeman, quoting Sismondi, remarks that, "when every count and baron acted as an independent prince, and claimed the right of private war, among the endless evils of such a state of things there was one countervailing good. The lord could not venture to oppress greatly men whom he expected to follow him to battle. When the days of greater peace and order came, the hand of the lord who was no longer a captain came down far more heavily on subjects who were no longer his soldiers." This is exactly true of Oudh.

Another point worth noting is that the hands of the Rent

Courts are bound by a provision of the Rent Act (XIX. of 1868), which prohibits them from taking into consideration circumstances, such as bad seasons, floods, drought, or hail, which may have caused a default in payment of under-proprietary rent, unless a remission of revenue has been allowed by competent authority for the same cause and in the same estate. Now it rests with the Taluqdár to apply for such a remission, and as it is his direct interest to get rid of privileged cultivators and sub-holders, and supplant them with hardworking low-caste tenants-at-will, it may often not be worth his while to apply for a remission of revenue which would put the privileged cultivators *pro tanto* out of his power. The sum of which he and they would thus escape payment may, especially if the cause of default extend over only a limited area, be a trifle to him, though possibly a matter of life and death to them. Still more is it the interest of the Taluqdár to destroy and break down under-proprietary rights in subsettled villages. It would often, therefore, be worth his while to allow arrears to accumulate up to the period of limitation, and then to sell up the under-proprietors. There are, probably, not many Taluqdárs who would be guilty of such nefarious conduct,—which, if it could be proved against them, would be a direct breach of the conditions of their *sannads*; and some, who might have no moral scruples, may have been restrained by impecuniosity. But it has been put on record by high authority in Oudh that some Taluqdárs have deliberately allowed the rents of subsettled villages to fall into arrears with a view to ultimately crushing the rights of the under-proprietors. Others, again, have deceitfully induced, or allowed their agents to induce, claimants of such rights to file relinquishments of their claims in the settlement courts, by promises, which have not been fulfilled, of maintaining them in possession of all the privileges they enjoyed. In any case the fact remains that we have left under-proprietors, with a tenure exceedingly difficult to maintain in its integrity, in the hands of men whose ultimate interest it is that they should default. And if, as Mr. Mill has somewhere observed, it is never safe to assume that any body of men will act contrary to their own

immediate pecuniary interest, it is almost equally unsafe to
assume that out of any body of two or three hundred men,
some will not be found to act for their own ultimate pecuniary
interest, however injurious that may be to the welfare of
others, so long as they can do so without running considerable risk of incurring legal penalties. Altogether, much
as has been said and written about the contumacy and recu-
sancy, the *sharárat aur nidihandí*, of the under-proprietor, it
may be that we have not left ourselves very much right to
be virtuously indignant with him if he has sometimes formed
the same determination, with regard to the Taluqdár and
the Deputy Commissioner, at which Goldsmith's vagabond
friend arrived, concerning his stingy master and the latter's
still more stingy housekeeper,—"As they determined to
starve me between them, I made a pious resolution to prevent their committing murder."

The only other high Hindú castes which are numerically
important enough to claim mention here, are Banyas (grain-
dealers and money-lenders), who number about 240,000, and
Kayaths, or writers, of whom there are nearly 150,000. Somewhat akin in character to both of these are the Khatris, of
whom, though they are little over 13,000 in all, eleven are
Taluqdárs.* Both Banyas and Kayaths are generally considered cowardly castes, and both, as also Khatris, have
considerable sedentary ability. The first are, strictly speaking, Vaisyas, the third division of Hindús, according to
Manu; but the term Vaisya is almost obsolete, and Banya,
though properly the name of a profession, not of a caste, is
that by which they are usually known. They can boast
of no Taluqdárs among their ranks. Kayaths are really
Sudras, and their right to be included among the higher
castes is rather a vexed question. The claim of their
women to be treated as *pardanishin*, *i.e.* never to show their
faces unveiled, was on one occasion referred to a leading Ta-

---

* They are generally traders, but sometimes landholders. They are
held in higher esteem in the Panjáb than in Oudh; and it is from the
Panjáb that most of the Khatris come who are in Government service
in Oudh.

luqdár as arbitrator, and decided in their favour. The *patwáris* are all but universally Kayaths, and write, as a rule, Hindí or Nágri in some one of its many forms, the most usual of which is that called Kayathí, after the name of this caste. The more educated generally write only Persian, and despise the ruder character. Many of them are in Government service as clerks; others practise as pleaders and law agents. They are excellent penmen, and very quick and shrewd, but have a reputation—not seldom, however, undeserved—for being unscrupulous and corrupt. Kánúngos are generally of this caste, which, though not often occupied with agriculture, includes not a few small landowners, and seven Taluqdárs. The circumstance which chiefly militates against their claim to belong to the higher castes is that they are very often addicted to drinking.

The lower classes of Hindús, all of whom are Sudras, are divided into 64 castes, many of them very minute. The most important are Ahirs, or cowherds, who number nearly 1,200,000; Chamárs, or tanners and labourers, of whom there are more than a million; Kurmis, the cultivators, *par excellence*, of Oudh, with 760,000; Muráos, or gardeners, with over 400,000; and Pásis, who are found all over the province as village watchmen, labourers, pig-keepers, and thieves, and number about 650,000. Lonyas, though but little over 100,000, perhaps deserve mention as the caste which has suffered more than any other by British rule, their profession, the manufacture of salt, having been prohibited, and rendered a penal offence. They are expert with the spade, and many of them have taken to work on the roads. Gaṛariyas, or shepherds, number 230,000, and Koris, or weavers, 360,000.

Of the non-agricultural castes, the chief are Bhujwas or grain-parchers; Barháis, or carpenters; Halwáis, or confectioners, some of whom are Musalmáns; Kalwárs, or distillers; Lohárs, or blacksmiths; Náos, or barbers; and Telis, or oilmen. Sunárs, or goldsmiths, number less than 50,000, but are often wealthy, and have an ill repute as being addicted to receiving stolen goods, especially gold and siver ornaments.

The most hopeful classes of the peasantry are the Kurmis,

Muráos, and Káchhis or Kisáns, whose aggregate numbers are about 1,180,000. They are hardworking, well-behaved agriculturists, who, with fixity of tenure, might be reasonably expected to rise to a fair degree of comfort. Even in their present defenceless condition, for it is very rare to find them in any position but that of tenants-at-will, they are, as a rule, less badly off than cultivators of any other low caste. Muráos and Káchhis generally cultivate very small holdings with very great industry, and pay very high rents, devoting themselves chiefly to garden produce; while Kurmis usually grow the ordinary staples on larger areas. It is a significant illustration of the divorce in Oudh of landed property from agricultural industry, that of these 1,180,000 only one, a Kurmi, is to be found in the list of Taluqdárs. A good many well-to-do Kurmis are found, under the names of Chaudhri or Mahto, in positions corresponding to that of the Mokaddams of Southern India. In taluqdári villages where Rájpúts and Bráhmans were few or none, Kurmis not unfrequently enjoyed a *quasi*-under-proprietary right, in return for their services as the medium of communication between the landlord and the other tenants. Many of this caste have shown themselves good soldiers.

Next to these, the most well-to-do castes are Ahirs and Garariyas, who, especially in the northern districts, have sometimes considerable wealth in flocks and herds. Ahirs, owing, doubtless, to their wandering, out-door life, and to their consumption of milk and curds as food, are an erect and stalwart race, and are generally to be recognised by their long silver ear-rings. Many of them are to be met with in charge of vast herds of cattle sent up for pasture to the great grazing-grounds of the Tarai. They are singularly fearless of wild animals, and, when one of their cattle has been attacked by a tiger or leopard, will often rush up to within a few feet of the assailant, and endeavour, sometimes with success, to drive him away by a demonstration with a brandished *láthi* or bamboo club, accompanied by terrific yells.

At the very bottom of the social scale come the Koris and Chamárs, who are not recognised as genuine Hindús, and are certainly not of Aryan blood. They are mere village drudges, employed to skin dead cattle, and as ploughmen and day-labourers. A few of them can make the rude shoes which the poorer classes of rustics wear; and some of those who are established in towns are very neat leatherworkers. Koris are also weavers, but anything more hopeless than their position, and that of the common village Chamárs, it would not be easy to imagine. Their best—indeed, their only—chance of escaping from a state of serfdom and, in hard times, of semi-starvation, is to obtain service as grooms or grass-cutters, and those who are fortunate enough to do so often show by their smartness and activity that, under better auspices, they are far from incapable of improvement. In the northern districts of Oudh almost every Bráhman or Chhatri cultivator has one or more Koris or Chamárs bound under what are known as *sánwak* bonds to serve as plough-men until the loan is paid off. Such bond-slaves must, of course, be kept in food and some kind of clothes, and no interest is charged so long as they go on working. These debts often descend from father to son, and to generations who were, perhaps, unborn when the bond was executed. Naturally, the debtors are apt to abscond, and their high-caste employers spend a good deal of their time in wander-ing about the country in search of fugitive ploughmen. Usually, the only resource of the runaway is to take refuge with some other employer in the same capacity, and if the latter sees fit to retain him when claimed, custom requires that he should pay his debt. This, of course, he only does on condition that a new bond for the amount so paid be exe-cuted in his own favour. The *sánwak* ploughman is thus practically a slave, but with liberty to change his master if he can find someone to buy him.

Outside the pale of Hindúism altogether are such abori-ginal tribes as Thárús (who are found only in the Tarai), Bhars, Nats, and Kanjars. The latter are wandering gyp-sies, thieves, and hunters. These aborigines are happier than Koris or Chamárs, in having "escaped," once more to quote Mr. Benett, "being assigned any definite functions in the Hindú caste system."

Religious sectaries and mendicants number more than

130,000, of whom some 57,000 are entered in the census returns as fakírs without distinction of sect, while the remainder, or some 73,500, are divided, if a few generic appellations be excluded, into twenty-three or twenty-four classes. These figures include only clerical members of many of the sects which admit of lay followers, who are shown in the returns under their various castes The principal division of the Hindú sects in Oudh, as in other parts of Upper India, is into Vaishnavas and Saivas. The Sáktas are, happily, almost unknown, their worship of the female generative principle in nature, as symbolised by Kálí, the wife of Siva, being the worst form of Hindúism. The Vaishnavas are generally respectable religionists, and live together in large well-ordered *maths*, or monasteries, of which there are a considerable number at Ajodhya, near Faizábád, where twice a year great crowds of pilgrims flock to bathe in the holy river and be purified from their sins. The Saivas, on the other hand, are often vagabonds, wandering over the country in search of offerings from their followers. Their ceremonies, however, are free from any gross indecency. Some of the larger monasteries have a good deal of landed property, and over most large estates held by Hindú proprietors are scatterred small patches of rent-free land, assigned by the piety of the owners for the support of petty shrines kept up by solitary Gosáyins and Bairágis. It is usual for wealthy Hindú families to maintain a resident Guru, or spiritual guide; while those in humbler circumstances receive annual or biennial visits from their pastor, according to the extent of his *clientèle*. These sects are open to men of any caste, high or low, but those who were previously Bráhmans are held in especial esteem. The cœnobitic monasteries are presided over by abbots, or *muhants*, who are elected for life by *pancháyats* of all the members. Pre-eminence in Sanskrit learning and austerity of life are the chief qualifications for the post.

Musalmán sectaries are, of course, much fewer and less important than those of the Hindús, and have no such elaborate organizations. The great majority are mere religious mendicants, without any special doctrines to distinguish them from other Muhammadans. They are to be found all over the country, in villages and isolated houses, and not a few hold small rent-free grants even in Hindú estates. Perhaps the most respectable among them are those who are attached to the shrines of the five Muhammadan saints, known throughout Oudh as the " Pánchón Pír." The chief of these shrines is the Dargáh of Syad Salár Mas'úd Ghází, at Bahraich.

The anti-sacerdotal character of the Muhammadan faith sufficiently accounts for the inferior importance of the Musalmán sectaries, and the small estimation in which they are held as compared with those of the Hindús. The respective numbers of Shias and Sunnis are not known. It is certain, however, that the latter are much the more numerous, though Shia doctrines, as having been those of the Nawábs of Oudh, are the more fashionable and the more richly endowed.

If it be asked what progress is Christianity making in Oudh, the only answer that can be made is, None that is perceptible by an ordinary lay observer. There are about two hundred and fifty native Christians in Lucknow, which is probably more than are to be found in all the rest of the province put together. The simple monotheism of Islám, and the elaborate theology and cosmogony of Hindúism, dissimilar as they are, present pretty equally impregnable fronts to missionary enterprise.

In speculating on the future of a country, it is of course never safe to omit from any calculation of forces to be reckoned with the possibilities of a revolution in religious thought. The probability of a revival of Islám has been a good deal talked of as a danger to the Empire. Such a movement is, perhaps, less unlikely than any other, but there is certainly not much sign of it at present. To produce any direct effect on the material condition of the people, nothing short of a great wave of religious enthusiasm, directed to philanthropic ends, would suffice. But of this the likelihood seems too remote to justify more than a mere passing reference to its possibility. Buddhism, with its marvellous renunciation and self-effacement, seems dead in Oudh beyond all chance of resuscitation. A revival of Islám would probably tend rather to military than humanitarian objects. The Hindú revival of the last hundred years, whether it is still going on or not, has probably not affected the richer classes so much as the poorer. Christianity, as already remarked, is making no progress that is appreciable by an outsider. Perhaps the religion least unlikely to get hold of and influence the wealthier landholders of Oudh is the theism of the Brahmo-Somáj, and on some few of them it has had a certain effect. Uneventful, however, as the horizon may seem at present, it should never be forgotten that in India, at any rate, the age of new religions is not yet past, and that "there are many events in the womb of time which will be delivered." Let us hope that if a great new teacher should arise, we may have the insight to recognise him ere it be too late, and to save us from endeavouring to crush a force which might be guided to precious results.

Much has been, and much more doubtless will be, written on the almost infinitely complex subject of native character. Almost every caste has more or less marked moral features of its own. But the broadest line of distinction which can be drawn is that which separates the character of the Hindú from that of the Musalmán. And the distinction appears to consist ultimately in this, that the Hindú mind, and habits of thought, and modes of life, are based on and moulded by a creed of pessimist asceticism; while those of the Musalmán are under the sway of a creed of optimistic hedonism. It may be doubted whether sufficient weight has been attached to the effect upon Hindú character of the influence of Buddhism, which was once the prevailing creed of Northern India, and nowhere reigned more absolutely than in the region which was then Kosála, but is now known as Oudh. The future happiness to which the devout Hindú looks forward is no sensual rapture of flowing wine-cups, or of black-eyed houris; it is not, indeed, happiness at all, in the ordinary sense of the term; but rather, escape from the misery of the ceaseless flux and decay of an eternally transient and illusive world. His ideal of virtue consists, primarily, of renunciation, the deadening of passion and desire; and, secondarily, of benevolence and an often extravagant generosity. It is only the small fractional minority of thinking Hindús who would, or could, explicitly avow these doctrines, but the idea has been unconsciously engrained into their nature until it has come to lend a distinctive colour, or rather, perhaps, a distinctive want of colour, to the character of the race. With the Muhammadan, on the other hand, a totally different set of theological and ethical doctrines have been at work, and have contributed, together with his history and traditions as a member of a conquering race, to make him what he is. More arrogant, more sensual, more materially civilised than the Hindú, he seems to have even less faculty for improvement, or for change of any kind. But the immobility of the Hindú is the result of despair of anything better; that of the Musalmán arises from contentment with a certain standard of material comfort, and a narrow range of ideas above which he does not seek to rise. The mind of the former tends to work inward, that of the latter outward; but though individuals of both races, here and there, are doubtless ambitious of individual worldly success, yet the mass, both of Hindús and Muhammadans, though from very different causes, are about equally apathetic.

The distinction which I have here sought to draw may to some extent explain, what is undoubtedly the fact, that gentleness, docility, and uncomplaining patience, often accompanied by mental inconsequence and instability of purpose, are the chief characteristics of the Hindú national character. What share of the first three of these qualities the Musalmán possesses, he has acquired mainly from long contact with his Hindú neighbours, or, if he be himself of low caste, probably from his own original Hindúism. Of the two latter he has little or nothing, being practically logical, clear-sighted, and persistent enough, but all in a narrow sphere. He is more educated, more cosmopolitan, more conversant with the course of affairs, knows very well what he wants, and is only dissatisfied because he can seldom get it. The Hindú mind, meanwhile, goes on groping vaguely, " in worlds not realised," for it knows not what, and looks forth with timid wonder on the actual world in which it finds itself. Elastic fluidity and tolerance characterise most of its religious and moral conceptions; it will not quit its own path, but willingly admits that what others do may be right for them. It cannot conceive of anyone being born out of a caste, and as caste customs differ, thinks that foreign ways are doubtless good for foreigners.

The ideas of the Musalmán, on the other hand, are rigid and stereotyped, so far as he is untinctured by Hindú influences. He knows more of our ways, but likes them less. He can remember, if of middle age, the time when Musalmáns ruled in Oudh, and it is hard for him to forget the past when brought into contact with the new order of things. He can understand and utilise the appliances of our civilisation, but dislikes, and affects, at least, to despise it, because it is not his own.

In their full extent, however, these remarks are only intended to apply to that small section of Oudh Musalmáns who have almost wholly escaped the influences of Hindú contact. And these are chiefly descendants, often greatly impoverished, of old and wealthy families, living principally in Lucknow, Faizábád, and a few other towns. The rural and the less aristocratic Muhammadans have become to a great extent Hindúised, and the process of assimilation is steadily going on under the compressive and welding forces of British rule.

Of the great mass of the people, Hindús and Musalmáns alike, it may be asserted, generally, that they are good-natured; honest among themselves; prone to verbal quarrels, but easily reconciled; considerate, after their own fashion, in their treatment of women and the aged; careful of and kind to their male children, but apt to be careless of their daughters; frugal in their habits, except on special occasions, such as births, deaths, and marriages; extremely submissive to authority; industrious, though, except in the case of the specially agricultural castes, such as Kurmis and Muráos, with a somewhat fitful and desultory industry; careless and unsystematic in most of their arrangements; very prone to lying, and still more to what seems to be lying, but is often, with Hindús at least, the result of imperfectly understanding what is said to them, and of a looseness of thought and mental limitations which are beyond the conception of a European interrogator; averse to any change of which the benefit is not very obvious to them, and craving few boons of Government except to be left alone as much as it can find it in its heart to leave them.

Perhaps the occasions on which they show to most advantage are large fairs and similar gatherings. It is difficult to watch those dense crowds of thousands, perhaps hundreds of thousands, of men, women, and children, in their clean, bright-coloured garments, so patient, so good-humoured, so simply amused, not a drunken or a quarrelsome man among them, without feeling that, whatever their other shortcomings, they are the best-behaved holiday-makers and sight-seers in the world. On the whole, a likeable, even a loveable, though, not unfrequently, a somewhat exasperating people; difficult to understand, but well worthy of study; who will repay with interest the expenditure, by all who have to deal with them, of the whole of their available stock of the four great qualities which they most require and most appreciate—gentleness, patience, firmness, and thoroughness.

CHAPTER III.

EARLY OUDH HISTORY AND LEGEND.

Ra'ma and Buddha—these are the two names, the two figures, which still stand prominently forth amid the mass of indistinct conceptions which are all that we can now form of ancient Oudh.

The former can be for us little more than a name, though he still lives in the hearts and on the lips of millions of Hindús, who revere his memory as the son of Dasáratha, the bender of the magic bow, the wooer of Síta, the patient exile, the loving and beloved brother of the faithful Bhárata, the triumphant slayer of the demon Rávana, the ideal type of the heroic king who ruled long and gloriously in Ajodhya the blessed, thousands of years ago. Ajodhya, the capital of the kingdom of Kosála, was founded, according to tradition, by Manu, the father of the human race, ascriptive author of the code that bears his name, and first of the line of Súrajbans, or Sun-begotten kings, of whom Ráma was the fifty-seventh in descent. The prosperity of the city has waxed and waned with the changing fortunes of the Hindú faith, and when, on the fall of the last of the line of Ráma, it became a desert, the royal kinsmen went forth into distant lands, and from them the noblest houses of Rájpútána still claim the honour of descent.

It was about the year 1426 B.C. that Nihadbála, last of the Súrajbans line, is supposed to have been slain in a great battle, and from that time it lay deserted until the days of King Vikramaditya of Ujjain, about 78 A.D. Modern Hindús, indeed, are in the habit of ascribing the achievements of all Vikramas to this Sákárí prince of Ujjain, so their opinion on the point is of little value. But Hweng Thsang, the Chinese Buddhist, who travelled in Hindústán between 629 and 642 A.D., states that a Vikramaditya, of Bráhmanical and anti-Buddhist tendencies, was reigning in Sravasti (Ajodhya) at about that period, and it is to him that General Cunningham, of the Archæological Survey, attributes the restoration of the city. Hindú tradition asserts that he found the site of the old city a jungle, but discovered all the spots sacred to Ráma by measurements made, according to ancient records, from a famous shrine known as Nageshwar Náth, and built three hundred and sixty temples in honour of Ráma and Síta, Ráma's three brothers, Lachman, Bhárat, and Satrughan, and his famous monkey ally, Hanumán, who constructed the bridge over the sea by which his army crossed to Lanka (Ceylon), the stronghold of Rávana. All the existing Ajodhya temples, except perhaps two, are comparatively modern; most of them have been built during the last two hundred, many within the last twenty, years; but the sites on which they stand are those of very ancient temples, destroyed either by old age or by eiconoclastic Musalmáns.

The other great name of Oudh, a name greater than that of Ráma, if human greatness be measured by the mark it makes on the world's history, is also closely connected with Ajodhya. Sakya Buddha was a prince of the house of Kápila (near the modern Gorakhpur), which was an offshoot of the Súrajbans line of Kosála. Ajodhya was the scene of his labours for a period of several years, and his favourite resting-place during the rainy season. Some fifty miles north-west of it lie the ruins of Sahet-Mahet, a very ancient city, where a line of Buddhist kings reigned for some five centuries. In the life-time of Gautama Buddha, Sahet-

Mahet was the capital of King Prasenajít, whom he converted to the new faith. But his son, Virudatha, persecuted the Sakyas, attacked their country, and put to death five hundred of their maidens who had been destined for his harem. For this impious deed he was destroyed by fire from heaven, in proof whereof the tank in which he vainly sought refuge was shown to Hweng Thsang. The city and kingdom of Sahet-Mahet seem to have flourished as a dependency of the Gupta dynasty of Magadha, and to have gradually declined after the fall of the latter in or about 319 A.D. Fa Hian, an earlier Chinese pilgrim than Hweng Thsang, who visited the city about 400 A.D., found it in ruins, and containing only two hundred families. Its remains, mere jungle-covered mounds, may still be seen a little south of the Rápti river, on the borders of Bahraich to the west and Gonda to the east. They would probably repay a far more thorough excavation than any they have as yet received.

The legend of the life of Buddha has been made familiar to us by the journals of Fa Hian and Hweng Thsang, and by the labours of St. Hilaire, Stanislas Julien, Burnouf, Beale, Max Müller, and a host of other modern writers; and, defaced as it is by wild extravagance, it is yet not difficult to catch sufficiently clear glimpses of a noble personality through the thick veils of Oriental embellishment. The "obstinate questionings" of the reality of outward things in which his "sad and philosophic youth" was passed; the agonizing sense of human misery which turned a prince into an ascetic, and rendered life intolerable to him until he seemed to himself to have found a way of escape and of salvation for mankind; the sombre grandeur of spirit which could look without quailing into the fathomless abyss of annihilation, and find in its dark depths the remedy for human woe—these should be no ineffectual claims to the reverence of an age like ours. If a creed may be judged by the highest outcome of its moral teaching, by the most perfect efflorescence of its spirit, it may be fairly doubted whether it has yet entered into the heart of man to conceive a loftier height of aspiration than that which

breathes in this utterance of a later Buddhist master—
"Never will I seek, nor receive, private individual salvation; never enter into final peace alone; but for ever, and everywhere, will I live and strive for the universal redemption of every creature throughout all worlds. Until all are delivered, never will I leave this world of sin, sorrow, and struggle, but will remain where I am."

Never, perhaps, has the spirit of self-negation found loftier or more complete expression, and the country which gave birth to a creed capable of rising to such moral heights as this, should never want a title to the regard and consideration of civilised men. There is no region in the world of such small extent, and, indeed, no region whatever, which can claim to be the Holy Land of two such faiths as Hindúism and Buddhism, which, between them, probably number half of the whole human race as their adherents. Though Ajodhya be now little more than a collection of modern temples, and though the great Buddhist city of Sahet-Mahet lie in ruinous heaps, yet the memory of the great part which she has played in the religious history of the world should secure tender treatment for Oudh, even at the hands of conquerors of alien creeds and of other blood.

The meagre records of Ptolemy, who visited India towards the end of the first century of our era, possess an undoubted interest for the antiquarian, but they are too obscure, and their interpretation too difficult, to be more than briefly alluded to here. From Mr. Benett's epitome of them it may be gathered that of the three peoples among whom he describes the country as divided, the Tánganoi, who held the country between the Ghághra and the hills, were an aboriginal tribe, nowhere else mentioned in history, and whose name now only survives in the Tánghans, or hill ponies, of lower Naipál; the Maracmdai, in central and eastern Oudh, were of Scythian origin; while of the Amanichai, who occupied a narrow strip along the Ganges to the south, nothing certain is known, but it is plausibly conjectured that from them the town of Mánikpur, near Allahábád, derives its name. Some ascribe it to the "ubiquitous Mánik Chand of Kanauj," who lived at the end of the twelfth century, but such a date is

5

far too modern for some of its remains. Among the towns mentioned by Ptolemy, Baraita, or Baraila, is identified by Mr. Benett with the modern Rai Bareli, and Sapolas, or Sapotas, with Sravasti or Ajodhya.

About the year 100 A.D. the Sravasti dynasty was overthrown by Samundra Pála, King of Patna—who, according to the legend of Ajodhya, cheated Vikramaditya out of his kingdom in the disguise of a *jogi*—after a desperate struggle which seems to have laid the country desolate. For centuries henceforward nothing is heard of Oudh, and it may be conjectured that the greater part of the country relapsed into jungle and forest, inhabited only by primitive wandering tribes. The great forest which covered the trans-Ghághra tract was known as the *Gandharb Ban*, while that to the south, embracing what is now Faizábád and Sultánpur, was termed *Banaudha*, or the forest of Oudh. Between 800 and 900 A.D. the Thárus, a hill tribe of Mongolian origin, began to assert their power. They partially cleared the northern forest, and were the dominant race in what is now Gonda and Bahraich at the time of Salár Mas'úd's invasion. Further south of the Ghághra than the immediate neighbourhood of Ajodhya they do not seem to have ever penetrated. They appear to have been in some sort of subjection to a Sombansi family of Rájpúts who were ruling at, or near, the ruins of Sravasti early in the eleventh century. Sohil Deo, otherwise Sohel Dál, the conqueror of Salár Mas'úd, and last of his line, had his head-quarters at Sahet-Mahet. The legend of his downfall is thus related by Mr. Benett:—

"Sohel Dál came in hot from the chase a few minutes before sunset, and his princess, fearing that the close of the day would prevent his eating his evening meal, sent up to the roof of the house the wife of his younger brother, whose surpassing beauty detained the sinking sun. Till the supper was ended, the damsel stood and the god watched, and then, as she left her post, a sudden night ensued. The prince inquired why there had been no twilight, and the guilty passion which arose from his discovery of the truth was followed by his punishment in the total destruction of his fort during an appalling tempest. The historical fact underlying the story is the subversion of this small northern kingdom by Sri Chandradeo, the Ráthor monarch of Kanauj, during the last quarter of the eleventh century." The battle in which Sohil Deo was defeated is said by Mr. Carnegy to have been fought at Satrikh, the burial-place of Salár Sahu, in what is now the Bárabanki district. The Ráthors appear to have followed up their victory by a general expulsion of the Buddhists from the Trans-Ghághra districts, and the family of Sohil Deo are said to have fled to Jumla in the territory of Naipál. It may here be added, on the authority of General Cunningham, that during the first half at least of the seventh century the kingdom of Kanauj itself was held by Buddhist kings. They were succeeded by dynasties of Tomár and Ráthor Chhatris, probably of Brahmanic tendencies. The later Ráthor kings were certainly Brahmanical, as is evident from the war waged against the Buddhist dynasty of northern Oudh by Sri Chandradeo. Jai Chandr, the last of his line, was vanquished in a battle at Banáras by Sháháb-ud-dín Ghorí in 1194 A.D., and is said to have been drowned in the Ganges. This defeat finally crushed the power of the Kanauj kingdom.

Until about 1050 A.D. the whole of Oudh, except the trans-Ghághra tract, seems to have been under the successive dominion of the kings of Patna and Kanauj. But somewhere about that period, the Bhars, an aboriginal tribe, who are still to be found in Faizábád and Sultánpur, revolted from the Kanauj dynasty, and extended their power considerably beyond the present limits of the province. Their sway culminated under the joint rule of two famous brothers, Dál and Bál, who held forts at Karra and Kálinjar, and are said to have mastered the country even as far south as Málwa. The record of their crushing defeat, and of the entire overthrow of the Bhar power by Nasír-ud-dín Muhammad, Emperor of Delhi, in 1246 A.D., is to be found in "Farishta." This event appears to have been succeeded by a *morcellement* of the whole country into petty Rájpút chiefships, which, under more or less subjection to Muhammadan governors, and in spite of frequent struggles with rival Muhammadan settlers, have to a great extent maintained their ground up to the present day. The greatest degree of antiquity claimed for their present settlements by most of the Chhatris of southern Oudh is twenty-two generations. It may be noted that twenty-one generations, of thirty years each, would almost exactly cover the period from 1246 A.D. to the present time.

It is something of a relief to turn from these disjointed fragments of information to a more connected narrative. The wild expedition of Syad Salár Mas'úd Ghází, almost, if not quite, the earliest Muhammadan invasion of Oudh, is also that regarding which our knowledge is least meagre. The story is told in the "Mírát-i-Mas'údi," a translation of which is appended to the second volume of Sir Henry Elliott's "Muhammadan Historians." He calls it an "historical romance," written by Abdur Rahmán Chishti, founded on an older book by Mulla Muhammad Ghaznavi, who was in the service of Salár Mas'úd himself, and also of his father, Salár Sahu, both of whom he survived. General Cunningham expresses his opinion that the work, "although a late compilation of the traditions current in the reign of Jahángír, is probably correct in its general outlines." A brief summary of the story may not inappropriately be inserted here.

Syad Salár Mas'úd was born at Ajmír, in the year 405 Hijri=1014 A.D. His father, Salár Sahu, was a general in the Ghaznavite army, and his mother was sister of Sultán Mahmúd himself. The favour shown by the latter to his nephew gave rise to so much jealousy against him at the court of Ghazni, that he found it expedient to start, at the age of eighteen, on an invasion of India, at the head of some twenty thousand zealous Moslems, eager to slay and plunder, if they could not convert, the infidel Hindú. After a campaign in the Panjáb, Syad Salár marched upon Satrikh, "the most flourishing of all the towns and cities of India." On the strength, apparently, of this somewhat vague description, General Cunningham identifies Satrikh with Vesákh, an old name of Ajodhya. It seems, however, at least as probable that the present Satrikh, some twenty miles east of Lucknow, is the place intended. Its situation fits in better than that of Ajodhya with the known movements of the army, while it contains the well-known tomb of Salár Sahu, father of our hero, who is said by the story itself to have died at Satrikh, and in whose honour an annual fair is still held there. Here Mas'úd took up his quarters, and sent out detachments to conquer the surrounding country. Salár Saif-ud-dín and Miyán Rajjab, *kotwál* of the army, were despatched against Bahraich, and as they were unable to obtain provisions, a supply of which had to be sent after them, we may infer that the intervening country was somewhat sparsely inhabited. Syad Azíz-ud-dín was sent against Hardui, but fell in battle at Gopamau on the banks of the Gumti, where his memory is still revered under the title of the Lál Pír. Mas'úd himself "continued to reside with great magnificence at Satrikh, enjoying the pleasures of the chase."

Satrikh is nearly half-way between Bahraich on the north, and Karra and Mánikpur on the south. The chiefs of the last two places now sent an embassy, with presents, to advise Mas'úd to retire. They urged, as was undoubtedly the fact, that he had no manner of business there, that the country had been theirs from time immemorial, and that it had been spared by Sultán Mahmúd himself, who had penetrated on one occasion as far as Kanauj. "But you," the message continued, "without any respect for the rights of property, establish yourself in a country that does not belong to you. The action is unworthy of a great mind like yours. It is an infinite sorrow to us that you should be the only child in the house of your father, and that he should have no other descendants. Consider, we pray you, the right. Satrikh is a pleasant place, but it is not fitting that you should remain there. We have ninety thousand picked soldiers"—this, it may be safely affirmed, was a lie—"the princes of Bahraich and other places will come to our help on every side, and you will find yourself in great difficulties. You had better take the prudent course of retiring of your own free will."

However great may have been the mind of Mas'úd in other respects, one cannot help suspecting it to have been somewhat deficient in sense of humour, for the only effect upon him of this most respectable, most reasonable, most unimpeachable message was to make him "rage like a fierce lion," and threaten destruction to the infidels who had sent it. He was soon after joined by his father, from Kábuliz, near Kashmir. Spies were captured on the Sarjú or Ghághra river, who were conveying letters from the Ráís of Karra and Mánikpur to those of Bahraich, calling on the latter to fall on the Musalmáns from the north, while the former attacked them from the south. Mas'úd, having ascertained by means of his own spies that the chiefs of Karra and Mánikpur were quite unprepared to resist an attack, despatched his father against them. Salár Sahu took them by surprise, destroyed their forces, "putting thousands of unbelievers to the sword," and sent the two chiefs themselves in chains to Mas'úd, who passed them on to Saif-ud-dín at Bahraich. Sahu returned in triumph, leaving Malik Abdullah in charge of Karra, and Kutb-Haidar at Mánikpur.

Meanwhile, Saif-ud-dín found himself surrounded by enemies, and wrote for reinforcements. Mas'úd, with difficulty, and on the pretext of a hunting excursion, obtained leave from his father to proceed to Bahraich in person. The mere news of his arrival was sufficient to quiet the unbelievers, "whose dimness of perception alone had caused the rising." He hunted in the neighbourhood of Bahraich, and took a fancy to a *súrajkund* (tank of the sun) temple, on which he fixed his desires for a dwelling-place. There was a stone image of the sun, called Bálarukh, on the edge of the tank, the fame of which had caused Bahraich to flourish. Here, every Sunday, flocked crowds of worshippers, who had a habit of rubbing their heads on the pedestal or feet of the idol, which practice much distressed the monotheistic piety of Mas'úd, and caused him to pray that he might some day convert these benighted pagans from the worship of the material to that of the spiritual sun. He had reached Bahraich on the 17th of the month Shábán, 423 Hijrí = 1032 A.D., and shortly after his arrival heard of the death and burial at Satrikh of his father, whereat he wept bitterly, and remarked that he now knew what it was to be an orphan.

The Ráís of Bahraich, who were probably for the most part Thárús, with perhaps a sprinkling of Bhars and Banjáras, now sent Mas'úd a message couched in terms similar to those which had been used by the ambassadors from Karra and Mánikpur, warning him that they were seventeen in number, and that they had two millions of cavalry and three millions of infantry under arms. The oriental mind appears to have been then, as now, without adequate perception of the eloquence of understatement. Malik Nekdil was sent to discuss affairs in general with the Ráís, and to take note of their numbers. He made deceitful proposals of peace, which a majority of the Thárú chiefs had the good sense to reject. One of them, Rai Karan, assured him that he did not yet understand what the rainy season of Bahraich was like, and that the climate would soon do their work for them. After this, "the unbelievers all began to talk like fools," and Malik Nekdil returned to Mas'úd, while the enemy advanced, and encamped on the Kasahla, probably the Koriála, river. A council of war decided Mas'úd to take the initiative. He advanced in a north-westerly direction—getting, probably, some good tiger-shooting on the way—defeated the enemy, and then fell back leisurely on Bahraich.

Rai Jogi Dás, of the Hindú Koh, sent a messenger with presents to Mas'úd. He was favourably received, and informed that if his master would embrace Islám, he might enjoy his country securely. Other Ráís also paid visits, but without ceasing to be hostile. They found a valuable ally in the Thárú chief Sohar Deo, Sohel Dál, or Sohil Deo, as he is variously called—it is by the latter name that he is still locally remembered—by whose advice they prepared large quantities of fireworks, and of poisoned spikes to be fixed in the ground when the Musalmán cavalry were about to charge. In two months the Ráís were again encamped, "with innumerable forces," on the banks of the Kasahla, and again sent word to Mas'úd, "that if he wished to save his life he had better leave that country and go elsewhere, as the land belonged to their fathers and ancestors, and they were determined to drive him from it." His reply was of the briefest and most simple :—" The country is God's, and the property of him on whom He bestows it. Who gave it to your fathers and ancestors?" The audacious casuistry of this argument, which at once reduced the question at issue to first principles, much impressed his opponents. A second council of war decided Mas'úd to remain on the defensive, but the enemy drove off his cattle, and forced an attack. Many " noble Turks " suffered martyrdom from the fireworks and the insidious spikes. The loss was great on both sides, and a third of the Musalmán army perished. Another quiet interval, however, followed, which Mas'úd, now nineteen years of age, devoted to religious musing at the *súrajkund*, under the shade of a huge *mahua* tree which he particularly affected. His meditations were disturbed by a fresh gathering of the foe, and he made up his mind for the worst. Assembling his forces, he advised all who cared for their lives to retreat to the Panjáb, but such as were desirous of martyrdom were left at liberty to remain. They all wept, and vowed never to desert him. " In fact, it was like the day of judgment, or even more solemn."

On the 18th and 19th of the month Rajjab-ul-Murajjab 424 Hijrí, continuous fighting went on. Two-thirds of what remained of the Musalmáns were slain, and among them Saif-ud-dín. The bodies of the faithful were cast into the *súrajkund*, "in the hope that through the odour of their martyrdom the darkness of unbelief might be expelled from that spot"—which strikes one as being a slightly equivocal aspiration. Mas'úd then "remounted his mare of sacred blood," charged the enemy, and put them to flight. But Sohil Deo, and a few others who had reserved their troops, attacked the body guard, which was all that was now left to him, and on Sunday, the 20th of Rajjab 424 Hijrí=14th June 1033 A.D., at the hour of evening prayer, a chance arrow pierced the main artery in the arm of the Prince of the Faithful. His sun-like countenance immediately became pale as the moon. Repeating the text in praise of martyrdom, he dismounted, was carried under his favourite *mahua* tree, and there expired. The remnant of his body guard was cut to pieces by Sohil Deo, to whom, however, Mas'úd appeared

EARLY OUDH HISTORY AND LEGEND. 73

the same night in a vision, and foretold his violent death, which came to pass as already related in this chapter. So ended this singular invasion, and Islám was in abeyance in Oudh for one hundred and sixty years, until the conquests of Shaháb-ud-dín Ghori, in 1193 A.D., enabled him to place Kutb-ud-dín Aibak as his representative on the throne of Delhi.

It was probably about the middle of the thirteenth century that the present Dargáh of Syad Salár was built. It was visited about 1340 A.D. by Sultán Muhammad Toghlak, after his suppression of the revolt of Ain-ul-Mulk, and is still the scene of a large annual fair held on the first Sunday in Jeth. Mas'úd is said by tradition to have condescended, while at Satrikh, to take to himself as wife the daughter of a converted Teli, or oilman, who dwelt at Radauli, in what is now the Bárabanki district, and on the great day of the fair—said to be the anniversary of the martyr's marriage as well as his death — a representative of his wife's family regularly arrives from Radauli, with a bridal couch and other offerings for the use of his shade. The Dargáh is a massive, battlemented building, in the centre of which stands the tomb itself, inside a dark and narrow cell, entered by a single door some five feet high. Till a year or two ago, there was no other means of ventilation, and as into this cell the pilgrims crush together all day long in successive batches of as many as a vigilant police, armed with knotted handkerchiefs to drive back the crowd, and assisted by barricades, will admit, the state of the atmosphere towards the close of a hot day in May may be more easily imagined than described. Some eight or nine years ago more than twenty people were crushed and suffocated to death, after which police supervision somewhat mitigated the crowding, but was powerless perceptibly to improve the vitiated atmosphere. Recently, however, an energetic Deputy Commissioner, among other "modern touches here and there," which redeem the shrine, if not from "nothingness," at least from annihilation of its worshippers, has succeeded in getting a window opened in the wall of the holy of holies, the application to which of a thermantidote considerably cools and purifies the heated horrors of the atmosphere within. The curious part of the matter is that though the *khádims*, or servants of the shrine, vehemently objected to this innovation before it was made, the pilgrims have quite accepted the *beláti pankha* as part of the sacred apparatus, and call the current of air which proceeds from it the breath of the martyred saint. They have even begun to place on it offerings of pice, cowries, and flowers; and in two or three years time these will doubtless form a recognised source of income to the *khádims*, and be mortgaged, fought over, and sued for, with as much earnestness as if the origin of the tribute were lost in the mists of antiquity.

The fair itself is essentially a poor man's fair, and is attended by low-caste Hindús quite as largely as by Muhammadans. This is a curious illustration of the laxity of Hindú religious conceptions, considering that the one object of Salár Mas'úd's life was the destruction of their faith and the slaughter of its adherents. This anomaly is noticed in Sleeman's "Tour in Oudh," and is there explained on the theory that thinking Hindús regard the invader as having been an instrument of divine vengeance, to whom power was given over them for their sins; while the ignorant masses hold " that the old man must still have a good deal of interest in heaven, which he may be induced to exercise in their favour by suitable offerings and personal applications to his shrine." It is, perhaps, a more probable explanation that the Hindú worshippers believe themselves, in some confused way, to be adoring, not so much Syad Salár, as the old Sun god, whose image, Bálarukh, has been already mentioned. It is, at any rate, certain that they speak of the personage whom they come, as they put it, to interview, as "Bála Bádsháh," or "King Bála"; and it is not easy to see how, except by some such confusion as this, the name should have come to be applied to the Musalmán hero and Ghází.

The crescentade of Salár Mas'úd has been dwelt on at what may seem undue length, mainly because it was the first impact of Islám on Oudh, and has left more traces, and is known in fuller detail, than any subsequent invasion; partly, also, to be perfectly candid, because its scenes are more familiar to the writer. Its hold on the popular imagination is testified to by the fact that "the Musalmáns of Oudh are apt to associate with Syad Salár every object or tradition of antiquity to which they can ascribe no certain origin."

It is a somewhat humiliating confession, but it is probably a true one, that of the history of Oudh, from the time of Syad Salár's expedition to the appointment of S'ádat Khán as Súbahdár of the province in 1720 A.D., a period of nearly seven hundred years, we have next to no real information. Written Hindú records there are almost none, and from Muhammadan chronicles little can be gleaned beyond such unfruitful items as that this governor was superseded by that, or that the infidels of such a place revolted, and were put down with great slaughter. Local Hindú traditions there are in abundance, but it seems almost impossible to connect them with any degree of certainty with such facts as are to be gathered from the Muhammadan historians. Thus we learn from the latter that in 1226 A.D. Malik Nasír-ud-dín was appointed as governor of Oudh, and "overthrew the accursed Bartúh (Bhars?), under whose hands and swords more than one hundred and twenty thousand Musalmáns had received martyrdom"; all of which was, no doubt, very vivid and real to him, and to the poor Bartúh, whoever they were, but is not quite so much so to us. In 1243 A.D. the Emperor Alá-ud-dín sent his uncle Nasír-ud-dín as governor of Bahraich, where he "devoted himself to peaceful pursuits, and the improvement of the condition of his subjects . . . In that country and in the hills he fought many battles against the infidels. Under his kind rule Bahraich attained great prosperity." This Nasír-ud-dín afterwards became Emperor, and it was he who again defeated the Bhars under the brothers Dál and Bál, as already related, in 1246 A.D. Or perhaps these two defeats of the Bhars may be really one and the same, and a confusion of twenty years have crept into the chronology. Or, again, the victory which is spoken of as if it followed immediately on his appointment as governor, may not in reality have occurred till twenty years after that event, when he had become Emperor.

Oudh and Bahraich were evidently two distinct governments or fiefs. The latter, including Gonda, seems to have been always held singly, owing doubtless to its isolated position, cut off from the rest of the province by a great unfordable river. The former was sometimes held jointly with Karra, sometimes with Badáun, and sometimes with Zafarábád.

It would be easy to accumulate such items as these, were it worth while to do so. But as mere isolated events they are useless. They might serve as landmarks, if we were in possession of general information as to the movement of society and popular life in Oudh. Taken by themselves, they are as worthless as would be an assortment of milestones in the absence of a passable road on which to erect them. Local details of the fortunes of particular families are plentiful enough, but scarcely any generalisations wide enough to be entitled to a place in a provincial history can be arrived at. It must suffice to say that for about a century and a half after the conquests of Shaháb-ud-dín Ghori, though Musalmán influence in Upper India was steadily becoming consolidated, yet Musalmán settlements in Oudh were few and insignificant. But from about the year 1350 A.D. the tide of Muhammadan immigration set steadily in, and continued with short intervals until nearly the middle of the eighteenth century. The course which it followed lay chiefly from the north-west to the south-east of the province, and formed a broad belt running through Harduí, Lucknow, Bárabanki, and Faizábád. In Unáo, Sítapur, and Sultánpur, the Musalmán colonies wese less numerous and sporadic; while in Kheri, Bahraich, and Gonda to the north, and Rai Bareli and Pratábgarh to the south, they were few and isolated.

CHAPTER IV.

THE NAWABI [1720–1856].

THE wheel of fortune was whirling at the very top of its speed in Upper India during the early part of the last century. Adventurer after adventurer rose like bubbles to the surface of the seething cauldron, floated there for a moment, and then vanished into an obscurity from which, in most cases, they had no apparent claim to have arisen. Some few, of tougher texture or more favourably environed than the rest, contrived to keep themselves with more or less permanence at the top of affairs. One of the most distinguished of these was S'ádat Khán, founder of the modern dynasty of Oudh. His original name was Muhammad Amín, and he came of a noble Syad family which derived its descent from the Prophet himself through the Imám Músa Kázim, and had long been settled at Naishapur in Khorásán. He was described by Alexander Dow as "the infamous son of a yet more infamous Persian pedlar," but this vigorous language may perhaps be to some extent explained by the fact that S'ádat Khán's grandson Shúja'-ud-daulah had refused to grant certain salt contracts to the historian who used it. Mirza Nasír, father of Muhammad Amín, had been in the service of the Emperor Bahádur Sháh, second son of Aurangzíb, and on the news of his death, Muhammad Amín, in his turn, set out for India. He was well received by the then Emperor Farukhsiyár, who appointed him commandant of his body guard, and afterwards made him governor of Agra. We need not do more than mention the murder of Farukhsiyár, in 1719 A.D., by the Syad brothers Abdullah Khán and Hosen Ali, who were then *de facto* masters of the empire; the subsequent elevation of Muhammad Sháh to the throne; and his release from the tyranny of the Syads, and the overthrow of the latter by means of a conspiracy, in which Muhammad Amín was a principal agent. As a reward for his services, he was appointed Súbahdár of Oudh in 1720 A.D., under the title of S'ádat Ali Khán, Burhán-ul-Mulk, and seems to have been occupied for several years in establishing some kind of order in his province. In 1736 he defeated the Mahrattas under Báji Ráo, in the Doáb, and about the same time his daughter married his nephew Muhammad Mukím, better known to fame as Safdar Jang, who, on his death, succeeded him in the governorship of Oudh. S'ádat Khán took a conspicuous—and, according to what is perhaps a calumny of Dow's, a treacherous—part in resisting the celebrated invasion of Nádir Sháh of Persia in 1738-39. He was taken prisoner at Karnál, and died before the year was out.* S'ádat Khán's policy in Oudh seems to have been to cherish the peasantry, and to keep in check the encroachments of the larger landholders; and he was probably the first to make the power of a comparatively strong and central government felt throughout the province. Ajodhya and Lucknow were the places at which he chiefly resided, and, having assumed for his crest the fish which is still, so to speak, the arms of Oudh, he changed the name of the wellknown fort of Lucknow from Kila Likna (so called after the

---

* The story goes that S'ádat Khán and his great rival, Nizám-ul-Mulk, were so grossly insulted by Nádir Sháh for their treacherous conduct towards the Emperor of Delhi, that they agreed to take poison rather than survive the indignity. The ingenious Nizám-ul-Mulk, however, only pretended to swallow the poisoned draught, and came to life again as soon as he was assured of his rival's death.

founder, one Likna, Ahir) to Machhi Bháwan, or the fish-house. Though he continued, after his appointment as Súbahdár, to play a prominent part in the politics, or rather, in the intrigues of the empire, yet he identified himself more closely with the province, and spent more of his time there than any previous governor had done. He was a keen but unsuccessful candidate for the office of Wazír of the Empire, an honour which was reserved for his successor to attain. He left a large treasure, said to have amounted to some nine millions sterling, three millions of which he is related to have offered to Nádir Sháh as a ransom for Delhi. The offer, however, was not accepted, and the city was sacked. His hoards must have been raised by unscrupulous exactions, but these seem to have been confined to the rich. His great object was the aggrandisement of his own family, in which he certainly succeeded, in spite, if the story may be trusted, of his own ignominious death by poison.

It may here be convenient to give a list of the eleven rulers who composed the Oudh dynasty, showing their dates and mutual relationships:—

1. S'ádat Ali Khán, Burhán-ul-Mulk . . . 1720–1739.
2. Mansúr Ali Khán, Safdar Jang, nephew and son-in-law of No. 1 . . . . 1739–1756.
3. Shúja'-ud-daulah, son of No. 2 . . . 1756–1775.
4. Asaf-ud-daulah, son of No. 3 . . . . 1775–1797.
5. Wazír Ali, reputed son of No. 4 . . . 1797–1798.
6. S'ádat Ali, half-brother of No. 4 . . . 1798–1814.
7. Ghází-ud-dín Haidar, son of No. 6 . . 1814–1827.
8. Nasír-ud-dín Haidar, son of No. 7 . . . 1827–1837.
9. Muhammad Ali Sháh, brother of No. 7 . 1837–1842.
10. Amjad Ali Sháh, son of No. 9 . . . 1842–1847.
11. Wújid Ali Sháh, son of No. 10 . . . 1847–1856.

Muhammad Mukím, under the style of Mansúr Ali Khán, Safdar Jang, succeeded his uncle and father-in-law. He was the first "Nawáb Wazír," a combination of his two titles of Nawáb of Oudh and Wazír of the Empire. This latter honour, as also the title of Mír Átish, or Commander of the Artillery, was bestowed upon him by the Emperor Ahmad Sháh, who succeeded Muhammad Sháh on the throne of Delhi in 1749.

Safdar Jang took an active part in the external politics and wars of the empire against the Mahrattas, and also against the Dúránis under Ahmad Sháh Abdálí, who were defeated in the Panjáb in 1748. With the assistance of the Rohillas, he drove the Mahrattas out of the Doáb in 1851. Of his relations with the people of Oudh, we know but little. He completed the city of Faizábád, the foundation of which had been begun by S'ádat Khán, and divided his time between it and Lucknow. Faizábád is still spoken of by the country-folk as "Bangla," the origin of the name being that, before the erection of the modern city, S'ádat Khán had a shooting-box or *bangla* (*anglicè*, bungalow), on the banks of the Ghághra, which may still be seen by the curious in the compound of what was the Dilkhushá palace, but is now the residence of the Opium Agent. Safdar Jang's most trusted instrument was Rája Newal Rai, a fighting Kayath, who was killed in an engagement with the troops of the Nawáb of Farukhábád, with whom the Nawáb Wazír's own treachery had embroiled him. He had induced Káim Khán Bangash, who was Nawáb of Farukhábád in 1746, to attack his own countrymen, the Rohilla Afgháns, who had shown themselves troublesome neighbours to Oudh. Káim Khán fell in fight, and Safdar Jang promptly seized his territory, and, pacifying his brother Ahmad Khán with a pension, went off to Delhi, leaving Newal Rai in charge of both Oudh and Farukhábád. Ahmad Khán, who at first sat down tamely under his injuries, was roused to action by the stinging reproaches of an Afghán woman, who had been insulted by one of Newal Rai's soldiers. He collected an army, defeated and killed Newal Rai, who marched to resist him, on the banks of the Kálínadí, crossed the Ganges, and was soon master of Oudh. Safdar Jang hastened to the scene of action with a large force, accompanied by Súraj Mal, the Ját chief of Bhartpur, but was completely defeated by Ahmad Khán with very inferior numbers. This victory left the Afgháns for a short time in full possession of Oudh and Allahábád. They soon, however, fell out among themselves, and Safdar Jang did not scruple to call in the Mahrattas, with whose aid Ahmad Khán was driven into Kumáon, cooped up under the hills, and forced to capitulate.

Shortly before his death, Safdar Jang lost the favour of the Emperor Ahmad Khán owing to his share in the murder of a eunuch named Jawíd, of whom the queen-mother had been enamoured. He found himself superseded as Wazír of the Empire by Ghází-ud-dín (grandson of Nizám-ul-mulk, the successful rival of S'ádat Khán), who had been a *protégé* of his own. He retired to Oudh in disgust, and died in 1756. About all that is known of his internal policy is that he made a Hindú, Newal Rai, his minister, and that he commenced the construction of a bridge across the Gumti at Lucknow, which was completed by his grandson Asaf-ud-daulah. The mausoleum of Safdar Jang at Delhi, whither his remains were removed for interment, is well known as one of the finest works of the kind in India.

Shúja'-ud-daulah, his son and successor, had married in 1743 the Bahu Begam, a Persian lady, whose grandfather had been Aurangzíb's head cook, and whose wrongs were to be afterwards immortalised by the eloquence of Burke. His claim to the succession was disputed, but unsuccessfully, by his cousin Muhammad Kuli Khán, Governor of Allahabad, who was supported by Ismail Khán, Kábuli, who had been the chief military adherent of Safdar Jang. The wretched nominal Emperor Álamgír II. was at this time a virtual prisoner in the hands of his tyrannical Wazír, Ghází-ud-dín, and his son Ali Gohar, the Crown Prince, was a fugitive from Delhi, wandering about India in search of support. In 1758 he joined Shúja'-ud-daulah and Muhammad Kuli Khán in an invasion of Bengal, where English influence had a year before been made paramount by the victory of Clive at Plassy, or, more correctly, Palásí. And now Shúja'-ud-daulah was guilty of what was probably the greatest crime of his life. He treacherously lingered behind Muhammad Kuli and Ali Gohar, seized the fort of Allahabad, and on the return of his cousin to recover it, captured and put him to death. Ali Gohar, meanwhile, on receipt of a moderate sum from Clive, withdrew across the Karamnása, a small river which served as a rubicon between Bengal and the upper provinces, and again fell into the hands of Shúja'-ud-daulah. In November 1759 the unhappy Álamgír was murdered by Ghází-ud-dín, and for some months there was no recognised Emperor of Delhi. Ali Gohar, however, claimed the title, and appointed Shúja'-ud-daulah, whose prisoner he practically was, Wazír of the Empire, an honour which, as previously mentioned, had been lost by Safdar Jang shortly before his death. When Kásim Ali, who had been set up by the "ring" of English adventurers who then ruled and exploited Bengal, as Nawáb of Murshidábád in supersession of Mír Jáfar, finally broke with his masters, he fled from Patna to Shúja'-ud-daulah, who had again, after a brief separation, got hold of Ali Gohar, *alias* Sháh Alam. A fresh invasion of Bengal followed, which was defeated at Baksár on the 23rd of October 1764.

Shúja'-ud-daulah now retired to his own territory, while Sháh Alam joined the English. It was proposed by the Calcutta Council to confer on the nominal Emperor all the Wazír's possessions, except Gházípur and Banáras, which were to be granted to the Company. Sháh Alam, indeed, went so far as to issue a *farmán*, dated 29th of December 1764, assigning "the country of Gházípur, and the rest of the Zamíndárí of Rajah Balwant Singh belonging to the Nizámat of the Nawáb Shúja'-ud-daulah," to the Company, on account of the expense and danger caused them by the latter waging war "unjustly, and contrary to our royal pleasure!" This arrangement, however, was disallowed by the Court of Directors as being onerous and profitless, and in 1765 Shúja'-ud-daulah was recognised as in possession of Oudh, Gházípur, and Banáras; Allahabad and Karra being reserved for Sháh Alam. The despatch of the Court of Directors forbidding the intended transfer of Oudh to Sháh Alam has always been deemed a laudable instance of their moderation. It is not surprising, at any rate, that Shúja'-ud-daulah should have regarded its effect in that light, though ignorant of the cause; for it was received just at the time when, after being defeated in an engagement near Karra, he had thrown himself on the mercy of the victors, from whom he could have little expected such easy terms. It is worthy of note, as Sir H. Lawrence has pointed out, that even under circumstances when he might have been supposed likely to agree to anything, Shúja'-ud-daulah insisted, and Clive consented, that "trade and factories" should not be so much as mentioned in the treaty—a pretty significant proof of the dread with which the Company's mercantile operations were regarded.

In 1768 the agreement of 1765 was confirmed at Banáras, and the Nawáb undertook to limit his force to 35,000 men, of whom 10,000 were to be cavalry, 10,000 infantry, 500 artillerymen, and 9,500 irregulars. Of these the infantry alone were to be armed and trained in European fashion.

In 1772 the Mahrattas threatened Rohilkhand, and Shúja'-ud-daulah entered into an agreement with the Rohillas for their expulsion, in consideration of being paid four hundred thousand pounds. It was about this time that an altercation took place between Hastings and Sir Robert Barker, who was commanding a brigade sent to co-operate against the Mahrattas, regarding the choice of a diplomatic agent with the Wazír. Hastings, writes Sir H. Lawrence, "carried his point after an angry correspondence, the commencement of that acrimony which prevailed in the discussion of Oudh affairs during Mr. Hastings' administration, and which has been so prominent a feature in most of the discussions regarding that province." It is, perhaps, some little consolation to reflect that if we too, in this our day, have been guilty of controversial bitterness, we are, after all, only treading in the footsteps of our fathers who were before us.

In September 1773 Hastings and the Wazír had a personal conference at Banáras, at which a new treaty was concluded, declaring that, whereas Sháh Álam, contrary to the treaty of the 16th of August 1765, granting him Karra and Allahabad for his expenses, had assigned those districts to the Mahrattas, his rights were forfeited, and transferred to the Wazír for a payment of fifty lákhs, or five hundred thousand pounds. It was also stipulated that Oudh should pay for all such troops of the Company's service as she, or rather her despot, required, at the rate of Rs. 2,10,000 *per mensem* for each brigade, consisting of two European and six sepoy battalions, with one company of artillery. Shúja'-ud-daulah had already conceived the design of crushing the Rohillas, and took the opportunity of this meeting with Hastings at Banáras to ascertain whether he might count on English support in the attempt. He alleged that they were about, under the lead of Háfiz Rahmat and other Sardárs, to seize Etáwah, which he could not permit, especially as they had not paid any part of the forty lákhs which they had agreed on as the price of the expulsion of the Mahrattas; and offered to pay forty lákhs to the Company for the loan of a brigade which he was to support himself, at the stipulated rate of Rs. 2,10,000 monthly, until it was discharged.

His proposals were accepted by Hastings, and the result was the battle of Bábul Nála, fought on the 23rd of April 1774. The Rohillas were defeated, after a gallant struggle, by the English force under the command of Colonel Champion, while the Nawáb's troops were very active in plundering the camp of their vanquished enemies. The whole transaction, exaggerated though the subsequent atrocities have probably been, will always remain an indelible blot on the record of the British power in India. In expiation of Shúja'-ud-daulah's share in the matter, perhaps all that can be urged is, that it was his interest, as a matter of policy, to crush such turbulent neighbours; that he was a Shia, while the Rohillas were Sunnis; and that he had on his side such moral force as the sanction of Sháh A'lam and the support of Hastings could convey—all of which, however, does not amount to very much.

It had been agreed by Hastings and the Wazír, during the Banáras conference of 1773, that a permanent British Resident should be appointed, and in that capacity a Mr. Middleton was sent by the Governor-General to Lucknow. By the time, however, that the Rohilla war was concluded, the opposition party, headed by Francis, were in a majority in Council, and one of the first assertions of their power was the supersession of Middleton by an agent of their own selection named Bristow. This bone of contention was the cause of quarrels which lasted for years, and of repeated shiftings of the rival Residents. In 1776, Hastings recovered his majority by the death of Monson, and promptly recalling Bristow, sent Middleton back to Lucknow. In

1780, Bristow was reinstated by the express order of the Court of Directors. In 1781 Hastings again displaced him, restored him in 1782, and finally ousted him in 1783. There was certainly no lack of personal acrimony at this period in the treatment of Oudh affairs.

But we have anticipated the course of events by several years, and must go back to 1775. Shúja'-ud-daulah was taken ill during that year, while engaged in the settlement of Rohilkhand, and died at Faizábád, of which city his tomb, the Guláb Bárí (or rose-garden) is one of the chief ornaments. He was the first of his line whose remains were not carried westwards. Whether his death was due to natural causes or not, is uncertain. Mr. Carnegy mentions two conflicting rumours on the subject; one, that he was worried to death by the triumphant opposition in the Calcutta Council; the other, that he was wounded by a poisoned dagger while insulting the modesty of a daughter of the Nawáb of Farukhábád. Of the two, the latter seems the least unlikely; the former probably originated in the lively imagination of some ardent partisan of Hastings. Shúja'-ud-daulah was a man of undeniable ability, and, Colonel Champion to the contrary notwithstanding, of marked personal courage. He was perhaps even less troubled with scruples than most Indian rulers of the time. Dow's description of him, though, as before pointed out, that of an enemy, is worth quoting. He speaks of him as "extremely handsome in his person, about five feet eleven inches in height, and so nervous and strong that with one stroke of the sabre he can cut off the head of a buffalo. He is active, passionate, and ambitious; his penetrating eye seems at first sight to promise uncommon acuteness and fire of mind, but his genius is too volatile for depth of thought, and he is consequently more fit for the manly exercises of the field than for deliberation in the closet. Till of late, he gave little attention to business. He was up before the sun, mounted his horse, rushed into the forest, and hunted down tiger or deer till the noon of day. He then returned, plunged into the cold bath, and spent his afternoons in the harem among his women. Such was the state of Shúja'-ud-daulah's mind till the late war (*i.e.* the campaign ending with the battle of Baksár) . . . . . . Stung with the loss of reputation, his passions have taken another course. His activity is employed in disciplining his army, and he now spends more time at the comptoir of his finances, than in dalliance with the ladies of his seraglio. His authority is therefore established, his revenues increased, and his army on a respectable footing. But with all his splendid qualities, he is cruel, treacherous, unprincipled, and deceitful."

His business capacities were undoubted. By 1768, four years after his defeat at Baksár, he had paid off all his debts, and had a full treasury and flourishing revenue. He reduced and, with French aid, remodelled his army, and founded an arsenal at Faizábád. It was English jealousy of the progress he was making which led to the treaty of 1768, limiting his army to thirty-five thousand men. Like Safdar Jang, he had a Hindú minister, Beni Bahadur, Bráhman. Such writers as Franklin and Scott, who were not, like Dow, prejudiced against him by a private grudge, speak of him as "an excellent magistrate, a lover of justice, and anxiously desirous for the prosperity of his country . . . wise and dignified in character, affable, humane, and generous . . . Sincerely beloved by his own subjects, even the sons of Háfiz Rahmat wept at his death." This last item sounds apocryphal, unless, indeed, their tears were tears of joy; but we may, at any rate, agree with Sir Henry Lawrence, that Shúja'-ud-daulah was "an able, energetic, and intelligent prince, and that he possessed at least the ordinary virtues of Eastern rulers." He was only forty-six years of age at his death, on the 26th of January 1775, an event which marks the close of an epoch in the external history of Oudh. The first three Nawábs had all been pre-eminently soldiers. S'ádat Khán and Safdar Jang had met the Persians, the Duránis, and the Mahrattas in the field. Shúja'-ud-daulah had crossed swords with the English; and the tale is still told in Oudh of how he would have been the victor at Baksár had not his gunners played him false, and loaded with trusses of straw instead of with ball.

THE NAWABI.

But with the accession of his son Asaf-ud-daulah, fourth Nawáb and third Wazír of the Empire, a great change came over Oudh politics. With Shúja'-ud-daulah there had been but little interference from Calcutta, and what there was, was owing mainly to his initiative. But his son, during the twenty-two years that he occupied the *masnad*, was little more than a passive instrument in the hands of successive Governors-General. His share in Delhi affairs was almost confined to a well-timed offering of men and money in 1776, which liberated Sháh A'lam from the tyranny of Zábita Khán, which was nearly as oppressive to him as that of Ghází-ud-dín had been to his father. For this service he was rewarded with the Wizárat of the Empire.

The Calcutta Council began their relations with the new Nawáb by assuming that the death of Shúja'-ud-daulah had put an end to all engagements entered into with him. After four months of discussion, Bristow negotiated a fresh treaty, which affirmed friendship between the contracting parties, and provided that the Nawáb should employ no Europeans without the sanction of the Company; that neither party should consent to any proposals made to it by the Emperor of Delhi against the other; that Karra and Allahabad should be confirmed to the Nawáb, and Banáras, Jaunpur, Gházípur, and the other possessions of Chait Singh—yielding an annual revenue of twenty-three lákhs—should be ceded to the Company. The monthly cost of a brigade was raised from Rs. 2,10,000 to Rs. 2,60,000. All arrears due by his father were to be paid up by the Nawáb. The Company, on its part, was to defend Oudh, Karra, Allahabad, and the recent acquisitions of Shúja'-ud-daulah in Rohilkhand and the Doáb. These terms were to be in force during the lifetime of Asaf-ud-daulah. In addition to the permanent brigade quartered on Oudh by the Faizábád treaty with Shúja'-ud-daulah, a "temporary" brigade was imposed on his successor in 1776 or 1777, and from time to time several detached corps were added, at a further aggregate cost of twelve lákhs a year. Besides the *Resident*, whose appointment had been agreed on by Hastings and the late Nawáb, a Major Palmer, as *Company's Agent*, at a moderate salary of

Rs. 2,20,000 a year, was also sent to Lucknow, whither the Oudh capital had now been permanently removed from Faizábád by Asaf-ud-daulah, with the object, it is believed, of escaping from his mother, the Bahu Begam, who continued to reside at the latter place.

Of the ill-feeling between these two, mother and son, the mistaken interference of the Francis majority in the Council, in the first place, and Hastings' subsequent unscrupulous repudiation of their engagements, in the second, were the principal causes. The anti-Hastings junto began the mischief by putting the Bahu Begam, Shúja'-ud-daulah's widow, in possession of her deceased husband's treasures, as well as of an enormous *jághír*, comprising Salon, Parsadipur, Jais, Karra, Tánda, Wazírganj, &c. &c. To these treasures it does not seem that she had any right, either rational or customary, though she did, indeed, produce a will, which was probably false, and which, whether true or false, would certainly never have been enforced in any native state. All that she was really entitled to was maintenance in a manner befitting her dignity, and this there is no reason to suppose that she would not have obtained from her son. By this alienation, Asaf-ud-daulah was deprived of the power of paying off his father's debts to the Company, as the treaty of 1775 bound him to do; and as a natural consequence, he soon fell into arrears with the current demands for the pay of the troops. As might have been anticipated, he endeavoured to set himself right by plundering his mother.

The Court of Directors, in a letter addressed to Hastings in 1783, wrote as follows :—

"In 1775, the Resident at the Wazír's Court not only obtained from the Begam, widow of the late Shúja'-ud-daulah, on the Nawáb's account, thirty lákhs of rupees, half of which was to be paid to the Company, but also the forbearance of twenty-six lákhs, for the repayment of which she had security in land, on the Nawáb's agreeing to renounce all further claim upon her; and to this agreement the Company were guaranteed."

In acknowledgment of these fifty-six lákhs, the Nawáb

gave his mother a written undertaking, dated the 15th of October 1775, renouncing all further claims upon her, and confirming her in the above-mentioned jághírs. The collections were to be made by her own agents, and she was to retain her mints at Ajodhya and Faizábád. This agreement was guaranteed by Bristow on the part of the Company, and however weak her claim might originally have been, the Begam was now fairly justified in considering herself as secure as the solemn engagements of her son and the Company could make her.

A period of nearly six years followed, during which the internal affairs of Oudh went on from bad to worse. The introduction of European officers into the Nawáb's army, and the discharge of a number of irregular troops, led to a serious mutiny, which was not suppressed without considerable loss. Asaf-ud-daulah abandoned himself to dissipation, leaving the management of affairs to his minister, Murtaza Khán, who was soon assassinated by Khwájah Basant, a eunuch in command of the army, who had got up a party in favour of S'ádat Ali, younger brother of the Nawáb. Khwájah Basant was promptly executed for the murder, and S'ádat Ali, who was destined to become himself Nawáb some ten years later, fled for safety to British territory. "Thus, in one day," to quote Sir H. Lawrence, "the Wazír lost his minister, his general, and his brother." The former was replaced by Haidar Beg Khán, a creature of Hastings, a man of considerable vulpine astuteness, and considerably less than no character. Meanwhile, arrears of subsidy accumulated rapidly. "The regular subsidy," as Sir H. Lawrence tersely puts it, "was originally twenty-five lákhs and a half; the Francis junto raised it to thirty-one lákhs and two-fifths, but what with the expense of the temporary brigade, extra troops, and numerous officers employed with the Oudh army, as well as various miscellaneous accounts, the demands, during seven years of Mr. Hastings' administration, averaged one hundred lákhs annually, while in spite of constant screwing, the receipts only averaged seventy lákhs; leaving in 1781 a deficit of two and one-tenth crores of rupees (=£2,100,000). To meet this frightful item, there was a materially decreased revenue." The pay of the Nawáb's servants and the allowances of members of his family were heavily in arrears. The ladies of the harem were in absolute want of food. While, to complete the picture, Colonel Hannay, who had been appointed farmer of the revenue of Bahraich, Gonda, and Gorakhpur, in 1778, made such good use of his time and opportunities that he "dropped off gorged" in 1781, with, if Burke's information, which is accepted by Marshman, may be trusted, three hundred thousand pounds in his pocket. The terror which this man established in the country and in the mind of the Nawáb, may be imagined from the terms in which the latter wrote to Hastings regarding a rumour that he was again to be quartered upon Oudh:—

"Colonel Hannay is inclined to request your permission to be employed in the affairs of this quarter. If, by any means, any matter of this country dependent on me should be entrusted to the Colonel, I swear by the holy Prophet that I will not remain here, but will go from hence to you. From your kindness, let no concern dependent on me be entrusted to the Colonel."

And this language, be it remembered, was used by a man whose letters to Hastings were usually of the most meekly submissive type. Whether owing to this letter or not, Hannay was not sent back to Oudh. But he left behind him plenty of imitators, though on a less gigantic scale. These men, whether forced into the Nawáb's service as revenue farmers, or on military duty, seem to have been the curse of the country, which they plundered with a thoroughness and audacity that were truly Verrine. They ill-treated and rack-rented the zamíndárs in the one case, and, in the other, interfered with the course of trade, established markets of their own, abolishing those which were already in existence, and collected the customs on their own account. Small wonder that the revenue dwindled.

In 1778 the Nawáb had petitioned for removal of part of the troops quartered upon him, as they were not needed, and were ruinously costly. This request was not granted until 1781, when, at a personal conference between Hastings and

Asaf-ud-daulah at Chunár, it was agreed, on the 19th of September :—

(1.) That all English troops, except one brigade and one extra regiment, were to be withdrawn from the Nawáb's territories; and

(2.) That "as great distress has arisen to the Nawáb's Government from the military power and dominion of the jághírdárs, he be permitted to resume such jághírs as he may find necessary, with a reserve that all such for the amount of whose jághírs the Company are guarantees, shall, in case of the resumption of their lands, be paid the amount of their net collections, through the Resident, in ready money."

At the time when this treaty was made, the Company's finances were in an exceedingly bad condition, and in order to better them, Hastings practically sold to the Nawáb permission to break his engagements, which had been guaranteed, whether rightly or wrongly, by the Company, for an immediate supply of fifty-five lákhs of ready money, and a stipulation for the payment of an additional twenty lákhs. The well-known outbreak at Banáras provoked by Hastings' outrageous treatment of Chait Singh, had occurred in the previous August; and on the utterly frivolous pretext, supported by the famous affidavits made before Impey, that the Begams had taken part in this *émeute*, the work of confiscation was begun.

No need to dwell here upon the oft-told, shameful tale. In justice, however, to Asaf-ud-daulah, it should be stated that, whether or not he had made the first proposal for resuming the jághírs—(the annual value of which was nearly thirty lákhs, or three hundred thousand pounds)—there can be no doubt whatever that when it actually came to the point, he was exceedingly loth to carry it out. Middleton's own letters to Hastings make it perfectly clear how reluctant he was to take such a step. Middleton himself hesitated to apply the pressure requisite to force him to sign the orders for resumption. Nothing but Hastings' imperious resolve and stringent commands compelled the unwilling Resident to goad on the wretched Nawáb to the execution of this nefarious scheme. Middleton wrote to Hastings that in consequence of the resumption of all the jághírs, so much against his inclination . . . a settled melancholy has seized upon the Nawáb, and his health is reduced beyond conception." Indeed, the orders for resumption were not issued by Asaf-ud-daulah, for he could not by any pressure be induced to sign them, but by Middleton himself, and were only enforced by a military demonstration. During the early days of 1782 the work of spoliation was carried out at Faizábád, by means of moral torture applied to the Begams themselves, and physical torture applied to their treasurers. The house, on the south bank of the Ghághra, in which the disgraceful scene was enacted, is now known as the Commissariat bungalow. Haidar Beg Khán, the minister, according to Middleton's well-known letter to Sir Elijah Impey, "supported him nobly" in his arduous task of terrifying two secluded old native ladies and a couple of aged eunuchs. Seventy-six lákhs (£760,000) were extorted, and all the jághírs resumed, but of the latter a great part was subsequently restored, and held by the Bahu Begam until her death, at a very advanced age, in 1815. To have their village included in the Begam's jághír was about the greatest stroke of good fortune that could befall the inhabitants thereof, for they thus obtained protection from the extortions of the revenue farmers and other leeches who harassed and drained the greater part of Oudh.

Faizullah Khán, the Rohilla Nawáb of Rámpur, who had been spared by Shúja'-ud-daulah, was another of the victims of the tyrannous necessity under which Hastings laboured of filling the Company's treasury. He was bound by treaty not to maintain more than five thousand troops, of whom three thousand were to be furnished to the Nawáb of Oudh on demand. In November 1780, Hastings ordered the Nawáb to call on Faizullah Khán for five thousand troops for the defence of Behar. The unhappy man promptly and humbly offered three thousand. For this meek refusal to comply with an unwarrantable demand, Hastings assented to the annexation of all his estates to Oudh, and he was only restored on payment of fifteen lákhs (£150,000), a sum equal to his whole annual income. For three years after the spoliation of the Begams, Oudh was under the merciless screw of Haidar Beg Khán, acting under the imperious menaces of the Governor-General. But the patient could not be made to bleed freely enough. Finally, after the failure of his own nominees, Middleton and Palmer, Hastings fell back on Bristow, on whom he bestowed almost unlimited powers. Better proof could hardly be found of the depth of shameless meanness to which, with all his great qualities, Hastings was capable of descending, than a comparison of the private instructions which he gave to Bristow, and his subsequent public condemnation of Bristow's conduct in carrying them out. The instructions ran thus:—The Resident must be the slave and vassal of the Minister, or the Minister at the absolute devotion (*sic*) of the Resident . . . It will be necessary to declare to him (the Minister) in the plainest terms, the footing and conditions on which he shall be permitted to retain his place, with the alternative of dismission, and a scrutiny into his past conduct, if he refuses." Little more than a year later, Bristow was for the third time removed from Lucknow by the Governor-General on the publicly recorded ground that he, "after an ineffectual attempt to draw the minister Haidar Beg Khán into a conspiracy with him to usurp all the powers of the Government, proceeded to an open assumption of them to himself."

Really, if his treatment of Oudh had been a fair sample of the whole of Hastings' Indian career, it would hardly be too much to say that no whit of Burke's invective could have been excessive or exaggerated.

"Owing to the weakness of the Nawáb's government," no troops were withdrawn as had been provided by the treaty of 1781, until a visit paid to Lucknow by Hastings in March 1784, when the province was relieved of a detachment. About the same time he caused the restoration of a part of the confiscated jághírs, and altogether does not seem to have inflicted very much injury on Oudh upon this occasion. Indeed, the state of the country was sufficiently deplorable to have excited even his compassion, and was in every respect worse than it had been under Shújá'-ud-daulah. Hastings himself, in a minute written at Calcutta in May 1784, previous to his visiting Lucknow, admits that the province "had fallen into a state of great disorder and confusion, its resources being in an extraordinary degree diminished"; and expresses a hope that he "may possibly be able to establish some plan by which the province of Oudh may be in time restored to its former state of affluence, good order, and prosperity." How utterly demoralised its actual condition was may be gathered from the following account by Bristow, written in December 1782:—

"Despotism is the principle upon which every measure is founded, and the people in the interior parts of the country are ruled at the discretion of the A′mil or Faujdár for the time being; they exercise, within the limits of their jurisdiction, the powers of life and death, and decisions in civil and other cases, in the same extent as the Sovereign at the capital. The forms prescribed by the ancient institutions of the Mughal Empire are unattended to, and the will of the provincial magistrate is the sole law of the people; the total relaxation of the Wazír's authority, his inattention and dislike to business, leave the A′mils in possession of this dangerous power. . . . I can hardly quote an instance, since the Wazír's accession to the *masnad*, of an A′mil having been punished for oppression, though the complaints of the people and the state of the country are notorious proofs of the violences daily committed; it is even become unsafe for travellers to pass except in large bodies; murders, thefts, and other enormities shocking to humanity are committed in open day."

He adds that A′mils were selected solely by favour, or capacity to pay a large sum in advance, and "entered upon their trust ruined in reputation" and pocket. They bullied the weaker zamindárs, and were cowed in their turn by the more powerful, whose forts covered the country; Almás Ali Khán, the famous eunuch, who for many years farmed the south-east portion of Oudh, having—though this estimate must have been greatly exaggerated—"not less than seven hundred in his districts." It was customary for an A′mil to keep some near relative of each zamindár as a hostage; "a great A'mil will sometimes have three or four hundred of these hostages, whom he is obliged to confine in places of security."

Captain Edwards, who was examined as a witness at Hastings' trial, deposed that " in the general aspect that the country bore, and the cultivation of the country, it was infinitely better cultivated in 1774 than in 1783 . . . In Shúja'-ud-daulah's time the country was in a very flourishing state in merchandise, cultivation, and every article of commerce, and the people then seemed to be very happy under his government, which lately was not the case, because the country in reality, in the year 1774, appeared in a flourishing state, and in the year 1783 it appeared comparatively forlorn and desolate."

The main cause of the unhappy change, described with such curious infelicity of phrase, is not far to seek. An Asiatic, or, indeed, any ruler, when the slave of a powerful external Government, whose only object is to get money from him, and which, so long as that object is attained, guarantees him against the results of his own oppression and misrule, is tolerably certain to lose interest in his affairs, to " let things slide," and to seek refuge in sensual pleasure. This was the course of every Nawáb or King of Oudh from Asaf-ud-daulah onwards, with the two exceptions of S'ádat Ali, and his son Muhammad Ali Sháh, of whom the first was a man of extraordinary natural force of character, and the second was favoured by the good early training he had received from his father, the quiet and decorous life he had led for many years previous to his accession to the throne, and an exceptionally good Resident, Colonel Low. The result must almost inevitably be a total collapse of administration, and particularly of land revenue administration; a tendency to shirk the trouble of supervising a large number of small landholders, and to hand them all over in a mass to the first large revenue farmer or powerful official who will pay, or undertake to pay, heavily for the privilege of plundering them at discretion. This was what was done by Asaf-ud-daulah, and the growth of " mushroom" Taluqdárs began during his reign, owing chiefly to the tremendous drain upon the resources of Oudh established by the Calcutta Council under Hastings, and continued with but little actual, though with some nominal, diminution under his immediate successors.

The first of these was Lord Cornwallis, and to him, in 1786, the Nawáb addressed an entreaty that his burthens might be lightened by the withdrawal of the troops from Fattihgarh and Cawnpore. This request was refused, on the ground that it could not safely be complied with. Negotiations between Lord Cornwallis and Haidar Beg Khán went on for some months, and on the 15th of April 1787 the Governor-General wrote a letter to the Nawáb, pointing out the superiority of the British troops to his own, and reminding him that their pay was expended in Oudh, which had enjoyed peace—such as it was—while the rest of India was disturbed. He promised, however, that future demands should not exceed the expenses actually incurred by the Company in their relations with the province, which amounted to "fifty lákhs of Faizábád rupees." The force was to be increased or decreased hereafter as circumstances required, and the Resident was no longer to interfere in the internal affairs of Oudh. "For several years past," wrote Lord Cornwallis, "the inhabitants of your Excellency's dominions, from motives of self-interest, have appealed to this Government, and this has been a source of injury to the affairs of your Government. I am determined to put a stop to this practice, and to disregard their applications; but, as the connection between the two governments is universally known, strict attention to justice on your part will add credit and renown to both."

The substance of this letter was discussed with Haidar Beg Khán, and on the 21st of July a florid reply was received from the Nawáb, still dwelling on the great weight of expense which his Government had experienced every year from these troops, and on the negotiations which had passed with "former gentlemen" on this subject; but agreeing to the continuance of the troops "with a view to preserve his Lordship's goodwill and satisfaction," and to the annual payment of fifty lákhs. A portion of the balance due to the Company was remitted.

On the 25th of July 1788 a commercial treaty was signed, providing that neither party should claim any exemption for the goods of their respective subjects from duties which were to be levied at rates of two and a half to five per cent. on permits granted by the respective Governments. The exaction of transit duties by zamíndárs was forbidden, under penalties. The office of Governor-General's Agent was abolished, an economy of one hundred thousand pounds a year, which seems a somewhat high price for the province to have paid for the services rendered to her by Major Palmer and his establishment; the claims of private creditors of the Nawáb were refused recognition; and sundry monopolies which had been acquired by European adventurers under colour of the Company's authority were abolished. Altogether, Lord Cornwallis did a good deal in the way of pruning the most flagrant of the evil growths by which Oudh was being suffocated, and it is possible to study the history of our relations with the province during his term of office, without feeling any very overpowering sense of shame; which, considering the events of the previous decade, is, comparatively at least, saying a good deal.

But as far as Asaf-ud-daulah was concerned, the mischief was done. Whether he might, under happier auspices, have turned out a respectable ruler, is of course an open question. His liberality and munificence are still proverbial in Lucknow, as is testified by the following slightly profane couplet, which the Banyas are wont to repeat on opening their shops in the morning:—

> Jis ko na de Maula,
> Tis ko de Asaf-ud-daulah;

which may be rendered,

> Who from Heaven nought receiveth,
> To him Asaf-ud-daulah giveth.

He spent money lavishly on public buildings, the principal of which were among the chief ornaments of Lucknow, such as the Daulat Khána, the Rúmí Darwáza, Hasan Bágh, the Bibiapur Kothí, the Chinhat Kothí, the Bara Imámbára, the

Aish Bágh, the Chár Bágh, and the Residency. The Martinière College, also, was built during his reign by General Claude Martin, a French officer in his service. But, whatever his potential good qualities, Asaf-ud-daulah had, by the time of Lord Cornwallis' Governor-Generalship, become utterly debauched and demoralised, and totally heedless of his affairs, which, being left to themselves, naturally grew worse and worse. The revenue farmers, as they grew powerful by draining the country of its wealth, shook off their allegiance to the Nawáb and defied his authority. Asaf-ud-daulah's own excuse for his reckless abandonment of business was that he had been rendered desperate by the insatiable demands of the Calcutta Council, who, however divided on other points, could always unite in any scheme for the plunder of Oudh, and only differed occasionally as to the choice of agents—a Middleton or a Bristow—for its execution.

Haidar Beg Khán died in 1795, and with him expired such little vitality as still lingered in the administration of the province. The finances were in a desperate condition when Sir John Shore, who succeeded Lord Cornwallis as Governor-General, visited Lucknow in 1797, and—by way of relieving them—established a fresh drain of five lákhs and a half, yearly, for the support of two additional regiments. In return for this concession, he bestowed "a sight of good advice" on Asaf-ud-daulah, which the latter was incapable of appreciating. It was not even stated that these extra troops were to be kept in Oudh at all, and the demand was made "in compliance with the Company's orders," owing to "the late very great increase in their military establishment." Poor Oudh!

The only other result of Sir John Shore's visit was the appointment, as minister, of Tafazzul Hosen, who had been the Nawáb's representative at Calcutta. He appears to have been an intelligent and respectable man; but the Nawáb would have preferred Almás Ali Khán, and for once it is probable that the Nawáb was right. Sleeman writes of him thus:—

"Miyán Almás was the greatest and best man of any note that Oudh has produced. He held for about forty years districts yielding to the Oudh Government an annual revenue of about eighty lákhs of rupees (£800,000). During all this time he kept the people secure in life and property, and as happy as people in such a state of society can be; and the whole country under his charge was, during his lifetime, a garden." He died a poor man, "for his immense income he had expended in useful works, liberal hospitality, and charity. He systematically kept in check the Taluqdárs or great landholders; fostered the smaller; and encouraged and protected the best classes of cultivators, such as Lodhs, Kurmis, and Káchhis, whom he called and considered his children. His reign over the large extent of country under his jurisdiction is considered to have been its golden age."

Such was the man who was set aside in favour of the worthy, but comparatively insignificant Tafazzul Hosen. Sir John Shore had given his consent to the appointment of Almás Ali, but revoked it on discovering an old order by Lord Cornwallis against his being employed. Had this order not been passed, or not been discovered when it was, the subsequent course of Oudh history might have been materially different. For Asaf-ud-daulah died very shortly after Sir John Shore left Lucknow, and it was mainly owing to the representations of Tafazzul Hosen that his putative son and successor, Wazír Ali, was set aside after a few weeks in favour of S'ádat Ali, second son of Shúja'-ud-daulah, and brother of the late Nawáb.

The news of Asaf-ud-daulah's death reached Sir John Shore at Calcutta, and he ratified the succession of Wazír Ali, reputed son of the late Nawáb. But reports soon came in apace of his illegitimacy, profligacy, and hostility to English interests, and the Governor-General again set out for Lucknow to dispose of the matter on the spot. He was met on the way by Tafazzul Hosen, who was full of Wazír Ali's transgressions and enormities, and whose zeal for his deposition was, perhaps, partly due to the fact that he had formerly been tutor to S'ádat Ali, in whose sight he hoped to find more favour than in that of the violent and intractable young Nawáb.

Sir Henry Lawrence felt " bound to record his opinion that

Wazír Ali was unjustly treated," and that his "spurious birth would not by Muhammadan law have interfered with his succession, and never would have weighed with the English authorities, had he not rendered himself obnoxious to them by desiring to degrade Tafazzul Hosen, who was considered as 'the representative of English influence.'" Mr. Eastwick follows suit, and writes that Wazír Ali was deprived of a kingdom upon evidence on which "a court of English law would not have decided against him a question of a few pounds."

To us it seems that the question of Wazír Ali's legitimacy or illegitimacy was one of very secondary importance, and that Sir John Shore was perfectly justified in taking into consideration his anti-English leanings as a part of the larger question of his general fitness or unfitness to rule the province. That he should have bitterly disliked all things English is not surprising, considering what he had seen of English influence in Oudh, and was certainly not to be imputed to him as a moral failing. Still, the fact remained that Oudh *was* under English influence, and was obviously destined so to continue, and Wazír Ali's hostility to that influence was, so far, a disqualification for the task of presiding over the affairs of a province that was subject to it. In other respects, moreover, there was no room for doubt that he was totally unfit to govern, and, indeed, as his subsequent conduct showed, hardly fit to live. However English influence over Oudh had been acquired, it was an existing fact, and Sir John Shore, being in possession of it, was bound to use it for the best interests of the province. That he did so use it in setting aside Wazír Ali and substituting S'ádat Ali, the subsequent career of the latter leaves as little doubt as the terms of the treaty which Sir John Shore exacted from him, as a condition precedent of his elevation, leave that his motives in making the selection were not unmixed.

Since he had fled from Oudh, as already mentioned, in fear of the consequences of Khwájah Basant's unsuccessful conspiracy, S'ádat Ali had been living in British territory, and was at this time at Banáras. It was there that the intention of raising him to the *masnad* was announced to him by the Resident, Mr. Cherry, and a draft treaty presented to him for his acceptance, the substance of which may be summarised as follows :—

(1.) The subsidy to the Company was to be raised from fifty-six to seventy-six lákhs *per annum*, payable by monthly instalments of Rs. 6,33,333 5. 4., commencing from the date of his accession (which took place on the 21st of January 1798); the arrears of the subsidy were to be at once discharged; a yearly allowance of a lákh and a half was to be paid to Wazír Ali through the Resident; and twelve lákhs were to be paid at once as *nazarána*, or douceur, to the Company, who had "incurred a considerable expense in their exertions in establishing his right."

(2.) In the event of the instalments falling into arrears, such security was to be given as should be deemed satisfactory, and "since by this treaty the amount of the subsidy is considerably increased, and many other permanent charges upon His Excellency are incurred . . . it becomes necessary, on a comparison of his disbursements with the assets of his country," to make reductions in expenditure; and S'ádat Ali agreed to act to that end in consultation with the Company.

(3.) No correspondence with foreign powers was to be carried on by the Nawáb without the knowledge and concurrence of the English Government; and he was to entertain no Europeans without its sanction.

(4.) The commercial treaty of the 25th of July 1788, which had been hitherto neglected, was to be duly enforced for the future.

(5.) The reputed children of Asaf-ud-daulah were to be maintained by S'ádat Ali.

(6.) The fort of Allahabad was to be made over to the Company, with the sum of eight lákhs to be spent on its fortifications—the Company, be it observed, paying *ghát*-fees—and three lákhs were to be made over to them for strengthening the fortifications of Fattihgarh.

(7.) In return, the Company agreed to maintain not less than ten thousand troops in Oudh. If at at any time the force amounted to more than thirteen thousand, or less than eight thousand, an increased subsidy was to be paid, or a decrease allowed accordingly.

The treaty contained no provision for the good government of the province, and, except for the look of the thing, the omission was not, perhaps, under all the circumstances, of much consequence.

Such as it was, it was accepted by S'ádat Ali, who was in no position to haggle about terms, and on the 21st of January 1798 he was proclaimed as Nawáb Wazír at Lucknow, whither he had been escorted by British troops. The treaty was formally signed on the 21st of February. Wazír Ali had maintained a threatening attitude during the course of these negotiations, but no outbreak took place, owing, it is only fair to say, in great measure to Sir John Shore's perfect coolness and tact, for which he was publicly thanked by the Court of Directors. One can only wish that the success of the cause in which these fine qualities were displayed had been signalised by the conclusion of a somewhat less one-sided treaty. A great *darbár* of all the Lucknow Court was held at the Bibiapur palace, at which Wazír Ali was informed of the order for his deposition, and sent off to Banáras under escort. With his subsequent adventures, culminating in the assassination of the Banáras Resident, Mr. Cherry, Oudh history has little further concern.

S'ádat Ali inherited from his father Shúja'-ud-daulah both his taste for pleasure and his business capacity, but in him the latter was far more marked and developed, and the former less so. His character seems to have been very generally misunderstood, and it was a character worth understanding rightly, for there was a great deal of it. He was about forty years of age when raised to the *masnad*, and had previously been known as a jovial spirit, fond of wine and hunting, but at the same time, prudent and economical. From that time forward, however, he was a changed man. He deeply felt his responsibilities, and struggled gallantly against the difficulties of his position to fulfil his duty to the province. His conduct was often misconstrued by those who imperfectly comprehended his situation and the needs of the country. But the people of Oudh, at least, appreciated him, and he is still remembered, even by the large landholders—whom to keep in check was one of the chief aims of his policy—as the best, wisest, and strongest administrator that the province has ever known. He underwent, in fact, "conversion," and solemnly vowed at the shrine of Hazrat Abbás to abandon his life of pleasure, and to devote himself to the task of government; and this vow he certainly kept to the end of his life.

But his circumstances, especially at first, were most unfavourable. The treaty which he had signed bound him to pay more than three-quarters of a million annually for the use of ten thousand of the Company's troops. This he seems to have done without fail, for the treaty forced upon him in 1801 contains no mention of any arrears. But he had also to contend against the earth-hunger of Lord Wellesley, who reached India shortly after his accession, stimulated by apprehensions, which for a period of about ten months were probably genuine enough, of an invasion of northern India by Zamán Sháh, son of Ahmad Sháh Abdálí, the redoubted victor of Pánípat. Lord Wellesley began by calling on S'ádat Ali to disband a great part of his own troops, of whom Asaf-ud-daulah had left some eighty thousand, and to substitute for them an increased British force. This proposal was very distasteful to S'ádat Ali, but objections were useless against the master of many legions and few scruples, the robust vigour of whose policy ran little risk of being weakened by any excess of urbanity in his mode of expressing it. The Nawáb at last threw out a hint of abdicating, at which Lord Wellesley eagerly caught, assuming as a matter of course that his abdication would be in favour of the Company. This, however, was by no means S'ádat Ali's intention, and he refused to resign unless he was to be succeeded by one of his own sons. The Governor-General put on record some very strong language concerning the "duplicity and insincerity" of the Nawáb, but the latter would not yield, and Lord Wellesley was not prepared forcibly to depose him without some better pretext that he had yet been able to obtain. For the charge o duplicity there was really no foundation, for the Resident, in his letter describing the interview at which the proposal to abdicate was made, expressly states that the Nawáb dwelt on the fact that his son would succeed him, and the dignity be continued in his family. Yet Lord Wellesley's reply to this letter was accompanied by a draft treaty for the Nawáb's acceptance, in which no mention whatever was made of his children except as recipients of a pension, and by which the entire civil and military administration of Oudh was to vest in the Company. It was not surprising that S'ádat Ali refused his consent to a proposal which, he declared to the Resident, "would bring upon him such indelible disgrace and odium that he could never voluntarily subscribe to it." It is impossible to read the correspondence which ensued between Lord Wellesley and the Nawáb without feeling that the latter had very much the best of the argument, as a mere question of fairness and reason. The Governor-General appeared to have convinced himself that S'ádat Ali was incapable of doing any good thing whatsoever; and if that conviction had been correct, he would surely have been justified in relieving Oudh of him, always providing that he was prepared to substitute a better government than that which he removed. But where Lord Wellesley seems to have been wrong, was in his axiom of S'ádat Ali's worthlessness. He had before him, perhaps the ablest and most enlightened native ruler then living, and failed to recognise him.

Vanquished in argument, Lord Wellesley threw his sword into the scale. A British force marched into Oudh, without the consent of the Nawáb, whose local officers were ordered by the Resident to receive it, and supply provisions for its use. This order they obeyed. The Nawáb's troops were vastly reduced, an invidious task which was well carried out by Colonel Scott, and twelve battalions of the Company's infantry and four regiments of cavalry substituted, at an additional cost to the Oudh exchequer of fifty-four lákhs annually. The total amount of the subsidy was thus increased to £1,300,000, while to balance this greatly augmented demand there was a saving of only £165,000, effected by the reduction of a great part of the Oudh troops. The

Nawáb, not very unnaturally, wrote to the Resident, dwelling on the difficulty of meeting this enhanced charge, and asking where the money was to come from. Lord Wellesley promptly declared that this was a confession of inability to satisfy the Company's demands, that the subsidy was no longer safe, and that it must be secured by the cession of "such a portion of the Wazír's territories as shall be fully adequate, in their present impoverished condition, to defray those indispensable charges," or, in other words, of rather more than half of the whole of his dominions. It was in vain that S'ádat Ali explained that he had merely wished to ask for the advice of the Resident, which he had been enjoined to take, and had frankly put his perplexities before him; and pointed out the regularity with which the subsidy had hitherto been paid. Lord Wellesley deputed his brother Henry Wellesley to Lucknow, and under threat of complete deposition, the treaty of the 10th of November 1801 was extorted, by which Rohilkhand, Farukhábád, Mainpuri, Etáwah, Cawnpore, Fattihgarh, Allahábád, Ázimgarh, Basti, and Gorakhpur, were ceded to the Company in perpetuity. The revenue then yielded by these districts amounted to Rs. 1,35,00,000, which, including stamps and excise, had risen in 1846-47 to more than Rs. 2,11,00,000. It is now considerably over Rs. 3,00,00,000. The principle on which the districts to be ceded were chosen was to isolate the remaining dominions of the Nawáb by surrounding them on three sides with a ring of British territory, while to the north, as before, they were shut in by the mountains of Naipál. Henceforward, with one or two trifling exchanges, the dimensions of the province continued as at present. The other provisions of the treaty were that the subsidy should cease for ever, and that no future charges should be made for the protection of Oudh. The Nawáb was to retain only four battalions of infantry, one regiment of Najíbs, two thousand cavalry, and three hundred artillerymen. Possession of the reserved dominions was guaranteed to him and to " his heirs and successors," as also full exercise of authority within the same; and the Nawáb engaged to introduce a good system of administration, in concert with the Company's officers. The ceded districts were to be made over at the commencement of the year 1209 Fasli=22nd of September 1801, though the treaty was not actually signed till the 10th of November, and the subsidy was to be continued until actual possession was obtained. The navigation of the Ganges and other boundary rivers was declared free.

And here, perhaps, it may not be inappropriate to point out, in some little detail, the changes which have taken place from time to time in the extension of the term Oudh.

Mr. Carnegy, on the authority of Sir Mán Singh, informs us that the old pre-historic Awadh, the kingdom of Ráma, contained five main divisions, viz. :—

(1.) Uttara Kosála, or the trans-Ghághra districts, now known as Bahraich, Gonda, Basti, and Gorakhpur.

(2.) Silliána, or Sáliána, consisting of the lower range of hills to the north of Uttara Kosála, as above defined, now belonging to Naipál, with the Tarai at its base.

(3.) Pachhimráth, which may be roughly described as the country between the Ghághra and the Gumti, bounded on the east by a line drawn from Ajodhya on the former river to Sultánpur on the latter, and on the west by a line drawn through Nímkhár in the Sítapur district so as to connect the same two rivers considerably nearer their sources. This division must have included about a third of the present district of Faizábád, a small portion of the north of Sultánpur, greater part of Bárabanki, and sections of the Lucknow and Sítapur districts.

(4.) Púrabráth, or the country between the Ghághra and the Gumti east of the line from Ajodhya to Sultánpur, including two-thirds of the modern Faizábád district, the north-eastern corner of Sultánpur, and parts of Ázimgarh and Jaunpur. How far it extended eastwards, it is difficult, if not impossible, to determine with any precision.

(5.) Arbar, or the country about Pratábgarh, extending southwards from the Gumti to the Sai river. Arbar, it may be noticed, is still the local name of the large pargana and tahsíl of Pratábgarh.

From the pre-historic period to the time of Akbar, the limits of the province and its internal divisions seem to have been constantly changing, and the name of Oudh, or Awadh, seems to have been applicable only to one of these divisions or *Sarkárs*, nearly corresponding to the old Pachhimráth. The title of Súbahdár of Oudh is mentioned as early as 1280 A.D., but it can only have denoted the governor of the tract of country above defined. The Oudh of Akbar was one of the twelve (or fifteen) súbahs into which he divided the Mughal Empire as it then stood, in the year 1590 A.D. As constituted at the end of the sixteenth century, the Súbah contained five Sarkárs, viz. Awadh, Lucknow, Bahraich, Khairábád, and Gorakhpur, and these, again, were subdivided into numerous *maháls* and *dastúrs*. It seems to have been of nearly the same extent as the present province, and to have differed only in including Gorakhpur, Basti, and Ázimgarh, and in excluding Tánda, Aldemau, and Mánikpur, or the territory to the east and south of Faizábád, Sultánpur, and Pratábgarh.

The wars and transactions in which Shúja'-ud-daulah was engaged, both with and against the East India Company, led to the addition of Karra, Allahábád, Fattihgarh, Cawnpore, Etáwah, Mainpúri, Farukhábád, and Rohilkhand, to the Oudh dominions, and thus they remained until the treaty of 1801 with S'ádat Ali, by which the province was reduced to its present dimensions. Since then, only a few slight alterations of frontier have taken place. Khairigarh, Kanchanpur, and what is now the Naipál Tarai, were ceded in 1816, in liquidation of Ghází-ud-dín Haidár's loan of a million sterling towards the expenses of the Naipál war; and at the same time the pargana of Nawábganj was added to the Gonda district, in exchange for that of Hándia, or Kawai, which was transferred from Pratábgarh to Allahabad. The Tarai to the north of Bahraich, including a large quantity of valuable forest and grazing ground, was made over to the Naipál Darbár in 1860, in recognition of their services during the Mutiny, and in 1874 some further cessions, on a much smaller scale, but without any apparent reason, were made in favour of the same Government. Except then for about thirty years during which it included Shúja'-uddaulah's acquisitions, the limits of the province have not differed very materially from the time of Akbar to the present day.

By the treaty of 1801, S'ádat Ali found himself left, after three years of trouble and humiliation, with half the dominions he had inherited, but with no subsidy to pay, an efficient military force, and comparatively little vexatious interference to contend against. For the remaining twelve years of his life, he devoted himself to the task of administration. His chief difficulties were due to the turbulence of the large landholders, whether Rájpút chiefs or successful revenue farmers, of which latter class a plentiful crop had, as before mentioned, sprung up in the time of Asaf-ud-daulah. He was perfectly aware, as Almás Ali had been before him, that the province could only be governed as an organic whole by keeping a strong hand on the large Taluqdárs, and he was fully determined to crush all lawless recusants. For this purpose it was necessary to use freely the troops at his disposal. This process was highly distasteful to the English officers in command, who called it "collecting taxes at the point of the bayonet," a phrase which sounds dreadful enough, but really only describes what was, under the circumstances, an inevitable operation. Sympathising, like most Englishmen of their class, with a turbulent landed aristocracy as against a central government, they threw as many obstacles as possible in the way of carrying out the work of suppression; and S'ádat Ali complained bitterly that after having given away half his kingdom for the use of the Company's troops, he was subjected to humiliating remonstrances from commanding officers whenever he asked for their assistance in putting down refractory and recusant landholders. However, in spite of all obstacles, the work was thoroughly done for the time, and the authority of the Government maintained.

S'ádat Ali resumed many of the rent-free grants which had been capriciously lavished by Asaf-ud-daulah, and a good deal of taluqdárí *nánkúr*. "He upheld," writes Colonel McAndrew, "the Government right to the whole assessment, which was *mauzahwár* (*i.e.* imposed village by village, and not in the lump), making an allowance for each *mauzah* called *dehí nánkár*. Besides the *nánkár*, which was originally allowed to the *málguzár* (revenue payer) only, the proprietors enjoyed their *sír* land," up to 10 per cent. of the cultivated area, at favourable rates. He abandoned the vicious *ijárah* system of getting in the revenue through irresponsible contractors, and adopted the *amáni* or trust mode of management, *i.e.* instead of letting out a district in farm for a fixed sum to the highest bidder, leaving the latter to make what he could out of it, he required his collectors to account for their collections, without binding them to pay any fixed amount. That the latter system, if genuinely carried out, is far the best for the people, needs little demonstration. But to prevent embezzlement, strict supervision of the collectors was necessary. And that supervision S'ádat Ali bestowed. Constant reports of the proceedings of every *chakladár* (collector of a *chakla* or circle) were submitted by the news-writers appointed for the purpose, and he himself constantly tested the correctness of these reports by personal local inspection. "The result of his administration," again to quote Colonel McAndrew, "was that the people became contented and prosperous, much waste land was broken up, and a very general conversion of rents in kind into rents in money took place in the more populous parts of the province. . . . At his death S'ádat Ali left behind him the name of the friend of the ryot, and a full treasury."

He has been accused of undue parsimony, a charge which any successor of the lavish Asaf-ud-daulah could hardly escape. S'ádat Ali was certainly not a man to throw away money, or even to spend it without getting the money's worth. But on fitting occasions he could be liberal enough, as witness the long list of public buildings which he erected, and especially the Dilárám, Dilkhúshá, Músa Bágh, Haiyát Baksh and Núr Baksh Kothis, the Khás Bázár, and the Dargáh of Hazrat Abbás Ali.

Colonel Sleeman, who travelled through Oudh when it was still comparatively a *terre vierge*, and who probably knew more of the province as it was under native rule than any other Englishman, writes of S'ádat Ali that he was "a man of great general ability, had mixed much in the society of

British officers in various parts of British India, had been well trained in habits of business, understood thoroughly the character, institutions, and requirements of his people, and above all, was a sound judge of the relative merits and capacities of the men from whom he had to select his officers, and a vigilant supervisor of their actions. . . . Men who served him ably and honestly always felt confident in his protection and support. He had a thorough knowledge of the rights and duties of his subjects and officers, and a strong will to secure the one and enforce the other. To do this, he knew that he must with a strong hand keep down the large landed aristocracy, who were then, as they are now (1850), very prone to grasp at the possessions of their weaker neighbours, either by force, or in collusion with local authorities. In attempting this with the aid of British troops, some acts of oppression were, no doubt, committed; and as the sympathies of the British officers were more with the landed aristocracy, while his were more with the humbler classes of landholders and cultivators, who required to be protected from them, frequent misunderstandings arose—acts of just severity were made to appear to be acts of wanton oppression, and such as were really oppressive were exaggerated into unheard-of atrocities." He would not tolerate peculation, and did not hesitate to make a detected peculator disgorge, but "he never confiscated the estates of any good and faithful servants who left lawful heirs to their property." An honest and able officer might count confidently on being maintained in his position, and had no need to make haste to be rich, *e.g.* Hakím Mehndi at Muhamdi, and Bálki Dás and his son Rai Amr Singh at Bahraich, were continued in office for many years consecutively, and made their respective districts like gardens.

Such was the Nawáb S'ádat Ali, whom Lord Wellesley had wished to set aside as incapable.

He died in 1814, leaving a treasure which is variously stated at three, and at fourteen, millions sterling. The former estimate is probably a good deal below, and the latter a good deal above, the mark. His yearly income during the last twelve years of his reign probably never exceeded a million and a half sterling, and it is not impossible that he may have put by half that sum annually. The rent (revenue) of good land in his time according to Dr. Butter's Report on the southern districts of Oudh, written in 1837, was from one to one and a half rupees per (standard) bigha. "Now," he adds, "the assessment is two, three, or four rupees per bigha, and can seldom be fully levied without ruin both to ryot and zamindár." Though the revenue demand was so much lower under S'ádat Ali's *régime* than under that of his successors, it is probable that he actually received considerably more than they did, the costs of collection and the amount intercepted by officials being much smaller than they became later.

Shams-ud-daulah, eldest son of S'ádat Ali, had died before him, and his children were therefore excluded from inheritance under the rule of Muhammadan law known as Mahjúb-ul-irs, in favour of the second son, Ghází-ud-dín Haidar. The latter had never been on good terms with his father, and had been left much in the hands of servants. One of these, Ágha Mír, otherwise known as Muhtamad-ud-daulah, who had been his *khánsámán*, was made minister, in supersession of Hakím Mehndi, who had been S'ádat Ali's right-hand man for several years before the latter's death. The cause of his fall was that he strongly objected to the interference of Colonel Baillie, the then Resident, and induced the Nawáb to remonstrate against it to the Governor-General. Ghází-ud-dín, however, became frightened at the notion of an open rupture with the Resident, and backed out of his remonstrance, pleading that he had been misled and misinformed by his minister, who was deprived of all his offices and much of his property, and was for a time imprisoned. On his release he went into British territory, and in 1824 was living in magnificent style at Fattihgarh. This, however, was not his final departure from the stage of Oudh politics, and he will be heard of again in the following reign. Ágha Mír plundered his master in almost every possible way, and is said to have appropriated half a million sterling which was entrusted to him for expenditure on public works.

It was not long before the Calcutta Government, then presided over by Lord Moira—who afterwards became Lord Hastings—began to tap the treasure which had been left by S'ádat Ali. In 1814 a million was borrowed for the Naipál war, at six per cent., the Resident being instructed to "make it appear as a voluntary offer on the part of the Nawáb." A second million was borrowed in the following year, but this debt was liquidated in 1816 by the cession of Khairigarh and the strip of Tarai country under the Naipál hills, extending from the Koriála on the west, to the border of Gorakhpur on the east. Mr. Eastwick represents this cession as a very doubtful benefit, and says that the Tarai became a stronghold for all the rebels and banditti of eastern Oudh. But it must, in fact, have very considerably strengthened the Oudh Government, and led to the suppression of the Banjáras and other hill tribes who had long been a thorn in the north side of the province. In addition to his money loan, it should be added, Ghází-ud-dín had furnished a fully equipped regiment of cavalry at his own expense, and supplied a large number of elephants which did very good service, and many of which he never saw again. These loans were not negotiated without a good deal of discreditable intrigue, in which the Residency Munshi seems to have duped both the Resident and the Nawáb, and all further interference in the affairs of the latter was peremptorily forbidden by the Governor-General. The prohibition, however, had been uttered before, and was destined to be uttered again.

In 1819 it struck Lord Hastings that Ghází-ud-dín, if created a king, would be a useful counterpoise to the Emperor of Delhi. He accordingly induced him to coin money in his own name, and to assume the title of Sháh. This was perhaps the most sterile stroke of the sterile science of diplomacy that was ever conceived or executed. The title never took much root out of Lucknow, and though Ghází-ud-dín and his four successors were all titular kings, their rule is far more commonly spoken of by the country folk as the "Nawábí" than as the "Sháhí."

We get an interesting glimpse of Oudh as it was in 1824

from Bishop Heber's journal. He entered the province from Cawnpore in October of that year, and went straight to Lucknow. He found the peasantry universally armed, and at Newalganj a body of them were besieging some of the King's troops who were escorting Rs. 30,000 of treasure to Lucknow. Warlike though they were, however, he found a crowd which was collected round a dying elephant of the King's, "civil and communicative," and saw, to his surprise, that the whole country between Cawnpore and Lucknow, with the exception of occasional barren wastes, was under cultivation. He had heard much before entering Oudh of the hatred of the English name which prevailed in Lucknow, but of this he himself, though he went about the city almost wholly unattended, could see nothing. He was politely entertained by the King, who asked him to breakfast, and whom he describes as a tall, long-backed man, who "had evidently been very handsome," and whose features were still good and his countenance pleasing. His manners were gentlemanly and elegant. He was well versed in Oriental philosophy and philology, had a taste for mechanics, and had, when younger, been fond of hunting. He was popular with the few who had access to him, and was never accused of any personal violence or oppression, but was averse to public business, and quite in the hands of his minister, the ex-*khánsámán*, Ágha Mír. The latter is described as "a dark, harsh-looking, hawk-nosed man, with an expression of mouth which seems to imply habitual self-command struggling with a naturally rough temper .... and exceedingly unpopular."

The Bishop, on leaving Lucknow, marched to Shahjahánpur through what is now the Hardúi district. On the whole, he thought the anarchy and distress of Oudh over-rated. He saw no mud forts or stockades, and the people whom he met with north of Lucknow were not so universally armed as those to the south. Between Lucknow and Sándi he found the country "as populous and well-cultivated as most of the Company's territories." Things, he was told, had improved somewhat since the aid of our troops was withheld from the King's officers. This, of course, was just the kind of thing he was likely to hear in Lucknow. He, however, "could not help observing that there really is a greater appearance of ease, security, and neatness among the middling and lower classes of the Company's subjects than among those of the King of Oudh."

As a fact, there was probably a good deal more wealth in Oudh at that time than in our own surrounding districts, taxation being lighter, and being expended inside the province. But the reputation of possessing it was too dangerous to admit of much exhibition of its outward and visible signs, such as handsome clothes or elaborate houses.

The *amáni* system of revenue collection, which S'ádat Ali had worked so successfully, soon fell into disuse under his son. It required close supervision, which Ghází-ud-dín Haidar had neither the will nor the power to bestow. The *ijárah*, or farming system, soon revived, with all its attendant abuses. The Taluqdárs again began to assert themselves, and to make head against the local officials, who, being unable to exact the full revenue demand from the large landholders, tried to make up the deficiency by piling it on the small zamíndárs and coparceners. These latter soon fell into arrears under the increased pressure put upon them, and were then in many cases handed over to the nearest Taluqdár who would undertake to pay the sum demanded, but who had generally no intention of paying it for more than a year or two, and was willing to submit to a temporary loss on the chance of ultimately evading or obtaining a reduction of the demand. The zamíndárs in such cases generally retained their *sír*, and sometimes their *dehí nánkár* as well; but there was a constant struggle, conducted in a spirit of watchful jealousy, going on between them and the Taluqdár, and their best chance of keeping their heads above water lay in being always ready to resist his encroachments. If, again, an open rupture took place between a Taluqdár and a Názim or a Chakladár, and the latter, with the aid of the King's troops drove out the former, the ejected party considered himself in a state of war with the Government, took to the jungles, and thought nothing of laying waste his own estate and harrying any tenants who presumed to cultivate it, until by this exhaustive process he compelled the Názim to restore him to possession. The state of things, in short, set in which lasted, with perhaps one short interval, for the forty-two years between the death of S'ádat Ali in 1814 and the deposition of Wájid Ali in 1856, and which was in full vigour and development when we annexed the province in the latter year. The short interval above alluded to was during the reign of Muhammad Ali Sháh, 1837–1842.

The cause of all this miserable imbroglio was the utter absence of anything worthy the name of revenue administration, and of any sufficient control over the turbulent land-holding classes, and more especially over the large Taluqdárs. The coparcenary bodies were lawless enough, but they seldom openly resisted the Government officers, except when rallied for the purpose by a Taluqdár in support of his own interest. This cause, indeed, was in full working for some eighty years, from the time of Asaf-ud-daulah onwards, with the exception already mentioned, during the reign of Muhammad Ali Sháh, and, much more markedly, during the twelve years from 1802 to 1814, when the indefatigable industry, clear perception, and great business powers of S'ádat Ali turned the tide for a time. It is not strange that both before and after that period the revenue had a constant tendency to fall off. It was only the large treasure left by S'ádat Ali which enabled his successors to carry on so long as they did. The difficulties which had been made about granting the aid of the Company's troops during his reign, to suppress local disorders and to enforce payment of revenue, much increased, and were, indeed, far more reasonable, in the time of Ghází-ud-dín Haidar. The Resident insisted, and the King and Minister admitted, that he had a right to be satisfied of the justice of the claim which he was asked to enforce by military aid. But the Resident was not in a position to hear both sides fairly, he being at Lucknow, and the defaulter, perhaps, in a jungle fort; and commanding officers had neither opportunity nor, in most cases, the requisite knowledge to enable them to arrive at any sound opinion. As the *morale*, too, of the Oudh Government deteriorated, it found such scrutiny into

8 *

the merits of its revenue demands grow more and more
distasteful, and the Minister, Agha Mír, began to increase
the King's troops to enable himself to dispense with the
aid of the Company's. Towards the end of this reign,
the treaty of 1801 to the contrary notwithstanding, the
Oudh force amounted to over sixty thousand men, of
whom twenty thousand were regulars, and the rest
undisciplined *Najíbs*, who "found themselves" in their
equipments. To do the British Government justice, it should
be said that at this time they were really willing and anxious
to support the King's authority so far as they justifiably could.
In November 1824 Lord Amherst wrote to the Resident that
our troops were to be " actively and energetically employed in
the Oudh territory in cases of real internal commotion and
disturbance." In July 1825 the Resident, Mr. Ricketts, was
censured for not sufficiently carrying out these orders, and
informed that the Governor-General was "sincerely disposed
to maintain the rights of the King of Oudh to the fullest
extent," as guaranteed by the treaty of 1801. It was added,
however, that the British Government was "clearly entitled,
as well as morally obliged, to satisfy itself, by whatever
means it may deem necessary, that the aid of its troops is
required in support of right and justice, and not to effectuate
injustice and oppression." This rider practically cancelled
the preceding declaration in something like four cases out of
five in which the aid in question was likely to be demanded.
For, however mischievous might be the turbulence of Taluqdárs, the Oudh Government was pretty sure to have contrived
by its mismanagement to put itself as much in the wrong as
its rebellious subjects.

Ghází-ud-dín Haidar died on the 20th of October 1827.
He had lent to the Company three millions and a half out of
his father's treasure. It was during his reign that the
system was begun of making the interest on these loans payable in perpetuity to the King's nominees, who were
guaranteed the protection of the British Government. It
led to great abuses, and created a class of pensioners who
were constantly arraying themselves against the King's authority under cover of that of the Resident. The character of

the King may be sufficiently gathered from this brief account of his reign. He was not an ill-disposed man, and, at the time of his accession, was inclined to spend his father's accumulations freely on public works. But his want of business habits prevented the money from being properly applied, and he does not seem to have been judiciously treated by the then Resident, Colonel Baillie. He soon sank into a life of voluptuous indulgence, and never emerged from it. He had, indeed, little motive to exertion. He had no lack of money; his position on the throne was secured by the presence of the Company's troops; and he was totally without the strenuous force of character and love of hard work for its own sake which were so conspicuous in his father. Perhaps the best that can be said of him is that he filled the post of *roi fainéant* not ungracefully, and was never personally guilty of any barbarity or outrage. But

> " 'Tis not mildness of the man that rules
> Makes the mild regimen,"

and so the people of Oudh found to their cost during the reign of Ghází-ud-dín Haidar.

Nasír-ud-dín Haidar, son of Ghází-ud-dín, and seventh Nawáb, differed from his father mainly in being considerably more debauched and disreputable. The father had been an outwardly decent hedonist and voluptuary, but the son was under no restraints of any sort or kind, and it is probable that his character was not unfaithfully depicted in that highly coloured sketch, the " Private Life of an Eastern King." " Any one," we are told, " was his friend who would drink with him," and "his whole reign was one continued satire upon the subsidiary and protected system." He inherited from his father the valuable services of that accomplished swindler Ágha Mír, and almost the only mark of good sense which he evinced during his reign was to discharge him, and attempt to make him disgorge his ill-gotten gains. The ex-minister, however, contrived to evade this drastic process under cover of British protection, and, taking up his abode at Cawnpore, started a printing press for the dissemination of attacks on the government which he had so long mal-administered. His son was an intimate of the Nána Sahib, and took an active part under him in the Mutiny.

Ágha Mír was succeeded by one Fazl Ali, who shortly gave place to Mehndi Ali Khán, better known as Hakím Mehndí, who had, as already mentioned, been living at Fattihgarh since his banishment by Ghází-ud-dín. He had great administrative ability, and though far from scrupulous, was, for his time and surroundings, indifferent honest. His character, however, is believed to have been stained by one conspicuous crime. In 1817 he offered Ghází-ud-dín to pay a lákh of rupees more than Rai Amr Singh, manager of Bahraich, had paid for that district in the preceding year. His offer was accepted, and the contract made over to him. He and his brother went down to Bahraich, where they were met by the Rai. They solemnly swore that they would do him no injury, but after putting him off his guard by compliments on his skilful management, and getting all his papers from him, they had him strangled at night, in his tent, by a couple of Mughal troopers. His property, amounting, it is said, to fifteen or twenty lákhs of rupees, was seized by the Hakím, who reported at Lucknow that his victim had poisoned himself to escape rendition of accounts. But it so happened that one of the murderers, whose name was Bábú Beg, had, in the struggle, thrust one of his fingers into Amr Singh's mouth, who had bitten it off in his dying agony. And there it was found by the dead man's relatives when they came to perform the funeral ceremonies, one of which consists of putting a sprig of *tulsi*, or holy basil, into the mouth of the corpse. Then the whole story came out, and Ágha Mír, who was at that time the Hakím's rival in the King's favour, was eager to have him tried for the crime. But

> "oft 'tis seen
> The wicked prize itself buys out the law,"

and judiciously-applied bribery having silenced all accusers, Bahraich was for the next three years rack-rented by the successful criminal. Such is the story as told by Sleeman. The episode of the bitten-off finger sounds apocryphal, and it is just conceivable that the whole story may have been fabricated by, or at the instigation of, Ágha Mír. But the probability seems in favour of its being substantially true, and the writer has been assured of its correctness by trustworthy residents of Bahraich. The scene of the murder, a little north-west of the town on the Nánpára road, is still pointed out. The house, in the centre of the town, where Amr Singh lived, is now a dispensary.

Whatever the real facts of the case may have been, Hakím Mehndi came back from exile about 1831, in April of which same year Lord Bentinck paid a somewhat notable visit to Lucknow. The Resident had reported in 1828 that "the country had reached so incurable a state of decline that nothing but the assumption of the administration could preserve it from utter ruin." Lord Bentinck now warned the King at a personal interview, and also by a written communication, that if his administration were not reformed from within, the task would have to be undertaken by English officers. The notion of assuming the administration of Oudh was, and had for some years been, familiar to the Government of India. In July 1831 Lord Bentinck reported to the Court of Directors that:—

"Unless a decided reform in the administration should take place, there would be no remedy left except in the direct assumption of the management of the Oudh territories by the British Government. . . . Acting in the character of guardian and trustee, we ought to frame an administration entirely native. . . . The only European part of it should be the functionary by whom it should be superintended, and it should only be retained until a complete reform might be brought about, and a guarantee for its continuance obtained, either in the improved character of the reigning prince, or if (he be) incorrigible, in the substitution of his immediate heir, or, in default of such substitute by nonage or incapacity, by the nomination of one of the family as regent, the whole of the revenue being paid into the Oudh treasury."

The Court of Directors, in reply, authorised him to take over the management at once, unless a marked improvement had taken place during the interval. But their final despatch was not dated until the 16th of July 1834, and Lord Bentinck considered the reforms effected by Hakím Mehndi, of whom he had a very high opinion, sufficient ground for granting the Oudh administration a fresh lease of life.

The new minister laid about him vigorously in his attack on the "tortuous, ungodly jungle" of misrule and corruption, which, centreing in Lucknow, overspread the province like a network. He reduced expenses, and especially the salaries and pensions of undeserving favourites. He systematised the revenue collections by introducing the practice of exchanging written agreements concerning the amount to be paid by each málguzár. Civil courts and police arrangements were to some extent reorganised. It has been asserted that he was desirous of seeing the province taken under British management. It is possible that he may have dropped a hint to that effect to some credulous English visitor. But that he could really have had any such wish is wholly incredible. He was emphatically a strong man, with a belief in himself, and in his own power of saving the country from misgovernment. Why should he have wished to abdicate a power which, while it lasted, was almost absolute? His pay as minister was Rs. 300,000, equal in itself to that of the Governor-General of India, while his perquisites, which included a deduction of one-fourth from all official salaries, were supposed to amount to Rs. 1,700,000 more—giving him a total annual income of £200,000 sterling. What could he have expected to receive in the way of pension from the British Government after Oudh had been annexed which could have in any way compensated him for the loss of such a position?

He worked nobly, and accomplished much during the short period, less than four years, that he held office. But he was not free from the vice of arrogance, and his want of courtesy to the men with whom he had to deal, and the harshness with which he carried out retrenchments which often pressed hardly on individuals, made him excessively unpopular, and contributed to his downfall. A reforming minister in Oudh necessarily had the whole army of corrupt officials and courtiers to contend against, and in this instance the King himself as well, and the natural difficulties of his situation were intensified by his lack of suavity. From Lord Bentinck he could obtain no active support, and "benevolent neutrality" was not enough to maintain him in his position. After a brief term of office, he was displaced, on some absurd pretext of want of respect for the Queen-mother, and superseded by one Roshan-ud-daulah, who is represented by some writers as an abandoned quack, a mere average specimen of the large class of "fools aspiring to be knaves" who surrounded Nasír-ud-dín; but by Mr. Shore, the author of a now somewhat rare work, "Notes on Indian Affairs," who was wont to understand his subject, is spoken of as "a well-disposed man, who is fully aware of the dangers of the path now followed, and who would gladly change its course and introduce a reform; but he wants nerve to face the storm which would be raised by those who profit by the present extravagance; so he is content to let things go on in their present train." However blameless may have been his tendencies, it is at least certain that under him such improvements as Hakím Mehndi had effected were speedily undone, and so far as the prosperity of the country depended on the efficiency of the central power, it markedly deteriorated from this time.

Of the state of the province during the latter part of Nasír-ud-dín's reign, the most detailed account which we possess is that given by Dr. Butter in his "Outlines of the Topography and Statistics of the Southern Districts of Oudh," written in 1837. As this work is now somewhat rare, a few excerpts from it may be given here.

Dr. Butter attributes "the present miserably depressed state of agriculture" partly to the prevalent insecurity of life and property, and partly from the diminution of rainfall resulting from "the extensive changes of the season and winds which have been remarked within the last twenty-two years, all over the Indian peninsula and seas," and the steady denudation of the north-western forest tracts. In the time of S'ádat Ali, the execution of three and five years' leases and counterparts for the payment of revenue was general, and the conditions agreed upon were strictly observed. But since his death, no lease for more than one year had been granted, and the demand was usually fifty per cent. higher. Consequently, cultivators were so impoverished as to be dependent on *mahájans* even for their seed, and were hardly ever out of debt. From the rapacity of the chakladárs, the only means of escape was the command either of influence at court, the possessors of which were known as *zor-wálas*, or of a body of fighting men strong enough to resist their encroachments. Some of the large landholders kept hundreds of armed retainers for this purpose. The smaller zamíndáris in Faizábád and the north of Sultánpur were being rapidly absorbed by Darshan Singh of Mahdona and Harpál Singh, the Gargbansi Thákur of Khapradíh. The ryots of these parts, according to Dr. Butter, were longing for the occupation of Oudh by the Company. This, however, is an assertion of which anything like proof is so difficult, and which has been so emphatically denied by trustworthy writers, that it could be wished that Dr. Butter had more distinctly stated the grounds on which he made it. That the sufferers from special acts of oppression may have desired annexation is probable enough, but that there was anything like a general wish for it on the part of a majority, or even a considerable minority of the people, is, to say the least of it, extremely doubtful.

The numbers and quality of agricultural cattle had markedly diminished and deteriorated during the previous twenty-five years. The area of the *dhák* jungles had been much narrowed by the increased demand for firewood during the same period, and that of the *jhíls*, or marshes, by frequent drought. The price of oxen varied from five to thirty rupees the pair, but they had become so few that it was usual to see men and women working at the well-rope instead of bullocks. Except along the Sai river, and in parts of Faizábád, where pasture was still abundant, the country cattle were extremely small, thin, and sickly, and the price of *ghí*, which was formerly twenty *sírs*, had risen to one *sír* and a half for the rupee.

Wells were less frequently constructed than of old, and for

forty years hardly a *pakka* tank had been built, except the Súraj Kund made at Darshannagar by Darshan Singh, and the Bhárat Kund at Bhadarsa by Bakhtáwar Singh. The existing tanks held less water, and dried in October instead of in December, so that their utility for irrigation was much reduced. Except in Baiswára, Salon, and the immediate vicinity of Faizábád, arboriculture was much decaying; few new groves were planted, and many old ones cut down.

The chief articles of manufacture were salt, soda, saltpetre, gunpowder, arms, cotton cloths, dye-stuffs, blankets, sugar, paper, and glass. The only exports of any importance seem to have been salt and saltpetre. Hardly any grain appears to have left the province in ordinary times, and exportation was legally prohibited whenever the price of wheat rose as high as twenty *sírs* for the rupee. The chief imports were cotton, silk, copper, brass, arms, and horses.

Apart from Lucknow, the province, or as it would, since 1819, be more strictly correct to term it, the kingdom of Oudh, was divided into eleven *chaklas*, viz. Sultánpur, Aldemau, Pratábgarh, Pachhimráth, Baiswára, Salon, Ahládganj, Gonda-Bahraich, Khairábád, Sándí, and Rusúlábád. In theory, each *chakla* should have been in charge of a separate *chakladár*, but it was not uncommon to put two or more *chaklas* under one officer, who was commonly called the Názim. Thus Darshan Singh for many years held the four first-mentioned districts under his sole authority.

The post of chakladár shared the tendency of all Indian office to become hereditary, though it carried with it no other income than the margin of difference between the sum which its holder contracted to pay into the treasury and the amount which he could succeed in collecting. Chakladárs spent eight months of the year in tents, and wherever their camp was pitched, their followers, military, civil, and miscellaneous, stripped the roofs of the neighbouring villages wherewith to make for themselves a temporary shelter. Each pargana, or subdivision of a chakla, of which, including Lucknow, there were seventy in all, was in charge of a Faujdár on twenty-five, and a Díwan on fifteen, rupees a month, salaries which, as may be imagined, were supplemented by perquisites, authorised and otherwise. The assessment of the year was divided into nine *kists*, or instalments, one of which fell due on the appearance of each new moon between Kuár (September) and Jeth (June). The penalties for default were sale of the defaulter's property, imprisonment in irons of himself and his family, and, in the last resort, torture. Powerful zamíndárs, however, were generally ready to fight, and skirmishes and cannonading were of frequent occurrence. "During the reign of S'ádat Ali a single cannonshot could not be fired by a chakladár without being followed by immediate inquiry from Lucknow as to its cause; now, a chakladár may continue firing for a month without question."

The army, excepting Colonel Roberts' brigade, was "an ill-paid, undisciplined rabble," divided into some forty-five *paltans*, or regiments, each of which, when complete, was about twelve hundred strong. The pay of the private soldier was three rupees a month, which was always kept much in arrears, and he had to find himself in arms and ammunition. His only uniform was a turban; as regards the rest of his dress, he was allowed to consult his own fancy. Fixed cantonments, parades, drill, leave of absence—except such as individuals granted themselves—and pensions were all alike unknown. In Shúja'-ud-daulah's time, the pay of the sepoy was seven rupees, and he was provided with uniform and a firelock. Some degree of discipline, too, was maintained, and grants of land were assigned to those who were wounded or otherwise disabled.

S'ádat Ali enforced the responsibility of zamíndárs for all thefts and violent crimes committed on their estates, but "since his death, no court of justice has been held by the Nawábs, and the chakladárs attend to nothing but finance. Nothing is said about a murder or a robbery; and consequently crime of all kinds has become much more frequent, especially within the last sixteen years." Gang robberies and dacoities were very common, and travellers went on their way armed to the teeth; "but such has always been the custom of Oudh." The only oases in this moral desert were to be found where power and good intentions were united in the person of some influential landholder, such as Shankar Singh, Rája of Tiloí in Salon.

The administrative state of the country in 1837 is summed up by Dr. Butter in the following scathing terms:—

"A sovereign regardless of his kingdom, except in so far as it supplies him with the means of personal indulgence; a minister (Roshan-ud-daulah) incapable, or unwilling, to stay the ruin of the country; local governors,—or, more properly speaking, farmers of the revenue, invested with virtually despotic power,—left, almost unchecked, to gratify their rapacity, and private enmities; a local army ill-paid, and therefore licentious, undisciplined, and accustomed to defeat; an almost absolute denial of justice in all matters, civil or criminal; and an overwhelming British force distributed through the provinces to maintain the faith of an ill-judged treaty, and to preserve—Peace."

Considering, however, the extent to which the negation of the principle of Government in its judicial and protective aspects was erected into a system, and the almost unbounded scope which was allowed to cupidity, revenge, malice, and almost every evil passion, by the absence of legal restraints, Dr. Butter thought that "the limited amount of crime attributable to private and individual motive that occurs in this country must be considered as highly creditable to the natural humanity, love of justice, and forbearance of its inhabitants. That rapine, burnings, and murder accompany the circuits of its revenue officers, and the predatory expeditions of the chieftains who rule the eastern and wilder districts, is the misfortune, not the fault, of the people, and the inevitable result of that maladministration which permits the accumulation of irresponsible power in the hands of unworthy persons, who, as private individuals, might prove harmless members of the community, but in whose unprepared and undisciplined minds the possession of unlimited power has produced its well-known and barbarizing effects."

The above is certainly not a flattering account of the state of the administration during the later years of Nasír-ud-dín. Anyone who wishes to see the opposite side of the picture, as painted by an ardent opponent of annexation and a firm disbeliever in the excellence of English rule as it then existed, will do well to consult a paper, already referred to, by Mr. Shore, on the " Present State and Prospects of Oudh," written in May 1835, about two years before the King's death. It was then generally believed that the province would be annexed within three or four years at most, and the measure was earnestly deprecated by Mr. Shore on the ground that the people were at least as well off, and much more contented, than was the case in our own territory. Some of his assertions may be open to question, and his criticisms on English methods of administration certainly do not err on the side of leniency. It is difficult, after a perusal of Dr. Butter's report, to concur in the opinion that " on the whole, the people of Oudh are not worse governed than our own subjects," or that its "civil and criminal administration is certainly not worse than ours," though the latter, whatever it may be now, was certainly far enough from perfection in 1835. It must be remembered, however, that Mr. Shore's remarks apply principally to western Oudh, while Dr. Butter was concerned only with the south and east. And, taking the country as a whole, the former was probably correct in his contentions that the mass of the population were " far more lightly taxed than those of the British dominions," and that they were " governed by their hereditary rulers, and benefited by the expenditure in the country of the revenue that is raised, instead of being subject to a few foreigners, by whom as much wealth as possible is carried out of the country."

" In every part," he continues, "are to be found respectable landholders and heads of villages, of various degrees of rank and wealth, forming the chain between the higher and lower classes, instead of, as in our provinces, the whole being reduced to the equality of a nation of paupers. They are not cursed with confiscation laws or with special commissions; nor with salt, opium, or other monopolies; they have not one system for realizing the demands of government, and another for individuals; . . . the people are not excluded from every office which a man of integrity could accept; .... and, without exception, there is not a single class which does not possess more wealth and property than the corresponding class in our own provinces. Such, and I fear not any inquiry properly conducted, is a true picture of the state of Oudh at this moment; and yet we are told that the people are sighing for the blessings of the British-Indian rule! When the voice of *the people* shall be really heard,—not that of courtiers and men in power, but of the landholders and peasantry,—they will be found to unite in one cry of 'Of all miseries keep us from that.' So far from their entertaining any such feeling, I can inform my readers, that in one part of the Doáb, not many months ago, the people, farmers and peasantry, held quite a rejoicing on hearing a report that that part of the country was to be transferred to the King of Oudh."

Pondering which conflicting opinions of two able and disinterested observers, the candid reader will probably arrive at the judicious, if not very startlingly original conclusion, that there was a good deal to be said on both sides of the question.

Meanwhile the career of Nasír-ud-dín was drawing towards its close. Colonel Low, who was Resident at the time, advocated setting up another member of the royal family in his place; but nothing was done. The belief was general in Oudh that the country would be taken over by the Company on the death of the King, and he himself is supposed to have had no dislike to the idea of being the last of his line. Such a course would have been highly acceptable to the horde of parasites who professed to govern the country, and who knew that in it lay their best chance of escaping a scrutiny into their malversations. Moral certainty, or even strong suspicion of peculation would, by a native government, be deemed amply sufficient ground for making them disgorge; while English officers would, as they were well aware, require legal proof, which it was almost always impossible to obtain.

Such was the state of things when, on the night of the 7th of July 1837, the sudden death of Nasír-ud-dín was reported to the Resident. The unsuccessful attempt on the part of his adoptive mother the Pádsháh Begam, widow of Ghází-ud-dín, to place his putative son Munna Ján on the throne, is too well known to be related here. The story of that tumultuous night has been strikingly told by Colonel Sleeman. A scene more wild, more utterly *bizarre*, than the Farhat Baksh palace presented from midnight till morning, can hardly be imagined. The dead body of the late King lay in one chamber; his uncle and successor, the respectable but decrepit Nasír-ud-daulah, sat cowering in fear of his life in another; while a furious mob of matchlockmen and dancing-girls filled the Lál Bárahdarri, or great hall of state, with mad acclamations in honour of Munna Ján and the Pádsháh Begam. Their triumph, however, only lasted for a few hours of frantic excitement. The guns soon opened fire, the palace was stormed by a handful of the Company's sepoys, and the insurgents fled, leaving some forty or more of their number dead on the ground. Nasír-ud-daulah, whose elevation to the throne in the event of the late King's death had been previously determined on, was proclaimed under the title of Muhammad Ali Sháh, and in a few hours more, all was quiet.

It is generally believed that Nasír-ud-dín died of poison. And it is also generally believed that Munna Ján was really his son, and was only repudiated by him to annoy the Pádsháh Begam, with whom he had for some years been on bad terms, and who was passionately fond of the lad. The boy himself seems to have been quite as vicious and unmanageable as a son of Nasír-ud-dín might have been expected to be, and his natural tendencies had been sedulously fostered by the Begam. The pair were speedily deported to Cawnpore and thence to Chunár, where they were kept in confinement, and perhaps no two prisoners of state ever deserved less compassion. Colonel Low and his assistants, Captains Paton and Shakespear, behaved admirably throughout. Their coolness and address both saved their own lives and probably prevented a general massacre. So ended the reign of the most contemptible specimen of the Oudh dynasty.

According to the principle of Muhammadan law already mentioned under the name of Mahjúb-ul-irs, Muhammad

Ali Sháh was the rightful heir to the throne on the death of Nasír-ud-dín without legitimate descendants. For, Shams-ud-daulah, as aforesaid, had died during the lifetime of his father S'ádat Ali, whose eldest son he was, and hence his children were excluded from the succession. His own elevation, however, seems to have been wholly unexpected by Muhammad Ali Sháh, and on the eventful night of Nasír-ud-dín's death he had signed a Persian declaration, drawn up for the occasion by Colonel Low, by which he agreed to consent to "any new treaty for the better government of the country that the British Government might think proper to propose to him." In accordance with this agreement, Lord Auckland obtained the new King's signature to the so-called treaty of the 18th of September 1837. This document certainly deserves the commendation bestowed by General Sherman on Mark Twain's celebrated map of Paris—"it is but fair to say that it is in some respects a truly remarkable" treaty. It recited that the Company was bound by the treaty of 1801 to defend Oudh, and had done so ; and that the King was bound to maintain only a limited number of troops, and had infringed the obligation ; that the treaty of 1801 was carried out with difficulty and required modification; that restrictions on the strength of the Oudh force might be relaxed, on condition that part of it was put under British officers; that the sixth article of the aforesaid treaty required the establishment of an improved administration in the reserved territories of Oudh, but provided no remedy for neglect of the requirement, which neglect had been "continued and notorious," and had "exposed the British Government to the reproach of imperfectly fulfilling its obligations to the Oudh people."

From these premises, it was deduced, as a "just and proper" consequence, that the King might maintain such force as he liked, subject to reduction when deemed excessive by the British Government; and that part of this force, not less than two regiments of cavalry, five regiments of infantry, and two companies of artillery, should be organized and disciplined by British officers, as part of the Oudh establishment, at an annual cost to the King of not more than sixteen lákhs of rupees! The year being one of great scarcity, and the pay of the King's troops and establishments heavily in arrears, the organization of the new force was postponed for eighteen months, to the 1st of March 1839. This force was to be employed whenever the King, with the concurrence of the Resident, deemed it necessary. But it was to be "clearly understood that such force is not to be employed in the ordinary collection of revenue."

Thus, after S'ádat Ali had given up half his territory on the distinct treaty stipulation that no further subsidy or military payments should be required of him or his successors, and that the whole cost of defending Oudh against external attack or internal commotion should, in consideration of this cession, be borne by the Company, Muhammad Ali Sháh was now called upon to contribute £160,000 yearly for military expenses on the strength of an agreement signed by him, when aroused in the middle of the night and offered the crown, to accept a new treaty "for the better government of the country."

The treaty further provided that the King was to take measures, in concert with the Resident, for improving the police, revenue, and judicial administration. In the event of his failing to attend to advice, "and if (which God forbid) gross and systematic anarchy, oppression, and misrule should hereafter at any time prevail within the Oudh dominions, such as seriously to endanger the public tranquillity, the British Government reserves to itself the right of appointing its own officers to the management of whatsoever portions of the Oudh territory, either to a small or to a great extent, in which such misrule as that above alluded to may have occurred, for so long a period as it may deem necessary; the surplus receipts in such case, after defraying all charges, to be paid into the King's treasury, and a true and faithful account rendered to His Majesty of the receipts and expenditure of the territories so assumed." In this event the Governor-General in Council would "endeavour to maintain as far as possible (with such improvements as they may admit of) the native institutions and forms of administration within the assumed territories, so as to facilitate the restoration of those territories to the Sovereign of Oudh, when the proper period for such restoration shall arrive."

This engagement was entered into with great reluctance by Muhammad Ali Sháh. But the Home Government, to their credit, altogether refused to sanction it, and directed restoration of the previous relations as they existed under the treaty of 1801. The abrogation of the treaty was never formally notified to the King, who was merely told that any expenses already incurred in organizing the subsidiary force would be borne by the Company, and no outlay required from him. Such was the history of this curious "treaty," which, though never ratified, was constantly referred to in subsequent discussions, as if it had been of binding force. It consisted of two distinct parts, the first of which would have involved a manifest breach of faith, while the second erred only in the excessive consideration for the King's rights with which it approached the question of reform. The latter portion probably expressed the views of Colonel Low; the former may be ascribed to the Calcutta Council.

With the accession of Muhammad Ali Sháh, commenced a period of something like administrative reform. The new King was an old man, who had long lived a retired life, but who, when young, had been well practised in the conduct of affairs by his father S'ádat Ali, and was now prudent, parsimonious, and generally decent and business-like. The court was no longer a paradise for fiddlers and buffoons. Roshan-ud-daulah was discharged from the post of Minister, and succeeded by Hakím Mehndi, who now, for the second time, came back from exile to assume the reins of office. Had he still been the man he was only six or seven years before, much might have been effected in the way of reform, for he had now the influence of the King on his side instead of against him, as had been the case with Nasír-ud-dín. But time had told heavily upon the old statesman, and both his brain and hand had forgotten much of their cunning. Death overtook him before he had time to do much towards improving the administration, and he was succeeded by Zakír-ud-daulah, who was also a man of ability. He, too, however, shortly died, and the post of Minister was bestowed on Hakím Mehndi's nephew, Manowar-ud-daulah, an honest man and good sportsman, but an indifferent administrator, who remained in office for only two years, after which he retired, and went on pilgrimage to Makka. It was by him that the great tomb of Hakím Mehndi at Lucknow, to the east of Golaganj, was erected. He was succeeded by Sharf-ud-daulah, a nephew of Zakír-ud-daulah, a business-like and respectable man, who remained in office for the rest of the short and uneventful reign of Muhammad Ali Sháh, which came to an end in May 1842. Its chief features were an attempt to revive the *amáni* system of revenue management over a portion of territory paying 35 lákhs of rupees, and the erection of the great Husenábád Imámbára, as a burial-place for the King. This institution was largely endowed out of the interest payable on investments in the Company's loans. Other works constructed during this reign were a magnificent tank near the Husenábád Imámbára, and a mosque, intended to rival the Jama Masjid of Delhi, but which was never completed. A curious *Satkhanda*, or seven-storied tower, was also commenced, but never rose beyond the fourth story. Muhammad Ali Sháh had found only £700,000 in the treasury at his accession out of the accumulations of S'ádat Ali, on which his two predecessors had drawn lavishly. He himself was careful and saving, and after expending some eighty lákhs in Company's paper and charitable funds, left £788,000 to his son and successor Amjad Ali Sháh.

This succession was another illustration of the doctrine of Mahjúb-ul-irs, Mumtáz-ud-daulah, son of Asghar Ali, the elder brother of Amjad Ali, being excluded, owing to his father's death during the lifetime of Muhammad Ali Sháh.

Sharf-ud-daulah, who was Minister at the time of the late King's death, resigned after two month's experience of Amjad Ali's caprices, and was succeeded by a favourite named Imdád Hosen, under the title of Amín-ud-daulah. This person was removed after five months' exhibition of his incapacity, and Manowar-ud-daulah, who had now returned from his pilgrimage to Makka, held the office for seven months. The mighty tide of Lucknow intrigue then swept him away, and Amín-ud-daulah was recalled. Such work as was done in his time was performed by his deputy, Syad-ud-daulah, "a low person who has rapidly risen from penury to power by the prostitution of his own sister." The choice of such a miserable *dilettante* as Imdád Hosen was not due to the absence of a better candidate. Sharf-ud-daulah was ready and willing to take office, but the King's personal dislike for him debarred him from employment.

Sir Henry Lawrence, writing in 1845, sums up the situation as follows:—

"The condition of Oudh is yearly becoming worse. The revenue is yearly lessening. There are not less than one hundred thousand soldiers in the service of the zamíndárs. The revenue is collected by half that number in the King's pay. In more than half the districts of Oudh are strong forts . . . surrounded with dense jungle . . . Originally the effect of a weak or tyrannical government, such fortresses perpetuate anarchy. The amils and other public officers are men of no character, who obtain and retain their position by court bribery. Only the weak pay their revenue; those who have forts, or who, by combination, can withstand the amil, make their own revenue arrangements. Throughout the country nothing exists deserving the name of a judicial or magisterial court. The news-writers are in the pay of the amils, generally their servants; nevertheless, not less than a hundred dacoities or other acts of violence attended with loss of life are annually reported; how many hundreds, then, pass unnoticed! . . . In short, the government of the country is utterly palsied; its constitution is altogether destroyed; no hope remains. Were any vitality left in Oudh, the country has, during the last twelve years, had a fair opportunity of recovering. If the system of a King, a Minister, a Resident, and a protecting army, could subsist without ruin to the country so ruled, it has had a trial. The scheme cannot be said to have failed for lack of good instruments. The Oudh rulers have been no worse than monarchs so situated usually are; indeed they have been better than might be expected. Weak, vicious, and dissolute they were" —some of them, not all—" but they have seldom been cruel, and have never been false. . . . Among her ministers have been as able individuals as are usually to be found in the East; and there have not been wanting good men and true as Residents. It is the system that is defective, not the tools with which it has been worked. We have tried every variety of interference. We have interfered directly, and we have interfered indirectly, by omission as well as by commission, but it has invariably failed.

"One great error has been our interference in trifles, while we stood aloof when important questions were at issue. Another crying evil has been the want of any recognised system of policy in our negotiations with the Lucknow Court. Everything seems to have been mere guesswork and experiment. . . . The King, the Minister, and the Resident have each had their turn. One or other has been alternately everything and nothing. . . . Each member of the triumvirate could vitiate the exertions of one or both of the others; any individual of the three could do incalculable evil; but the three souls must be in one body to effect any good. Such a phenomenon never occurred, there never was an approach to it, unless perhaps for a few months in Colonel Low's time. . . . Is it to remain thus for ever? Is the fairest province of India always to be harried and rack-rented for the benefit of one family, or rather, to support in idle luxury *one* individual of *one* family? Forbid it, justice! forbid it, mercy! Had any one of the many Governors-General who spoiled Oudh remained a few years longer in office, he might have righted her wrongs. But unhappily, while several have been in authority long enough to wound, not one has yet had time to bind up and heal. Hastings began the 'Stand and deliver' system with the Nawábs. More moderate Governors succeeded, who felt ashamed to persecute a family that had already been so pillaged. They pitied the monarch, but they forgot that misdirected mercy to him was cruelty to his subject millions. . . . Let the management of the province be assumed under some such rules as those which were laid down by Lord W. Bentinck. Let the administration of the country, as far as possible, be native. Let not a rupee come into the Company's coffers. Let Oudh be at last governed, not for one man, the king, but for him and his people."

No apology is needed for this long excerpt, so instinct with the clear vision of a statesman, and with the righteous indignation of an honest man. While the words were being penned, Amjad Ali's frivolous reign was drawing towards its close. He died in February 1847, leaving as memorials of his better impulses the iron bridge across the Gumti, and the metalled road between Cawnpore and Lucknow. He was succeeded by his son Wájid Ali, the last, and, with the exception of Nasír-ud-dín, perhaps the most despicable of his line. Ever since the unhappy Afghán expedition of 1838-39, Oudh questions had been kept in abeyance by wars and rumours of wars in different parts of the empire—in Sindh, the Panjáb, and Central India. In 1847 there was a breathing space, and in November of that year Lord Hardinge visited Lucknow, and administered to Wájid Ali the sort of warning, now become somewhat hackneyed, which had been so often addressed to his predecessors. The young King, however, was not so much accustomed to these admonitions as he afterwards became, and is said to have been too much affected to speak, and to have been able to signify his good intentions only on paper. He was allowed two years' grace —it would have been of as much, or as little, use to allow him a couple of centuries—in which to cleanse his Augean stable, and informed that if a marked improvement were not visible in that time, the result would be the assumption by the Company of the management of Oudh. Previous to this warning, for the first few months after his accession, Wájid Ali had held a few *darbárs*, and made some faint show of attending to public business, but he had abandoned the effort before Lord Hardinge's visit, and never resumed it. Colonel Sleeman, as Resident, reported in 1849 that no improvement whatever had taken place; but the second Sikh war, the Burmese war which followed, and political complications in southern and central India, at Satára, Nágpur, Jhánsi, Tanjór, and elsewhere, once more staved off the inevitable. In his diary of February 1850, Colonel Sleeman recorded that "the King has natural capacity equal to that of any of those who have preceded him in the sovereignty of Oudh since the death of S'ádat Ali in 1814, but he is the only one who has systematically declined to devote any of that capacity, or any of his time, to the conduct of public affairs." He was a poetaster in a small way, and dabbled, in his loftier moments, in music and painting, and if he had had to earn his living by these accomplishments he might have passed muster in a crowd as a decent member of society. But the proverbial "pumpkin as a shade tree" could hardly have been a greater failure than was Wájid Ali as King of Oudh.

The three recognised branches of the Oudh-constitution were, as Sir H. Lawrence, in the lately quoted extract, remarks, the King, the Minister, and the Resident. But, besides these, there was generally a fourth personage at work, viz. the great revenue contractor, or Názim, whose influence, whether for good or evil, was extremely effective. Several of these men have left traditions, either of benevolence or destructiveness, which still survive in the country. Greatest and best of the class was Miyán Almás Ali, who flourished under Shúja'-ud-daulah, and his successors Asaf-ud-daulah and S'adat Ali, and of whom mention has already been made. His mantle seems, to a certain extent, to have descended on Hakím Mehndi, who was contractor of Muhamdi from 1804, and of Khairábád from 1809 up to the time of his disgrace and banishment in 1819. His influence in both these districts—the present Kheri and Sítapur—was beneficial. He vastly increased cultivation, and doubled the rent-roll without resort to oppression. But in 1816 he obtained the contract of Bahraich, and, as is generally believed, murdered his predecessor Rai Amr Singh in the manner already described. Whether he was guilty of this crime or not, his management seems to have been pernicious. He raised the revenue $12\frac{1}{2}$ per cent. all round, *i.e.* two annas in the rupee—or one-eighth. Whether he would, had he remained longer in office, have mended his ways, and produced as good results as he had shown in Muhamdi and Khairábád, is uncertain. Out of the money which he had obtained by the death of Rai Amr Singh, he bribed the confidants of the then minister, Ágha Mír, to persuade the latter to postpone the attempt to get him punished on the charge of murder until a more convenient season, and then, after sending away his available wealth into British territory, took a favourable opportunity of following it himself to Sháhjahánpur. The part which he subsequently played in Oudh affairs was as minister rather than as revenue contractor, and has been already noticed. It may here be added that his successor, Hádí Ali Khán, who held the contract of Gonda and Bahraich—now for the first time united under one Názim—for nine years, up to 1827, enhanced the assessment of Hakím Mehndi by another two annas in the rupee, and when difficulty was found in the collection of this exorbitant demand, began the vicious system, which had been strictly prohibited by S'ádat Ali, of making over *khálsa* (or allodial) lands held by small proprietors paying directly to the State, to Taluqdárs, whose first step was generally to crush or drive out the zamíndárs, and who, until that feat was accomplished, could make nothing of the villages assigned them. Sometimes the contending parties contrived to arrange some *modus vivendi*, but this was the exception. The extent to which small zamíndáris were absorbed in taluqas, may be gathered from the fact that during Hádí Ali Khán's tenure of office alone, 439 villages were thus transferred; while between 1827 and 1856, as many as 349 more villages were similarly absorbed, making a total of 788 villages, paying a revenue of more than 5 lakhs, which were lost to the zamíndárs during a period of forty years. According to some figures given by Colonel Sleeman, the three parganas of Bahraich, Hisámpur, and Hariharpur contained in 1807, during the reign of S'ádat Ali, and under the management of Balkidás Kánúngo, father of Rai Amr Singh, *khálsa* lands paying a revenue of Rs. 5,75,000; while in 1849, during the reign of Wájid Ali and the Nizámat of Muhammad Hosen, the *khálsa* villages of the same three parganas yielded a revenue of no more than Rs. 54,000. How completely the zamíndárs were crushed is apparent from the small number of them who were found at annexation to have kept alive any proprietary right.

The next great Názim was Darshan Singh, founder of the Mahdona estate, the typical instance of a "mushroom" taluqa. He was fourth son of Purandar Rám, a Páthak Bráhman, who came from Gorakhpur about the end of the last century, and settled at Palia, a village twelve miles south-west of Faizábád, and close to Sháhganj, the present abode of the family. Bakhtáwar Singh, eldest son of Purandar Rám, was a trooper in the Bengal Cavalry, and being stationed at Lucknow, his fine physique attracted the attention of S'ádat Ali, who bought him out of the Company's service, and made him a Resildár in his own. By Ghází-ud-dín he was created a Rája, and Muhammad Ali Sháh conferred on him the title of the Premier Rája of Oudh, and the Mahdona estate of forty-two villages. Through his influence at court, Darshan Singh, his younger brother, was in 1822 appointed Chakladár of Salon and Baiswára, and Názim of Sultánpur in 1827, and in 1836 was given the contract of Gonda-Bahraich, but held it only for a short time, during which he contented himself with acquiring information, and did but little. But in 1842 he was again appointed to the same districts, and this time he proceeded to lay about him unsparingly among the large taluqdárs, for which purpose, indeed, he had been sent there. He was the hammer with which the Oudh Government attempted to crush refractory barons, and for a time, at any rate, he was certainly an effective instrument. His name was great throughout his Nizámat, and he is still spoken of by the country folk as the "Rája Bahádur." But in 1843 he pursued Dirg Bijai Singh, the young Rája (now Mahárája) of Balrámpur, into Naipál territory, where he had taken refuge under the protection of the then minister Mátbar Singh. The Oudh Government was thus brought into collision with the Naipál Darbár, and the latter was very insistent in its demands for reparation, which being backed up by Lord Ellenborough, Darshan Singh was, in March 1844, dismissed from all his employments, and banished the kingdom. This decision was only arrived at after much intrigue on the part of three of Amjad Ali Sháh's wives, the father of one of whom, Hosen Ali, was desirous of succeeding to the estates of the disgraced Názim. Both Darshan Singh, and his brother Bakhtáwar Singh, in whose name the revenue contracts stood, were heavily fined, and their estates made over to Hosen Ali, who undertook to pay Rs. 4,40,000 for them, or one lákh more than had been paid by Darshan Singh.

It was soon found, however, that things would not work in the absence of the powerful exile. Landholders everywhere refused payment, the collections came to a standstill, and in May 1844, after only two months' banishment, Darshan Singh was recalled from Gorakhpur where he had taken up his abode. He was now restored to all his estates, invested with additional honours and titles, and appointed Inspector-General of Oudh, with unlimited powers to reduce everything and everybody—always excepting the Lucknow court—to order and submission. His strenuous energy, and utter unscrupulousness as to means might, had he lived long enough, have evolved some system out of the chaos. He must have been a man of great force of character, and certainly established a wonderful awe of himself in the minds of all who had to do with him. Faizábád folk will still tell one how a frown from Darshan Singh, accompanied by an imperious "Dastkhatt kar! Kalam chú!" ("Sign! Touch the pen!") would drive the most recalcitrant taluqdár or zamíndár into signing any agreement that was put before him. He died, however, in August 1844, at Ajodhya, leaving his possessions to his three sons, Rám Adhín Singh, Raghbar Dyál Singh, and Mán Singh. Of these, the first was a man of little note; the second earned conspicuous infamy as the tyrant of Gonda-Bahraich; while the history of the third is tolerably well known. Mán Singh was Názim of Dariábád and Radauli in 1845, and Sultánpur was soon added to his charge, which he held till 1847, when he was superseded by Ágha Ali, better known as the Aghai Sáhib. His most celebrated exploit was the murder of Harpál Singh, the Gargbansi chief of Khapradih, whom he had induced by the most solemn oaths to come out of his fort to meet him, on the false pretence of bestowing on him a dress of honour from the Lucknow court. Harpál Singh was sick at the time, but was brought out in his bed, and after a long and seemingly cordial conversation with Mán Singh, was cut to pieces by the attendants of the latter as he himself rode away. Colonel Sleeman says that the whole family, with the exception of Bakhtáwar Singh, who accompanied him on his tour through the province, had been brought up in the camp of a revenue contractor, than which there is "no school in the world more adapted for training thoroughbred ruffians." Darshan Singh, and Mán Singh after him, had amassed an enormous estate by means which earned them the bitter hostility of almost every zamíndár upon it. No one who knows anything of the history of the Mahdona taluqa can be surprised that its management should have collapsed under a revenue system which, whatever its defects, does not permit indiscriminate torture and imprisonment at the discretion of the landlord. For some forty years the family was the most powerful in Oudh, and something like half the province was, with occasional breaks, in the hands of one or other of its members as Názim. Their influence at court was great, and without it their power in the districts could not have been maintained. Ghází-uddín married one of Darshan Singh's daughters, and placed another in his harem. This Darshan Singh, the Shankaldwípí Bráhman of Mahdona, must not be confounded with a notorious Kurmi Rája of the same name, who, like Bakhtáwar Singh, brother of his namesake, rose to favour under S'ádat Ali, and under the title of Ghálib Jang experienced many vicissitudes of honour and disgrace during the reigns of later Nawábs.

One other great Názim remains to be mentioned, A'gha Ali, but his career may be more conveniently noticed in its place in a brief review of Sleeman's "Tour in Oudh," a work which bears much the same relation, to compare small things with great, to the subsequent annexation of the province and the course of the mutiny, that Arthur Young's "Travels in France" bears to the first French Revolution. The "Tour" is the record of a three months' march through Oudh, from the 1st of December 1849 to the 28th of February 1850. During that short period, Colonel Sleeman acquired a surprising amount of information, of which subsequent experience has shown the general accuracy, and it was on this information, mainly, that the province was annexed six years later, though by no means in the manner which the author himself would have advocated. Starting from Lucknow, his route lay through Chinhat, Nawábganj-Bárabanki, and Bahrámghát, northwards to Bahraich; thence south-east to Gonda and Faizábád, and then almost due south to Sultánpur and Pratábgarh. From Pratábgarh he marched west-north-west to Rai Bareli, and on to Purwa and Safipur, in what is now the Unáo district. Thence due north to Sandíla, from which his course swept round by Sáudí, Sháhábád, and Gokarnnáth to Sítapur and Biswán, thence south-east again to Dariábád, and from that point, due west, back to Lucknow. He thus passed through every one of the twelve districts into which Oudh is at present divided. He made his marches principally on an elephant, talking freely with the native officials and zamíndárs who accompanied him; and his great powers of observation and knowledge of and keen interest in native ways and traditions, combined with his easy and unpretentious style, make his journal at once a most trustworthy and attractive *compagnon de voyage*. He of course found considerable local variations in the condition of the country. Even so near the capital as Bárabanki, the king's officers and the landholders were at open war, and the large Muhammadan taluqdárs plundering the small Hindú zamíndárs. Crossing the Ghághra into Bahraich at Bahrámghát, he found the tables turned, and the Kalhans Rájpúts of the Chadwára or Guárich pargana despoiling the Syads of Jarwal and other Musalmán proprietors. The Raikwár estates of Baundi, Rahwa, and Hariharpur—the first of which is now held by the Mahárája of Kapurthala—had been frightfully devastated three or four years previously by the notorious Raghbar Dyál, who held the contract of Gonda-Bahraich in 1846-47. Under pretext of collecting the revenue, this most pernicious villain, who was the son of Darshan Singh and elder brother of Mán Singh, harried the whole country, extorted hidden hoards by torture, seized all the cattle he could lay hands on, and, generally, behaved more like a fiend broke loose than any officer, even of the Oudh Government, before or since. He and his agents Karm Hosen, Gauri Shankar, Mahárái Singh, and Bihárí Lál, are said to have seized twenty-five thousand head of cattle, and two thousand men, women, and children, in the Baundi estate alone. Of the latter, those who could not ransom themselves were sold for what they would fetch. Great numbers of the peasantry fled northwards to the Tarai to escape his exactions, and not a few died under the treatment they received. Even now, the effects of his atrocities, in the shape of a comparatively sparse population in the Bahraich district, have scarcely ceased to be perceptible. Many square miles of fertile soil were thrown out of cultivation, much of which has not yet been reoccupied, and is still covered with long grass which affords shelter to pigs and *nilgai*, whose depredations are a severe check on all attempts to reclaim the waste. "No oppressor," it has been said, "ever wrote his name in a more legible hand" than Raghbar Dyál. And all his extortions were for his own private benefit, not for the King's treasury. The cattle sold by him must have been worth, according to Colonel Sleeman, at least a lákh; but all that was credited to the Baundi estate on account of them was one hundred and thirty-seven rupees! His atrocities were, of course, but feebly reported by the news-writers, or *Akhbár Navís*, attached to his office, all of whom were propitiated by a share in the plunder. Thus we are told that "Jiorákhan, the news-writer at Baundi, got one anna for every prisoner brought in; and from two to three rupees for every prisoner released. He got every day subsistence for ten men from Karm Hosen. All the news-writers in the neighbourhood got a share of the booty in bullocks, cows, and other animals." And on their absurdly inadequate reports, the Lucknow Darbár passed utterly imbecile and ineffectual orders, which were never carried out. "Several times during the two months" of September and October, when these iniquities were at their height, "Raghbar Dyál paid off heavy arrears due to his personal servants, by drafts on his agents for prisoners, to be placed at the disposal of the payee, ten and twenty at a time."

The barbarous cruelty of Raghbár Dyál and his minions, and the shameless acts of treachery by which it was supplemented, fill many pages of Colonel Sleeman's diary, and really beggar all description. All representations made by the Resident were useless to secure the punishment of these ruffians, who were, Colonel Sleeman tells us, " by all I saw considered more as terrible demons who delighted in blood and murder than as men endowed with any feelings of sympathy for their fellow creatures; and the Government, which employed such men in the management of districts with uncontrolled power, seemed to be utterly detested and abhorred." Raghbar Dyál Singh went off into British territory, to evade demands for balances, and nothing was done towards punishing him until Colonel Sleeman assumed charge of the office of Resident in January 1849. He induced the King to proclaim him an outlaw, and to offer a reward of three thousand rupees for his arrest, if he failed to come in within three months. " He never appeared, but continued to carry on his negotiations for restoration to power at Lucknow, through the very agents whom he had employed in the scenes above described." These latter, Bihári Lál, Gauri Shankar, Karm Hosen, and Maháráj Singh, had been arrested by Colonel Sleeman's influence and sent into Lucknow, with abundant evidence of their guilt. But they promptly purchased their way out of prison, and were never punished. Soon after this, Raghbar Dyál engaged in a contest with his brother Mán Singh for the estates which had been acquired by the latter and Darshan Singh in Sultánpur and Faizábád, by means of deeds of sale, or *bainámas*, which subsequently became notorious in our settlement courts. Mán Singh, however, proved too strong for him, and drove him out.

Raghbar Dyál had been succeeded in the contract of Gonda-Bahraich by his uncle Incha Singh, who obtained it at a reduction of four lákhs. He, also, absconded before the end of the year, and was followed by Muhammad Hosen, who raised funds to meet an enhanced demand by the murder of Rám Datt Pánde, the great agricultural capitalist of the Gonda district, all whose property he seized. This crime was committed less than a year after Colonel Sleeman had passed through the district, attended by both the future murderer and his victim. Muhammad Hosen sent in a report to Lucknow to the effect that Rám Datt had defaulted on account both of his own estate, and of other landholders for whom he had given security, and when pressed for a settlement of his liabilities had attacked the Názim and his men, and been killed by the latter in self-defence. The real facts were that, only eight days before he was murdered, the banker had advanced Rs. 80,000 to the Názim, and had declined to increase his pledges of security until he had further consulted the landholders for whom he had given them. The minister, however (who was "certainly an accessory to this murder after the fact, while there are strong grounds to believe that he was so before the fact"), by order of the King, presented Muhammad Hosen with a dress of honour, and conveyed to him the thanks of His Majesty for having crushed so notorious a rebel! The Resident, with the assistance of the British magistrate of Gorakhpur, Mr. Chester, elicited the truth, and Muhammad Hosen was pressed so hard that he came back from Gorakhpur where he had taken refuge, and surrendered himself at Lucknow. Being, however, a Syad and a Shia, he could not be convicted of murder for the killing of a mere Hindú, and was acquitted by the *mujtahid*, or judge. "No Shia," writes Colonel Sleeman, "could be sentenced to death for the murder even of a Sunni, at Lucknow, much less for that of a Hindú. If a Hindú murders a Hindú, and consents to become a Musalmán, he cannot be so sentenced; and if he consents to become so after sentence has been passed, it cannot be carried into execution. Such is the law, and such the every-day practice." It only remains to be added that none of the plundered property of the banker was ever recovered by his family.

The Gonda district had had the advantage of being in great part included in the Bahu Begam's *jághír*, until her death in 1815. It suffered heavily under Raghbar Dyál, though less so than Bahraich. Colonel Sleeman found but a small portion of it under tillage, and the better classes of cultivators, Kurmís, Muráos and Káchhis, almost non-existent. In 1854 Captain Orr reported that it was fast recovering under the beneficent rule of Sadhan Lál, Kayáth, who was *de facto* Názim, though nominally only the Názim's Náib, or deputy. He had an excellent lieutenant in Bhya Shioratan

Singh, Chauhán, an old gentleman who is still alive and much respected. Sadhan Lál paid seventeen lákhs of rupees for Gonda and Bahraich, and governed leniently.

Crossing the Ghághra at Faizábád, Colonel Sleeman found himself in the Sultánpur Nizámat, which included, besides the modern district of Sultánpur, Aldemau, Jagdíspur, Pratábgarh, and Pachhimráth, by which latter is here intended, not the old division of that name, which comprised more than a fifth of Oudh, but the modern pargana, lying to the south and west of Faizábád. This huge tract, as well as Dariábád and Radauli, amounting in all to more than one-third of Oudh, had been held by Darshan Singh, and after him by Mán Singh, for several years previous to 1847. In that and the preceding year, Raghbar Dyál was in possession of Gonda-Bahraich, and thus the family held between them, with practically unlimited powers, more than one-half of the province. In 1847, A'gha Ali, the "Aghái Sahib," was appointed Názim in place of Mán Singh, nominally on the *amání* principle, but it was perfectly well understood that he was to pay a fixed sum. Spasmodic attempts had been made from time to time since the death of S'ádat Ali to enforce the *amání* system which he had worked so successfully, but they had always failed. Ghází-ud-dín, within two years of his father's death, reverted to the *ijára* method, and though he allowed trust management to be re-adopted at the instance of Colonel Baillie, it was given up in despair after two years' trial. Under Nasír-ud-dín, Hakím Mehndi being minister, and Mr. Maddock and, after him, Colonel Low, Residents, the effort was renewed, but again abandoned after two years. Under Muhammad Ali Sháh, while Sharf-ud-daulah was Minister, and Colonels Low and Caulfield, Residents, lands yielding an annual revenue of thirty-five lákhs were made *amání*, and both Sharf-ud-daulah, and his successor Amín-ud-daulah, seem to have done their best to make the system work, but without success. The *ijára* system, however, does not seem to have been much abused under this king, for Colonel Low recorded in 1841 that any farmer who paid his revenue regularly might feel confident of being allowed to retain his farm, and some motive was thus provided for conciliation and good management. In 1847, Lord Hardinge had urged Wájid Ali Sháh to try *amání* collection once more, and a specimen of it was now to be seen in A'gha Ali's management of Sultánpur. So far as the change was anything more than nominal, it seems to have been for the worse. Nothing like a fixed assessment for a term of years was attempted, and every collector was really bound to pay a fixed sum. The more frequently changes took place among the higher officials, the greater were the profits of the Lucknow parasites, whose influence made and unmade Názims and Chakladárs. There were the same abuses of authority, the same rack-renting, the same uncertainty, the same bribery and corruption, under both systems, and Major Troup, Captain Bunbury, and Captain Patrick Orr, of the Oudh auxiliary force, and Captain Alexander Orr, of the police, were all agreed that while the Government was far more robbed, the condition of the peasantry was still worse under *amání* management as it was then worked, than it had been under *ijáradárs* like Darshan Singh. A'gha Ali saved himself the trouble and expense of collecting the revenue by a free resort to the device known as *kabz*, *i.e.* collection by troops on their own responsibility. *Kabz* was of two sorts, *lákalámí*, or unconditional, and *wusúli*. The first was where a commandant gave a pledge to collect and pay, either to the Názim or to his troops, a fixed sum assessed on the estate made over to him. In the second he only agreed to pay whatever he might be able to collect. The difference between the two was analogous to that between *ijára* and *amání* management, and, so far as the rent-payer was concerned, was practically very little. The *lákalámi* pledge alone was theoretically accepted at the Lucknow treasury as equivalent to an actual disbursement; but both had the same practical effect, for the troops might be fully trusted to get their pay out of an estate, if they had to sell every living thing on it to do so. A more ruinous or demoralising system it would be hard to conceive. The only reason for its adoption was its convenience to the Názim, and the troops had no alternative but to accept the *kabz* or remain unpaid.

A'gha Ali had immense power throughout the Sultánpur

Nizámat. He had the control of a considerable military force, including two of the *komakhia*, or auxiliary regiments, which were the least inefficient troops in Oudh. All his Chakladárs were his relatives. Thus, A'gha Haidar, Chakladár of Sultánpur, and A'gha Hosen, of Aldemau, were his brothers; Ata Ali, collector of Pachhimráth, and Syad Hosen, of Radauli, were his uncles; and they all played into his hands. The chief Taluqdárs of Baiswára were at this time, *i.e.* 1849–1850, under *Huzúr Tahsíl*, *i.e.* they paid their revenue directly into the head-quarters treasury, and not through the medium of the Názim or Chakladár. This privilege, which was shared by the Mahdona estate of Mán Singh, saved its possessors from arbitrary official exactions, and the cultivators were not liable to forced labour. It was, however, as a matter of course, distasteful to the collectors, and in 1851 A'gha Ali stipulated that it should be abolished throughout his Nizámat. The gross revenue of Sultánpur was estimated, roughly speaking, at thirty-six lákhs, of which nine lákhs were payable on account of *Huzúr Tahsíl* estates. Of the remaining twenty-seven lákhs which passed through his hands, A'gha Ali "accounted for" seventeen lákhs to the Government, and retained the other ten for administrative purposes. Out of the seventeen lákhs accounted for, came the *samjhota*, or pay of troops, and all costs of repairs to forts, erection of cantonments, ammunition, and feed of cattle and elephants. The real amount expended on this latter item was almost *nil*, but the nominal sum was very considerable. Another lákh probably found its way into the Názim's coffers in the shape of *siráe*, or extra items, in addition to the regular revenue demand, and of fees from *firáris*, or absconded landholders, who were returned in the accounts as paying nothing, but who really paid very highly for protection. The maintenance of the news-writers, who had been hitherto kept up as a check on collectors, was regarded as an unnecessary precaution under *amíni* management, and discontinued. That this, however, was no great loss may be gathered from the glimpse which we have already been afforded of the efficiency of the members of this body who were attached to Raghbar Dyál's camp during the perpetration of his worst atrocities in Bahraich.

A'gha Ali's management was unfavourably contrasted with that of Darshan Singh by Captain A. Orr, of the Oudh frontier police, in a letter to the Resident, dated "Camp, Faizábád," 9th of January 1855, one passage of which may be quoted :—

"Rája Darshan Singh is cited as having levied, under *ijára*, the highest amount of revenue, *i.e.* thirty-two lákhs."

"Aghai has levied, on *amáni*, thirty-six lákhs" (from which sum, however, as Captain Orr himself remarked elsewhere, nine lákhs should be excluded which were paid into the Huzúr Tahsíl direct).

"Darshan Singh taxed rich and poor in equal proportion."

"Aghai fears the one and ruins the other."

"Darshan Singh was the sworn enemy of dacoits and thieves."

"Aghai has ever spared them."

"Darshan Singh never gave, on the average, less than twenty-two lákhs to Government."

"Aghai gives *nominally* seventeen."

"Darshan Singh made for himself by oppression a vast estate, styled the Baináma, assessed at two lákhs and a half, and yielding from five to six lákhs, but ruled it "—as far as mere cultivators were concerned—" with the utmost leniency."

"Aghái, instead of seizing on lands, seized on hard cash."

Probably no people ever got less return for their money in the way of administration than did the people of Oudh at this period. Out of the huge funds at his disposal, A'gha Ali maintained four deputies, one in each district, on salaries of from Rs. 150 to Rs. 200 a month, and fifty or sixty *tahsildárs* or *jamoydárs*, on from Rs. 15 to Rs. 30 each. Such order and stability as existed were mainly due to strong Taluqdárs, who, when not at war with the Government, found it expedient to keep their estates well cultivated, and their tenants contented. They had at least the merit of "redeeming the country from the dead level of powerless slaves under an all-powerful Sultan." They formed a breakwater behind which it was possible for the artisan to keep alive the germs of manufacturing industry, and the justice which they administered, rude though it was, was at least preferable to the article dispensed under the same name by the King's officers. The town of Sháhganj, under the protection of Darshan Singh and Mán Singh, contained large numbers of traders and artisans, who are said to have been more secure there than anywhere else in Oudh. An enlightened self-interest, too, prompted them to protect their humble, low-caste cultivators, so that their estates were well tilled. But this was quite compatible with the grossest oppression towards the small proprietors whose villages they had incorporated in their taluqas. Two such men were found by Colonel Sleeman in the hands of Mán Singh. They had refused to sign *bainámas*, or deeds of sale, of their property, which he demanded from them, and had been six or seven years in confinement, "I have never," writes Colonel Sleeman, "seen enmity more strong and deadly than that exhibited by contending co-sharers and landholders of all kinds in Oudh,"—a sentence worth remembering with a view to assertions, in the course of recent controversies, that the zamíndárs did not value the recognition of their rights.

The Taluqdárs of Baiswára were Rájpút lords, not upstarts, and in writing of them in his monograph on the Rai Bareli clans, Mr. Benett remarks that—

"The chieftain and his retainers were the only unit of Hindú society susceptible of development . . . . nor were signs wanting that the throne was soon to fall before the rising national life. The central executive was already paralysed, while the ties of family and clan were widened and consolidated on a territorial basis. Had we stayed our hands, it is possible that even now a Hindú Rája would be ruling a Hindú nation from the ancient seat of Hindú religion and empire (Ajodhya), on a throne supported by a landed aristocracy lately developed from the hierarchy of chieftains, whose ancient ranks had been enforced by the addition of all that was most vigorous in the late *régime*. . . . . The mistake which vitiates almost all our political theories in India, is that we are the successors of the Musalmán emperors; were we only that, we should not be here now. The vital fact is that we have, or at any rate think we have, succeeded, where the Muhammadans, in their strongest days, never attained complete success, in taking the places of the local princes, and in substituting our own for native law and organization. The Commissioner has supplanted not so much the Názim as the Rája."

It may seem strange that the barons were so often able successfully to resist the King's troops. This was mainly due to the fact that their retainers had much stronger motives to fight for them than the Názim or Chakladár supplied to his soldiers. If a Taluqdár's retainer was killed in his lord's quarrel, his family was provided for by a grant of land rent-free, called *marwat*. But if one of the King's *sipáhis* was killed in action, his family, though nominally entitled to a gratuity equal to his pay for two months, did not even obtain the arrears of pay actually due to him; and if disabled by wounds, he was at once dismissed without a pension. From men with such prospects, devotion was scarcely to be expected.

All through Sultánpur and Baiswára, Colonel Sleeman found the large Taluqdárs on bad terms with the Názim, and in Unáo and Hardui, the most zamíndárí districts in Oudh, the small landholders were quite as turbulent in their way. In Unáo, especially, they were at perpetual feud with the detested Chakladár, Bhadrínáth. From Hardui, the "Diary" takes us through Muhamdí, or Kheri, and thence into Khairábád, or Sítapur. These districts, as already mentioned, had been held by Hakím Mehudi for several years previous to his first banishment in 1819. For the greater part of the following thirty years they were held separately. Muhamdí had suffered most of the two, having fallen into the hands of worse contractors. It had had no less than fifteen *ijára* and two *amání* collectors, and the revenue had sunk from seven lákhs, with the people contented, to three lákhs, with everybody miserable. Not one-tenth of the soil was in cultivation, or one-tenth of the nominal villages inhabited. Rája Loní Singh of Mithauli, whose conduct during the Mutiny afterwards earned him peculiar infamy, was the great man of the district, and was increasing his possessions after the usual manner. Khairábád was comparatively quiet and better cultivated. Here Nawáb Ali, Taluqdár of Mahmúdábád, was extending his estate by means less undisguised, but scarcely less efficacious than had been employed by Darshan Singh and Mán Sing in Sultánpur and Faizábád. Like them, he kept his own lands well cultivated, and was not disliked by low-caste tenants, though detested by zamíndárs.

The four great evils of rural Oudh at this period are represented by Colonel Sleeman to have been :—
(1.) Depredations of refractory Taluqdárs ;
(2.) Rack-renting by contractors ;
(3.) Dissensions among landholders, created or fostered by contractors ;
(4.) Depredations of troops and camp-followers.

The first of these scourges needs no elucidation.

Of the second, an instance may be quoted from Captain Alexander Orr. The assessment of Chandausi, a zamíndárí in the Sultánpur Nizámat, was officially supposed at Lucknow to amount to Rs. 5,338. A'gha Ali, however, assessed it at Rs. 7,200, and further imposed demands for Rs. 1,500 as his own *nazaráná*, Rs. 1,200 as that of A'gha Haidar, his brother and chakladár, Rs. 1,100 as that of Bande Hosen, A'gha Haidar's deputy, and lastly, Rs. 113 as the due of Rám Baksh, Díwán of Bande Hosen, making a total of Rs. 11,113, or considerably more than double the Lucknow assessment. Nor was this an isolated instance.

To turn to the third item in Colonel Sleeman's list, so long as Rájpúts remained united, the King's officials could do nothing with them. The warrior caste certainly possesses, or did possess, a capacity for coherent action which is wanting to Bráhmans ; and where they were powerful, Názims and Chakladárs could only make head against them by taking advantage of their disputes among themselves, or creating quarrels where they found none ready made. According to old Bakhtáwar Singh, brother of Darshan Singh, who had been deputed by the Darbár to accompany Colonel Sleeman on his tour, there were more well-to-do landholders in Oudh in the time of S'ádat Ali than were to be found in 1850 ; but they did not dare to hold their heads so high, the local officers being all able men, and supported by a wing of one of the Company's regiments, and some good guns. Since then, the strength of the Taluqdárs had been waxing and that of the Government waning, while the aid of the Company's troops had been gradually withdrawn. Landholders kept ten armed men where formerly they had kept only one, and spent on their maintenance the rents which they withheld from the Government. The chief object with which they kept up their armed retainers was to resist all attempts at reduction of their informally granted *nánkár* allowances. None of these grants had been sanctioned at Lucknow since the death of S'ádat Ali in 1814 A.D., corresponding to 1222 Fasli; but they had been made and acquiesced in, by a usurpation of authority on the part of Názims and Chakladárs, to the amount of some forty lákhs. In 1850, orders were issued for the resumption of all such grants of any later date than 1222 Fasli, but it was, of course, impossible to carry them out, and their only effect was a change in the nomenclature employed in the revenue accounts. Henceforth the sanctioned grants were known as "*nánkár san báís*," or the allowances of the year twenty-two, and the subsequent informal reductions as "*kamí ruqúmát*," or deficiency of assets.

With regard to the oppression and plundering which the people had to endure at the hands of troops and camp-followers, without any wish to exaggerate them, and even with a readiness to believe that the sins of the Oudh Government have often been painted in blacker colours than they deserved, it is still impossible to doubt that the suffering from this source was really very great. Colonel Sleeman was certainly not prejudiced against native governments as such, and though it has been said, probably with some degree of truth, that he looked at things "through Darbár spectacles," and unconsciously exaggerated the enormities of the Taluqdárs, the very people whom he met on the roads being tutored what to say to him, yet there can be no ground for supposing that the Oudh Government would go out of its way to make the conduct of its own troops or servants appear more odious or oppressive than it actually was. Yet it would be difficult to imagine more lamentable scenes of tyranny and hardship than those which he describes as of constant occurrence, whenever the Najíb corps, of which there were thirty-two, were moved from one cantonment to another. And they were incessantly on the move; for if kept long in one place, they created an artificial famine. "The line of march," he writes, "of one of these corps is like the road to the temple of Jagannáth." Captain Orr speaks in equally strong terms of this subject, and of the *begárí*, or forced labour system, he writes:—

"The Chamár, Lodh, Kurmi, and all inferior castes are the prey of all, caught at every hour of the day or night, made use of as beasts of burthen, beaten and abused, treated as if incapable of feeling pain or humiliation, never remunerated, but often deprived of the scanty clothing they may possess."

This is one of the few points on which it is possible to feel a satisfactory assurance that the poor are better off under British than they were under native rule.

Even so mere a sketch in outline as is here attempted, of the condition of Oudh during the few years previous to annexation, would not be complete without some portrayal of the state of affairs at Lucknow as well as in the provinces. Colonel Sleeman's "Diary" is full of digressions relating to the affairs of the court. His well-known character and personal leanings toward any tolerable native government are sufficient guarantees for the freedom from adverse prejudice of the picture which he draws in these oft-repeated touches. It leaves no doubt that Wájid Ali, though not naturally a stupid or unamiable man, was as deeply sunk in the slough of sloth and effeminacy as it is possible for any man, even an oriental prince born in the purple, to be, or that he was surrounded by as profligate and insatiable a set of knaves as any such prince ever succeeded in attracting to himself. A strange life it must have been that he led in that "enchanted Armida palace" of his, where we catch glimpses of him through the motley crowd of singers, fiddlers, sorcerers, cock-fighters, negroes, eunuchs, and buffoons, who hovered round him, like moths round a very flickering and faint-coloured lamp. As for his minister, Ali Nakki Khán, whom he had appointed in August 1847, contrary to the urgent advice of Colonel Richmond, the then Resident, it is enough to quote Colonel Sleeman's report of 1851, in which he writes, " He appears to me to be the most deeply interested of all in maintaining the worst abuses of the present system of administration, and I consider it painful and humiliating to be obliged, by my public duties, to hold, any longer, communication with such a person on the subject of the many evils which he could, but will not, remedy; of the many wrongs which he could, but will not, redress; and of the many fearful sufferings which he could, but will not, relieve."

One or two instances of the way in which the Kings of Oudh were plundered by their own officials may not be out of place here.

S'ádat Ali had a favourite garden at Muhamdi, where he kept up a large establishment of gardeners and bullocks. This fell into decay after his death, and all the cattle save two bullocks were sold off, and all but two of the gardeners were discharged. But up to 1847, thirty-three years after the death of S'ádat Ali, Rs. 60,000 a year was charged in the royal accounts for pay of gardeners and feed of cattle supposed to be employed in the Muhamdi garden.

Again, one thousand seven hundred and thirty bullocks were charged for in the accounts of the artillery park at Lucknow. The actual number of bullocks maintained was twenty.

Again, Ghází-ud-dín Haidar had a favourite dog, the barking of which happened one day to annoy him. He was told that the best remedy to stop the dog's barking was a daily dose of a *sir* of conserve of roses and a bottle of rose-water, and gave orders accordingly. The dog died in 1816, but the charge for its daily allowance of conserve of roses and of rose-water was continued up to 1850.

In spite, however, of the King's incapacity and of the maladministration of his officers, it was natural enough that he should be popular in the capital where his resources were so profusely lavished. The shopkeepers of Lucknow were probably wealthier than those of any other town in India except Calcutta. Manufactures of all sorts of costly and useless products flourished luxuriantly. With the traders and artisans of Lucknow, annexation could hardly be otherwise than unpopular, and the decay of these classes during the last twenty years, though inevitable, has been pitiful in the extreme. Artificially stimulated by the lavishness of the court, they have necessarily declined since the stream of expenditure has been stayed. Probably the only class in Lucknow to whom annexation was not altogether distasteful was that of the ministers and other officers who had amassed large sums by peculation, and were not wholly unwilling to see the source of their gains stopped for the future on condition of secure enjoyment of what they had already acquired.

CHAPTER V.

ANNEXATION.

THE annexation of Oudh has perhaps incurred more unsparing condemnation than any other act of the East India Company's Government since the days of Warren Hastings. It has been denounced, under the name of "Dacoity in Excelsis," as the last and most glaring, if not the worst, illustration of the Dalhousie policy, and as one of the proximate causes of the Mutiny. Some brief account, often though the tale has been told already, should perhaps be given here of the circumstances under which the step was adopted, the motives and reasons by which the persons chiefly responsible for it were actuated, and the mode in which it was carried out. Of the condition of the province during the closing years of the reign of Wájid Ali Sháh a description has been attempted in the previous chapter; and it is in that condition that the measure of annexation finds its best and, indeed, its only possible justification.

On the 21st of November 1854, General Outram being about to proceed to Lucknow to take over charge from Colonel Sleeman, Lord Dalhousie indited a minute, proposing that the new Resident should be instructed to make "an enquiry into the present state of that country; with a view to determine whether its affairs still continue in that state in which

Colonel Sleeman from time to time described them to be; whether the improvement which Lord Hardinge peremptorily demanded seven years ago at the hands of the King, in pursuance of the treaty of 1801, has in any degree been effected; and whether the duty imposed upon the British Government by that treaty, a duty recognised by Lord William Bentinck in 1831, and reiterated by Lord Hardinge in 1847, will in truth any longer admit of our honestly indulging the reluctance we have felt to have recourse to those extreme measures which alone can be of any real efficacy in remedying the evils from which the state of Oudh has suffered so long."

The Members of Council at this time were Mr. Dorin, Colonel John Low, formerly for eleven years Resident at Lucknow, Mr. Barnes Peacocke, and Mr. John Peter Grant. The first three briefly assented to this proposal, while the fourth recorded the grounds of his assent at some length, declaring that " in the case of Oudh, a state wholly supported by the British Government, and bound to be wholly guided by that Government, he had never been able to understand how the policy of even temporary non-interference could be justifiable, on any other ground than that, for the time being, non-interference was better for the people of Oudh than interference. How many years ago it is since any statesman has maintained that ground, we need not stop to count."

Accordingly, by Mr. Secretary Edmonstone's letter of the 24th of November 1854, General Outram was instructed to inquire into and report on the condition of Oudh.

In obedience to these instructions, the Resident, on the 15th of March 1855, submitted a voluminous report, divided into seven heads, relating respectively to:—

(1.) The Sovereign and his Minister.
(2.) Revenue and Finance.
(3.) Judicial Courts and Police.
(4.) The Army.
(5.) Roads and Public Works.
(6.) Statistics of Crimes.
(7.) Oppressions and Cruelties.

The general character of this report may be sufficiently imagined by anyone who has read the preceding chapter.

There had been, in short, no improvement, and there was no prospect of improvement, on the state of things described by Colonel Sleeman. All that could be said for the last five Kings of Oudh was that they had been always ready and desirous to comply, as far as possible, with all demands made by the British Government relating to its own interests; and almost the only redeeming features about the administration were the Frontier Police, under the command of European officers, maintained at a cost of Rs. 77,000 annually, and sundry institutions kept up for the benefit of Europeans at a yearly cost of Rs. 47,000.

The revenues of Oudh were derived almost entirely from the land, and its sources were four, viz.:—

(1.) Allodial lands, or Crown estates, known as *khálsa*.

(2.) Huzúr Tahsíl estates, paying revenue directly to Government.

(3.) Districts held under contract by *ijáradárs*, or farmers.

(4.) Districts held under *amání*, or trust management.

The transfer of *khálsa* lands to Taluqdárs, which has been described in the Bahraich district, had been going on all over the province. The Huzúr Tahsíl system which had "always proved more successful and popular in Oudh than any other mode of management," was much abused by the Díwán Rája Bálkishn at Lucknow, who was supposed to superintend it. He and his subordinates were in the habit of raising rents for their own benefit, by the threat, if their demands were not acquiesced in, of handing over the estate of the recusant to a Chakladár. Of the *ijára* and *amání* methods of collection, enough has been said already. With regard to the expenditure and financial arrangements generally, the Resident found it almost impossible to obtain any statistics or information. Those who possessed any official knowledge of the subject dared not communicate it, and the Minister, Ali Nakki Khán, demurred to furnishing any accounts, on the ground that there was no precedent for such a course. Pensions of the royal family and other stipendiaries were heavily in arrear. The annual cost of the civil and police establishments seems to have been about 38 and $12\frac{1}{2}$ lákhs respectively. The pay of the

Minister was Rs. 114,000 yearly, and his perquisites amounted to more than seven lákhs, or a total of more than £80,000, nearly thrice the salary of the Governor-General. The total revenues of 1853 and 1854 appear to have amounted to about £1,200,000. Of this sum only between £300,000 and £400,000 found its way to the Lucknow treasury, the remainder being "accounted for" by the Názims as expended in the districts on different branches of Government service. The amount actually disbursed was probably little more than half a million, something like £350,000 being absorbed by Názims and their subordinates, with the assistance of the Darbár officials at Lucknow.

As for judicial courts, there were none, except at the capital, and such as were there maintained were worthless, being presided over by men of no character, who treated their position simply as a means for extortion. The total cost of the judicial establishments for the whole of Oudh was less than Rs. 16,000 a year. Their efficiency was sufficiently illustrated by the acquittal of Muhammad Hosen, who, while Názim of Gonda-Bahraich, murdered the banker Rám Datt Pánde, as already related, and a host of similar, though less conspicuous, instances might be quoted. Revenue courts there were none. The charge of district police stations was farmed out by the Názims to the highest bidder.

The military force numbered about 60,000 men of all arms, costing rather more than £420,000 yearly. The *komakhia*, or auxiliary regiments, commanded by European officers, of which there were four, were fairly efficient. The rest were an undisciplined rabble, paid at the rate of three to four rupees a month, and always kept in arrears, but allowed to compensate themselves by living at free quarters on the peasantry. Their numbers, moreover, were merely nominal, though pay for their full strength was of course drawn by the paymasters, or *Bakshis*, acting in collusion with the Názims.

Roads and public works could hardly be said to exist. The only metalled road in Oudh was that between Cawnpore and Lucknow. There were about half-a-dozen permanent bridges, besides two spanning the Gumti at Lucknow; and General Outram, after mentioning these, adds that, "with the exception of a few Government forts, there are literally no other public works in Oudh." Immense sums were charged in the accounts for the erection of royal palaces and tombs, of which but a small proportion was actually thus expended.

As for the remaining heads of the report, Crimes and Outrages, and Oppressions and Cruelties by Government Officials, little or nothing need be said. The killed and wounded in dacoities and riots were estimated at about two thousand annually, and irresponsible officials of all sorts continued to do after their kind, with a psychologically curious disregard of the amount of pain they might inflict in gaining their end of extorting money. In conclusion, General Outram felt himself bound to declare, though with great reluctance, his wish to uphold native states wherever possible being well known, that "the lamentable condition of this kingdom has been caused by the very culpable apathy and gross misrule of the Sovereign and his Darbár"; that the improvement of administration demanded by Lord Hardinge seven years before had been in no degree effected; and that there was, in his opinion, no doubt that the British Government could no longer honestly refrain from "those extreme measures which could alone be of any real efficacy," or, in other words, from taking the administration of Oudh into its own hands.

At the time of the receipt of this despatch at Calcutta, Lord Dalhousie was absent at Utakamand, and thither it was transmitted to him by General Low, who recorded his concurrence in the opinion expressed in its concluding paragraphs, because:—

"The public and shameful oppressions committed on the people by Government officers in Oudh have of late years been constant and extreme; because the King of Oudh has continually, during many years, broken the treaty (of 1801) by systematically disregarding our advice instead of following it, or even endeavouring to follow it; because we are bound by *treaty* (quite different in that respect from our position relatively to most of the great native states) to prevent serious interior misrule in Oudh; because it has been fully proved that we have not prevented it, and that we cannot prevent it by the present mode of conducting our relations with that State; and because no man of common sense can entertain the smallest expectation that the present King of Oudh can ever become an efficient ruler of his country."

To these words, weighty from their author's long experience as Resident at Lucknow, as well as from his individual leanings in favour of native states, General Low added that he had good grounds for believing that the long delay to interfere in Oudh, after repeated warnings, had created a general impression that such interference was prohibited by orders from England; and that Oudh officials had thus less fear of the Resident or the Company, as regards internal mismanagement, than they had felt at any time previous to Lord Hardinge's visit in 1847.

From Utakamand, Lord Dalhousie wrote his monster minute of the 18th of June 1855, the greater part of which consists of a review of our relations with Oudh from the time of Warren Hastings, and of the information furnished by General Outram, Colonel Sleeman, and others regarding its present condition. Passing to the immediate practical question of what was to be done, the Governor-General remarked that as the so-called treaty of 1837 had never been sanctioned by the Court of Directors, regard must be had exclusively to the treaty of 1801. This latter, he pointed out, unfortunately contained no provision for the course to be adopted in the event of the Oudh Government failing to maintain a tolerable administration; and also barred the employment of English officers in Oudh by providing that the system of administration to be introduced by the Nawáb was "to be carried into effect by his own officers."

So long, therefore, "as observance shall be paid to the letter, and to the obvious spirit, of the treaty of 1801, that instrument will prohibit the admission of British officers to take any part in the management of Oudh, and will ever stand as an insurmountable barrier to the employment, by the British Government, of those means which can alone be effectual to introduce into Oudh 'such a system of administration as shall be conducive to the prosperity of' the King's 'subjects, and be calculated to secure the lives and property of the inhabitants.'"

On the assumption that active interference in Oudh was, in some shape or other, inevitable, Lord Dalhousie proceeded to consider the various modes in which effect might be given to it. And here it will be well to quote his own wording of the alternative courses open:—

"1st. The King may be required to abdicate the sovereign powers he has abused, and to consent to the incorporation of Oudh with the territories of the British Crown.

"2nd. The King may be permitted to retain his royal title and position, but may be required to vest the whole civil and military administration of his kingdom in the Government of the East India Company, for ever.

"3rd. His Majesty may be urged to make over his dominions to the management of British officers, for a time.

"4th. The King may be invited to place the management of the country in the hands of the Resident; under whose directions it shall be carried on by the officers of the King, acting with such British officers as may be appointed to aid them."

Of these alternatives, Lord Dalhousie believed the first to be abstractedly the best, but from a regard to the fidelity which had always been shown to the Company by the Nawábs and Kings of Oudh, he did not recommend its adoption. "The rulers of Oudh," he wrote, "however unfaithful they may have been to the trust confided to them—however gross may have been their neglect, however grievous their misgovernment, of the people committed to their charge—have yet ever been faithful and true in their adherence to the British power. No wavering friendship has been laid to their charge. They have long acknowledged our power; have submitted, without a murmur, to our supremacy; and have aided us, as best they could, in the hour of our utmost need."

The first proposal, then, being too severe; the fourth, insufficient, as had been pointed out by Lord Wellesley in

1799; and any merely temporary arrangement, such as was contemplated by the third, being self-condemned, as well as by the precedents of the Nizám's territories and of Nágpur; Lord Dalhousie strongly advocated the adoption of the second. To attain the end aimed at by that proposal, he advised that the King should be informed that the treaty of 1801 was at an end, owing to his failure to fulfil the obligation which it imposed upon him of maintaining a decent administration in Oudh, and that the Resident was under orders to quit Lucknow, and to withdraw the subsidiary force, unless the King gave his consent to a draft treaty which was to be laid before him. The main features of this instrument were to be the annulment of all previous treaties; the transfer of the "whole civil and military administration, with all power, jurisdiction, rights, and claims thereto belonging" from the hands of the King to those of the Company's Government; the allotment of a liberal provision for the King, and also for the members of the royal family, not being his own children; and, last and most important of all :—

"That the revenues of Oudh shall be applied, first, to the payment of the expenses of the civil and military administration of the province; secondly, to the payment of the stipends secured in the preceding Articles to the King and to the royal family; and thirdly, to the improvement and benefit of the province. *The residue of the revenues, after the foregoing deductions, shall be at the disposal of the East India Company.*"

In reference to this last Article, Lord Dalhousie wrote: "For many years to come, while the reform of the administration of Oudh is still in progress, and while its natural resources are not yet fully recruited, the provision will remain altogether inoperative. But in process of time, the revenues of the country will largely increase under the management of British officers, and a surplus will probably remain, after meeting all ordinary charges of the administration, and after providing for those measures of gradual improvement to which the increase in the revenues of the province ought unquestionably to be made applicable in the first instance."

The Governor-General considered the appropriation by the Company's Government of the surplus revenues "perfectly consonant with justice and equity, and founded upon a just consideration for the general good of that Empire of which Oudh originally was, and still is, no more than a province." But if the Court of Directors desired that the interference of the British Government should be "not only virtually, but in the very letter, a disinterested act," he was prepared to omit any such provision (which had been borrowed from the treaty with Tanjor) from the proposed compact; only stipulating that in any new relations to be entered on with Oudh, it should be at least arranged that all civil charges and all charges of troops which it might prove necessary to station within the province, should be defrayed from its revenues; as it would no longer, the treaty of 1801 having been declared at an end, be needful to maintain any military force in the province, "were it not for the contemplated renewal and extension of our relations with the King of Oudh."

The Governor-General's minute was circulated in due course to the four Members of Council, all of whom expressed opinions, more or less weighty, on the subject.

Mr. Dorin, the senior member, advocated the adoption of Lord Dalhousie's first proposal, for simply incorporating Oudh with British territory, and deprecated the continuance to Wájid Ali Sháh of the title of King.

General Low was of opinion that the Oudh Government was, "from the Prime Minister down to the meanest chaprási," so thoroughly and inveterately corrupt, that there was no remedy left but the exclusive, permanent, and direct assumption of the management of the country by the Company. He protested, however, against the notion of withdrawing the Resident and troops, as dangerous and unnecessary; and in the event of the King's refusing to sign a new treaty, recommended that Lord Wellesley's precedent in the case of S'ádat Ali in 1801 should be followed, and orders issued to the native collectors to pay no more revenue into his treasury.

Mr. Grant's line of argument was that the British Government had always occupied towards Oudh the position of paramount state towards subordinate province; that what the Emperor of Delhi nominally was, that we had really been; that the arrangement of 1801 was not founded on any previous treaty; and that this fact was fully recognised by Lord Wellesley, who always addressed S'ádat Ali as a subordinate ruler—(he might almost have added, as a convicted pickpocket)—and by S'ádat Ali himself, so much so that when he proposed to abdicate, he only requested to be succeeded by any one of his sons whom Lord Wellesley might choose. From all this it followed that if the treaty of 1801 were set aside, the position of Oudh to the Company would still be, as it was previous to that treaty, the position of subject province to paramount state; and the King would have no rights as against us in 1855 which the Súbahdár had not in 1800, except such as might be guaranteed by intermediate agreements. Thus, "the decision as to what ought to be done now must follow the decision that shall be pronounced upon the historical point of the justice of Lord Wellesley's conduct in 1801." Mr. Grant held that Lord Wellesley was justified in what he did, and quoted James Mill's opinion, that if his premises were correct, he ought to have gone still further, and annexed the whole instead of only half of the Oudh territories.

It apparently did not occur to Mr. Grant, or to any other Member of Council, that if the *status quo ante* the treaty of 1801 was to be reverted to, Wájid Ali might not unplausibly have asserted a claim to be restored to possession of all the territory which had been ceded to the Company under that treaty. The ceded territory, yielding a revenue of £1,300,000, was made over to the Company as security for the charges of the troops to be employed in the defence of Oudh. If those troops were to be withdrawn, and the Company was to be relieved of all responsibility for the defence of Oudh, it would seem to follow logically that the ceded districts should have been restored, on the principle of *cessante causâ cessat et effectus*.

The Súbahdárs of Oudh, to return to Mr. Grant's minute, never claimed, before they came into contact with the British power, to be independent sovereigns, or professed any right to retain the Súbah if it had pleased the Emperor of Delhi to recall them. Shúja'-ud-daulah, when he espoused the cause of Mír Kásim, complained, not that the Calcutta Council had driven him out of Bengal, but that they had driven him out without the Emperor's authority. "How is it," he asked, "that you turn out and establish Nawábs at pleasure, without the consent of the Imperial Court?" We stand, Mr. Grant contended, in the place of the Mughal, and our position only differs from his in the respect that we have the power to do that which it would have been his duty to do if he had been able, while he had not that power. "Our practice has accorded with no other theory," *e.g.* the deposition of Wazír Ali in 1798, and the setting aside of Munna Ján in 1837. "These were doubtless very proper acts on our part; but if such acts were not founded on the assertion of our having supreme dominion over the kings and people of Oudh, I ask on what doctrine they were founded, and by what reasoning they can be justified? Is it only when the People are concerned that we should hesitate to assert our supreme dominion?"

Mr. Grant preferred the first of Lord Dalhousie's proposals, as involving no fiction, to the second, and so agreed with Mr. Dorin; but differed from him in wishing to allow the King, though not his descendants, to retain the royal title. He condemned, as at once needless and hazardous, the proposal to withdraw our troops and sever all relations; and recommended that Oudh should be at once incorporated with British territory, with the King's consent if it were procurable; if not, then without it.

Mr. Peacocke—afterwards Sir Barnes Peacocke—discussed the question from the legal point of view, and argued that the Company had a right to compel enforcement of the treaty of 1801, so far as it had been broken by the King, *i.e.* in his failure to secure good government, quoting Vattel in support of his position. He preferred the second of the Governor-General's alternatives, but was of opinion that "no pecuniary benefit should be derived by the East India Company," and therefore "could not recommend that any part of the revenues of Oudh should be applied to the payment of the military administration of the province"; seeing that under the treaty of 1801 we agreed to defend Oudh in consideration of the ceded territory. He argued that, our interference being for the sake of the people, they should not be made to bear any burthen which they would not have had to bear if the treaty of 1801 had been fulfilled by the King. He therefore thought that all except military expenses should be defrayed out of the revenues of Oudh, and that the whole surplus should be spent on the province.

It is easy enough to fancy Lord Dalhousie muttering to himself as he read Mr. Peacocke's minute that this was mere ideology; but not perhaps quite so easy, except by a return to first principles and a total abandonment of all legal grounds, to suggest an adequate answer to Mr. Peacocke's scruples.

On the 21st of November 1855, the Court of Directors despatched their reply to the questions raised by General Outram's report, and the minutes of the Governor-General and Members of Council. They had no hesitation in deciding that the government—or misgovernment, they were much the same thing—of the King of Oudh must be put an end to, once for all. But unless Lord Dalhousie felt morally certain that the announcement to the King that all existing treaties were cancelled, and that all connection between his Government and that of the Company was at an end unless he accepted the new treaty to be proposed to him, would at once have the effect of inducing him to accept it, the alternative should not be offered to him. With regard to the terms of the treaty to be laid before him, and the mode to be adopted of disposing of the surplus revenues of Oudh, the Court of Directors, beyond an expression of opinion that the reigning family should be very liberally provided for, maintained a discreet and significant silence. The question had been expressly put to them by Lord Dalhousie in his minute, and certainly seems one which demanded an answer. But answer came there none. And this, perhaps, was hardly so odd as it at first sight seems, for the Honourable Court may have been of opinion that the matter, if left in the hands of the Governor-General, would arrange itself in a manner not wholly unfavourable to their pecuniary interests, while the issue of explicit instructions might have been awkward, not to say embarrassing. A considerable sense of decorum always pervaded the proceedings of the Honourable Court.

On the 23rd of January 1856 instructions, framed by Lord Dalhousie and concurred in by the other Members of Council, were despatched to General Outram concerning the steps to be taken for the assumption of the Government of Oudh. Troops were to be moved up to Cawnpore, and such a force as the Resident thought requisite to be marched to Lucknow, under the immediate command of Colonel Wheler as Brigadier. If hostilities appeared imminent, the Resident was authorised to assume control over all the troops in Oudh. The news of his deposition was to be broken to the King through his Minister, Ali Nakki Khán, after which the Resident was to obtain an interview with Wájid Ali himself, at which he was to inform him that "the time had now come when the systematic violation of the treaty of 1801, by every successive Ruler of Oudh, from the date of its signature to the present day, rendered it the imperative duty of the British Government to declare the treaty null and void, and to proceed either to form new engagements with the King of Oudh, or to assume to itself the administration of his territories."

The King was then to be handed a letter from Lord Dalhousie, which recapitulated the relations between the British Government and that of Oudh from their beginning, in a manner which left little to be desired, except that it made no mention of the extortions of Warren Hastings, and was grossly unjust to S'ádat Ali. The letter concluded, after fervidly denouncing the existing misrule, and declaring that the British Government would be "guilty in the sight of God and man, if it were any longer to aid in sustaining, by its countenance and power, an administration fraught with suffering to millions," and that the violated treaty of 1801 was at an end, with an exhortation to the King to accept the proposals which would be made to him by General Outram, and a warning of the consequences of refusal.

The perusal of the letter was to be followed by the presentation of a draft treaty, which the king was to be invited to sign. The purport of this treaty was much the same as had been proposed by Lord Dalhousie in his minute of the 18th of June 1855. Wájid Ali and his successors were to retain the title of "King of Oudh," and to receive an annual pension of twelve lákhs, in addition to which a body-guard was to be maintained for Wájid Ali himself, at a cost of not more than three lákhs yearly. All collateral members of the royal family who were at that time provided for by the King were in future to be maintained by the Company. Wájid Ali and his successors were to retain "full and exclusive jurisdiction" in the palace at Lucknow, and in his favourite parks of Dilkhushá and Bibiapur, but were not to inflict the punishment of death without the previous consent of the Governor-General in Council. The bitter pill of which the above provisions formed the sugared coating was that "the sole and exclusive administration of the civil and military government of the territories of Oudh shall be henceforth vested, for ever, in the Honourable East India Company, *together with the full and exclusive right to the revenues thereof.*"

Not in vain was the confidence of the Honourable Court of Directors.

Two draft proclamations addressed to the people of Oudh were forwarded to the Resident along with his instructions. The first was to be issued in case the King consented to sign the treaty; the second in the event of his refusal. The difference between them consisted entirely in the recitals. In either case, it was proclaimed that the government of Oudh was henceforth vested in the East India Company, to whose officers all classes of the inhabitants were called upon to render obedience, under penalties. In conclusion it was declared that:—

"The revenue of the districts shall be determined on a fair and settled basis.

"The gradual improvement of the Oudh territories shall be steadily pursued.

"Justice shall be measured out with an equal hand.

"Protection shall be given to life and property; and every man shall enjoy, henceforth, his just rights, without fear of molestation."

The Resident was instructed to afford to the King all possible explanation of the reasons for the course adopted, and to do all in his power to persuade him to sign the treaty, offering, should it seem necessary, a yearly pension of fifteen lákhs instead of twelve. All promises of amendment of his administration on the part of the King, and all attempts to argue the point, or to procure postponement of the assumption of his powers by the Company, were to be met by an assurance that the intentions of the Government were fixed and irrevocable, and that Lord Dalhousie had been ordered by the Court of Directors, with the approval of the Ministry, of which Lord Canning, the Governor-General elect, was a member, to carry them into execution before leaving India. In case the King referred to the "treaty" of 1837, he was to be informed that that instrument had now no existence, having been annulled by the Court of Directors as soon as it was submitted to them; and that the Governor-General regretted that, owing to inadvertence, the annulment had not been notified to the then King of Oudh, Muhammad Ali Sháh. Three days, if required, were to be allowed the King for deliberation.

According to his instructions, General Outram communicated the intentions of the British Government to Nawáb Ali Nakki Khán on the 30th of January. The Minister expressed himself much surprised and distressed at the news, deprecated the advance of the troops as unnecessary, and "attempted to contrast the reign of the present King with those of his predecessors, and to point out the manifest reforms which were to be seen on all sides."

The Resident in reply assured him that the advance of the troops was necessary, and the resolve of the Government unalterable.

On the following day, Ali Nakki Khán again waited on General Outram, according to agreement, and after reading the draft treaty and proclamation, "declared that he was authorised by the King to state that His Majesty was the servant of the British Government, and was, of course, ready to do what was required." He proposed, however, that the King should personally visit Lord Dalhousie, or even go to

England, in the hope of obtaining a more favourable decision.

These proposals the Resident met, as before, by a simple assurance that any reconsideration of the merits of the case was out of the question, and asked the Minister to request the King to appoint a day on which he might wait on him with the treaty.

The following day, the 1st of February, the King wrote a piteous letter to the Resident, pleading that he had "never wilfully performed aught that could offend the British Government; on the contrary, for the least of its servants, every step has been taken to please . . . everything has been done to obey whatever instructions may have been received. For instance, after the admonition of Lord Hardinge, the whole country has been placed under a new arrangement, and transferred from the *ijára* to the *amáni* system; police stations have everywhere been formed; and the number of culprits who have been punished is manifest." The letter ended with entreaties to the Resident to "intercede most imploringly" with the Governor-General to "put off the adoption of the new policy."

To all this General Outram once more gave the only possible answer. On the same day he visited the Queen-mother, the Janáb Aulia Begam, at her own request, at the Zard Kothí palace, in the hope that she, being a sensible woman, would influence the King to accede to the proposed terms. There was a dense crowd in the palace courts as he passed, but the demeanour of the people was, as usual, perfectly courteous. The Queen-mother poured forth supplications in a style similar to that of the King's letter; "entreated the Resident to inform her what His Majesty had done, and why he had incurred the wrath of the British Government"; and begged hard for delay, "during which the King might be enabled to show to the world, by the adoption of vigorous reforms, how anxious and eager he was to obey" the advice of the British Government.

Poor Wájid Ali! Poor Queen-mother! The period of "vigorous reforms," as understood in the Lucknow palace, was passed, and not to be recalled by any entreaty.

All attempts to discuss the question were met by General Outram with the same irresistible *non possum*. He urged on the Begam the risk which the King would run of losing the liberal terms offered him if he refused to accept the proposed treaty, but could elicit no response but protestations.

At last, on the morning of the 4th of February, at the Zard Kothí palace, an interview took place between Wájid Ali and General Outram. The palace courts were almost deserted, the foot guards unarmed, the artillery dismounted, and not a weapon was to be seen among the officials who received the Resident, who was accompanied by his assistants, Captains Hayes and Weston. On the side of the King were present his brother, Sikandar Hashmat, the Minister, Ali Nakki Khán, the Financial Minister, Rája Bálkishn, and the Residency Vakíl and his Deputy, Mahsí-ud-daulah and Sáhib-ud-daulah.

The King had already received through Ali Nakki Khán a copy of Lord Dalhousie's letter. He was now presented with the original, after reading which, he turned to the Resident, and put to him the same question which his mother had asked, " Why have I deserved this ? What have I done ? " After reading the treaty, the unhappy man " gave vent to his feelings in a passionate burst of grief, and exclaimed :—

" ' Treaties are necessary between equals only : who am I, now, that the British Government should enter into treaties with me ? For a hundred years this dynasty has flourished in Oudh. It has ever received the favour, the support, and protection of the British Government. It had ever attempted faithfully and fully to perform its duties to the British Government. The kingdom is a creation of the British, who are able to make and to unmake, to promote and to degrade. It has merely to issue its commands to ensure their fulfilment; not the slightest attempt will be made to oppose the views and wishes of the British Government; myself and subjects are its servants.' "

Taking off his turban and placing it in the hands of the Resident—the utmost token of humility which an Oriental can display—he declared that it was not for him to sign a treaty, that for him there was nothing left but "to seek in Europe for that redress which it was vain to find in India."

Three days later, on the 7th of February, the briefest possible note informed the Resident that the King's resolution not to sign the treaty remained unaltered. Immediately on receipt of this ultimatum, the charge of the city and various departments of State was formally assumed; the civil officers who had been appointed to the Oudh Commission were despatched to their several divisions and districts under military escort; and the annexation of Oudh was an accomplished fact. This was the last important event of Lord Dalhousie's administration, and before the end of the month he had given place to Lord Canning.

Two days before this the King had issued a proclamation to all civil and military officials, and to his subjects generally, enjoining them to make no resistance to the British officers who were about to assume the administration; and prohibiting everyone from making any attempt to accompany or follow him when he quitted Lucknow for Calcutta, and Calcutta for England—his intention being to bring his case in person before the Governor-General, and to intercede with the Queen.

General Outram, who from the 7th of February became Chief Commissioner of Oudh, having commented to the Residency Vakíl on the latter part of this proclamation, the King wrote to explain that his reason for issuing it was that "ever since his subjects have heard of the new arrangements they have altogether abstained from food, and have never ceased to lament and wail; hence, if immense multitudes of His Majesty's subjects should forsake the country to accompany the King, there would be a great loss to the collection of the revenue; therefore, the King deemed it necessary to forbid them."

Whether this was a mere flourish, or whether the King really believed that his own departure would be followed by a general exodus of his subjects, it is difficult to say. Probably he, in all good faith, believed himself to be a very estimable monarch. There had always been plenty of people to tell him so, and no one but a Resident, and occasionally a

Governor-General, to convey a hint to the contrary. By Lord Hardinge and Colonel Sleeman he had certainly been addressed in as plain and unflattering terms as it often falls to the lot of an Oriental prince to listen to, but the idea does not seem to have ever penetrated his mind that he had duties to perform toward his people, or that the British Government could have any ground for complaint against him so long as its own immediate interests were consulted, and its own requirements obeyed. On behalf of his view of the case it may at least be said that it would probably recommend itself to a large majority of Asiatic minds. I remember on one occasion discussing the subject of the annexation of Oudh with a well-to-do zamíndár, a man perfectly well affected to English rule, whose father, moreover, had been put to flight, and his estate harried and laid waste by Raghbar Dyál, the infamous Názim of Gonda-Bahraich, so recently as 1847. "Why," he asked, "had the *Sarkár* deposed Nawáb Wájid Ali? He was a poor meek creature, a humble servant and *tábidár*, or follower, of the British. What had he done to be so summarily wiped out?" And it appeared to be quite a new light to him to be told that the misrule and disorder of Oudh had become more than the British Government could tolerate. If this is the point of view of one who was a severe sufferer from the ex-King's administration, and who gained immensely by its subversion, it is to be feared that the judgment of those who suffered and gained less than he will hardly be more favourable. The question of whether the masses of the people of Oudh, in whose interest we believed ourselves to be acting, really desired to be incorporated with the Company's dominions, seems scarcely to have been raised at all in the course of the discussion. The question was certainly one to which, in the nature of things, it would have been hard to find means of furnishing a trustworthy answer. But it seems highly probable that the result of a perfectly honest *plébiscite*, could such by any possibility have been taken, would not have been in favour of the course adopted. That the people were generally grossly misgoverned, and often cruelly oppressed, there can be no doubt. But had they been allowed a choice, it is almost certain that they would have chosen still to bear the ills they knew rather than to be brought under the rigid, irresistible action of a bureaucracy of foreigners, whose ways were not as their ways, whose principles and motives were generally beyond their comprehension, and whose laws and regulations, though not intentionally unjust, appeared to be hemmed in by every species of pitfall and mantrap, from which a plain man, however innocent and well-meaning, could hardly hope to escape.

However, if our policy in India is not to be determined by the soundest judgments we can ourselves form, rather than by the unenlightened notions of the masses of our native fellow citizens, we have no *raison d'être* in the country. The set of native opinion must always be one of the main elements to be considered in all problems of Indian politics, yet it should not be so far the paramount consideration as to be allowed to over-ride the distinct behests of a higher law where such can be discerned. And the question of the annexation of Oudh seems to be a case in point. It is difficult to rise from a study of the Blue Book of 1856, without feeling that the motives which led to the adoption of that measure were not mere vulgar lust of conquest, or mere greed of pecuniary gain. There can be no doubt that Lord Dalhousie, and the Members of his Council, and General Outram, were, one and all, firmly convinced that by assuming the administration of Oudh, they were acting in the interests of humanity, and conferring a great blessing on several millions of people. And they were certainly right in their belief that the misrule and oppression prevailing in the province were intense. Their confidence, or at least the confidence of Lord Dalhousie, in the positive excellence of English methods, and in the beneficent effects of English rule on the populations subject to it, was, no less certainly, exaggerated. But, having that confidence, they would surely have been neglecting their duty had they omitted to act on it when they had the power, or allowed regard for the feelings of a King like Wájid Ali Sháh to outweigh what they believed to be the welfare of millions. The true test by which the policy of the annexation of Oudh must be judged is, whether the people were, to a considerable degree, more likely to prosper, and to rise in the scale of civilisation, under British than under any practically attainable form of native rule. Whether they actually have thus risen and prospered, is a question of fact, on which there may be, and are, differences of opinion. But if the then Government of India firmly and honestly believed, as it unquestionably did, that the only effective means of securing a tolerable government to the people of Oudh was to assume the administration of the province, then were they more than justified in assuming it.

Human motives are seldom wholly unmixed, and it may perhaps, without uncharitableness, be doubted whether the reluctance to interfere would not have been greater than it was, had Oudh been a country from which no surplus revenue could be derived. It may be regretted that Colonel Sleeman's advice was not followed, and taxation reduced to the level of expenditure within the province. In a letter to Sir James Hogge, dated from Lucknow, on the 28th of October 1852, he wrote as follows:—

" Were we to take advantage of the occasion to *annex* or *confiscate* Oudh, or any part of it, our good name in India would inevitably suffer; and that good name is more valuable to us than a dozen of Oudhs. We are now looked up to throughout India as the only impartial arbitrators that the people generally have ever had . . . . and from the time we cease to be so looked up to, we must begin to sink. We suffered from our conduct in Sindh; but that was a country distant and little known, and linked to the rest of India by few ties of sympathy. Our conduct towards it was preceded by wars and convulsions around, and in its annexation there was nothing manifestly deliberate. It will be otherwise with Oudh. Here the giant's strength is manifest, and we cannot 'use it like a giant' without suffering in the estimation of all India. Annexation or confiscation are not compatible with our relations with this little dependent state. We must show ourselves to be high-minded, and above taking advantage of its prostrate weakness, by appropriating its revenues exclusively to the benefit of the people and royal family of Oudh. We should soon make it the finest garden in India, with the people happy, prosperous, and attached to our rule."

The course of our relations with Oudh was not destined to follow the path here sketched out for it, and the garden of India has, for good or evil, become a part, and perhaps the most heavily taxed part, of the British Indian Empire. All wishes that it had been otherwise, and speculations as to what might have been, are now fruitless; and any scheme for reversing the current of events must be regarded much as would be a proposal to restore the Heptarchy, and relegated to the region of "lunar politics." But this much, at least, may be fairly asserted, that the province from which we have taken so much, and to which we have hitherto given so little, has a historic claim to exceptionally liberal treatment; and that, should it ever come to be generally acknowledged that only by a considerable pecuniary sacrifice can she be raised from her present poverty-stricken condition, that sacrifice ought not to be refused.

NOTE.—It was not until this chapter was in type that I had the advantage of seeing Major Evans Bell's "Retrospects and Prospects of Indian Policy." The article on "Oudh" in that work appears to demonstrate that the treaty of 1837 had never been abrogated as a whole; that its provisions for administration by British officers on behalf of the King still held good and should have been acted on; and that reform, without annexation, was practicable and should have been aimed at.

CHAPTER VI.

FIFTEEN MONTHS OF ZAMÍNDARÍ POLICY [1856-1857].

"Séparé du passé," says Lamennais, "le présent est muet sur l'avenir," and it is practically impossible to understand the present, or to devise schemes for modifying the future condition of Oudh, without a general acquaintance with the more salient features and more important issues of the controversies regarding the land questions of the province, which have filled so many Blue Books and excited so much acrimony during the last twenty years or more. In this chapter and the next it will be attempted to give something like a connected view of the course of the discussions which, since annexation, have been carried on concerning the rights in the soil of Taluqdárs, zamíndárs, under-proprietors, and cultivators.

The modern history of Oudh may be said to begin with the deposition of Wájid Ali Sháh, and its formation into a Chief Commissionership under Sir James Outram. The first phase of this modern history lasted little more than fifteen months, during which the administration was carried on upon the lines laid down in the Government of India's letter of the 4th of February 1856. This very able State-paper is an excellent embodiment of all that was best in the system of political philosophy preached and practised by

Lord Dalhousie, and was the logical outcome of his famous annexation minute of the 18th of June 1855, which has been referred to in the preceding chapter. Probably no bureaucracy, certainly no bureaucracy of foreigners, ever had the good of the people so sincerely at heart as that over which Lord Dalhousie presided. All that was noblest and most vigorous in the spirit of the English Liberalism of the day breathes through the minutes of the Governor-General, and of the ablest Member of his Council, Mr. John Peter Grant. The instructions of the 4th of February might have been written by Bentham himself in his least unimaginative mood, so clearly do they insist on the popular welfare as the one aim to be steadily kept in view, so determined are they that "everybody shall count as one, and nobody as more than one," so confident of the justice and reasonableness of the policy which dictated them.

They directed the Chief Commissioner to proceed to the formation of a summary settlement of the land revenue, to be made "village by village with the parties actually in possession, but without any recognition, either formal or indirect, of their proprietary right." It was declared "as a leading principle, that the desire and intention of the Government is to deal with the actual occupants of the soil, that is, with the village zamíndárs or with the proprietary coparcenaries which are believed to exist in Oudh, and not suffer the interposition of middlemen, such as Taluqdárs, farmers of the revenue, and such like," whose claims, " if they have any tenable claims," might be more conveniently considered at a future period. " The tenures being identical, the existence of coparcenary communities of village proprietors being certain, and the nature of the country, as well as the agricultural usages of the people, being similar, the system of village settlements in the N.W. Provinces," as laid down in the *Directions to Settlement Officers*, " should unquestionably be adopted."

Lord Dalhousie's trumpet, as Sir John Kaye might have said, gave no uncertain sound.

With regard to rent-free grants, it was laid down that, though such grants were to be generally maintained, "the

Government revenue should be assessed on each village or tract which constitutes a separate tenure, so that the holder, if his tenure be maintained, may not have it in his power to rack-rent his tenants, or derive more from the land than would be taken by the Government whose place he will occupy." It is to be feared that Lord Dalhousie had not clearly grasped the great doctrine of non-interference between landlord and tenant, which has since been worked out in Oudh with such happy results as are now apparent.

It is customary to represent this first Summary Settlement as having been made with the village proprietors to the exclusion of Taluqdárs. How far removed this notion is from the truth, may be gathered from the fact that out of 23,543 villages included in taluqas at the close of native rule, 13,640, paying a revenue of Rs. 35,06,519, were settled with Taluqdárs in 1856, while 9,903 villages, paying Rs. 32,08,319, were settled with persons other than Taluqdárs. The barons of Oudh thus retained considerably more than half the villages included in their taluqas, which, considering the state of society during the last forty-two years of the Nawábi, from the death of S'ádat Ali in 1814, was probably quite as much as they were entitled to. Individuals may have received hard measure, but such cases were exceptional, and were chiefly confined to parts of Faizábád and Sultánpur. The general rule was that where village proprietors were found, the settlement was made with them; where there were none, it was made with the Taluqdár. Much has been made by opponents of the peasant proprietary system out of the case of Mahárája Mán Singh, who is said to have been deprived of all his villages but three. But of this, even if he had not been, as he was, a defaulter to the King's collectors at the time of annexation, the history of the Mahdona estate affords ample explanation. It was got together "by fraudulent and extorted *bainámas*," to quote Mr. Gubbins, which "were treated at their proper worth and generally rejected." The writer remembers alluding to these celebrated three villages to which Mán Singh's estate was reduced, while in conversation with a Taluqdár's agent, living in quite another part of Oudh, and who could have had no personal prejudice against him, and his comment was that if Mán Singh was left with three villages, it was three more than he was entitled to. This was doubtless an exaggeration, but not insignificant as illustrating the tendency of native opinion. There is, moreover, every ground to believe that cases of real injustice, where they occurred, would have been considered and redressed before any regular settlement was concluded. The Government of India, however, after reoccupation,—

> "marked this oversight,
> And then mistook reverse of wrong for right."

The official view of the policy of the first Summary Settlement may perhaps be taken to be that indicated in the "Introduction to the Oudh Gazetteer." There we read that "our first essay in administration was based on ignorance and ended in disaster. The officers who were entrusted with the all-important work of settling the land revenue had been imbued with the principles of the so-called Thomasonian school"—Mr. Wingfield, for example, the Commissioner of the Bahraich Division—"and shared the prejudices of the only native society with which they had been personally acquainted, that of the Court"—a description which can scarcely have been intended to apply to the Financial Commissioner, Mr. Martin Gubbins. "The first told them that the village communities were the only element in the country which deserved to be maintained; the second, that the Taluqdárs were a set of grasping interlopers, in arms against the officials, and tyrants to the people, whose sole object was to defraud Government of its revenue. The result was that *orders were issued to disregard them wherever it was possible, and to take the engagements everywhere from the yeoman classes.* In fact, the policy which Lucknow had for so many years been endeavouring to put in practice, was to be carried out at once by main force. *The instructions were well acted up to. The chieftains were stripped of nearly all their villages, and a settlement made in which they were entirely left out of consideration.*"

Of the accuracy of the passages italicized, the figures already given, showing that, out of 23,543 villages held by Taluqdárs at annexation, no less than 13,640 were settled with them in 1856–57, are sufficient comment. As for the assertion that our officers forcibly carried out the policy which the Lucknow Court would have executed if it had had the power, it is enough to remark that the Court had always asserted a claim to the whole rental of the soil, while our officers limited the revenue demand to just one-half of that rental, as nearly as they could ascertain it. The King of Oudh's officials had no abstract passion for village proprietors, and only objected to Taluqdárs because they absorbed a larger proportion of the rental than petty zamíndárs. Our officers, on the other hand, assessed Taluqdárs and zamíndárs alike at half assets. Moreover, the great extension of the Taluqdárí system during the forty years preceding annexation had been the direct result of the measures adopted by the Názims and Chakladárs. This being so, it is surely misleading to say that the Lucknow Darbár would, if it had had the power, have made revenue arrangements bearing any real resemblance to those of the first Summary Settlement. It is really surprising that such a statement should have received the *imprimatur* of a Local Government, the head of which was Secretary to the Chief Commissioners of Oudh, under whom that settlement was carried out.

For a statement of the other side of the case, a passage may be quoted from Mr. Gubbins' account of the Mutinies in Oudh, and readers may be left to decide for themselves which has the truer ring, and which indicates the most fitting policy for a Government whose professed *raison d'être* was the redress of popular suffering and oppression.

"There are those," writes Mr. Gubbins, "who take the part of the Taluqdárs, who, misled by appearances, think that they should have been left in undisturbed possession of their blood-stained spoils, and that justice should have been refused to the long-expectant villagers. So, however, did not rule the Government of India presided over by Lord Dalhousie. And surely, if no redress was to be granted, and no wrong to be repaired, to what end was our mission in Oudh, and what business had we in the country? So long as the native Government remained, redress was most hopeless. No tenure was a fixity, and a Taluqdár who possessed himself of a county to-day, might be driven from every village to-morrow. Such was not the case, however, under British rule. A title once declared and recognised was as immutable as the Government itself. And the admission of the title of the Taluqdár by a British court would have been the consummation of his fraud, would have stereotyped his usurpation! As a rule, the right of the villagers to recover their own was admitted."

Of the course run by the Mutiny in Oudh, no account can be attempted here. The story has been told in ample detail by Mr. Gubbins, who of the events he related *pars magna fuit*, and by other writers whose works are easily accessible. The events, moreover, are so well known to all who take any interest in the subject, that a mere sketch in outline could possess neither use nor interest even for the most " general" reader; while anything more than a sketch would be out of the question. Suffice it, therefore, to say that the Mutiny broke out at Lucknow on the 30th of May 1857, and that by the 10th of June all the out-stations were lost to us, and the civil officers and their families were either massacred or fugitives. A year later, Sir Robert Montgomery, then Chief Commissioner, found himself with a staff of officers, but no province to govern. He called on Taluqdárs to come in, and two-thirds of them obeyed the call by the end of the year. When the cold weather of 1858 began the country was comparatively tranquil, though fighting went on in the Tarai for some months longer.

The author of the Introduction to the "Oudh Gazetteer" follows the example of previous apologists of the Taluqdárí system in laying stress on the re-assertion of their influence by the barons during the mutiny, from which he concludes that " one thing at least had been made evident, that policy and justice alike forbade their being overlooked in the new settlement which the pacification of the province necessitated." How far it is correct to say that they had been "overlooked" at the first Summary Settlement has been already pointed out.

Lord Canning's view of the case is contained in his letter of the 6th of October 1858, addressed to Sir Robert Montgomery, as Chief Commissioner, which sounded the knell of the zamíndárí system. Arguing that the conduct of the petty proprietors, both in the N. W. Provinces and in Oudh, almost amounted to "an admission that their own rights, whatever these may be, are subordinate to those of the Taluqdárs; that they do not value the recognition of those (their own) rights by the ruling authority; and that the Taluqdárí system is the ancient, indigenous, and cherished system of the country"; and that though it might be true, as Sir James Outram had stated, that the zamíndárs had not influence and weight enough to assist us, yet they had numbers, and, if they valued their restored rights, might have given us active aid, Lord Canning declared that :—

"On these grounds, as well as because the Taluqdárs, if they will, can materially assist us in the re-establishment of our authority, and the restoration of tranquillity, the Governor-General has determined that a taluqdárí settlement shall be made. His lordship desires that it shall be framed so as to secure the village occupants from extortion," and that the tenures should be declared to be "contingent on a certain specified service to be rendered."

Now, how far, if at all, were Lord Canning's conclusions correct? That they were sincere, no one will for a moment question.

The facts were that during the Mutiny the villagers for the most part remained passive. Some joined the revolted Taluqdárs, but the large majority stayed quietly in their villages.* Of all the European fugitives betrayed and butchered, two only, Mr. Block and Mr. Stroyan, were betrayed by the treachery of a zamíndár, Yasín Khán of Sultánpur. For the fate of the rest, Taluqdárs were responsible. Many of the refugees received assistance from villagers in making their way to Lucknow, without which they could never have escaped. But quite apart from such

---

* In June 1857, Mr. Wingfield wrote that "confidence in our power was fast departing; and *zamíndárs who had recovered their villages from Taluqdárs at settlement were writing to propitiate the latter, or making preparations for flight.*"

instances of good will to ourselves among the peasantry, no proof that they were ill-affected to our rule, careless of their own rights, or well-affected to the rebel barons, can be found in the undoubted fact that they did not lend us active assistance. As Sir Charles Wood pointed out in his despatch of the 24th of April 1860, the mass of the mutineers were kinsmen and co-religionists of the petty zamíndárs. There were some sixty thousand Bráhmans and Rájpúts from Oudh in the Company's army, most of whom were in revolt, and it is surely not surprising that the fathers and brothers of these men did not take up arms against them. Their attachment to our rule must indeed have grown with marvellous rapidity, if, after only fifteen months' experience of it, they had cast aside all ties of blood and religion to come to our assistance. The Taluqdárs had forts and cannon. It was surely not strange that those of the zamindárs whose disaffection towards ourselves, *i.e.* whose sympathy with their own brethren, was sufficiently strong to drive them into action, should have joined the revolted chiefs without whose assistance they could have done little or nothing. The utmost inference that can logically be deduced from their conduct is that their dislike of the great landholders who had oppressed them was not, in some instances, strong enough to prevent their taking part with them, in the cause of their own relatives, fighting what they believed to be the battle of their own religion, against an alien and newly imposed power. This seems a somewhat fragile moral foundation for the weighty edifice of Taluqdárí policy which Lord Canning proceeded to construct upon it.

The fact is that the zamíndárs were in an exceedingly perplexing situation. All around them was raging a war in which their kinsmen were slaying or being slain by a race of foreign conquerors, of alien blood, creed, and colour, whose rule had been imposed upon the province for little more than a year, and whose claim to govern rested on that very superiority of civilisation, and of civilisation of a wholly different type, which rendered their aims and measures generally incomprehensible and mysterious, and sympathy with them well-nigh impossible. All around them, too, were feudal chieftains, who had indeed deprived many of them of great part of the rights in the soil that had once been theirs, but who were still their countrymen, whose motives they could understand, who had often rallied them to resist the aggressions of Názims and Chakladárs, who were fighting the battle of their brethren and their faith, and with whose assistance and leadership alone it was possible for them to take any effective part in the struggle. The antagonism between yeoman and landlord was still there; but in the intoxicating whirl of the moment it was thrown temporarily into the background.

To set against all the ties which bound the zamíndárs to the barons, the British Government had only two claims to their allegiance, that it could put an end to the disorder and misrule of the Nawábí, and that it had in a great measure restored them to the rights in the soil of which that disorder and misrule had led to their being deprived. These were solid and substantial reasons, no doubt, for throwing in their lot with ourselves, and the latter, at all events, they fully appreciated. But it is just this sort of solid and substantial reason which in time of revolution so often seems to lose its weight, and to be outbalanced by considerations which appeal to imagination and the passions. So it was in the present instance, and the grim old proverb, *Quem Deus vult perdere prius dementat*, received one more grim illustration. The large majority of the zamíndárs were passive, but a minority, sufficient under the circumstances to pass for the whole, yielded to the solicitations of the rebel Taluqdárs, and thus ruined the prospects of the peasant proprietors as a body, bringing all, active and inactive alike, under the same condemnation.

The effect of this identification of themselves, such as it was, by the peasantry with the Taluqdárs, was of course enormously to strengthen the hands of the official party who desired to maintain and extend the Taluqdárí system, and proportionally to weaken the advocates of a settlement made with the village zamíndárs. This unnatural alliance rendered the extinction of the Mutiny, by any other means than that of offering their own terms to the Taluqdárs, a task of so much difficulty and danger, that it can hardly be a matter of wonder that those terms were offered. It is impossible now not to regret that we did not persevere, and save the people in spite of themselves, even by the slow, costly, and vexatious process of destroying fort after fort until the revolt was stamped out. But though it may be matter of regret, the policy adopted can hardly be matter of wonder. The Summary Settlement of 1856 to 1857 made with the village communities, to the exclusion in many cases, as has been seen, of the usurping landlords, was doubtless one of the main reasons of the discontent of the latter, which, combined with the disaffection of the native army, so largely recruited from Oudh, culminated in the Mutiny. [It should be remembered, however, that in no part of the province had annexation produced less change in the *status quo* than in the trans-Ghághra districts of Gonda and Bahraich, where very few villages were lost by the barons. Yet in no part of Oudh did the latter join more readily in the revolt.] It was then that so many villagers whom the Summary Settlement had recognised as independent landholders, cut their own throats by joining the Taluqdárs by whom their lands had previously been absorbed, thus putting at the service of the upholders of the Taluqdárí system an argument which, under the circumstances, was so nearly irresistible that one cannot be surprised at its success.

"The people," it was argued, "evidently regard the Taluqdárs as their natural leaders. Why, then, should we go out of our way to force on them a more democratic system for which their own conduct shows them to be unfitted? Let us make terms with the Taluqdárs, and the country will be pacified."

Military considerations, also, tended to make these counsels prevail. Besieging numberless petty forts in the hot weather, losing men at every one, is about as inglorious and heartbreaking a task as can well be proposed to a general, and it is not surprising that Lord Clyde hesitated to undertake it. The work, if attempted, would probably have cost many lives, and have prolonged the disturbances in Oudh for another year, and though the teaching of subsequent events may make us bitterly regret the course adopted, we can hardly blame the men of the time for acting as they did.

It was determined, then, to pacify the Taluqdárs by allowing them to engage for the payment of the Government revenue of all villages included in their taluqas at the time of annexation in 1856, and on this principle the second Summary Settlement, which followed the Mutiny, was based. Thus, to borrow a phrase from Mr. Matthew Arnold, the people of Oudh re-entered the prison of feudalism whence for a brief space they had emerged, and the key was turned upon them for a period of which the end is not yet.

Of this policy it is usual to speak of Lord Canning as the author. How far the scheme was his own it is difficult to determine. Sir James Outram, indeed, contemplated the necessity of recognising the Taluqdárs more fully than had been done prior to the Mutiny, but for a time only, and under strict limitations on their power over subordinate occupants. In January 1858 he had addressed a memorandum to the Government of India, which deals principally with questions of general administration, but contains the following passages relating to the subject in hand :—

"The system of settlement with the so-called village proprietors will not answer at present, if ever, in Oudh . . . . . I see no prospect of restoring tranquillity, except by having recourse, *for the next few years*, to the old Taluqdárí system. There will be no difficulty in settling the rent (revenue) to be paid from each taluqa, and this should be distributed rateably over the several constituent villages, the exact amount to be paid by each villager being settled among themselves. *By this arrangement the Taluqdár will be unable to raise his rents.*"

Sir James was not one of the "picked men of a picked service," and his notions of land revenue policy would very likely be considered somewhat crude by a modern settlement officer; but one may be permitted to think that he had got hold of one or two sound notions on the subject, notwithstanding.

And now the writer ventures to hope that he has made the motives and aims of the three main actors in the drama, the

Taluqdárs and the yeomen during the Mutiny, and our own administrators before and after it, fairly intelligible to readers who have little or no previous acquaintance with this period of Oudh history. Those who have made of it a special study will, he trusts, find much that is true, if little that is new, in what has been advanced. The yeoman was in a puzzling predicament,' and might, if he had ever read *King John*, have exclaimed with Blanche—

> "Whoever wins, on that side shall I lose,
> Assurèd loss before the match be played."

His choice was not a wise one for his own material interests, but the mistake has, perhaps, been sufficiently expiated by a penalty which has been already prolonged over more than twenty years. Lord Canning doubtless believed sincerely in the policy which he initiated, and *ex post facto* wisdom is proverbially cheap; but for a right comprehension of the subject it should never be forgotten that that policy was a *pis aller*, and of the Taluqdárs it may be fairly said that—

> "In a rebellion
> When what's not meet, but what must be, was law,
> Then were they chosen."

Lord Canning went so far as to assert that the Taluqdárí system was the "ancient, indigenous, and cherished system of the country." It would doubtless be an exaggeration to describe it as "the modern, extraneous, and detested system imposed upon the country by the exactions of the British, and by the fiscal necessities and incapacity of the native government," but it would not be hard to demonstrate that such a definition would be at least as little incorrect as that adopted by Lord Canning. Still, though it is easy, after the event, to perceive that "confusion's cure lay not in these confusions," and that the attempt to maintain feudalism, without the sentiment and the customs which can alone make feudalism tolerable, was a deplorable mistake, yet it would be unjust to forget that there was much in the circumstances of the time to make the course determined on seem specious and plausible. Even by readers who sincerely dislike the political morality which pervades the greater part of Mr.

Froude's "English in Ireland," no apology will be felt necessary for the following extract:—

"The forces which govern the evolution of human society are so complex that the wisest statesman may misread them. The highest political sagacity, though controlled by conscience and directed by the purest motives, may yet select a policy which, in the light of after history, shall seem like madness. The 'event' may teach the inadequacy of the intellect to compass the problems which at times present themselves for solution. The 'event' alone will not justify severe historical censure where a ruler has endeavoured seriously to do what, in the light of such knowledge as he possessed, appeared at the moment most equitable." Lord Canning need not be condemned for yielding to "arguments at the moment unanswerable, which later history has too effectually answered."

CHAPTER VII.

TEN YEARS OF TALUQDA'RI' POLICY [1858–1868].

THE profound change of tone and altered standpoint which have marked the policy of the Government of India since the Mutiny, could hardly be more strikingly illustrated than by a comparison of the instructions addressed to Sir James Outram on the 4th of February 1856 with those issued to Sir Robert Montgomery on the 6th of October 1858. The judgment which the reader may pass upon their respective merits is likely to depend to some extent on the opinion which he holds as to the true aims and duties of the English in India. The object of Lord Dalhousie's Government was to benefit the masses with a lofty disregard of the impression which by so doing they might produce upon the native aristocracy. And to this end they sought to put themselves into direct contact with the people, " with no miscrowned man's head " between them. They were resolved, in short, that "everybody should count as one, and nobody as more than one."

When we turn to Lord Canning's instructions of the 6th of October, everything is changed. Not the good of the masses, but, as a writer in the " Calcutta Review " of September 1860 approvingly puts it, " to hold the Eastern Empire with the least strain on the population and finances of Great Britain is the problem of Indian Government." Popular welfare has retired into the background, and its place is taken by the "urgent necessity of pacifying the country." The Taluqdárs, who for Lord Dalhousie had been mere middlemen, had for Lord Canning become an "ancient, indigenous and cherished" institution of the country, with whom the settlement was to be made wherever they were found to exist. It was even declared that, prior to annexation, "village occupancy, independent and free from subordination to Taluqdárs, had been unknown" in Oudh, an assertion so monstrous, and so obviously and notoriously incorrect, that one is at a loss to understand how it can have found its way into an elaborate State paper. Lord Canning, however, had the excuse that he was writing comparatively in the dark, and after a great crisis.

Whatever may be thought of the process by which he arrived at it, his conclusion was that "these village occupants, as such, deserve little consideration from us." He argued that they had behaved as if regardless of their own rights, and ungrateful to the British Government for maintaining them; and that if they had not considered themselves as wholly subordinate to the Taluqdárs, they would certainly have afforded us active assistance in resisting them when they went into rebellion. "On these grounds," of which one was an entire misconception of fact, and the other a false inference, "as well as because the Taluqdárs, if they will, can materially aid us in the re-establishment of our authority and the restoration of tranquillity," it was determined that a Taluqdárí settlement, "so framed as to secure the village occupants from extortion," should be made. This settlement was begun without any expectation that it would be final, was crowded into six months, and then declared irrevocable as regards the superior proprietary right. There can be no doubt that mistakes were made, and that villages were decreed to Taluqdárs of which they had not been in possession at annexation, and even, in some cases, of which they had not been in possession for some years previously. This, however, is somewhat anticipating the course of events, and it must be admitted, in justice to Lord Canning, that if in this respect he went beyond the advice of Sir James Outram's farewell memorandum of the 29th of January 1858, yet in others he did much to mitigate the spirit of blood and iron which pervaded its counsels. Sir James recommended the exclusion of natives from judicial employ; that there should be no appeal in criminal cases; that the native bar and native *amlah* or office establishment should be abolished, and the place of the latter supplied by "respectable European serjeants"; that any one found in possession of arms after one month from the issue of a proclamation for their surrender should be put to death; and that the lash should as far as possible be resorted to as a means of punishment, the number of lashes, up to two hundred, "to be determined only by the pulse of the offender under the fingers of the civil surgeon." He paid what was perhaps an unintentional compliment to civilians by "earnestly requesting" that the officers appointed to carry out the system which he advocated might be selected "principally from the military services." Without any desire to cavil at the utterances of one who was undoubtedly a great and good man, one cannot but remark the spirit of severity, almost ferocity, which inspires this memorandum, as an instructive illustration of the extent to which even a great and good man may be overpowered by reactionary impulses. If such was the effect of the Mutiny upon Outram, what was to be expected of lesser men, when armed, as was, *ex officio*, every Commissioner and Deputy Commissioner in Oudh up to the beginning of 1859, with irresponsible power of life and death? The system of administration imposed upon Oudh after reoccupation was the outcome of a deadly and ferocious struggle between alien races. It is not in a crisis such as that of the Mutiny, or by men "fresh from war's alarms," that schemes of broad, humane, and far-seeing statesmanship are likely to be conceived. The change which since 1857 has come over the attitude of the Government of India towards its subjects has been perhaps more marked in Oudh than in any other province of the Empire. Everywhere is discernible the tendency to treat the native aristocracy as a species of breakwater between ourselves and the masses, and to subordinate to them the interests of the latter. But more especially has this been the case in Oudh. The province was made over to the advocates of feudalism as a subject on which they were at liberty to work their will, and try what experiments they chose.

It must be admitted that the Dalhousie policy had the defects of its qualities, and the policy of Lord Canning the qualities of its defects. The North-West Provinces Collector, brought up in the school of Bird and Thomason, was doubtless prone to treat the native gentleman with scant ceremony, and in this respect it may be gladly conceded that his successor of the present day is more commendable than he. Insufficient regard was, no doubt, often shown both to the feelings and the vested rights of the chieftain, who was apt to be mistaken for the mere revenue contractor, and not unfrequently suffered by the confusion. But all this to the contrary notwithstanding, it must still be maintained that the Dalhousie-Thomason doctrine contained in it the root of the matter; that the welfare and independence of thousands are of more intrinsic importance than the feelings and privileges of individuals. It is to be regretted that natives of rank were not always treated with due deference by the Thomasonian school, and that in some cases their claim to engage for the revenue was not admitted in villages where it was well-founded. But these, after all, are lesser evils than that millions who might have been raised into peasant proprietors should be degraded to tenants at will; than that robbery of the worst type should be sanctioned and upheld by a civilised government; than that the statute book should be defaced by invidious and arbitrary laws in the interests of an exceedingly limited class. The policy of conciliating the strong by allowing them to lord it over the weak may be safe, but it is not noble. If we are not here to uphold the cause of the poor and of him that hath no helper, we have no right to be here at all. Therefore, while but too gladly admitting that in many respects we have advanced much during the last twenty years, in conciliatoriness, in thoroughness, in mastery of details, in systematic method, in laboriousness, in the desire to do things elaborately; it must still be maintained that in the broad scope and tendency of our policy and aims, we have retrogressed and fallen short of our fathers who were before us; that we have not shown their straightforward, downright courage, their single-minded, fervent resolve to rule for the good of the people, and for the good of individuals only so far as they were a part and portion of the people. The first aim of the State, the great aim of all social and political arrangements whatever, should be to secure as far as possible an equal chance of success, moral and material, to all, and the highest possible average chance of success to each of its subjects; while the policy of the Government of India since 1857, in Oudh, at any rate, has been in favour of territorial aristocracy and landlordism, and, generally, of giving more to him that hath abundance. It is very well, no doubt, to conciliate native gentlemen, and, indeed, natives of every rank and degree, by courteous treatment, and to respect their vested rights of property. But "'tis not very well, nay," with Roderigo, I "think it is scurvy," to conciliate them by the sacrifice of the security and independence of an entire peasantry, and by the maintenance of "rights" acquired by usurpation, violence, and treachery. *Aristocrat par mœurs, démocrat par principes* is a praiseworthy combination of method and object; but if we must choose between them, let us have the democratic principles, even without aristocratic manners, which characterised the policy of Lord Dalhousie, rather than the system of aristocratic manners, divorced from democratic principles, which the Government of India, "wise with the cynical wisdom of the Mutiny," has since his day inaugurated.

In March 1858 the Governor-General issued a proclamation declaring that with the exception of the six specially exempted estates of Balrámpur, Padnaha, Katiárí, Sisaindi, Gopál Khera, and Moráwan, the "proprietary right in the soil of the province is confiscated to the British Government, which will dispose of that right in such manner as to it may seem fitting." The owners of the six exempted estates were declared "sole hereditary proprietors of the lands which they held when Oudh came under British rule." One of these six, however, Padnaha, was afterwards confiscated, owing to subsequent discoveries regarding the conduct during the Mutiny of its owner Kulráj Singh. This estate is now part of the Naipál Taráí. Kulráj Singh is dead, and his sons are in the service of the Naipál Government.

Everyone knows how this proclamation was denounced by Mr. Bright in the House of Commons, in his great speech of the 20th of May 1858. It was supposed at the time that the measure was intended as a preliminary to the introduction of the never-to-be-sufficiently-inveighed-against "dead-level" system, under which, as the eloquent member for Birmingham put it, "the whole produce of the land of Oudh and of the industry of its people will be divided into two most unequal portions; the larger will go to the Government in the shape of tax, and the smaller share, which will be a handful of rice per day, will go to the cultivator of the soil. Now this," continued Mr. Bright, "is the Indian system. It is the grand theory of the civilians, under whose advice, I very much fear, Lord Canning has unfortunately acted. . . . I believe that this proclamation sanctions this policy. . . . It has been stated in the course of the debate that this sentence of confiscation refers only to certain unpleasant persons who are called Taluqdárs, who are barons, and robber chiefs, and oppressors of the people. This is by no means the first time that, after a great wrong has been committed, the wrong-doer has attempted to injure by calumny those upon whom the wrong has been inflicted."

Mr. Bright, like most other people at that time, was still in ignorance of the use that it was intended to make of this proclamation. Perhaps, when he found out, he was not very much consoled. But it was certainly a curious instance of the irony of circumstance that the Oudh Taluqdárs should have found their champion in the most strenuous assailant of feudalism at home.

This confiscating proclamation was speedily followed by another, which called upon all Taluqdárs to come into Lucknow, and to receive from the Chief Commissioner grants of the proprietary right in their respective taluqas, as they had existed in 1856. The terms thus offered were so extremely favourable as, probably, in some cases to defeat their own object. Not a few of the rebel chiefs were unable to believe in the promises held out to them, who might have risen to a hook baited with less suspicious liberality. The great majority, however, did come in, and the second summary settlement was promptly commenced. Its effect in modifying the previous allotment was, briefly, as follows:—

In 1856–57, as has already been remarked, out of 23,543 villages included in taluqas at annexation, 13,640 had been settled with Taluqdárs, and 9,903 with other persons. In 1858 to 1859, of these same villages, 22,637 were settled either with the same Taluqdárs or with loyal grantees, and only 906 with other persons, either as having been redeemed from mortgage, or in consequence of the conduct of the Taluqdár during the Mutiny. A tabular statement furnished in June 1859 by Major L. Barrow, then Special Commissioner of Revenue, shows the total distribution of the soil of Oudh to be as follows:—

	Villages.	Revenue demand.
1. Taluqdárí	23,157, paying	Rs. 65,64,959
2. Zamíndárí	7,201, ,,	28,45,183
3. Pattídárí	4,539, ,,	18,19,214
Total	34,897, ,,	1,12,29,356

It should be observed that, for the purposes of this classification, " zamíndárí " villages are those of which the proprietorship vests undivided in the hands of either a single individual or a coparcenary community; while " pattídárí " villages are those in which the lands have been divided among the shareholders. Where all the lands have been thus divided, the village is said to be held in " perfect," where only a portion has been divided, the remainder being occupied jointly, it is said to be held in " imperfect " pattídárí tenure. Zamíndárí villages are constantly becoming pattídárí, as, in course of generations, the sharers become more numerous. But it rarely happens that a pattídárí village becomes zamíndárí, except by sale, when a single owner, the purchaser, takes the place of the coparcenary body. It should also be noted that the number of separately demarcated villages now borne on the revenue records of the province is only 23,591, as many as 11,306 "nawábí" villages having, for convenience of survey, been doubled up with others.

Out of the total land revenue of Rs. 1,12,29,356, about six lákhs was assessed on revenue free grants not resumable during that settlement, and the actual demand was, in round numbers, 104 lákhs, of which, to quote the Secretary to the Government of India—Mr. Beadon's—epitome of the situation, "77 lákhs have been settled as they were before annexation, and $14\frac{1}{2}$ lákhs with the persons recognised in the settlement of 1856. These latter are chiefly zamíndárí villages which were in wrongful possession of Kabzdárs . . . . and which were restored in 1856 to their rightful owners. The remaining $12\frac{1}{2}$ lákhs are from confiscated lands. Under the old settlement, the Taluqdárs engaged for only 35 lákhs of the entire revenue; they have now been admitted to engage for 62 lákhs," or, in other words, for more than three-fifths, instead of for about one-third of the whole. This assessment was sanctioned by the Government of India "for three years certain, from the 1st of May 1858, or until a detailed settlement can be carried out in combination with the survey." In Gonda and Bahraich it was prolonged up to 1867, much to the advantage of the zamíndárs of those (then) very lightly assessed districts. The revenue demand of the last year of Wájid Ali Sháh's reign—the *demand*, be it observed, not the actual collections,—had been, in round numbers, 138 lákhs. The amount actually realised by Názims, Chakladárs, and other officials was probably more; that credited to the King was certainly considerably less.

Other sources of revenue tapped by our administration yielded about 15 lákhs, of which 8 were derived from salt, 5 from spirits and drugs, and 2 from stamps. The total product of Oudh taxation in the year 1858, was thus somewhat short of 120 lákhs, or £1,200,000 sterling. At present, the land revenue yields somewhat less than a million and a half sterling, an increase of more than 40 per cent; at least £200,000 is derived from salt duty; while the income from excise and stamps has risen from 5 and 2 lákhs, respectively, to not less than 7 and 9 lákhs.

The second Summary Settlement was completed before the middle of 1859, and everybody concerned in carrying it out was highly applauded by his official superior, in a graduated scale of laudation. The Assistants were praised by their Deputy Commissioners, the Deputy Commissioners by the Financial Commissioner, the Financial by the Chief Commissioner, and the Chief Commissioner by the Government of India. And so far, at least, as regards the rapidity with which the work was performed, the praise was doubtless well-deserved. "A down-hill reformation," as Dryden has told us, "rolls apace."

For some time everything went on smoothly, without any sign of the acrimonious controversies which were destined soon to break out. The most important external event was the cession to Naipál of a large strip of Tarai, as a reward for the services rendered by the Darbár under the guidance of Sir Jang Bahádur Singh, during the Mutiny. Vast quantities of valuable forest—not to speak of exquisite scenery—were thus transferred from ourselves who were, and are, in urgent need of both, to the Naipális, who had already an abundance of the latter, and have since been busily engaged in the transmutation of the former into cash. Two good results the cession undeniably secures. As long as the Naipál Darbár holds this strip of Tarái, so long is all likelihood of border raids into our territories by the Gurkhias annihilated; it being obvious to the meanest capacity that this, probably the most paying district in their possession, could be resumed with the utmost ease on any sufficient provocation. And, secondly, the Naipál Government thoroughly identifies itself with the welfare of its tenants, who hold land at very easy terms, with perfect security of tenure, and with no fear of being rack-rented in the interest of some needy landlord or greedy contractor, and in the name, falsely invoked, of political economy. The Naipál Tarai has therefore become, what it would not have been under British rule, a land of refuge for the cultivator whom exaction in our own territory has irritated to the bolting point. The existence of such a haven of security has some effect in keeping landlords from attempting, and tenants from submitting to, extortionate enhancement. But this effect is scarcely appreciable beyond the three northern districts, where it is least needed; the fear of fever, still more than the distance, preventing the cultivators of central and southern Oudh from availing themselves of the abundant waste lands and security from rack-renting which invite them across the Naipál border.

In June 1859 Mr., afterwards Sir Charles, Wingfield, who had succeeded Sir Robert Montgomery as Chief Commissioner in May of the same year, reported to the Government of India that distrust in the permanence of the Taluqdárí Settlement was widely diffused throughout all classes in Oudh, the Taluqdárs fearing, and the village proprietors hoping, that it was only a temporary arrangement, and that so soon as the province was finally pacified the former policy would be reverted to. Hence "a spirit of antagonism is kept alive. The Taluqdárs dread making any concession that may hereafter be construed into a recognition of the independent right of the village proprietors, and the latter will accept no benefit that may look like a renunciation of it." This uneasy feeling Mr. Wingfield wished to see set at rest by the formal accord by the Government of India of its sanction to the finality or perpetuity, as regards proprietary right, of the second Summary Settlement. Such sanction once accorded, he felt "no doubt of the complete success of the Taluqdárí Settlement"; and was unable to "see the use of giving the village proprietors hopes of a rehearing at next settlement; *if, after having then ascertained what everyone knows already, that they are the rightful proprietors of the soil, we are to tell them our policy will not permit us to recognise their claims.*" The most noteworthy points in these extracts are two: first, that the tenacity with which Mr. Wingfield describes the village proprietors as clinging to their hopes of being settled with hereafter, is in strong contradiction to that carelessness of their rights and independence which Lord Canning in his letter of the 6th of October 1858, less than nine months previously, had ascribed to them;

and, secondly, that *on Mr. Wingfield's own showing, it was, in June* 1859, *a matter of general notoriety that the village zamíndárs, wherever they were to be found, were, as opposed to the Taluqdárs, " the rightful proprietors of the soil."*

The first of these points carries its own comment with it, and need not be dilated on here. But the second is probably the most singular revelation to be found in the whole course of the voluminous Oudh land controversy. It is really startling, if the reader will but consider it. Here is a highly placed English officer, who for nearly seven years was Chief Commissioner of Oudh, and who during the whole of that time was the most strenuous upholder of the Taluqdárí system, did his utmost to carry it to lengths which the Government of India had never contemplated, and was unwearied in his laudation of that system on the ground that it secured the *maintenance of existing rights*, admitting, actually admitting, within two months of assuming charge of his office, that it was universally known that the village zamíndárs, and not the Taluqdárs, were the rightful proprietors of the soil, and plainly hinting that any inquiry to ascertain the truth of so notorious a fact would be little better than a farce! Such an assertion, coming from such a source, is indeed so surprising, that on first perusal of it one can but " gasp and stare," like Quintilian, and try to imagine that the words might have some other than their obvious meaning, or that Mr. Wingfield's purport might have been incorrectly expressed by his Secretary. But there can be no mistake. The sense of the words is perfectly plain, and in that plain sense they were quoted *verbatim* more than once in the course of subsequent discussion, and were never, so far as appears from the Blue Books, retracted or explained by their author. If an imaginary parallel will help the reader to realize the full significance of such a confession, let him try to fancy Lord Beaconsfield stating in the House of Lords that the Turks had notoriously not a shadow of right to be at Constantinople, or M. Gambetta announcing in the Chamber of Deputies that the Comte de Chambord was, beyond all possibility of doubt, the rightful ruler of France. Such assertions would scarcely be more out of keeping with the professed convictions of Lord Beaconsfield and M. Gambetta, than was the passage above italicised with those of Mr. Wingfield.

The Government of India concurred with the Chief Commissioner in thinking it desirable to remove all doubts as to the fixity of the Taluqdárí Settlement, and in a letter (No. 6268) dated the 10th of October 1859, declared that "every Taluqdár with whom a Summary Settlement has been made since the occupation of the province, has thereby acquired a permanent, hereditary, and transferable right in the taluqa for which he was engaged, including the perpetual privilege of engaging with the Government for the revenue of the taluqa." This right, however, was conceded, according to paragraph 2 of the letter, "*subject to any measure which the Government of India may think proper to take for the purpose of protecting the inferior zamindárs and village occupants from extortion, and of upholding their rights in the soil in subordination to the Taluqdárs.*"

The Chief Commissioner was directed to prepare a list of Taluqdárs who had thus acquired a permanent proprietary right, and to have in readiness *sannads*, running in his own name, to be distributed on the arrival of the Governor-General at Lucknow. In reply to this letter, Mr. Wingfield wrote strongly deprecating the proviso contained in the third paragraph, on the grounds that it would "unsettle the minds of the inferior proprietors, and encourage extravagant hopes of independence. It would alarm the Taluqdárs, and make them regard the gift of the proprietary right as a mockery and a delusion. Moreover, it will place an engine in the hands of any future Chief Commissioner and Governor-General adverse in principle to Taluqdárs, which would enable them virtually to annul this settlement, and oust the Taluqdárs nearly as effectually as was done in 1856."

If Mr. Wingfield's cynical candour had not already nearly exhausted all capacity for astonishment at his acts and utterances, it would perhaps be surprising to find that susceptibilities so delicate as to be "alarmed" at the reservation to itself by Government of the power—which, it need hardly be remarked, no Government can by any possibility morally consistent with its *raison d'être* profess to abdicate,—of protecting the cultivating community from extortion, and of upholding their rights in the soil, should have met with such ready sympathy from an English Chief Commissioner of Oudh. For the sake of the Liberal electors who have since those days had the honour of being represented in Parliament by Sir Charles Wingfield, one may hope that the old saw to the effect that those who cross the sea change their climate only, and not their minds, is not of universal application. But what really is surprising is that the Chief Commissioner's fears of the consequences to be apprehended from a declaration that the Government of India would not renounce its first duty towards its subjects, a duty for the non-fulfilment of which it had brought the native administration of Oudh to a violent end, should have been acknowledged to be well founded by a statesman of the calibre of Lord Canning. So it was, however, and this dangerous proviso was omitted from the *sannads* which were distributed by Lord Canning to 177 Taluqdárs on the 25th of October 1859. The omission, however, has had no practical effect in limiting the power of the Government to interfere in any way it may think desirable; for the letter of the 10th of October 1859 has been declared to possess the force of law, and was appended as Schedule I. to Act I. of 1869, which declares and defines the legal status of the Taluqdárs. The proviso of paragraph 3 is, therefore, just as legally binding on the Taluqdárs as if it had been actually inserted in their *sannads*, and the controversy on the subject is only noteworthy as an illustration of the spirit by which the then Oudh administration was actuated.

The *sannads*, in the shape to which Mr. Wingfield succeeded in reducing them, conferred on the recipients " full proprietary right, title, and possession " of the estate therein specified, subject to the conditions of paying revenue, and showing all possible loyalty and rendering all possible assistance to the British Government, and concluded with the following words :—

" Another condition of this *sannad* is, that you will, to the best of your power, try to promote the agricultural resources of your estate, and that whatever holders of subordinate rights may be under you, will be preserved in their former right. As long as you and your heirs will, in good faith, adhere to the conditions above mentioned, so long will the British Government uphold you and your heirs in the proprietary right of the said estate."

Such was the form of *sannad* conferred on such Taluqdárs as were restored to the estates which they had held at annexation. For loyal grantees, a much shorter form was adopted, the only conditions of which were that the grantee and his heirs " shall pay to Government the revenue which will, from time to time, be fixed for that estate, and that he and his heirs shall continue at all times firm in their allegiance, and shall do good service to the British Government."

The condition which binds Taluqdárs to uphold subordinate rights has not, in some instances, been strictly observed, some Taluqdárs having done all in their power to smash under-proprietary tenures. It must be admitted, however, that in such cases they have almost always received considerable provocation from the under-proprietors in the shape of persistent default, and have kept, at any rate, as a rule, on the windy side of the law. Even were it otherwise, the condition is one of the breach of which satisfactory proof, proof such as would justify so stringent a measure as the resumption of an estate, must, in the nature of things, be extremely difficult of attainment. Circumstances, of course, are easily conceivable in which such conclusive proof of flagrant breach of this condition might be forthcoming as would not only justify, but should compel, enforcement of the penalty. A Taluqdár, for instance, if such a case may be imagined for the sake of illustration, who should be convicted of resort to systematic bribery and corruption, in order to procure the destruction or falsification of judicial records, decreeing under-proprietary rights in his estate, might be fitly deprived, on the strength of this condition of his *sannad*, of the powers and position which he would, by the supposition, have so grossly abused. But nothing short of adequate proof of conduct of this or of a similar nature would be at all likely to draw down the penalty of resumption, unless, indeed, the duties of property should come to be interpreted with a degree of strictness which, at present, there seems little ground for anticipating.

Of a very different degree of importance is the condition binding the Taluqdárs to do all in their power to promote the agricultural resources of their estates. If it should come to be generally recognised as an unquestionable truth that there is one indispensable condition of agricultural prosperity, to confer which, consistently with the maintenance of his own position, is in the power of every Taluqdár in his own estate, and of the government in every village not included in a taluqa, ample warrant would be made out for calling upon the Taluqdárs to follow the example of government, and confer the benefit so urgently needed. I believe it will one day be recognised that fixity of cultivating tenure is such an indispensable condition, and that under this provision of the *sannads* its introduction might be enforced in taluqas, quite apart from the effect of paragraph 3, Schedule I. of Act I. of 1869. This latter, however, has the advantage of applying to Taluqdárs of every kind and degree, while, for some not very apparent reason, the obligation to improve the agricultural resources of their estates was not imposed upon loyal grantees.

In April and May 1860 further signs of the coming storm of controversy became visible in a seemingly innocent enough correspondence between Colonel Abbott, Commissioner of the Lucknow Division, and Mr. Charles Currie, afterwards Judicial Commissioner of Oudh, and at that time officiating as Secretary to the Chief Commissioner. In this controversy, two questions were started by Colonel Abbott—(1) the meaning to be attached to the term "Taluqdár"; and (2) the effect on subordinate rights of the confiscating proclamation of March 1858. Mr. Wingfield held that "Taluqdár" meant simply "an opulent landholder," and that confiscation, where carried out, annulled proprietary rights of every kind, inferior as well as superior. A few days later, Colonel Barrow, while officiating as Chief Commissioner, elaborated Mr. Wingfield's doctrine into this, that there were three species of Taluqdárí tenure in Oudh, " ancestral, acquired, and conferred "; and further asserted that, with regard to the first two, confiscation had not been practically carried out, and that, therefore, though the tenure was held under a new title, the inferior rights in the land were not affected. But in "conferred" taluqas, Colonel Barrow was of opinion that, confiscation, having been carried out, all subordinate rights whatever were abolished, and the estates made over to the grantees free from all encumbrances whatever.

"The sub-proprietors, if there formerly were any, do not possess any definite interest whatever, beyond what they may have derived from the grantee, who will seldom oust under-proprietors whose rights are clear and defined and not unreasonable, but the necessity for declaring this rule was justly felt in many cases where estates had been given in reward, or the parties on whom they have been conferred would have gained nothing. The Officiating Chief Commissioner cannot understand on what principle you would urge the sub-proprietor into an hereditary cultivator. The location of a class of cultivators of small holdings and no capital, possessed of a recognised right of occupancy at fixed rates of rent, is in the Officiating Chief Commissioner's opinion a great evil. The grant of an estate hampered with such conditions would not be a boon but a burthen to the recipient, and the Officiating Chief Commissioner cannot in any way recognise such rights."

It thus appears, on Colonel Barrow's own showing, that where an estate had been confiscated for the rebellion of a Taluqdár, and conferred upon a loyal grantee, the "clear, defined, and not unreasonable" rights of under-proprietors, who might have taken no part whatever in the revolt, were to be left entirely at the pleasure of the grantee. And although the legal recognition of such rights would, according to Colonel Barrow, have rendered the grant "not a boon but a burthen to the recipient," who would, in many cases, have "gained nothing" by such a gift, it was yet expected that the grantee, having unrestrained power to do so, would "seldom oust under-proprietors" who possessed them. In other words, it was expected that the grantee would voluntarily submit to a dead loss from his grant, rather than interfere with rights which, though clear, definite, and reasonable, had been authoritatively declared entirely at his discretion to recognise or disallow. Why, the mere fact of a man's claiming a shadow of right in the soil would, in the eyes of four out of five of even hereditary Taluqdárs —not to speak of extraneous grantees from the Panjáb and elsewhere—be deemed ample ground for ousting him if they could, *i.e.* for getting him ejected, and then, if he proved submissive, allowing him to hold on, at an enhanced rent, as a mere tenant-at-will. There is no need to comment on the parenthetical implication that the existence of a "class of cultivators of small holdings and no capital" is "a great evil," if they are protected from rack-renting by a right of occupancy, and so afforded opportunities, at least, of acquiring capital; whereas, if they are not so protected, and therefore have less opportunity of acquiring capital, their existence is either a minor evil, or no evil at all. On the whole, however, though no one would for a moment dream of hinting that the Officiating Chief Commissioner did not sincerely believe that the policy which he advocated was the right thing for Oudh, yet it will not perhaps be unfair to say that he arrived at his conclusions on grounds of what appeared to him to be expediency, rather than by deduction from the legal effects of Lord Canning's proclamation, or from considerations of abstract justice.

Such, at any rate, was the opinion of Lord Canning, who called for the correspondence, and on the 12th of September 1860 wrote to Mr. Wingfield, who had by that time resumed the post of Chief Commissioner, to the effect that Colonel Barrow's declaration of the course to be adopted towards under-proprietors in "conferred" taluqas, was alike opposed to the intentions of the Government of India, and to the Royal Proclamation of the 1st of November 1858. No such distinction between ancestral and acquired taluqas on the one hand, and conferred taluqas on the other, had ever been recognised by the Government, whose policy was—

"To leave the confiscation of 1858 in force only in the case of persons who persisted in rebellion, and generally so far as to restore in its integrity the ancient Taluqdárí tenure wherever it had existed at the time of the first occupation of Oudh in 1856, but had been set aside by our revenue officers. But the Governor-General in Council never intended that in Taluqdárí estates confiscated under the general order, and conferred in consequence of the persistent rebellion of the Taluqdár upon a new grantee, all the holders of subordinate rights, though themselves not persisting in rebellion, and though pardoned by the Queen, should be merged in the consequence of the Taluqdár's guilt, and become partakers in his punishment."

It was explained that the confiscation order of March 1858 had been carried out *throughout the province*, except in the six estates specially exempted, and the effect of such confiscation was laid down to be that all estates which came under it are now held by a title derived directly from the British Government, and that the relations between the Taluqdár and his subordinate holders are "those which subsisted between them before annexation, modified or regulated by such obligations as the Government has imposed, not those which were established between them by our officers acting under the instructions issued at annexation." In fine, Colonel Barrow's orders were to be cancelled, and instructions in conformity with the above remarks to be issued.

This correspondence instructively illustrates the difference which so early as 1860 separated the points of view from which the Government of India and the local administrators of Oudh respectively regarded the validity and importance of under-proprietary rights in the soil. Mr. Wingfield, it should be added, cordially coincided in Colonel Barrow's view of the question, and strenuously opposed the recognition of any subordinate rights in taluqas of which the superior right had been confiscated for rebellion, and bestowed upon loyal grantees. His main arguments were—(1) that, otherwise, preposterous claims would be asserted by the under-proprietors, "which, in the absence of the old Taluqdár, no one would care to refute"; and (2) that most of the confiscated estates were either north of the Ghághra, where subordinate rights were few and weak, or in Baiswára, where the under-proprietors themselves had very generally joined in the rebellion. Mr. Wingfield thus seems to have been of opinion that the possibility of preposterous claims being preferred was sufficient ground for refusing to listen to any claims, whether preposterous or not; that loyal grantees would not care to protect their own interests by refuting preposterous claims, if urged; that where under-proprietary rights were weak and few, they might justly be wholly ignored; and that where under-proprietors had, generally speaking, been guilty of rebellion, no attempt should be made to discriminate between the guilty and the innocent.

In September 1860 Mr. Wingfield submitted to the Government of India a copy of the instructions regarding the record of rights and assessment which he proposed to issue to the officers appointed to carry out the regular settlement of the province. These instructions, which were destined to attain notoriety under the name of the "Record of Rights Circular," were, on the whole, approved by the Government, and such modifications as were ordered are not material to the present purpose. They contain, amid much that is sensible and clear, a proposition which is clear, but scarcely, perhaps, sensible:—

"Only the subordinate rights existing in 1855, or subsequently conceded, are now to be recognised and recorded."

This, of course, amounts to saying that no act of oppression, however gross, committed, say, in 1854, could be redressed by our courts. A zamíndár might have been killed, and his family driven out of their village in 1854; but if the Taluqdár had been in full possession throughout 1855, no claim of the murdered ex-proprietor's descendants could be recognised. This cannot be called an extreme, for it is the obvious and immediate result of the rule. And of the meaning of the rule there can be no doubt, for it is added:—" If those persons who once held an intermediate interest in the land, between the Taluqdár and the ryot, are found to have been reduced, prior to annexation, to the position of mere cultivators, they will not be raised from it now." The subsequent extension of the period of limitation for claims to under-proprietary right to twelve years prior to annexation will be noticed hereafter. The Government of

India did not touch on the question at this time, and for the present no more need be said of it.

But the 31st paragraph of the circular is of such vital importance to the condition of something like three-fifths of the population of Oudh, that it must be quoted entire :—

"The Chief Commissioner has determined to make no distinction in the records between cultivators at fixed rates and cultivators at will. Abstractedly viewed, he considers that to give a permanent right of occupancy at an unvarying rent to the tiller of the soil, is an invasion of the rights of property, and a clog on enterprise and improvement. It must be shown that nothing less will suffice to guard the ryot from ill-usage to justify such a measure. There is not the slightest possibility of this result happening in Oudh; consequently the measure is utterly unsuited to the province. In three-fourths of Oudh there is a deficiency of cultivators. They are so valuable that no landlord would seek to dispossess a good one, and a bad one he should be free to get rid of. Even in those parts where the population is more abundant, no symptom that the cultivator needs protection has been manifested. The question has not been stirred by the cultivators themselves. To create an element of present discord, to provide against a contingency that cannot possibly occur for the next thirty years throughout three parts of the province, or for seven or eight years to come at least in the remaining fourth, would demonstrate a wanton spirit of meddling. The abandoned and waste lands of Oudh will furnish occupation to any number of cultivators for many years yet, and if increase of population in the already thickly peopled districts of the south-east of Oudh should eventually have the effect of driving cultivators across the Ghághra, it would be the greatest benefit that could be conferred on the province. It need further be observed that the extension of the system of granting *pattas* down to every one who holds land of another, which the Chief Commissioner contemplates, will afford ample protection to everyone."

The first point to be noticed in this paragraph is that Mr. Wingfield was, at the time of writing it, of opinion that there were two classes of cultivators—tenants at fixed rates, and tenants-at-will. He did not wish the distinction to be recognised in the record of rights in the soil, to frame which is one of the principal duties of a settlement officer, but he believed that it existed, and would have allowed, as he elsewhere explained, each case to be determined on its own merits by the rent courts, as occasion arose. This belief he afterwards disclaimed, and he was probably so far right, that there was no such hard and fast distinction as he had at first acknowledged to exist. There was, in fact, as later inquiries showed, no class of tenants pure and simple possessed of a right recognised by law to hold their lands at unchanging rent rates against the will of the proprietor, just as there was no class of landlords entitled to hold their estates at unchanging revenue rates. Rent rates in practice, probably fluctuated less than revenue rates, but the rent-payer had no more right to hold at a perpetually fixed demand than the revenue-payer. The idea of the one right was as alien to the state of society prevailing in the Nawábí as that of the other, and the only surprising thing about the matter is that the contrary supposition should ever have been entertained. Where all things were in a state of perpetual flux, it was not among the weakest and most down-trodden classes of the agricultural community that a beneficial fixity of tenure could have been expected to exist. Modern advocates of tenant-right in Oudh must abandon all attempts to justify its creation now on the ground that it existed then. It did not, and in the nature of things could not reasonably have been expected to exist. To concede this to the opponents of tenant-right is really to concede nothing.

Next comes to be considered the Chief Commissioner's "abstract view" that the grant of a "permanent right of occupancy at an unvarying rent to the tiller of the soil is an invasion of the rights of property, and a clog on enterprise and improvement." Thinking, as Mr. Wingfield then did, that tenants with a permanent right of occupancy at fixed rents did exist, it seems strange that it should not have occurred to him that to confiscate or ignore such a right, or even to expose it to the risk of being destroyed by the hasty disposal of a summary rent suit, was a decided "invasion of the rights of property." 'As, however, it is now generally agreed that he was mistaken, as he himself afterwards admitted, with regard to the matter of fact, there is no need to dwell upon the apparent inconsistency. It is enough to assert the general principle that society, acting through the State, has an indefeasible right to regulate the mode in which the rights of property in the soil are to be exercised, and to restrict any particular exercise of such rights which can be clearly shown to be seriously injurious to the community at large. This is a truth fully recognised in Asia, obscured though it has been in Europe, and especially in England, by an exaggerated worship of individualism. There is no need to demonstrate that society would be justified in preventing a large landlord from depopulating and laying waste his estate in order to turn it into a hunting-ground; and this once admitted, any minor interference becomes a mere question of degree. The utmost that can be asserted on behalf of the right of the landlord to do what he will with his own, is the right to have his property taken off his hands by the State at a fair valuation, if he prefers that to the alternative of exercising his control over his land subject to such checks as society sees fit to impose. Even so much as this cannot be asserted on behalf of Oudh Taluqdárs, whose lands were bestowed on them after confiscation, on the condition of doing their utmost to promote their agricultural resources, and with an express reservation to Government of the power of taking any steps it might deem necessary for the protection of subordinate holders and village occupants. It surely needs no demonstration that the Taluqdárs will have no just cause to complain of a breach of faith if Government sees fit to exercise the power which it has thus expressly reserved to itself.

As to the existence of occupancy rights being "a clog on enterprise and improvement," this is a question of political economy on which there is good ground for believing Mr. Wingfield to have been wholly mistaken. Most modern economists are agreed that *petite culture*, under favourable circumstances and conditions, yields economical and, still more, moral results at least equal to those afforded by large farming. The out-turn per acre of the soil of France and Belgium is probably little, if at all, inferior to that of England, and the condition of the French and Belgian peasant proprietors and small farmers will certainly bear comparison with that of the English farm labourer. This, however, is apart from the real question at issue. The rival systems in Oudh are not *grande* and *petite culture*, for the simple reason that the former cannot be said to exist. Wealthy capitalists cultivating farms of, say, five hundred acres with their own stock are practically unknown. The nearest approach to such farms is the *sir* land of an extensive proprietor, which is not a compact plot, but consists of a number of scattered patches lying in, perhaps, twenty different villages, and certainly no better cultivated than the petty holdings which surround them. The choice for Oudh lies between *petite culture* carried on by tenants-at-will, without security of tenure, and liable to indefinite rack-renting and capricious eviction, which is the state of things at present existing; and *petite culture* carried on by tenants secured in their holdings at fixed rents, and stimulated to exertion and improvement by the certainty that no caprice or greed of an individual can ever deprive them of the fruits of their labour, which is the system here advocated. *Petite culture* by tenants-at-will has never yet succeeded in any country known to history; but when worked by peasant proprietors, or by tenants enjoying fixity of tenure, it has succeeded in, perhaps, every country where it has been tried. It is easy to understand, while differing from, those who prefer a system of large farms worked by a comparatively small number of wealthy capitalists with hired labour, to small farms worked by a large number of cultivators. But it is very hard to comprehend the mental process by which some people arrive at conclusions in favour of small holdings worked by tenants at will, as against the same small farms worked by tenants enjoying perfect security from enhancement and eviction, and only differing from peasant proprietors in their liability to pay rent. It is not too much to say that all *à priori* reasoning, all historical experience, condemn the former and uphold the latter. Large landlords who are also improving landlords are the exception and not the rule, all the world over, and this is as true in Oudh as elsewhere. Four-fifths of the sums expended by an Oudh landlord in "improving" his estate are devoted to alluring cultivators from other villages to settle in his own, or to deterring them from leaving his villages to settle elsewhere. Such real improvements as are made consist chiefly of new wells and watercourses, and far the greater part of these are the work of tenants. On the whole, Mr. Wingfield's dictum would be much nearer the truth if transposed into the assertion that the greatest clog on enterprise and improvement in Oudh is the feeling of insecurity among the actual cultivators of the soil, which is the result of the general absence, especially among the most industrious of those cultivators, of occupancy rights. For it must be remembered that the fortunate few who do at present enjoy security from enhancement, and from fear of eviction so long as they pay a fixed and generally moderate rent, are nearly all Rájpúts and Bráhmans, the most idle and least improving classes of the agricultural body; while the unprotected masses include the Kurmis, Muráos, Káchhis, and all the rest of the most industrious and hard-working castes.

Mr. Wingfield's next argument, that tenant-right was unsuited to the province owing to the deficiency of cultivators over three-fourths of its area, is one which cannot now be urged, unless it be admitted that in no country in the world is there a sufficiency of cultivators. For the population of Oudh is four hundred and seventy-six to the square mile, a higher average than is known to prevail in any other part of the globe, and in no country probably is the proportion of urban to rural population so small. The common belief in 1860 was that the people of Oudh numbered only about five millions; while the census of 1869 disclosed the startling fact that there were more than eleven millions of them. Even Mr. Wingfield contemplated the necessity of protection for cultivators arising in thirty years in three-quarters of the province, and in seven or eight years in the remaining fourth. He could scarcely have expected that the population would have more than doubled even in thirty years. Nearly twenty years have passed since he wrote, so that we are already considerably past the point as regards time in one-fourth of the province, and as regards population, which is of course the essential matter, over the whole of it, at which he contemplated the possibility of its being needful to introduce tenant right. It is now generally known that cultivators from southern Oudh will not migrate to the waste lands of the Tarai, for the simple reason that if they do they die of fever during the rains. Cultivators acclimatised to the *hawá páni* (air and water) of the trans-Ghághra districts do not suffer so much, but an emigrant from Faizábád or Baiswára would almost certainly be struck down. Therefore it is not to be expected that the pressure of population in the south and east of Oudh will lead to the waste soil of the Tarai being brought under the plough. Nor is such a result to be desired. It is only in the Tarai that good and extensive grazing grounds for cattle are still to be found, and it is to be hoped that it will be very long before its beautiful green pastures are converted—or perverted—to cultivation.

As for Mr. Wingfield's contention that no landlord would seek to dispossess a good cultivator, and should be free to get rid of a bad one, it is probable that his definition of a " good " or " bad " cultivator would not altogether coincide with that which would recommend itself to an Indian landlord. A " good " tenant in the estimation of the latter is one who is content to live on one meal a day and, in native phrase, to sell his wife and children, rather than fail to pay the highest possible rent for his holding; who submits unquestioningly to any cesses it may please his landlord to demand; and who is always willing to work for him without payment, to give evidence for him in court, and, speaking generally, to do any conceivable thing he is told. Such is undeniably the ideal of a " good " tenant cherished by five Indian landlords out of six, as it is, *mutatis mutandis*, by a large majority of landlords all the world over. Such a tenant as this, it may be admitted that no landlord would seek to dispossess; but the converse proposition can scarcely be conceded, that any landlord should be at liberty to get rid of any tenant who may fall short of this lofty ideal. It would be hard to imagine any more effective device for wholly extinguishing anything like manliness and independence in a national character already sadly deficient in those qualities, than to render all assertion of them only possible at the risk of house and field.

It only remains to be observed that "the extension of the system of granting *pattas* down to every one who holds lands of another," which Mr. Wingfield contemplated as likely to "afford ample protection to everyone," would not have afforded any protection at all beyond the term for which the leases were granted, which is the essential point; even if it had, which it has not, ever got beyond the sphere of the then Chief Commissioner's contemplation.

Mr. Wingfield's instructions that no distinction was to be made in the "record of rights" between cultivators at fixed rates and cultivators at will, were "generally approved of" by the Governor-General. The question, however, was not allowed to rest. Sir George (then Mr.) Campbell, being at the time Judicial Commissioner of Oudh, pointed out in his report on the administration of justice for 1861, that the grant of judicial powers to Taluqdárs was often equivalent to making them judges in their own causes, which, where subordinate rights came before them judicially, was not likely to conduce to equitable decisions. As an instance of the mode in which these powers were employed he cited Mahárája Mán Singh's proceedings. This Honorary Assistant Commissioner had "from the first declined civil cases as an unprofitable labour." Of nineteen persons convicted by him during one month, eleven were punished for opposition to his own revenue processes, and four, as Mr. Campbell thought, were "illegally so punished for resisting the Mahárája's own servants engaged on executive duties."

Mr. Campbell did not maintain that there existed in Oudh any class of tenants with a permanent right of occupancy at a fixed rent. Neither rents nor revenue were ever so fixed in any part of India, though the former were so far more fixed than the latter, that what was by ancient law and practice claimable from the cultivator was a fixed proportion of the produce. This principle still exists in its integrity wherever grain rents prevail; but is obscured, if not wholly lost sight of, where these have been commuted to cash. But there were, he contended, tenants who differed from tenants-at-will by holding at *regulated* rates, and he maintained that—

"The holding of the superior zamíndárs from (the native) Government was of the same nature, but less distinctly regulated. The British Government regulates its demands by fixed rates short of the utmost limit. It is then for the Government to determine by its own laws whether the margin created by this limit is to be given exclusively to the superior holder, or is to be in any degree shared by the inferior holders; and, at any rate, it does seem that to permit, under our strong rule (which destroys the right of resistance), such unlimited enhancement at the discretion of the zamíndárs as to render the ancient tenants, in practice, mere tenants-at-will, would put them in a decidedly worse position than they previously occupied. .... It is clear that as the country advances great rent questions must arise between the superior and inferior holders; and I cannot but think that there is some ground for apprehending that if, while the rights of the latter are not recorded, the former are allowed for a series of years to decide cases which affect their own interests, the inferior rights may be obliterated more quickly than under ordinary circumstances they would have been."

One may be permitted to think that Sir George was wrong in admitting that a right of occupancy should be maintained only as the privilege of a favoured few, instead of as an indefeasible right of every cultivator whomsoever, and yet feel refreshed at finding that there was in Oudh one highly placed officer who had not wholly bowed the knee to the Baal of landlordism, and the sacred right of every man to do what he would with his own, including a good deal which belonged to other people. Naturally, however, this was not how it struck Mr. Wingfield, who, on the 15th of December 1862, addressed to the Government of India an eager protest against Mr. Campbell's "unwarranted and misleading inferences on a subject not coming within his department." Mr. Wingfield's protest amounts to this, that there were cultivators with a right of occupancy, but that the right could not be made to depend on occupation for any arbitrarily assumed period, and merely "entitled the tenant to hold at market rates and be protected from wanton eviction"; and that this right, such as it was, should not be recognised at settlement, but that the rent courts should deal with each case as it arose. He was also of opinion that many evils had arisen in the N. W. Provinces from interference between landlord and tenant, of which the only one he specified was that the value of property had been impaired. Why, he asked, should rents be fixed which must tend to rise with the extension of public works, and the consequent diffusion of wealth? Under native rule, he was of opinion, "there was no limitation on the power of the landlord to raise the rent," except his own interest.

To these arguments it is perhaps a sufficient answer to observe: (1) that it is probably a less evil that land should sell for a year or two's less purchase than that the people who cultivate it should be liable to rack-renting enforced by eviction, and all the misery which that implies; (2) that if rents rise in proportion to the increase of wealth, such increase will be *concentrated*, not *diffused*; and (3) that, though it is perfectly true that under native rule there was no limit on the power of the landlord to raise the rent of a tenant, except the violent resistance of the latter, or his own pleasure or interest, yet this is a poor argument for the course which Mr. Wingfield advocated of taking away the tenant's power of violent resistance, while leaving the landlord's power unrestrained, or rather increased by legal appliances and all the processes and paraphernalia of the rent courts. Moreover, it is probable that the average market value of land is considerably higher both in the Panjáb and N.W. Provinces, where tenant right to a greater or less extent prevails, than it is in Oudh.

Mr. Wingfield's orders to settlement officers to ignore the distinction between tenants with a right of occupancy, as he himself defined it, and tenants-at-will, though sanctioned, as has been seen, by Lord Canning, were called in question by Lord Elgin, who on the 18th of May 1863 directed the Chief Commissioner to report "whether the omission of all reference to their rights (those of occupancy tenants) in the settlement records, coupled with the judicial powers conferred on Taluqdárs, will not have a tendency to obliterate them altogether, and thus to prejudice unjustly the status of the holders." This inquiry, however, so far as appears from the Blue Books, was never answered; and so the matter remained for a time, occupancy tenants being admitted to exist, with a right to hold at fair rates, which rates were to be determined by the rent courts in each case of summary suit for rent or ejectment as it came before them, but not to be recognised by settlement officers. Mr. Wingfield's views on the subject of tenant right, however, had not yet attained their full development, as will shortly be perceived.

Meanwhile let us turn to the district of Pratábgarh, which was being settled by Mr. Moss King, C.S., who put on record some remarks worth noting.

"The Taluqdárs," he writes, "intend to fight every point, and yield nothing. They have been so successful hitherto under the strict view taken of under-proprietary claims, that their ambition now soars to the annihilation of all subordinate rights. . . . . I often regret to see that claims are rejected which are brought forward by men whom common report and estimation point out as possessed of rights. No doubt in a strictly legal sense they have failed to prove their points, but the Taluqdár proves nothing either. It is the *onus probandi* on the claimant which puts him at such a disadvantage. The Taluqdár is in the saddle, and the under-proprietor has to unhorse him. This he can seldom do, and he loses all in the encounter. A few of them (the Taluqdárs) are evil disposed, some are simply apathetic and incapable, others are grasping and lavish alternately. All are more or less in the hands of agents, whose reputation is usually bad. The fact is, *they have more land than they can manage*, (the italics are Mr. King's), and they do and will manage it ill. Made masters now of villages which have often defied them, and do not acknowledge them as their true head, they will have a very difficult task to perform, and I fear will confine their exertions towards these villages to such hostility as our rule permits, rather than manage them with a liberal hand. There is no disguising the fact that a Taluqdárí settlement, such as it will be made in Oudh, will be the commencement of a new era in landed property. The effect cannot be limited to the bare right to engage for the payment of the revenue, but the Taluqdár is made actual owner of much that was debateable before. And the spirit of our instructions for settlement may be briefly described as giving the Taluqdár the benefit of all doubts which may arise in the thousand questions concerning the particular parties in whom particular rights rest. Now I suppose there is no country in the world where so much margin for doubts to work will be found as in India; and if the Taluqdár is to have the benefit of them, he will be an immense gainer. I do not think that the inner history of village tenures will be found out in this Taluqdárí settlement; it is not the interest of either party to disclose the real facts of their cases, as we find that they did in the village settlements of the North-Western Provinces. I would have the settlement officer get as near as he can to the true facts of the position of the parties; and if he cannot find any precise amount of land to which good title can be shown, but still that a title to something is made out, I would have him weigh the position mentally, and match it with under-proprietary right in so much land."

In reply to this latter proposal, the Chief Commissioner could not "consent to give authority to a settlement officer to provide an equivalent in land for rights that he cannot define"; and to the Government of India, whose attention had been attracted by Mr. King's remarks, he represented that that officer's description should not be taken as applicable to Taluqdárs in general, that the importance of "tact" had been impressed upon him, and that he, Mr. Wingfield, felt "confident that the reports from other districts for the present official year will make the Taluqdárs appear in a much more favourable light."

In such wise laboured Mr. Wingfield, perfecting his theory, not, like the National Deputies, according to Carlyle, of "irregular verbs," but of a somewhat unregulated landlordism.

With Sir John Lawrence's accession to the Viceroyalty began a new phase in the history of the Oudh land question. Hitherto Mr. Wingfield had carried out his principles with but little interference. He was now to encounter opposition of a more serious character.

The first note of the coming conflict was sounded in a letter of the 17th of February 1864 to the Chief Commissioner from Colonel H. M. Durand, afterwards Sir Henry Durand, who was then Secretary to the Government of India. "A careful perusal," the letter begins, "of the official correspondence having reference to the settlement operations in Oudh has not satisfied his Excellency that the scope of the instructions of the Secretary of State for India has been clearly comprehended, or suitable measures adopted for carrying fully into effect the orders of the Government of India." After quoting at length despatches from the Secretary of State of the 24th of April 1860, and of the 17th of August 1861, the letter continues:—"By the foregoing instructions, it was decided that, while the arrangements made in favour of the Taluqdárs by the British Government should be respected, the subordinate rights of other classes of people in the soil should be ascertained and defined. It is the opinion of the Governor-General in Council that these instructions embraced all rights whatever under those of the Taluqdár, whether those of former proprietors, or hereditary tenants holding their lands on fixed rents; or on rents more advantageous in their character than those of mere tenants-at-will; or whether they are tenants with the simple right of occupancy." In other words, the Government made, as it had an unquestioned right to do, a sacrifice of a certain portion of its own rights in favour of the Taluqdárs, but it had no right to sacrifice the welfare, or to bind itself not to remedy the sufferings, of other classes. Such an agreement, had it been entered into, which it need hardly be said was not the case, would have been no more binding than an agreement in restraint of legal proceedings. The instructions of the Chief Commissioner that no under-proprietary rights not enjoyed in 1855 were to be admitted, and of the Settlement Commissioner, Mr. Currie, that no hereditary tenant right was to be recognised, were described as "at variance with those of the Secretary of State, and contrary to sound policy." The Chief Commissioner was requested to report with all speed whether any measures had been taken for the recording of occupancy rights, and whether settlement officers had, as a fact, been directed not to make any inquiry with a view to such record. A complete series of the settlement circulars issued by the Oudh administration, and also the settlement reports of Messrs. King and Clifford (Pratábgarh and Unáo) and of Captain McAndrew (Rai Bareli) were called for.

The Oudh policy was thus put upon its defence. On the first point—the practice enjoined of ignoring all under-proprietary rights except those actually exercised in 1855—the Chief Commissioner, in his letter of the 2nd of March 1864, justified his instructions by a reference to paragraph 5 of the Government of India's letter of the 19th of October 1859, which runs as follows:—

"This being the position in which the Taluqdárs will be placed, they cannot with any show of reason complain if the Government takes effectual steps to re-establish and maintain, in subordination to them, the former rights, *as these existed in* 1855, of other persons whose connection with the soil is in many cases more intimate and more ancient than theirs."

Mr. Wingfield pleaded that this rule had been sanctioned by the Government of India when embodied in his Record of Rights circular issued on the 29th of January 1861, which had been submitted for its approval, and had acquired the force of law under the Indian Councils Act; and that "the basis on which the rule rests is that on the reoccupation of the province we adopted as the principle of our summary settlement the *status quo* at annexation."

It may be remarked that these pleas seem to overlook the fact that a right may *exist* without being actually exercised. A man forcibly dispossessed of his land, without any other title than that of the strong hand on the part of his dispossessor, has surely a *right* to recover possession of his property; and to rule, as Mr. Wingfield had ruled, that if he were not in actual occupation in 1855, though he might have been expelled in December 1854, his claims could not be recognised, is clearly not to "maintain his *rights as they existed* in 1855." For in 1855 he had a *right* to recover possession, which Mr. Wingfield's ruling wholly ignored and annihilated. This is surely to maintain the *status quo* with a difference. Under the native Government there was practically no law of limitation, and to introduce a law of limitation so stringent as to bar all rights not exercised within 13 months and 13 days prior to annexation, must be admitted to be a sufficiently violent alteration of the *status quo* of 1855.

With regard to the non-record of occupancy rights, Mr. Wingfield opined that, though the terms of the Secretary of State's despatch, No. 33 of the 24th April 1860, were "sufficiently comprehensive to embrace every form of interest in land," yet, under the circumstances, "it could hardly be doubted that mere ryots were not then under consideration."

[The exact words of the despatch referred to were as follows:—

"You were quite right in rejecting at once the proposition of the Chief Commissioner, that all under tenures should be abandoned to the mercy of the Taluqdárs, and I observe from your Lordship's more recent proceedings that the engagements into which you have entered with the Taluqdárs provide for the protection of the under-proprietors, and that where a regular settlement is made, in all cases where there is an intermediate interest in the soil between the Taluqdár and the Ryot, the amount or proportion payable by the intermediate or subordinate holder to the Taluqdár will be fixed and recorded after careful and detailed survey."]

The Chief Commissioner's letter concluded by promising a further report on tenant-right, and by a deprecation of the opinions unfavourable to Taluqdárs expressed in Mr. King's report on settlement operations in Pratábgarh in 1862-63, which had been called for by the Government of India.

The further report thus promised was submitted on the 26th March 1864. And now, for the first time, the Chief

Commissioner announced his conviction that his previous admission of a "modified" right of occupancy was a mistake, and that such a right on the part of "non-proprietary cultivators had never in theory or practice existed in Oudh."

Not being careful to dispute the correctness of Mr. Wingfield's conclusion as to the matter of fact, one need not cavil at the suddenness of his conversion to the doctrine here propounded. Rights of occupancy among tenants pure and simple, *i.e.* rights capable of being legally enforced, or which were recognised by universal custom, may have existed in times beyond the reach of our investigations; but if so, they had certainly been effectually stamped out by years of lawlessness. It is probable that the genuine Hindú theory of tenure contemplates only the Rája on the one hand, and a body of hereditary cultivators on the other, removable, indeed, by him, but only in his capacity as head of the State, not as landlord, and paying him a fixed share of the produce as revenue, not as rent. Such, there is reason to believe, was the Hindú ideal, the first great departure from which, the first grand heresy, was the absorption by individuals, in the shape of rent, of a part of the dues of the State; and the second, the pretension to collect rent at rates in excess of the revenue rates. To say that this ideal rarely, if ever, practically existed, is only to say that it resembled the large majority of other ideals, in seldom or never being realised. The power of evicting a tenant, like the power of killing him, was one of which the exercise lay in the discretion of the King, and against the mode in which he chose to exert one power or the other there was no appeal. When the Hindú kingdoms were broken up into petty chiefships, a process which seems to have occurred every two hundred and fifty years or so, the powers of the King were assumed by petty Rájas, and even by small zamíndárs. It would, of course, be an exaggeration to say that, even in the later days of the Nawábí, a Taluqdár had as much theoretic right to kill a cultivator as to eject him; but it is certain that there was about as much, or as little, likelihood of his being brought to account for the one act as for the other. A low-caste, uninfluential cultivator had *no* rights which he could enforce against the owner of the soil he tilled. He was entitled by the custom of all tolerably good landlords to retain his holding as long as he would agree to pay something not much less than the highest rent for it that anyone would *bonâ fide* offer. But even this right he could not enforce; and no one with any adequate conception of the state of society then prevailing in Oudh would ever have thought it likely that he should be able to enforce it. As already remarked, it is not among the weakest and most down-trodden class of an anarchical society that a beneficial fixity of tenure is likely to be found. As to the matter of fact, then, one may quite agree with Mr. Wingfield, while differing from him in maintaining that the previous absence of tenant right was no reason against conferring it then, and is not a reason now.

Mr. Tucker, Commissioner of Baiswára, had pleaded the cause of the high-caste peasantry of his division, the Bráhmans and Rájpúts who had held their fields for generations at low rents, who were forbidden by caste prejudices from driving the plough, and who had suffered much from loss of military service. But the Chief Commissioner could not for a moment sanction the proposal to limit the demand of the Taluqdár on such persons, and thought "that we should rather look forward with satisfaction to the arrival of the time when caste will confer no advantages." A most unimpeachable aspiration, no doubt, but a somewhat fragile basis of expectation for a thirty years' settlement. Mr. Wingfield could not admit that "caste prejudices give a claim to privileges which must be denied to the humbler and more industrious races." Quite so; security from rack-renting and capricious eviction should not be a *privilege* of any caste, but should be regarded as what it is, an essential condition of healthy agriculture, and conferred upon every cultivator whomsoever. Any rights arising from high-caste, relationship to the landlord, or length of occupancy, should find expression in a lower rent-rate.

Even improvements of the soil effected by the tenant could not, according to Mr. Wingfield, confer any right of permanent occupancy, "except on conditions agreed to by the landlord"; for "to hold otherwise might have the effect of compelling landlords to interdict all improvements." Unless the object in view was effectually to prevent all improvement of the soil, this really seems a sufficient *reductio ad absurdum* of the tenancy-at-will system.* The argument might have some force in a country like England, where landlordism has established itself with a rigidity and a weight of ancient custom which few seem prepared to dispute. But in Oudh, though of course it was the cue of the Taluqdárs and their advocates to maintain the sacred duty of upholding the "ancient, indigenous, and cherished system" in its integrity, and to insist that to alter one jot or one tittle thereof—except, indeed, in favour of the Taluqdárs—would have been to shake society to its depths, yet there can be no real doubt that the "system" was in a very fluid condition indeed for several years after reoccupation, and quite capable of being considerably modified in favour of the cultivator without the slightest shock to the sense of justice of any landlord. Mr. Wingfield, no doubt, had done all that one man could do to impress them with a sense of their own importance, and of the inviolability of their right to rack-rent and evict at pleasure, and by 1864 these great moral lessons had to a considerable extent been brought home to them. But these warnings of the importance of conciliating the prejudices of landlordism would perhaps have been more impressive if urged by an authority who had done somewhat less to foster those prejudices into a condition of morbid rampancy than Mr. Wingfield.

The Chief Commissioner's next argument was that as no right of occupancy on the part of non-proprietary cultivators could be proved, to confer such rights would be to rob those landlords whose *sannads* only provide for the maintenance of rights previously enjoyed. That the conditions on which the *sannads* were conferred were exceedingly meagre and unsatisfactory, is indeed true, and for this Mr. Wingfield himself was,

---

* It is notorious that, in some parts of Oudh, landlords have been known to bring suits to prevent tenants from building wells, for fear they should thus acquire a temporary right of occupancy and become too independent.

as we have seen, responsible. But these oft-quoted *sannads* cannot abrogate the right, or rather the duty, of the State to impose such conditions on the enjoyment of property in the land which it allows individuals to hold, as it may from time to time deem necessary for the common welfare. Quite apart, moreover, from general considerations of this kind is the particular fact that power to take such steps as it might consider needful for protection of village occupants was expressly reserved to itself by Government at the time it conferred the *sannads*. If it be maintained, as it has been maintained, that the term "village occupants" was not intended to include all who occupy, *i.e.* live in, a village, this can only have been the case because Lord Canning, when he used the phrase, believed, as a matter of course, that occupancy rights existed and would be carefully protected, as had been done, though on an insufficient scale, in the N. W. Provinces.

That rights of occupancy had been recorded at the settlement of the N. W. Provinces in 1833, was due, Mr. Wingfield thought, to a reaction against the principles of the permanent settlement in Bengal, " by which it was supposed " —a mere supposition of course—" that the interests of the peasantry had been unduly neglected"; while in the Panjáb, " the right of hereditary occupancy was entirely created by our Government on arbitrary and varying rules," but—though this he forgot to add—with most admirable results. But, even on the supposition that rights of occupancy did exist, Mr. Wingfield could not see that they would be of any use to the holders, as they only meant, under the High Court ruling in the Hill's case, the right to hold at the market rent, "and no landlord wants to get rid of a tenant who will pay the market rate for the land." He must surely have been aware that it is only a very exceptional landlord who does not do all he can to get rid of a tenant who has had the temerity to complain of ill-treatment on his part, or given evidence against him, or refused to give evidence for him, or thwarted him in any way whatsoever.

After repeating his favourite comparison between the right of the landlord to get the utmost he can for his land, with the right of the shopkeeper to sell his goods at the highest obtainable price, Mr. Wingfield proceeded to denounce the claim of "the lowest form of agricultural interest" to protection as "opposed to modern principles." "Every attempt to legalise it under the guise of tenant right in Ireland has been defeated in Parliament, and the idea of limiting the power of the landlord as to the rent he may put on his land, or the choice of a tenant, has been denounced as communistic by an eminent living statesman." The argument from Irish precedents has been sufficiently refuted by recent history. The "communistic idea" has been at last introduced into Ireland with excellent results, the chief complaint now heard being that it has not been carried far enough. "The supposition that raising the rent lessens the peasant's means of subsistence," Mr. Wingfield considered "erroneous; any measure that would keep down rents is injurious to the interests of all classes, and of none more than the cultivators themselves, to whom the stimulus to exertion and improvement would be wanting." This amounts to saying that, if the yearly produce of a farm be 200 maunds, and the rent 75 maunds, the peasant's means of subsistence will not be diminished from 125 to 100 maunds, if 100 instead of 75 maunds be taken as rent. As for stimulus, what stimulus can a cultivator have to increase his out-turn if in constant danger of having the increment—not, be it observed, an "unearned increment"—taken from him in the form of enhanced rent. Mr. Wingfield's faith in the efficacy of rack-renting to foster industry and improvement is really a curious psychological phenomenon. His liberalism and devotion to "modern ideas" remind one of Lord St. Aldegonde. He seems to be always murmuring to himself as he writes, "As if a fellow could have too much land, you know!"

The conclusion at which he arrived was that the rent courts should take no cognizance of any suit by a tenant against a landlord which was not based upon a breach of contract by the latter, and that the Oudh peasantry should be taught to "seek the wide field of industry open to them." Where that field was, however, he omitted to specify. Probably he was thinking of the fever-stricken jungles of the Tarai.

This reply of the Chief Commissioner, with a memorandum by Mr. C. Currie, Settlement Commissioner, and letters from fifteen district and settlement officers, were submitted to the Government of India on the 26th of March 1864. These papers contain the Oudh Administration's defence of its policy. The views of Mr. Wingfield himself, as developed up to date, have been already analysed. The gist of the opinions given by other officers may be briefly stated, dividing them into *cons* and *pros*.

The *cons* amounted to this: that there was no class of non-proprietary cultivators possessed of a right which they could enforce against their landlord to resist eviction; that the *Ashráf* or high-caste tenantry—(with whom, under the name of "Shatrafs," an ingenious combination, apparently, of *Chhatri* and *Ashráf*, Mr. Caird has made the readers of the "Nineteenth Century" familiar)—rendered suit and service to their lord, in return for which they held lands at low or nominal rents; that, when not cultivating with their own hands, these were "idle middlemen," and not fit objects of compassion; that the right of occupancy at the market or rack-rent was a mere shadow, not a substance, and that a right of occupancy at any more favourable rate could not be recognised without injustice to the landlord.

The *pros* may be summed up thus: that the custom of the country was opposed to the ejectment of hereditary cultivators except for non-payment of a fair rent; that the idea of tenant-right, *as a legal and indefeasible claim*, was totally new to the province; that cultivators, however, who had constructed wells, tanks, embankments, &c., were allowed to hold on favourable terms *as long as the improvement lasted;* that though the same families had held the same land for generations, it "had never occurred either to the proprietor or to the tenant to speculate on the exact nature of the right enjoyed by the latter"; that complaints had been made by cultivators of ejectment from fields which they had occupied for centuries; that the general *consensus* of opinion that a *pahikasht* (or non-resident) cultivator had no right to retain his lands, pointed to a distinction between his *status* and that of the resident (or *chapparband*) cultivator, implying a *quasi* right of occupancy on the part of the latter; that, though public opinion was against the ejectment of old cultivators, it would not, in the absence of a positive enactment, suffice to restrain large landholders from increasing their incomes by this means; and that if eviction of high-caste cultivators or enhancement of their rent were allowed, crime would seriously increase, and a general sense of injustice prevail.

One officer alone, Dr. Wilton Oldham, a North-West Provinces civilian, who was then officiating as Deputy Commissioner of Sultánpur, broadly affirmed that rights of occupancy existed which should be recognised and recorded. His letter to that effect, dated the 18th of September 1863, seems to have been sent up to the Supreme Government, but Mr. Wingfield, in his summary of the opinions of officers, appears to have overlooked it. The following extract from it is sufficiently to the purpose to be quoted here:—

"It appears to me that a right of occupancy, where it exists, is a lower kind of property, and that the dictum of Savigny, that all proprietary right is based on 'adverse possession ripened by prescription,' applies most completely to this lower form of property. When, therefore, a cultivator has cultivated fields at rents lower than was usual in the neighbourhood for land of the same kind, as it was obviously the interest of the zamíndár to oust him, unless the contrary be proved, his possession may be presumed to have been 'adverse possession.' .... When this possession has continued for a long time, it may justly be considered to have become ripened by prescription, and a right of occupancy has arisen. .... If it be said that custom and respect for public opinion deterred zamíndárs from raising the rent of certain cultivators to a rack-rent, or ejecting them, then this is a proof that the right had not merely begun to form, but was actually in existence and recognised."

Readers must judge of these arguments for themselves. But it may be here observed:—(1) That when, under our stable rule, the high-caste tenant ceased to render suit and service, the lord also ceased to render the correlative of that suit and service, viz. protection, and it by no means follows that holdings at a low rent should be liable to resumption merely because the holders formerly rendered suit and service and now render none ; (2) that if the idea of absolute tenant-right was totally new to the people of Oudh, the idea of absolute proprietorship of the soil *by an individual* was almost equally novel ; (3) that when a fluid state of society is being deliberately and consciously crystallised, which was the process going on in Oudh for several years after reoccupation, beneficial customs, such as that which protected cultivators on all decently managed estates from eviction and rack-renting, should be consolidated into law, and the practice of good landlords made binding upon all.

In April 1864 Mr. Wingfield met Sir John Lawrence and Mr. H. S. Maine, then legal Member of Council, at Cawnpore, and the differences of opinion which prevailed between the Governor-General and the Chief Commissioner were discussed at length. The points in issue between them were mainly two, viz. :—

(1.) Should the period of limitation allowed for the assertion of under-proprietary claims be extended for twelve or twenty years backwards from 1855, or should it, as was then the rule, be reckoned from 1855 only ?

Sir John Lawrence maintained the former, Mr. Wingfield the latter, alternative.

(2.) Should the question of tenant-right be gone into by settlement officers, and the rents of all tenants who were found to possess a right of occupancy be judicially determined and recorded ?

Sir John Lawrence answered, yes ; Mr. Wingfield, no.

The Governor-General offered to leave the supervision of the settlement in the Chief Commissioner's hands, on condition of his agreeing to accept and carry out the principles which he had hitherto resisted ; otherwise he proposed to appoint a Settlement Commissioner to relieve him of the financial branch of the administration.

Mr. Wingfield asked for time to consult some of the leading Taluqdárs, and to consider " whether he could conscientiously give the necessary assurance," and, on the 15th of May, wrote to Sir John Lawrence to the effect that he himself and the leading Taluqdárs whom he had consulted were ready to agree to the extension of limitation for under-proprietary claims to twelve years computed from the date of the summary settlement of 1858–59, on condition that "where villages have been annexed to the taluqa within twelve years, the persons who were in full proprietary possession will not be entitled to recover the equivalent of their former rights (viz. a sub-settlement at the Government demand *plus* 5 per cent. as the due of the Taluqdár), but only to the most favourable terms they enjoyed in any one year since the incorporation of their lands with the taluqa."

Thus, (the example is not Mr. Wingfield's), if a zamíndár had been in full proprietary possession of a village up to 1850, and in that year had been forcibly dispossessed by a Taluqdár, who left him, say, five acres of land rent-free, and nothing else, for the following six years, those five acres rent-free would be all that he could be decreed by our settlement courts.

To this concession, thus guarded, he had no doubt that the Taluqdárs, as a body, would assent, and so far he was ready to conform to the Governor-General's views. But on the second point—"the record of any non-proprietary cultivators as possessed of a right of occupancy, and the limitation of the rent to be demanded from them during the term of settlement"—Mr. Wingfield was satisfied that the Taluqdárs would never give way, and he himself held that they would be justified in their refusal. He repeated his conviction that non-proprietary cultivators had no right of occupancy, and that to recognise such rights would be a breach of the *sannads* (for the terms of which Mr. Wingfield was himself responsible), and fatal to the progress and prosperity of the province. He held it to be "impossible to deduce from any length of permissive occupancy"—a somewhat question-begging description of adverse possession—"the conclusion that it establishes an interest adverse to that of the landlord"; predicted that the Taluqdárs would fight every case to the uttermost; urged that the Government of India should hear what a deputation of Taluqdárs had to advance before any change was resolved upon; and avowed that by carrying out any policy which recognised a right of occupancy, he would be doing violence to his own convictions.

On the 28th of May Sir John Lawrence replied to this letter, thanking Mr. Wingfield for writing so frankly, expressing approval of the Taluqdárs' concession on the first point in issue, and accepting the proviso with which they had coupled it, though of opinion that the period of limitation should count from 1856; but, for the rest, denying Mr. Wingfield's facts and repudiating his inferences as regards tenant right. "If this," he wrote, " were a mere question in which the interests of a few individuals were concerned, I might hesitate in maintaining my own views. But it is really a question in which are involved the interests of a great body of men, many of whom, I have no doubt, are the descendants of the old proprietary communities of the province of Oudh, whose rights are now enjoyed by the Taluqdárs of the present day. When these Taluqdárs talk of their rights, they should recollect that the chief value of these rights, viz. their permanence and security, is derived only from the British Government, and that under native rule they were always liable to lose their possessions in the same fashion as they won them. The value which British rule has given to their property is enormous. . . . . I do not myself believe that the admission of the ancient tenants of land, the old hereditary cultivators, and the broken-down, ill-treated descendants of former proprietors to the right of occupancy, and to fair and equitable rates, will infringe in the least degree the policy of Lord Canning." Sir John did not wish to introduce Act X. of 1859 (the N. W. Provinces Rent Act) into Oudh, but thought that if the Taluqdárs would not consent to some fair compromise, there would be nothing else for it. As for the proposal that a deputation of Taluqdárs should wait on the Government, he saw no good likely to arise from such a step, and thought that the Chief Commissioner could continue to urge all that was to be said on their behalf.

Mr. Wingfield wrote again on the 6th of June, to say that the Taluqdárs would not object to reckoning the period of limitation from 1856, but, *au reste*, reiterating his objections to tenant-right. Finally, weighing, with perfect candour and disinterestedness, the arguments for and against his retaining the office of Chief Commissioner, he left the issue in the hands of the Governor-General.

While this demi-official controversy was going on, and after considering the voluminous defence of the Oudh policy which has been summarised a few pages back, Sir John Lawrence took refuge in the usual resource of an Englishman in difficulties—he went to his lawyer. On the 21st of May 1864, extracts from the correspondence between Lord Canning and Mr. Wingfield regarding the wording of the Taluqdárs' *sannads*, from Mr. Wingfield's "record of rights circular," and from despatches of the Secretary of State for India issued in 1860 and 1861, were submitted, with a letter signed by Colonel Durand, but really drafted by Mr. Maine, to the Advocate-General, Mr. Cowie, whose opinion was requested as to (1) "the effect of Section 25 of the Indian Councils Act, 1861, on the statements, orders, and directions contained in the documents presently cited"; and (2) "whether persons claiming to be under-proprietors in Oudh, that is, persons claiming an interest in the soil intermediate between the Taluqdár and the ryot, are restricted to establishing such rights as were actually enjoyed in possession at the moment of annexation, or, what is the same thing, whether all rights existing previous to annexation, but not actually enjoyed when Oudh was annexed, are destroyed, unless revived by legislation."

The second of these queries, it will be perceived, was only a more specific form of the first.

The Advocate-General took nearly four months to consider the questions thus raised, and it was not until the 13th of September that he delivered himself of the opinion that Section 25 of the Indian Councils Act "must be read as applicable to such rules and regulations as were in the nature of laws affecting rights or imposing punishments, and that any rules or orders which in their nature were only rules for the guidance of a department or for the action of the executive, and which could be, and always have been, issued by the Government in its executive capacity merely, do not come within the section." From this he deduced the conclusion that of the documents relating to Taluqdárs and under-proprietary rights which had been submitted to him, the only one that came within the scope of Section 25, and received from it the force of law, was the declaratory order of the Government of India, dated the 10th of October 1859, which laid down that every Taluqdár who was admitted to engage for the revenue at the second summary settlement, " thereby acquired a permanent, hereditary, and transferable proprietary right in the taluqa for which he has engaged, including the perpetual privilege of engaging with the Government for the revenue of the taluqa. This right is, however, conceded subject to any measure which the Government may think proper to take for the purpose of protecting the inferior zamíndárs and village occupants from extortion, and upholding their rights in the soil in subordination to the Taluqdárs." This declaration and proviso (which have been appended as Schedule I. to Act I. of 1869), were given the force of law by Section 25; but all the other documents in question, and more particularly "the so-called record of rights," even apart from the absence of the Secretary of State's sanction, had not, in the Advocate-General's opinion, any such validity. " Practically," he concludes, " it appears to me that the reservation introduced in the Governor-General's order declaring the proprietary rights of the Taluqdárs is so wide that it leaves the rights of the under-proprietors where they were. And those rights remain as they were prior to annexation, and will so remain (subject, of course, to the effect of the Limitation Act), except in so far as they may be affected by express legislation."

Before being fortified by this legal opinion, Sir John Lawrence had indited a minute, dated the 20th of June 1864, in which he declared that " ever since the reoccupation of Oudh, it has been the uniform aim of the Chief Commissioner to sweep away, as far as practicable, all subordinate rights and interests in the soil in all the Taluqdári villages of the province . . . . and when he could not accomplish this, to restrict them to the narrowest limits. The struggle between the Taluqdárs and the village proprietary bodies, which had commenced on the annexation of Oudh, ended in 1859 in the almost complete success of the former class. Out of 23,522 (query: 23543?) villages " included in taluqas in 1856, "the Taluqdárs succeeded, after a mere nominal inquiry, in establishing their claims to 22,637. The mode in which this inquiry was made was criticised by the Secretary of State, but it was nevertheless maintained. . . . . We have the example in Bengal before us (a very similar instance to that of Oudh in more than one respect), in which, when enormous interests were conferred on one class, the interests, and indeed the rights, of another class were to a great extent sacrificed. The condition of the weak and friendless village proprietors and hereditary cultivators of the soil was undoubtedly very wretched under the late rule in Oudh; but their position will become gradually still worse under the British Government, if the principles and policy advocated by the Chief Commissioner are allowed to become the rule and law of the country. In the days of the Nawáb, the chiefs had some interest in protecting the yeomen of the country, and in conciliating their kinsmen and tenantry; but under a strong Government like ours, such friends and followers are not necessary, and will therefore be treated accordingly. Such considerations are of peculiar importance in India, where the cultivators are greatly attached to the soil, and where the masses have very limited and uncertain means of employment except in agriculture. In 1859 the Chief Commissioner of Oudh proposed that the proprietary right in the land should for ever be considered to rest absolutely in the parties with whom the summary settlement had been made—a practice, I may say, unknown in India. Now, such a decision would have given the *coup de grace* to every village proprietor and hereditary cultivator in all the taluqas of the country." Here Sir John Lawrence would seem to have somewhat overstated what Mr. Wingfield actually did propose, but he goes on to say that though the proposition was disallowed by the Government of India, investigation into subordinate claims was "limited to rights which existed" —it would have been more strictly correct to say, which were enjoyed—"in 1855, whereas it ought to have extended back for full twenty years, for it was during that period that the greatest misrule had prevailed."

Mr. Wingfield's instructions to settlement officers, prohibiting the record of occupancy rights, were, in Sir John Lawrence's opinion, "unsound and impolitic, as well as unjust. He denies that the cultivator needs any protection, or has ever stirred in his own interests. He thinks that it is no evil men being forced to abandon their own homesteads; and that the system of granting leases will form a complete protection to the ryot, totally forgetting that everything will depend on the terms of each lease." There was no valid ground for Mr. Wingfield's distinction between Taluqdárí and zamíndárí estates, which barred all claims to subordinate rights in the former which were not actually enjoyed in 1855, while in the latter it allowed a twelve years' period of limitation. The Chief Commissioner's suggestion that a three years' period should be prescribed for suits to contest decisions of settlement officers was described as "an excellent plan when the investigations and decisions have been made on proper principles, but out of the question in regard to the present settlements." Sir John then alluded to the reference which he had made to the Advocate-General as to the legal validity or otherwise of the "Record of Rights Circular." If Mr. Cowie decided in favour of its validity, a bill should be brought before the Legislature for its modification. "In the meantime the system of inquiry into and record of the landed tenures of Oudh should be altered as early as possible, for much time has already been lost." After referring to the conference in April at Cawnpore between Mr. Wingfield and himself, he proceeded to ask his colleagues what was in their opinion the proper course to pursue. Hitherto, he declared, no real inquiry into tenant-right had been made or permitted. "The Chief Commissioner assumes that which should be the subject of examination. . . . . All the orders which have emanated from the Government of India connected with the points now under consideration, from the time that Mr. Wingfield has been Chief Commissioner until my arrival in India, have been founded solely, so far as I can judge, on the reports of that gentleman. No information from any of the Commissioners or Deputy Commissioners has been forthcoming until especially sent for in February last. The instructions of the Secretary of State for India practically remained a dead letter." Mr. Wingfield in his capacity as Financial Commissioner, being the ultimate appellate judge in all suits relating to land, able to lay down what claims should be heard, and the mode in which they should be investigated, and his views, moreover, being shared by the Settlement Commissioner, Mr. Currie, " it may be judged what chance any man in Oudh has to substantiate a claim as an hereditary tenant in the land."

To remedy this state of things, and to give every man a fair chance of being heard, Sir John proposed that the original arrangement should be reverted to, and Mr. Wingfield be relieved of the duties of Financial Commissioner, which should be entrusted to a separate officer. The four Commissionerships of Oudh had been reduced to three when, two years previously, the post of Settlement Commissioner had been created and conferred on Mr. Currie. Sir John suggested that the fourth division, that of Rai Bareli, should be re-formed, and Mr. Currie put in charge of it, the office of Settlement Commissioner being abolished. These changes seemed to the Governor-General urgently required in Oudh, nd he accordingly proposed them for the consideration of his colleagues.

The first Member of Council who took up his parable in reply to Sir John's invitation was Mr. H. S. Maine, whose cultivated lucidity of style is a pleasant change from the comparatively headlong and unfinished writing through which we have been wading so long. " No quality," he declares, " is rarer or more useful in India than a healthy scepticism," and he laments that the virgin field for inquiry into the question of hereditary occupancy which Oudh had presented after the Mutiny had not been explored in an impartial spirit. The results of a dispassionate investigation " would have been of the utmost political and social, and even of the utmost historical value." He himself believed that " the inquiry would have ended in establishing the existence of hereditary tenants; but it was possible that the evidence to the contrary might have been so strong as to render doubtful their existence in any part of India. Or, again, the Oudh tenures might have been shown to be *sui generis*, or, lastly, it was not improbable that beneficial rights of occupancy might, through long years of anarchy, have been reduced to the level, as regards liability to rent, of tenancies at will."

But Mr. Wingfield had fallen into the same mistake with which he had reproached his opponents. He had assumed his own conclusions, and simply opposed those assumptions to the contrary ones. A perusal, while at Simla in 1863, of the demi-official correspondence between the Chief Commissioner and the Foreign Secretary had strongly impressed Mr. Maine with the "persistency of the Oudh officials in making assumptions instead of stating facts. It seems impossible to get them to answer *aye* or *no* to plain questions, and every inquiry about the hereditary tenants produced either observations on the fallacious basis of the North-Western system, or an assertion that the recognition of beneficial occupancy was an invasion of the rights of property." The same peculiarity struck Lord Elgin also. Had Mr. Wingfield's assertions as to the non-existence of hereditary tenants been made before the issue of his "so-called record of rights" circular, they would have been important as at least indicating the "impressions of an acute observer." But in the earlier documents relating to the controversy, the question had never been discussed as one of fact, and Mr. Wingfield's later declarations, after his policy had been long settled and partially carried out, could only be regarded "as another illustration of the ductility of men's impressions of fact under the influence of a foregone conclusion. All evidence of the subordinate Oudh officials unfavourable to the hereditary cultivators which is subsequent to the date of the record of rights, we are justified, I think, in regarding as vitiated in its source." The hands of these, the only persons who could satisfactorily have investigated the question, had been tied. Mr. Wingfield himself did not seem to have had much opportunity of examining it at first hand; while "the very character of his eminent services in managing, educating, and training to public functions and public spirit the new aristocracy created by Lord Canning, would seem to show that his intercourse has chiefly been with persons who, even if they had not had a strong interest in denying the existence of these tenures, have probably very imperfect ideas as to the difference which in a settled society is recognised between might and right." No one had such opportunities for getting at the real state of facts as settlement officers, but their " priceless testimony " seemed to have been " sacrificed in Oudh .... vitiated by the strong language of the record of rights ; and yet there is just enough of it to lead us to suspect what result could have been arrived at if the inquiry had been unfettered."

The course which Mr. Maine recommended was to join issue with the Taluqdárs on the question which they had raised as to the existence or non-existence of beneficial rights of occupancy, and to institute a full and free inquiry. He also advised the appointment of a Financial Commissioner, but deprecated the introduction into Oudh of Act X. of 1859, inasmuch as it contained provisions for the manufacture of hereditary cultivators, whether previously existing or not, and this, he considered, would be an act of "injustice to the Taluqdárs, if not a breach of faith."

And here it may readily be admitted that, in the then state of the question, and on the only grounds that were then recognised, which were grounds of right on the part of the cultivator, not of economical necessity, and consequent duty on the part of the State, the act would have been a breach of faith. Landlords, moreover, could have easily defeated that part of the Act which makes a right of occupancy result from twelve years' possession by ejecting wholesale all ordinary tenants of less than twelve years' standing. On these grounds, as well as on the principle that partial reforms are the greatest enemies of complete ones, and that it was necessary that the state of the Oudh cultivator should become worse before it can be made better, there is room for satisfaction that this opinion prevailed, and that Act X. of 1859 was not introduced into Oudh.

Turning to the question of extending the period of limitation for claims to subordinate rights in taluqas, Mr. Maine held that the arguments against extension derived from the *sannads* and Lord Canning's declaration were of no weight. For the *sannads* did not limit the recognition of under-proprietary rights to rights commencing in any particular year; and the Secretary of State had distinctly withheld his approval from Lord Canning's declaration. The Taluqdárs, moreover, had assented to the extension, or were ready so to assent.

But apart from this, Mr. Maine held that there are—

"Grave objections to admitting that any course of policy adopted or announced by the Government of India carries with it a pledge or promise to any class affected by it. It is too much the habit in India to complain of the abandonment by the Government of any particular principle or line of action, as if it involved a breach of faith to those who had profited by it. In old times, when the British Government had just succeeded to a despotic power which dealt with its subjects as if it were a single person, and did not affect to regard any interest but its own, it was not unnatural to look upon our declarations of policy as amounting to a personal engagement; but such a view of our position is irreconcilable with the functions of a government which now pretends to exist for the advantage of its subjects, which is bound to carry out every measure which is likely to contribute to their happiness and prosperity, and which is not ashamed to admit that it learns by experience. In point of fact, the very existence of a regular legislature in India is inconsistent with the notion of our faith being pledged to the policy of any particular year or period. The indistinguishable blending of executive and legislative functions in the Government of India at the time when the permanent settlement of Bengal was effected does seem to me to furnish some ground for looking on that measure in something like the light of a compact, but I think it would be preposterous now-a-days to put the same construction on the policy pursued in 1858 and 1859 towards the Taluqdárs of Oudh."

These are words so weighty, both in themselves, and as coming from an authority of such calibre as Mr. Maine, that no apology is needed for quoting them at length. They were intended, however, only to apply to the question of good faith. As a matter of policy, Mr. Maine fully recognised the inexpediency of "abrupt recoils from one line of action to another." He thought that in the present instance there was a "justification for interference in what he would not assume, but could not help suspecting to have been a cruel injustice"; but one ground on which he preferred his own recommendations to the Governor-General's proposal certainly was that they did not involve what was, on the face of it, so open a departure from the policy of Lord Canning.

In Mr. Maine's conclusions and advice as to the steps that should be adopted, Mr. Taylor and Sir Charles Trevelyan concurred. The latter argued that by the common law of India the land belonged to peasant proprietors, generally associated in village communities, and bound to pay to the ruler a portion of the produce generally known as *Hákimí Hissa*, or the share of the sovereign ; and that all that the State could bestow on an intermediate holder, Jághírdár, Taluqdár, or whatever other name he might be known by, was its own (or, as is more usual, a portion of its own) share of the produce.

It would, perhaps, be more strictly correct to say that both in Hindú and Mughal theory the ownership of the soil vested jointly in the King (or Emperor) and the cultivator, the former being the sleeping, and the latter the active, partner in the business of agriculture.

Sir Charles Trevelyan further maintained that the clause in the *sannads* reserving subordinate rights wholly obviated the possibility of any breach of faith being involved in the proposed measures. A similar clause had been one of the conditions attached to the permanent settlement of Bengal; but, except in Banáras, the failure to carry it out by an inquiry into and record of subordinate tenures had led to "the greatest of the evils which had afflicted that province during the best part of a century, and one of the greatest causes of weakness and discredit to the British Administration." A similar omission would, he feared, lead to as bad or worse results in Oudh.

So far, opinion in Council was dead against Mr. Wingfield's policy. But in Mr. Grey he found a staunch defender. As the Taluqdárs were willing to give way on the question of limitation for under-proprietary claims, he would only remark on that point that he thought the Governor-General was unjust to Mr. Wingfield in saying that he had steadily endeavoured to sweep away all subordinate rights. In Mr. Grey's opinion, the Chief Commissioner had been loyally endeavouring, as shown by his instructions to settlement officers, to carry out the orders of Lord Canning. With regard to occupancy rights, Mr. Grey despaired of convincing anyone who had remained impervious to the arguments of Messrs. Wingfield and Currie, and would therefore confine himself to a statement of the case as it actually stood, merely remarking that he entirely concurred with the views of those gentlemen. The conclusion which he drew from the reports of the Oudh officers was that Mr. Campbell's " general theory " of the existence of rights of beneficial occupancy was wholly baseless; and, believing that the object now in view was really the setting up of this general theory, and not an inquiry into " individual rights susceptible of being substantiated by tangible proof," he strongly deprecated a reversal of " the deliberate action of a former Government." He could not admit that the question was an open one on which the Government of the day was free to act as it thought best. The *sannads* did not expressly reserve the right of old cultivators to occupy their lands on favourable terms. Lord Canning's letter, No. 23 of the 19th of October 1859, explained the reservation clause to mean that " whenever it is found that zamíndárs or other persons have held an interest in the soil intermediate between the ryot and the Taluqdár, the amount payable by the intermediate holder to the Taluqdár will be fixed and recorded." The tenor of the correspondence relating to the *sannads*, between Lord Canning and Mr. Wingfield, clearly indicated that it was only under-proprietary rights, and not occupancy rights of cultivators, that were intended to be reserved. The Secretary of State's despatches of the 24th of April 1860 and the 17th of August 1861 did not allude to occupancy ryots, and only withheld approval of limiting recognition of under-proprietary claims to such as had been actually enjoyed in 1855. It was true that when Mr. Campbell's plea for the record of what he called rights of occupancy at "regulated rates" attracted the attention of the Secretary of State, the latter, in his despatch of the 9th of June 1863, certainly wrote of these occupancy rights as if they were of the same class as the rights referred to in his despatch dated the 17th of August 1861. But Mr. Grey thought that it was impossible so to interpret that despatch. The actual position of the question appeared to him to be that :—

(1.) Mr. Wingfield had reported that no mere cultivators in Oudh, whether of high caste or low, had any right to hold land at less than market rates ;

(2.) Lord Canning had accepted this report, and authorised its being acted on ;

(3.) Therefore the Taluqdár's *sannads* did not contain, and were not meant to contain, any reference to such rights ;

(4.) This form of *sannad* was approved by the Secretary of State ;

(5.) It was now proposed, in consequence of Mr. Campbell's report of the existence of "regulated rates," to "re-open and investigate afresh the question as to the general rights of the cultivators in Oudh."

Mr. Grey himself had no doubt that, whatever might have been the case in more ancient days, no such rights existed under the native rule which we superseded, and that any recognition of them now would be an act of injustice to the Taluqdárs.

Sir John Lawrence wrote a second minute in reply to that of Mr. Grey. The answer is most crushingly complete, and, from the style in which it is couched, it is difficult not to suspect that Mr. Maine had some share in its composition. It points out that Mr. Wingfield's whole course of action indisputably showed that he desired, no doubt with perfect sincerity and conviction of purpose, to sweep away, so far as he possibly could, all subordinate rights in taluqas. The offer of the Governor-General to leave under his control the execution of the measures now proposed was ample evidence of his trust in Mr. Wingfield's "official uprightness and capacity"; while the latter's refusal to accept the task under the conditions imposed by the Governor-General was "additional proof, were any needed, of the tenor of his conduct and of the bias of his mind." The sanction by Lord Canning, on the 8th of January 1861, of Mr. Wingfield's instructions of September 1860, directing settlement officers to record no distinction between tenants with a right of occupancy and tenants-at-will, could afford no possible ground for any inferences as to the original intention with which the form of *sannad* framed by Mr. Wingfield was approved of by Lord Canning in his letter of the 19th of October 1859. Mr. Grey, in fact, had transposed the order of time in which the proceedings took place. The Chief Commissioner, in his record of rights circular stated that "*he* has determined to make no distinction" between occupancy and other tenants; adding that the introduction of a right of permanent occupancy could only be justified by showing that nothing less would protect the ryot from ill-treatment. "This is not the language of a man who feels that he is restrained by a formal document from taking a particular step."

The terms, moreover, in which Lord Canning "approved generally" of Mr. Wingfield's instructions make it abundantly clear that he never dreamt that he was barred by the *sannads* from withholding his approval, and that he regarded the question simply as a matter of revenue detail. That the Secretary of State, while withholding his full opinion on the record of rights circular, of which he had received a copy from Mr. Wingfield while the latter was in England, had not expressly commented on its 31st paragraph, was no proof, as Mr. Grey had contended, that it had escaped his notice, or that if he had had any serious objection to make he would have made it. He probably regarded it as a question which should be first thoroughly discussed by the local authorities before being dealt with by him. Mr. Grey went even further than Mr. Wingfield himself in his zeal for the rights of the Taluqdárs. The latter did admit that no recognition of any really existing rights could infringe Lord Canning's pledges; while the former maintained that, whether rights of occupancy existed or not, they could not be recognised without a breach of faith. The obvious meaning of the saving clause in the *sannads* clearly was to cover "all persons holding any interest in the land under Taluqdárs," and if anyone had been misled into the belief that rights of occupancy were not protected, this "must be attributed, not to the wording of the *sannad*, but to the practical limitation given to its terms by the refusal to admit the claims of cultivators." In short, the refutation of Mr. Grey's argument was so complete, that it would really be little less than brutal to pursue the subject further.

Only one more contribution to this "modern symposium" remains to be considered—that of Sir Hugh Rose, which was, perhaps, the most original of all. The gallant general candidly admitted that he was not master of "this purely civil question," but was strongly opposed to the disturbance, by an inquiry which might prove needless, of the "propitious calm of one of the most influential positions of India." He also expressed, not, he assured his colleagues, for the first time, "the opinion that in their own interests, and those of the people, the Taluqdárs of Oudh should not be allowed to collect revenue," which he considered to be "the duty of a Government, and not the right of an aristocracy." What Sir Hugh imagined to be the functions of a Taluqdár, if not to collect the rents out of which he pays the revenue assessed upon his estate, can only be matter of speculation. It is strange enough that he should have expressed such an opinion once, but that he should, on his own showing, have done so a second time, is stranger still. Thus, somewhat grotesquely, ends the debate.

Its practical outcome was a letter, dated the 30th of September 1864, to the Chief Commissioner from the Government of India, much of which was a *resumé* of the minutes which have just been summarised, and need not, therefore, be repeated. Claims to under-proprietary rights in taluqas were to be tried on their merits if the rights claimed had been actually possessed in or after 1844, *i.e.* within twelve years prior to annexation. But all that could be decreed to the claimants was "the most favourable terms enjoyed by the suitors in any one year since the incorporation of their lands with the taluqa, and not the equivalent of their former rights, viz. a sub-settlement at 5 per cent. on the Government demand."

With regard to occupancy rights, the substance of the arguments in favour of a full and free inquiry into their existence was recited, and it was ordered that provision should be made for the impartial hearing of all such claims. To relieve the Chief Commissioner of this additional work, and in compliance with his own request, the appointment of Financial Commissioner of Oudh was revived, and conferred on Mr. R. H. Davies—then Secretary to the Panjáb Government, and since, successively, Chief Commissioner of Oudh and Lieutenant-Governor of the Panjáb—whose orders in all judicial matters were to be final, while he was to be subject, administratively, to the general control of the Chief Commissioner. The office of Settlement Commissioner was to be abolished, and the Baiswára (Rai Bareli) division, which had been absorbed, was to be reconstituted, and placed in charge of Mr. Currie.

Finally, Mr. Wingfield was enjoined to "carefully impress upon the Taluqdárs that, whilst His Excellency in Council has no desire or intention of infringing the terms of the *sannads* granted them so long as they abide by the conditions binding on themselves, His Excellency is equally resolved that the just and benevolent intentions of the Government towards the holders of subordinate rights and interests secured by the same documents shall not be frustrated."

Brave words! How far they have hitherto been anything more than words will appear in due time.

The much vexed question was once more threshed out by the Secretary of State and his colleagues of the Indian Council. Sir Charles Wood, in his despatch of the 10th of February 1865, conveyed a general approval of the Governor-General's action, accompanied by a caution against doing anything more than was strictly necessary to satisfy justice, or taking any measures likely to lower the dignity of the Taluqdárs. Perhaps the only passage in this despatch which can be considered a contribution to the subject is the following:—

"It appears to me that the grants in the *sannads* are necessarily co-extensive in their operation with that of the confiscation on which they are based. If only proprietary rights were forfeited, it was only necessary to re-grant proprietary rights, and then the occupancy rights remained on their former footing, whatever that was. If occupancy rights were forfeited, then they were restored and preserved under the *sannads*."

This despatch was approved of by a majority of nine to three in the Council. Sir James Hogg, Sir Erskine Perry, and Mr. Macnaghten, the three dissentients, wrote more or less elaborate justifications of their dissent, while Sir Frederick Currie and Captain Eastwick recorded their reasons for concurrence. Any attempt, however, to analyse their arguments would be an abuse of the patience of the most long-suffering reader, and our attention may again be turned from Calcutta and London to Oudh itself, and centred, for a little, in Lucknow.

Shortly after his appointment as Financial Commissioner, Mr. Davies, on the 15th of October 1864, issued a circular to all commissioners and settlement officers in Oudh, laying down as a general rule of limitation that all suits for rights in the soil, whether in taluqas or in zamíndáris, should be "heard and decided on their merits, provided that the dispossession of the claimant cannot be proved to have endured for twelve years from the date of annexation," *i.e.* from the 13th of February 1844 to the 13th of February 1856. This circular was followed on the 24th of October by a second, declaring that "rights of cultivators, other than tenants-at-will, must be carefully investigated, and if judicially proved to exist, recorded in the settlement records." An inquiry was to be commenced simultaneously in each of the districts under settlement, *i.e.* in all the twelve districts of Oudh, except Gonda, Bahraich, and Kheri. Lists of non-proprietary cultivators claiming a right of occupancy "in an equal number of villages (say twenty-five of each) whether held by Taluqdárs or proprietary communities," were to be drawn up, and each case was to be investigated by the settlement officer or his assistant. Among the points to which inquiry was to be directed were (1) the *khasra* (or field book) numbers of the lands in which a right of occupancy was claimed; (2) whether occupancy of the same fields had been continuous, or, if it had been changed, whether, by local usage, such change injured the right or not; (3) the duration of the occupancy, and the number of successions in the family of the claimant; (4) the mode in which the occupancy arose, "whether by breakage of waste, by grant, or agreement, or otherwise"; (5) whether the proprietor had ever evicted, or could evict, the claimant or his ancestors; (6) the mode in which rent had been paid, variations, if any, in its amount, and the terms claimed in regard to it. The decision was to explain clearly the "nature of the right of occupancy, if any be decreed; whether it carries with it the right to pay anything less than the rack-rent demandable from the tenant-at-will, or a fixed rent, or nothing but a preferential title to cultivate so long as the proprietor's demands are fulfilled." Mr. Davies hoped to be able to issue further general instructions as to the disposal of this class of cases, after reviewing a certain number of decisions.

It was not, of course, to be expected that the Taluqdárs would fail to exert themselves to discredit the Governor-General's action. The local papers abounded in denunciation of Sir John Lawrence and Mr. Davies. The "Englishman," the "Indian Daily News," and the "Delhi Gazette" were not behindhand. The British Indian Association held meetings to condemn the "communistic" policy, at which the eloquence of Mahárája Mán Singh, "the patriotic Bráhman," as the local organ of the Taluqdárs fondly styled him, was especially conspicuous. One of the favourite arguments of the opponents of the inquiry into tenant-right was an appeal to experience of what had been done in this way in the Panjáb after its annexation, or, in other words, a warning that, by the introduction of tenant-right, the state of one of the least flourishing provinces of India might be assimilated to that of one of the most prosperous. For it can scarcely be denied that the condition of the Panjáb is economically better than that of Oudh. Another bulwark of the opposition was the assertion that "the universal practice of exchanging *pattas* and *qabúliyats* (leases and counterparts) which prevails in Oudh incontrovertibly falsifies such an idea" as that of the existence of a right of occupancy. The practice, however, so far from being universal, was, and in many parts of the province still is, rather rare than otherwise.

"The ryot rose in the morning, and went to his bed at night, fully aware that his landlord had the power to drive him out of his house and field if he had sufficient reason to do so," and any measure likely to weaken this satisfactory conviction in the mind of the cultivator could not fail to be ruinous to society. "A high rent is the true sign of national prosperity," and Government was adjured not to hurl India back to "the darkness and stagnation of its past ages," by interfering between landlord and tenant, but rather to "leave them free to work out their several good, to go forward in the bright career before them, and to establish peace and prosperity to its loyal subjects." The "Hindoo Patriot," the organ of the Bengal landlords, was even of opinion that whatever "might have been the usages of the country or the ancient rights of the people, they had all been annulled by the edict of confiscation." Such are a few of the gems with which this somewhat ephemeral literature was lavishly decorated.

All this is bad enough, certainly, but after all it is not worse than much that has been said and written by landlords in other countries when they thought their privileges were in danger. When, moreover, the assiduity with which the Taluqdárs had for five years previously been educated by Mr. Wingfield is remembered, it must be admitted that a good deal of allowance is to be made for them, and even that, on the whole, they displayed a creditable moderation. Perhaps the most eager invective against the proposed measures was that indulged in by one of the most *parvenu* Taluqdárs in Oudh, "the patriotic Bráhman," some account of whose previous history, and of the rise of his family from obscurity, together with the mode in which their estate was put together, has been already given. If the Mahárája Mán

Singh was half as clever a man as he is generally supposed to have been, he can hardly have failed to perceive the comical nature of the situation, and must have felt very like Lord Beaconsfield expounding the virtues of fat oxen to an audience of Buckinghamshire farmers. Viewed in this light, his address to the British Indian Association was really a piece of exceedingly gracious fooling. "If these rights belong to our tenants," he declared, "we cannot overbear them. I do not suppose there is one among us who would deny this, and would be willing to take away the property of those who have eaten his salt for ages. Religion, morality, law, and social usages would all compel us to give up what is not our own." The orator omitted, indeed, to mention for how many ages the tenants of the Mahdona estate had eaten the salt supplied by his family, or how far "religion, morality, law, and social usages" had been effective in leading him to restore to the plundered zamíndárs of Faizábád the lands of which his father Darshan Singh and he himself had deprived them. But these, after all, were matters of detail, and his period was perhaps quite as effective without them. "You are all aware," he continued, "that our ryots live on our estates only by sufferance." Of course they were all aware of it, or they would not have been the men they were. "They have been allowed to retain hold of our lands for generations, not because they had any right to what they held, but because we were kind enough not to deprive them of their homes and comforts every now and then. . . . . . The ryots all along knew, however, that we had power to deprive them of their holdings, *if they in any way crossed us*. . . . Possession, however continued it may be, is not right. I may keep in my possession a golden ornament of another for centuries together, but still it is his, and I have no right thereto."

Disinterested native opinion is generally opposed to the doctrine that the recovery of a right should be barred by any definite lapse of time, so that this view of the law of limitation, though peculiar in itself, was not unsuited to the audience to whom it was expounded, always providing that it was not intended to apply to the claims of ousted zamíndárs.

What is more noteworthy is the phrase italicised, which is not without instructiveness for those, if there are still any such, who maintain that no landlord would ever think of ousting a tenant who was willing to pay a fair rent for his holding. I have perhaps lingered too long over the spectacle of the Mahárája Mán Singh posing in the attitude of the hereditary feudal chief, but the humorous aspects of the Oudh land question are so rare, that when one does come upon one of them, it is not easy to let it go at once. It is high time, however, to plunge once more into the grave realities of the tenant-right inquiry, an account of which can best be given district by district.

The investigation in Rai Bareli was conducted by Captain (now Colonel) Macandrew—at present Commissioner of Sítapur, and author, among other kindred works, of a valuable little treatise on "Some Revenue Matters"—and by his assistant, Mr. Lang. Its result was, in Captain Macandrew's own words, that "tenant-right did not exist in any shape under native rule in the Rai Bareli district," and that "the only idea" which the people had on the subject was "that they have a sort of right to cultivate their holdings, so long as they pay the rent which may be demanded."

Turning to the records of the cases themselves, which are printed in their entirety in the tenant-right Blue Book, we find a general consensus of opinion among the cultivators examined, or those of them, at any rate, who were of high caste, that they had a right to complain to the Chakladár if oppressed or ousted by the landlord. None of them had ever done it themselves, but they had heard that their fathers used to do so. Some said that the Chakladár never listened to *asámis*, but there was evidently a general impression that the proper thing for an oppressed *asámi* to do was to complain to the Chakladár. "Of course," said one, "the Taluqdár could loot an *asámi* if he would; it was always a state of disturbance during the Nawábí." There was also a general notion that under British rule, cultivators, as a matter of course, enjoyed fixity of tenure. Indeed, there seems some ground for supposing that there was a tendency on the part of many of the cultivators examined to exaggerate the misrule which had prevailed under the King of Oudh, by way of paying a compliment to the new order of things, *e.g.* in one village belonging to Rána Shankar Baksh of Khajúrgánw, all the tenants who were questioned stated that " in the Nawábí, the zamíndár could do as he liked, either raise the rents, or oust them, but that he cannot do so under British rule. When asked why he cannot now, Hewanchal, Tirbedi, says he gave a *sawál* (petition) at Bareli some four years ago that he was ousted, and was put back in possession." Again, Goka, Sukul, when asked if the Taluqdár could have turned him out in the Nawábí, answered, "No, he should not," on which the following dialogue ensued :—

" Q. If he did, what would you have done?

" A. I would have complained to the Hákim.

" Q. Would he have listened to you?

" A. I can't say. I don't know of any instance in which he gave an order in such a case.

" Q. Do you consider, if you paid a less rent than the value of your land, the lambardár has a right to raise it?

" A. Formerly he had the right, now he has not.

" Q. Why has he not that right now?

" A. In the Nawábí he could have beaten me and turned me out; now he cannot do so."

Again—the witness being Jagannáth, Dichit, in another village :—

" Q. Then you allow he had the power to oust you?

" A. Yes, but it is not right for him to do so."

Low-caste cultivators, however, generally speaking, disclaimed all rights of any kind.

The cases investigated in Sultánpur are not instructive, being nearly all claims for what was really under-proprietary right, brought by zamíndárs or founders of hamlets, not claims to rights of occupancy by cultivators pure and simple. Some of Captain Perkins' remarks, however, are worth quoting :—

" The tenants of this district can scarcely understand the rights which it was supposed they might possess: they are an ignorant body, and have been too much in the condition of serfs to have any clear notion of rights based only on long occupancy. . . . . If possession of the same fields for a course of years at equitable rates creates a right of occupancy, the rights to be recognised would still be very few, for tenants, as a rule, have held their fields at inequitable rates. . . . . Occasionally, the landlord is found to have brought rents" of high and low-caste cultivators alike "almost to a uniform level. The high-caste man groans under what he considers oppression, but he does not dispute the right to oppress him." A right of occupancy seemed to be conferred by founding a hamlet, locating cultivators, or planting a grove, "but the difficulty of making such inquiries has been considerably enhanced by the fact that the chief landholders have learned, through the medium of circulars, to deny the existence of such rights. . . . . The practice of the Revenue Courts has tended to teach old cultivators that they cannot be ousted, and they bless Government for the boon, but do not think that the right exists independently of the pleasure of the Administration."

The Pratábgarh inquiry was conducted by Mr. R. M. King, and his assistant, Captain Ralph Ouseley. Mr. King seems to have felt too vividly the ludicrousness of the views of tenant-right entertained by many of the cultivators he examined to make a very laborious or exhaustive investigation of the subject. And many of them certainly are funny, very funny, *e.g.* as an illustration of moral force, one Bráhman alleged that he could not be rack-rented because "he could grow his hair at the zamíndár, who would at once desist, terrified at such a danger." Beni, Muráo, "would sue if ousted, because he has made his *khets* (fields) so nice, and spent so much in manure; would not stand being turned out by anybody but the *Sarkár* (Government)." Girje, Kurmi, "is a cultivator, and is fully aware of it, and thinks it a poor position." Another "would refer the question of his ouster to Government, if it occurred; all such ouster is *zabardastí* (oppression)." A fifth "has a cultivator's rights; says these are a right to fill his belly." A sixth "has a cultivating right; has done so much in tilling and manuring that it would be a shame to turn him out; would not live if he were ousted."

The most noticeable discovery made by Captain Ouseley in the course of his inquiry was that of two *parwánas* issued by native officials, dated 1251 Hijrí, and 1243 Faslí, forbidding the zamíndárs of Rání Mau to raise the rents of certain Bráhman cultivators of that village.

But if Mr. King's records were somewhat meagre, his report is exceedingly valuable. In it, for the first time in the history of the controversy, is the question of tenant-right placed upon its true footing, as a matter of public policy.

"What," he asked, "were the relations between the Taluq-dár, the cultivator, and the native Government of Oudh, which we have promised (by the *sannads*) to maintain? I hold it to be a true view that the Government of Oudh looked upon itself as sole owner of the land of the country it governed, except in those cases where it had alienated that right by its own act, and that this idea was only modified in practice by the limited power of the Government. . . . The only beneficial use to which Government could put its assumed property in the land was the raising of revenue from it; and therefore they practically recognised the existing facts of the appropriation of the land by the so-called owners, and the cultivation of it by the lower classes; and I think in their treatment of each class may be found the view they held of them. The landowner was, they thought, too much of an opposite interest to their own to be altogether approved of; but being a fact, and also capable of doing much to thwart the Government, was tolerated and kept in check. The lower classes, or cultivators, were to them the working bees of the hive, from whose labours the revenue was to be drawn. The old traditions of the Mughal Empire, and probably of all Hindústání dynasties, wisely inculcated the maintenance of a contented peasantry as the firmest basis of their power, and though they succeeded remarkably ill in carrying out their intentions, yet the legend was not abandoned, and may be traced in the majority of the *pattas* for the annual payment of revenue from the native officers to zamíndárs, or even farmers. In these deeds '*riáya rází rakhna*' (to keep the ryots contented) is, next to the punctual payment of the revenue, the most indispensable condition of the tenure. It may be conceded, however, that the latter condition was not much more irreligiously observed than the former and I do not think that it can be argued from the misadventures of the Oudh Government in this particular, that they either never had, or ever abandoned, a power to exert themselves on behalf of the cultivators. To come to later times, it is a matter of history that the reforms which the British Government urged upon that of Oudh included some measure for the better security of the cultivating classes, and it is quite possible that had the King adopted any sound system for such an end, he would be at this moment reigning in Oudh, and have obviated the necessity for our present inquiries. Arriving, then, at the period of annexation, I believe the above sketch to represent truly the then status of the cultivator, *i.e.* that there was a Government tradition afloat as to the duty of protecting him; that there were some excessively poor attempts to protect him; but that at any time the Oudh Government might by caprice or design have interfered in his behalf in a more or less effective manner. Passing over the annexation, rebellion, and recovery of the province, we come to the epoch of the *sannads*, which guarantee to the Taluqdár the rights which he had enjoyed at annexation. If my statements are so far correct as they apply to the power which resided in the Oudh Government at annexation, it follows that the Taluqdár was then liable to interference on behalf of the cultivator, and can it be, then, that the *sannad* guarantees him from all interference now? . . . . The guarantee of the *sannads*, as far as it affects, or will in time be found to affect, the interests of others than the Taluqdárs or the Government, must be as if it did not exist, and the question of tenant-right, like all other similar ones, must be debated on its own merits and the demands of policy."

This extract puts the gist of the whole matter in the clearest possible light. The inquiry into the existence of tenant-right, as a question of fact, was no doubt an interesting historical research; but it was a grave, though, happily, not an irreparable blunder to separate it from the wider question of the desirability of establishing tenant-right as a matter of public policy; or to use language that might imply that Government was in the slightest degree debarred by the result of an inquiry into what had been in the past from taking steps which might be necessary or expedient for the public welfare in the future.

The settlement officer of Hardui, Mr. Bradford, reported that "such tenant-rights as are contemplated in Book Circular No. II. of October 1864 do undoubtedly exist," and he divided the persons whom he considered to possess them into three classes, viz. (1) descendants of ex-proprietors; (2) high-caste cultivators, such as Bráhmans and Rájpúts; and (3) low-caste *chapparband asámis*, who had held the same fields for generations at unvarying rents. The rents of these three classes of cultivators should, he considered, be fixed and recorded.

Many of the first of these three classes had claims to under-proprietary right, and therefore did not come within the scope of the inquiry. As to the high-caste cultivators pure and simple, Mr. Bradford dwelt on the universality and antiquity of the custom by which they held their lands at beneficial rents; and urged the significant fact that fighting men of low castes, such as Báris and Pásis, and sometimes Kurmis, or even Mihtars, did military service for their Thákurs, but did not hold, like Bráhmans and Chhatris, at low rents. This seems a sufficient answer to the assertion that low rents were merely the reward of military service, and to point to the conclusion that the true reason for granting them was one which still continues to exist, viz. the conventional inability of high-caste men to cultivate, or to live, as cheaply as men of inferior caste. In favour of the right of *chapparband asámis* to be confirmed in their holdings at the rent which they had been paying for generations, Mr. Bradford, while allowing that "the landlord could, during the Nawábí, have exacted more, had he chosen to disregard the law, the custom of patriarchal India, for they are synonymous," argued that this only proved the state of lawlessness and misrule which then prevailed. Where, in short, a beneficial custom had been found to prevail, it should be upheld, even though, under native rule, there was no authority which actively enforced its observance. Generally speaking, the cultivators examined by Mr. Bradford made no claim to retain the land against the will of the zamíndár, and admitted that he could turn them out and enhance their rent if he liked, which, indeed, went without saying, though it was not customary, and not the proper thing for a well-disposed landlord to do.

The result of the Sítapur inquiry, conducted by Major Thompson, was reported by him to be that "a right of occupancy under native rule, on the part of non-proprietary tenants, cannot be traced." The most instructive part of his researches was the examination of kánúngos, some of whose answers are worth recording. They generally agreed that the zamíndár could do what he liked with land held by tenants, for "the landlord was the Hákim over his cultivators; the Chakladár was Hákim over the landlord." The zamíndár, from a regard to his own safety, always tried to keep on good terms with high-caste cultivators, or *ámneks*. "Disputes were very rare, because it was the interest of both to agree." Panchayats to arbitrate on claims to cultivating occupancy were unknown, for "a cultivator's right was not such a commendable (? desirable) thing as to form the subject of a claim or reference to arbitration."

Munshi Har Prasád, Extra-Assistant Commissioner, stated that the only persons who enjoyed complete immunity from eviction were the *Bhyas*, or relatives of the landlord. Even they, however, *could* be ejected:—"*The Taluqdár had the power to do it undoubtedly, for he had the power of life and death*, but he did not exercise it because they were his own relations." Exactly so. A powerful landlord during the Nawábí could evict a tenant, or enhance his rent, or take away his wife from him, or cut his head off, with as much, or as little, likelihood of being called to account by Názim or Chakladár for one act as for another. That claims by dispossessed cultivators to be reinstated were almost unknown, was not surprising, for "the cultivation of the soil"—it is still Munshi Har Prasád who speaks—"was not considered a valuable thing. A man turned out of his holding by one landlord could get another holding immediately from another, and every cultivator could get the same terms which his caste usually got. Even the Bhyas, who had slightly better terms than the *ámneks*, could get holdings on their own terms, for it was thought a very fine thing to get the Bhyas of a neighbouring Taluqdár to settle on an estate."

Kesri, Bráhman, stated:—" I have never had a difference with my landlord, and he never interfered with me or raised my rent, but he could do what he liked. *He took away all the crop together from a cultivator if he was angry with him.*" It is a pity this witness was not asked whether he would have had any remedy in this latter case, and whether the Chakladár would have done anything for him.

" In the case of a man who had cleared jungle," says Major Thompson, " zamíndárs have admitted to me that the clearer would be entitled to hold the land as long as he paid rent, and that the rent would only be liable to enhancement if the Government demand were raised."

In Faizábád, Mr. Carnegy, with the aid of his Assistant, Captain Edgar Clarke, made an extremely elaborate inquiry, the result of which was, in his opinion, to disprove not only the existence of any occupancy rights in that district, but also in the adjoining N.W. Provinces district of A´zimgarh, up to the time of its annexation, or "cession," in 1801. This, it may be observed, was in accordance with Mr. Wingfield's contention, that tenant-right throughout Upper India was unknown until created by ourselves; and if by tenant-right is meant a right to occupy land at a fixed rent, which could be enforced by the tenant, through a legal tribunal, against the will of the zamíndár, there can not only be no doubt that he was right in denying, but it may be questioned whether anybody ever asserted, its existence under native rule. " The cultivators of a powerful but prudent landlord," wrote Mr. Carnegy, " will be found, almost to a man, to have held at unchanging rates for years, while in the badly managed estates the changes were frequent." This is pretty strong evidence that it is not in well-managed estates that the introduction of universal tenant-right would prove injurious to the landlords. Nearly all the cultivators examined by Mr. Carnegy agreed that, if turned out by the zamíndár during the Nawábí, they were helpless, "because," said one, "there was no one to listen to disputes between landlord and tenant." "The Taluqdár," said another, "could have ousted us without redress, because there was none for our class under native rule." As Mr. Carnegy himself puts it, "the zamíndár could have ousted them if he liked, or could have driven them away by overtaxing them; and in either case they were helpless, because there was, under the King's government, no tribunal for the redress of tenant grievances." It was generally agreed, however, that no zamíndár would oust a tenant and give the land to another, except in the event of a refusal to pay the rent demanded. Enhancement of rent was rare, and when it did occur, was general throughout a village, and rateable.

A number of Kurmi cultivators examined by Captain Clarke said that they and their ancestors had held the same lands for ten generations, but made no claim to a fixed rent. They had only one request to make, which was that the assessment of their village might be reduced, "because then the proprietor will have to pay less, and consequently we shall too." This is strongly suggestive of a little tutoring on the part of the zamíndár, but there is no doubt that an increase of revenue is always followed by an attempt—usually successful—on the part of the málguzár to raise rents. Some Bráhmans, endowed with more speculative acumen than most of the witnesses exhibited, declared, "We consider it to be our right to enjoy the same fields we now hold always; like as the Government lets the Taluqdár hold his villages always, so we are entitled to our fields always; and as regards the rents, the Court may do as it likes."

Ori, Hajjám (barber), stated that "during the King's time, the *asámis* were ground down, and dared not complain against the zamíndár, and even if they had so desired, there were no courts to grant redress; but now things are altered, and he expects justice."

Shiodín, Khewat, said, "During the Nawábí the zamíndár was all-powerful; as long as the cultivator paid his rent, he was generally maintained, but could not claim to hold as a right; he could be ousted at any time at the will of the zamíndár, and if he offered active resistance, was likely to be tortured, or perhaps killed. There was no redress in any court as under the British Government now. The zamíndár ousted him in Asárh last. He complained to the district court, and was put in possession in spite of the zamíndár, as there is nothing to fear. He could not, and dared not, complain in the Nawábí." By this time he has probably learnt the folly of complaining under British rule as it at present exists.

Here, as in other districts, the cultivator pure and simple had *no* rights which he could practically enforce against the will of the zamíndár, and the occupation of particular fields was not, under native rule, valuable enough to make him struggle very much to retain it; it was, in fact, not recognised as a right at all, but rather as a duty. The only right in the matter was deemed to be the right of the zamíndár to get his fields cultivated at the highest possible rent, not that of the tenant to cultivate them at the lowest. It should, moreover, be remembered that under the rules in force at the time this inquiry was made, ordinary cultivators in Oudh actually were, and believed that they would continue to be, better protected against eviction and enhancement of rent than in any other part of Hindústán, exclusive of the Panján. The protective rules have since been swept away, and it is very doubtful whether, if the inquiry were now to be made over again, cultivators would dwell with the same freedom on their helplessness during the Nawábí as a thing that was past and gone, and quite certain that they would not speak with the same easy unconcern of their security under British rule.

> "It so falls out
> That what we have we prize not to the worth,
> Whiles we enjoy it; but being lacked and lost,
> Why, then we rack the value; then we find
> The virtue that possession would not show us
> Whiles it was ours."

To the same effect as the Faizábád evidence, though of still stronger tendency, was that recorded in Unáo by Mr. Maconachie. In this district there were, until annexation, hardly any considerable Taluqdárs, nearly the whole of it being held by small zamíndárs, who were incessantly harried by the King's officers. Holdings and rents were constantly changing, and there was probably no part of Oudh in which, during the later years, at any rate, of the Nawábí, oppression and disturbance were more habitually rife. Cultivators were perpetually absconding, and to keep them from doing so was the main object of the zamíndár. A few extracts from the evidence seem sufficiently instructive to be worth quoting.

Subha, Bráhman, lambardár of Nigohí, said:—"Since annexation, the land has become more valuable, and no one will give up the holdings which formerly we had great difficulty in inducing them to retain."

Gulíb, Kúchhí:—"I allow that he (the zamíndár) had right to oust me in the Nawábí, but not now, the system being different. I mean, Government officials would not allow him to oust me. ... I was always leaving the village; every two or three years I absconded, and was brought back."

Rám Singh, Bráhman:—"I never heard of any cultivator's rights. Only those obtained anything who had assistance from friends in Lucknow. Without them, nothing could be obtained; with them, almost anything."

Raghbar Dyál, Kayath, kárinda of Guláb Singh, zamíndár:—"The land was not worth cultivators' fighting about in the Nawábí, and consequently no one cared much whether they lost or held."

Rámdín, Lodh:—"The only right a cultivator who built a well ever received was to pay a higher rent."

Rám Ghulám, Kayath:—"I never saw a cultivator who built a *pakka* well ousted. A zamíndár would not do so, as he would be ashamed to oust a man who had expended money on the property. Of course, if right is inquired about, he had right, but he would consider it wrong to do so."

Debidín, Kayath, an ex-Kánúngo:—"*Right* was never recognised. When zamíndárs were turned out, what chance had cultivators?"

Chote, Barhái (carpenter):—"We were forcibly made to cultivate the land, and punished if we wished to give it up."

Mohan Lál, Bráhman, speaking of another Bráhman:—"In

the Nawábí no one cared about the land; now land is not to be got anyhow, and he wishes to retain the land he now holds as a means of livelihood. What is he to do, or where to go, if he loses the land he now holds?"

Similar extracts might be quoted *ad libitum*, but these will probably suffice to convey a pretty distinct notion of the state of society to which they relate. Yet even here, the legend of the duty of Government to protect the cultivator was not wholly extinct, *e.g.* Thákur, Káchhi, said:—"My family have been fourteen generations in this village. . . . If I were ousted, I should complain. Had I been ousted in the Nawábí, I would have complained to the Wazír at Lucknow: I would plead that I had held for a long time, and had always paid what was demanded of me. My uncle once went to Delhi, and complained of increase of rent, and obtained an order letting him off. This was before I can remember, and before Oudh was a separate country." This statement being made in 1865, and Oudh having been a "separate country" since 1720, or, at latest, since 1739, it can hardly have been Thákur's uncle who went to Delhi, but this trifling inaccuracy does not impair the survival of the legend.* On the evidence before him, Mr. Maconachie naturally came to the conclusion that the cultivators of Unáo had no rights which they could enforce, and that, under the circumstances, they could not reasonably have been expected to possess any such rights.

No record of evidence from the Lucknow district is to be found in the Blue Book, but the settlement officer, Mr. Copeland Capper, furnished a report on the subject, which has a least the merit of reducing the matter of the inquiry to fairly definite terms. He presumed that "rights" include all benefits or powers which (1) accrued from written law, and were or could have been enforced by the constituted courts or the administration of the former government; (2) those not dependent on written law, but recognised as customary by the local panchayats of the village or dis-

---

* Perhaps the allusion may have been to the assumption of the kingly title by Gházi-ud-dín Haidar in 1819.

trict, and enforced by them with the common consent of the people; or (3) such as, though unknown to the ruder organisation of the native government, would, on the introduction of our rule, from the analogy of European common law, give the holder a prescriptive title against his lord.

Of rights of the first two classes, Mr. Capper could find no trace. As for the third class, or prescriptive rights, while admitting that such a title might arise, he concluded that "when one considers the condition of this district for many years prior to annexation, and the difficulty with which even proprietors and lords of manors maintained their rights, and that disorganisation arising from the prevalence of the law of might against right was, as we were informed at the annexation in 1856, the main reason for the introduction of British rule, I cannot but think that there will be very few cases in which a title cognisable under the analogy of common law will be shown." In short, the disintegration of society, in order to remedy which Oudh was annexed, rendered the existence of occupancy rights which could be enforced, an impossibility; and, if they had existed, they would have been, in the then state of society, of very trifling economical value. This, however, is a much better reason for than against the creation of such rights now.

The Bárabanki inquiry, made by Mr. H. B. Harington, was perhaps the most thoughtfully conducted, and his report, next to Mr. King's, the most valuable of any. "The right of the landlord to oust his tenant or to raise the rent was on all hands admitted to be absolute." But has he an equally uncontrolled power over the distribution of the produce? "Are we to look to caprice, to competition, or to custom as determining the position of the cultivator and the adjustment of his rent?" To these questions Mr. Harington answers that so far as his inquiries extended, he found custom exercising a very great influence, competition existing only to a very limited extent, and usage regulating in a remarkable degree the exercise of the landlord's power, both as to ousting tenants and adjusting rents. It was generally agreed that, of the gross produce of the soil, the landlord was entitled to receive from ordinary cultivators one half, and from privileged cultivators two-fifths; and on this principle were grain rents commuted to cash payments. In enhancing rent, the zamíndár was supposed to be bound to conform to the usage of the country, and not to be at liberty to demand more than the cash equivalent of that portion of the produce which was really his due, *i.e.* two-fifths from the privileged or high-caste (*ámnek*) cultivator, and one half from the unprivileged. There was further a general feeling that no cultivator but "a fool or a foe" would offer more than that equivalent. Hence Mr. Harington considered that competition was so limited by custom as to have, practically, no existence. He therefore held that the true parallel to the cultivating tenures of Oudh is, not the cottier system of Ireland, but the metayer system of Tuscany or Limousin. He recognised, however, the likelihood of the metayer being transformed into the cottier system by the growth of competition, and being fully aware that "no greater evil can befall a state than a cottier system in which, as in Ireland, competition is only tempered by assassination," advocated the authoritative limitation of the rise of rents to the bounds imposed by custom. He thought the Taluqdárs would, "without exception, subscribe to an agreement which would bind them to raise no rent, and evict no tenant, except in accordance with the usage of the province." That usage, he thought, might be easily defined. "It is true that the existence of the custom would seem to justify the introduction of the law," but if the good results of the law could be obtained without it, Mr. Harington thought it would be better to abstain from legislative interference.

A number of minor points were, of course, brought out in the course of this careful inquiry, but the most noteworthy were the following :—

(1.) Such right of occupancy as existed resolved itself into the right of refusal of land at a higher rent if any *bonâ fide* higher offer were made by an outsider.

(2.) An old tenant, or one who had improved his holding, would be allowed by any well-disposed landlord to retain his fields at a somewhat lower rent than the highest which an outsider would offer.

(3.) Twenty years' possession constituted an old tenant (*qadim asámi*).

(4.) Landlords admitted that rents should not be raised unconditionally (*be hisáb*), but only with reference to the rates paid for neighbouring fields or the quality of the soil.

(5.) No low-caste cultivator would bid against an *ámnek*, i.e. one receiving the allowance known as *kúr* or *bháta*—which amounts to a deduction of one-sixth of the gross produce (or its cash equivalent where grain rent has been commuted to a money payment)—on account of wages of the ploughmen who do the work which custom forbids a high-caste man to do for himself.

To this it may be added that Káchhis and Muráos, who pay very much higher rents than any other class, will not bid against one another; nor will a man of either of those castes consent to cultivate land from which one of his fellow castemen has been ejected.

It is doubtless true, as Mr. Harington asserts, that when rent is paid in kind, the proportion of the produce to which the landlord is entitled is strictly determined by custom, and that the share of the tenant is never supposed to be less than one half or, in some cases, than nineteen-fortieths of the gross out-turn. It is also true that high-caste cultivators are almost always, where grain rents prevail, allowed *kúr* or *bháta*. The more favoured of these *ámneks* pay, after deduction of *bháta*, one-third (*tíkur*), one-fourth (*chaukur*), or sometimes only one-fifth (*pachkur*), of the gross produce as rent. Landlords, however, generally maintain a chronic struggle to increase this proportion to one-half, which, when *bháta* is allowed, is known as *ádhá bháta*, and without it, as *karra ádhá*. To this extent competition is certainly limited, and rents thus determined are rather metayer than cottier rents.

It *may* also be true that when grain rents are commuted to cash payments, the amount of the latter is calculated on the basis of equivalence to the proportion of produce previously paid, or, at least, that such proportion is sometimes regarded as an element of the question. But it is very doubtful, indeed, whether in money rents of old standing any such reference to the actual produce can be traced, and the influence of custom in determining such rents is very much less marked. Rise of rents is due far less to competition of one cultivator against another, which is, indeed, somewhat rare, than to pressure applied by the landlord, enforced by the threat of eviction. The process is very simple. A landlord in want of money persuades himself that the cultivators of a given village will stand an extra turn of the screw without bolting. He demands, perhaps, an additional two annas in the rupee, or four annas per *bigha*. There is a long wrangle over the demand. Probably nine tenants out of ten finally agree to accept his terms, rather than abandon their homes and holdings. The recusants are served with notices of ejectment, and if this does not reduce them to what the landlord considers reason, they are probably ejected. If no other tenant will take up their fields at the enhanced rent, the landlord will bring them into his own cultivation, or *sir*. Here there has been a general rise of rents all round, but if the cause be competition at all, it is the competition of the landlord, as cultivator of his *sir*, against the tenants, not that of one tenant against another. Perhaps it would be more simple, without being less accurate, to say that the rise of rents is due to the landlord's "desire of wealth," which here, and in many other cases, as Mr. Cliffe Leslie has remarked, is not so much a productive as a predatory impulse.

The inquiry into tenant-right having been completed by the end of the cold season of 1864–65, Mr. Davies, on the 19th of June, submitted to the Chief Commissioner his report on the result. After reviewing the evidence from each district, he concluded that no prescriptive right on the part of cultivators pure and simple to retain their holdings against the will of the zamíndár was to be found in Oudh, and that it was therefore impracticable, "at present," to register in the settlement records as occupancy tenants all who had been in possession for a certain number of years, as had been done in the N. W. Provinces at the settlement of 1822–1833. He held, however, that the inquiry established that the status of tenants in Oudh at annexation was the same as that of tenants in the N. W. Provinces in 1822. The records then framed were only intended to show the existing state of possession, and were liable to be altered by civil suit, while in Oudh no rights were recorded which had not been judicially decreed by the settlement officer acting as a civil court.

Turning to the economical side of the question, Mr. Davies took his stand on the doctrine of which Mr. Mill has been the leading English exponent, that rents paid by labourers raising their wages from the soil cannot safely be abandoned to competition. Hence he deduced an answer to Mr. Wingfield's favourite question, "Why allow competition for grain, and not for the rent of land paid by peasants?" His answer was, "Because competition for grain has no tendency to multiply the number of mouths to be fed; but by adjusting its price in proportion to the supply, rather puts people on their thrift; whereas competition for rack-rent leases by encouraging false confidence, by eventually lowering wages, and by minimising the prudential checks, has a direct tendency to stimulate the increase of population, and in course of time to lessen the fund for its support."

Mr. Davies "entertained no hope whatever of the improvement of agriculture in Oudh by the expenditure of capital on the part of large landholders. Similar outlay by the corresponding class in Europe has been rare and sparing; and the traditions, habits, and idiosyncracy of Oudh Taluqdárs are not such as to render it probable that they will differ much in this respect from the Russian, French, and Hungarian nobles."

The fact is that a "good landlord" in Indian parlance does not mean an improver of his estate, but one who refrains from oppressing his tenants, is economical in his own habits, and keeps his accounts in good order.

If any interference on behalf of the cultivator should hereafter be needed, Mr. Davies was "decidedly of opinion that, apart from political engagements, Act X. of 1859 is as much adapted to the circumstances now existing in Oudh as it is to the North-Western Provinces. Its introduction would merely transmute customs into rights. . . . . I concur generally in the remarks occurring on this subject in Mr. King's report; and *if, at any future time, the condition of the cultivating classes should become such as to demand legislative interference, if it should be found that from the operation of causes familiar in their effects to modern science, the country is reduced to a worse state than that from which the British annexation was intended to rescue it, I conceive that the duty of dealing with such an emergency cannot be evaded by the Government.*"

In submitting all the papers to the Government of India, Mr. Wingfield expressed dissent, more or less modified, from nearly all Mr. Davies' conclusions, except the primary one, that no rights of occupancy against the will of the zamíndár had been proved to exist. He maintained that competition had been shown to be already far from uncommon; that the fate of the ryots of south-eastern Oudh could not be considered hard if they were driven by pressure of population to Kheri and the trans-Ghághra districts; and that, though cultivators may be protected against their landlords—" not that the Chief Commissioner means to imply that any such protection is needed "—they cannot be protected from the consequence of an increase in their numbers.

That competition was already not uncommon, was proof of the urgent necessity of fixing rents; not as Mr. Wingfield argued, that as custom had begun to give way to contract, the process should be allowed to continue unchecked, and no beneficial usages reduced to law. The fate of a cultivator driven from his ancestral village to a strange region where he will probably die of fever within five years is not exactly soft. And though no State can protect its subjects from the consequences of over-population, it can do something to check the too rapid growth of population by adopting institutions calculated to increase, and not to diminish, the force of prudential checks. That tenants enjoying security of tenure at a fixed rent are more likely to be prudent, than if they were subject to rack-renting and eviction, scarcely needs demonstration.

Mr. Davies had asserted that when rent was enhanced, it

was generally raised in proportion to the capacity of the land. Mr. Wingfield thought it was "not easy to see on what other principle than the capabilities of the soil the rent could be raised." It never seemed to occur to him that the helplessness of the cultivator may be such a principle, and that it is only capitalist rents that are determined by the capacity of the soil. At any rate, he declined to "enter into speculations in the field of political economy," and contented himself with saying that he did not "share the apprehensions of the Financial Commissioner," and thought the ryots were "perfectly well aware of their own interests." On the political question, Mr. Wingfield, of course, held that tenant-right being proved not to exist, the *sannads* were a bar to its creation. How truly was it said by one of old, "Where there is no *vision* the people perish!"

The local authorities having thus said their say, the running was taken up by Mr. (soon to become Sir William) Muir, who was then Secretary to the Government of India, in a very able "Memorandum on the Investigation into Tenant Rights in Oudh," dated the 20th of October 1865. To this memorandum were added three appendices, on (1) the existing law and practice of Oudh courts in regard to cultivating tenures; (2) the result of the local inquiry into rights of non-proprietary cultivators; and (3) tenant-right in the N. W. Provinces and other parts of India. These appendices were intended by Mr. Muir to be read before the memorandum. The summary of the first appendix may be stated in his own words:—

"The right of occupancy at a fair rent, *i.e.* the prevailing or customary rent of the neighbourhood, was early recognised and inculcated in our administration of the province, as inherent in ryots generally, and specially so if they had long cultivated the land; the principle has been (with some occasional expressions in the abstract reserving the right of ousting tenants-at-will) consistently reiterated from time to time, and it now forms the rule of the district courts which have the jurisdiction in this class of cases." A perusal of the circular orders issued on this subject by the Chief Commissioner clearly shows that, after directing, in April 1859, that wherever under-proprietary rights were "doubtful, the doubt should be given in favour of the Taluqdár," he proceeded to lay down that, except in the case of cultivators who paid a beneficially low rent in consequence of prescriptive right, and not by mere favour or caste privilege, there was "nothing to prevent the Taluqdár from now raising the rents to the fair rate of the pargana." But in May of the same year these latter orders were modified by a second circular directing that in the case of cultivators holding at beneficial rates by virtue of caste, "the Taluqdárs will not be considered authorised to raise the rents during this settlement, without the full consent of the tenants, if they have held at such reduced rates for at least twenty years." Only under-proprietary cultivators were to be deemed entitled to hold at fixed rates, all others being "simply *káshtkárs* or *asámis*, whose rents may be raised to fair rates, and among whom there is no distinction of *qadím* (ancient) and *jadíd* (modern). . . . The Chief Commissioner, however, must not be misunderstood to authorise the Taluqdárs to raise their rents beyond the fair rates of the country, merely because, at them, their incomes are not double the Government *jama*" (revenue demand). This obviously implies, and in subsequent orders it was expressly declared, that any cultivator, not holding merely under a terminable lease, was entitled to contest in the revenue courts any claim to enhancement which he considered unfair, and to obtain a lease at rates which he might call upon those courts to fix.

Mr. Wingfield afterwards stated, in his review of the tenant-right inquiry, that the above orders were needful to protect under-proprietary tenants from injustice, until the record of rights was completed. But it is obvious that such a precaution was, according to Mr. Wingfield's own doctrine, only needed where the tenant claimed under-proprietary right, and could have no justification where he professed to be a mere cultivator. And a perusal of the circulars themselves is quite enough to show that they were "framed independently on their own merits, and with no reference anywhere expressed to the temporary necessity noticed by Mr. Wingfield," who had himself admitted that it was not till March 1864 that he had come to the conclusion that occupancy rights had no existence in Oudh. It was clear that the belief was general among ryots, and after these rulings, indeed, it could hardly have been otherwise, that it was the intention of Government to afford them the same protection and security as it had afforded to their brethren in the N. W. Provinces. And it was equally clear that they hailed the boon with delight. While, on the other hand, "Taluqdárs and other, landlords must have received the successive rulings detailed above as indicative of a settled course of administrative action in favour of the right of occupancy. It was probably viewed as part of the system enunciated by Lord Canning in conferring their property upon them, viz. that 'the right was conceded subject to any measures which the Government may think proper to take for the purpose of protecting the inferior zamíndárs and *village occupants* from extortion.' And the only objection which seems to have occurred to any of them was the inapplicability of the principle to holdings of which the rent was paid in kind." This objection, which was perfectly reasonable, merely amounted to this, that a tenant should not be allowed to retain more land than he had means of cultivating, so long as his rent was payable in kind; and under a circular order of September 1863, the tenant had only to agree to pay a fair money rent in order to resist ejectment from any portion of his holding, whether imperfectly tilled or not. With this exception, no Taluqdár or zamíndár had uttered a word of complaint against what, according to the contention of Mr. Wingfield and his school, was so flagrant a violation of the pledges of Government as the recognition and enforcement, extending over a period of nearly seven years, of occupancy rights on the part of cultivators pure and simple.

Turning to Appendix II., it is not necessary to follow Mr. Muir into his digest of the evidence recorded by settlement officers. Let the quotation of one passage, of the nature of a general comment, suffice:—

"The degree in which the cultivator is attached to the soil appears to vary in different parts of the province. In the centre, exposed in its full force to the misrule and tyranny of the Lucknow Court, there was constant change even among the proprietary classes, and a corresponding absence of fixity in the tenure of the cultivator. . . . . In districts at a distance from the heart of this disorder, greater permanence and security prevailed among the landholders, and . . . . also among the cultivating ranks. . . . . In the central and more disorganized parts, we find rent often settled by the field in a manner approaching competition; while in more remote and settled quarters rent is adjusted by uniform and customary rates, and by them competition, wherever traceable, is in practice limited."

The third appendix consists of a masterly and most valuable sketch of tenant-right in southern India, Bengal, and the N. W. Provinces. Speaking broadly, Mr. Muir thought that, " on our accession to the empire, ryot proprietorship prevailed in the south of India, official zamíndárship in Bengal, and village proprietorship in the North-Western Provinces." With regard to the first, his conclusion was that "throughout India, excepting the Gangetic valley and adjoining tracts . . . . there exists the general law of ryot right. With few exceptions, no proprietary title intervenes between the Sovereign and the cultivator. The individual occupant, as a rule, is either proprietor or permanent holder. The exactions of the State may often have reduced the title to a mere shadow, but the moment tyranny and oppression are withdrawn, the occupancy resumes its substantial character, tending to acquire more or less of a beneficial interest. Such is the tenure which in every quarter exists, or which springs up naturally in the soil." In Bengal also, ryot right existed, and was not "displaced or materially weakened " by the official zamíndárship which we made the mistake of transforming into actual proprietorship; and it still survives, though in a sadly dilapidated condition, owing to the neglect of proper precautions for its protection.

But as our rule advanced up the valley of the Ganges, through Bahár into the North-West Provinces, our officers began to come in contact with real zamíndárs, village proprietors, and, occasionally, feudal chiefs. Here the zamíndár was no mere middleman or tax-collector, but *owner of the soil*. This may have been due to the martial character of the landholders, who seem to have been originally a conquering class. From this, coupled with evidence of a converse state of things in the Dakkhan and Bengal, may be deduced the inference that "ryot-right is in the inverse ratio of village proprietorship." In Banáras the two systems meet each other—the strong proprietary and weak tenant-right of the North-West, and the weak proprietary and strong tenant-right of Bengal—and this may account for tenant-right being weaker in the north and west of Oudh than in the south and east. Judging from the inquiry of 1818, it would seem that occupancy tenures in the N. W. Provinces, when they came under British rule, were on much the same footing as in Oudh at annexation, the present difference between them being mainly due to the fostering influence of the Bengal system, or rather theory, which in the N. W Provinces was, to a certain extent, reduced to practice.

After this glance at the appendices, let us turn back to the memorandum of which they form the bases. It begins by remarking that the right of cultivating occupancy had been steadily supported by the Oudh Administration from 1856 up to date, and on even a wider footing, embracing tenants of all classes, after reoccupation than before the Mutiny. So thoroughly was this recognised, that even where summary eviction would, under the ordinary law, be justifiable, landlords applied to the courts, as a matter of course, for leave to evict. For instance, Rána Shankar Baksh, the well-known feudal chief of Khajúrganw in Rai Bareli, having sued out execution against a defaulting tenant in his own court as an Honorary Assistant Commissioner, was reported by Mr. Wingfield to have applied to the Collector of his district, "stating that as defaulter was imprisoned by order of Government for arrears of rent, his land was lying uncultivated, and there was no one in his family to take his place; he therefore prayed that arrangements might be made with another cultivator."

There could hardly be stronger evidence than this of the extent to which the doctrine of Mr. Wingfield's circulars protecting tenant occupancy had found acceptance in the most unlikely quarters. Nowhere had a whisper been heard from any landlord, small or great, that the *sannads* were infringed by this policy. Indeed, had the tenant-right inquiry not been made when it was, occupancy rights must, under the existing rules and practice of the revenue courts, have acquired such prescriptive strength that they could not have been uprooted. The evidence of the ryots showed that the more enlightened among them regarded themselves as being now emancipated and secure, while the more ignorant seemed unable to understand what constitutes a right until it was taken from them. The spirit of the settlement rules in force in Oudh was to regard nothing as a right which did not fulfil all the tests of a complete proprietary title. "If a right be not divisible on succession by inheritance, if it be not transferable, if it do not possess a money value, if it could not have been successfully defended under native rule by litigation or arbitration, it is immediately concluded that there can be nothing left to look at or examine; whereas it is evident from a survey of agrestic (*sic*) affairs in other parts of India, that customary rights exist, and are recognised, although they constitute only an imperfect and partial interest."

After a parenthetic comment on the injustice of Mr. Wingfield's order that, where the evidence regarding a claim to under-proprietary right was doubtful, "the doubt should be given in favour of the Taluqdár," Mr. Muir went on to sketch, much as Mr. King had done, the attitude of the native Government towards the cultivator. That it had duties to perform towards tenants was recognised by the wording of the *sannads* by which the Mughal emperors appointed officers to serve in Oudh:—"He is to conduct his duties with truth and mercy, to comfort the ryots, to be careful that none of the A'mils should take more than half the produce, that the ryots may not suffer. . . . . If the A'mils have collected any forbidden cesses, he is to restore the amount to the villagers in the A'mil's presence." The design, indeed, was allowed to fall into desuetude. As one of the old *ziladárs* (collectors) of the King of Oudh's Government told Mr. Macunachie, "no complaint of increased rent or ouster was ever listened to; the zamíndár would at once have pleaded that, unless allowed to manage his village as he pleased, he could not pay the rent demanded of him by the Chakladár; and *that would have been sufficient.*" But the right to interfere, though dormant, was "perpetuated in the stereotyped engagements entered into by the landholders; and on any thorough reform of the native administration, no doubt the well-known form of words would have been turned into a reality, if anywhere the cultivators were found to have become the subjects of oppression."

Some officers had argued that though, outside taluqas, we were entitled to declare any occupancy rights that might be deemed expedient, yet the *sannads* were a bar to the recognition of any such rights in the estates which they covered. Mr. Muir, on the contrary, thought that if there were any restriction at all on our competence to declare occupancy rights, it would exist, not so much in taluqas, as in ordinary zamíndáris, held by prescription without *sannad*. For the proprietary right is equally full and complete in both cases, while Taluqdárs are expressly bound, which zamíndárs are not, to "promote, so far as in their power, the agricultural prosperity of their estates." Such prosperity in a country "where large farming is unknown" is incompatible with the oppression or over-taxation of the cultivators. "Agricultural prosperity, and a prosperous and justly taxed peasantry, are in India convertible terms. A distressed and straitened tenantry is synonymous with agricultural depression. And it cannot be questioned that the Taluqdárs, as well as the Government, understood the condition in this sense." This being so, Mr. Muir thought there could be no doubt that any measure for protecting the cultivator which might fitly be introduced in zamíndáris might with at least equal fitness be applied to taluqas.

The immediate question for decision was whether the protection actually enjoyed by the cultivator, under the existing orders and practice, was to be wholly or partly withdrawn. Mr. Wingfield advocated its entire withdrawal; Mr. Davies recommended the introduction of Act X. of 1859. Mr. Muir did not concur in either proposal, but suggested that all cultivators who had held land on an estate for twenty years, "and in whose family cultivating occupancy may have descended at the least to a second generation," should be held entitled to be maintained in possession at the rent rates prevailing in the neighbourhood. Ordinary ryots, however, should still find the courts open to them if their possession was interfered with, and their claims should be decided according to local custom, which would also regulate claims based on implied contracts growing out of custom, such as claims to compensation for improvements. From decisions in such suits, a code of precedents would in time spring up.

To those who believe that security of tenure at a fixed rent should be regarded as a necessity for all cultivators, not the privilege of a favoured few, this cannot but seem a somewhat disappointing conclusion; for Mr. Muir's premises appear to justify far more thorough measures than these.

We must now turn from the question of occupancy rights of cultivators to that of under-proprietary rights in general, and subsettlement in particular. There is no formal connection between the two, but the logic of events requires that they should be treated concurrently. It will be remembered that Mr. Wingfield's "record of rights" circular had barred from hearing all claims to under-proprietary rights in taluqas except such as were enjoyed in 1855, and that in September 1864 the Taluqdárs agreed to the extension of the period of limitation for such claims to twelve years from the date of annexation, *i.e.* to the 13th of February 1844, subject to the stipulation that the claimants of such rights should not be decreed anything more than the most favourable terms which they had enjoyed in any one year since the incorporation of their lands in the taluqa. The question soon arose whether, if the under-proprietors had held the lease of the whole village from the Taluqdár at any time during the twelve-years period of limitation, they were now entitled to be decreed a sub-settlement of the whole village, *i.e.* a lease at a rent amounting to the Government demand on the village, *plus* a certain proportion of the assumed profits, fixed for the term of settlement, and payable to the Taluqdár. It might seem, indeed, that the matter was not open to doubt,—that the right of engaging for the village having been kept alive by exercise within the period of limitation, must, as a matter of course, have been decreed. And this was the principle adopted by Mr. Davies in what is known as the Morárkhera case, decided on the 26th of November 1864.

This was an appeal from the order of Mr. Currie as Settlement Commissioner, rejecting the claim of Dáljít Singh and others to the subsettlement of the village of Morárkhera, in the estate of Mahesh Baksh Singh, a Taluqdár of the Rai Bareli district. The court of first instance found that the claimants were the hereditary zamíndárs of the village, had held leases from the Taluqdár within the period of limitation, and had engaged direct with the Chakladár when the village was held *khám*. But it dismissed their claim to subsettlement on the ground that they had not held at a fixed rent. The Settlement Commissioner upheld this decision, on the ground that "there was not even a terminable lease allowed to run on without renewal, for a regular lease was not given until one crop had been cut, and the prospects of the next ascertained." Mr. Davies, however, upset these decisions, holding that "the main point, namely, that the appellants are the hereditary zamíndárs, being fully established, it follows that if they have held a lease of any sort within the term of limitation, they are entitled to subsettlement under the British Administration. For it was of such a tenure that the Government of India, in their letter dated the 19th of October 1859, observed that 'it is not a new creation, and is a tenure which, in the opinion of the Governor-General, must be maintained,' and that 'the only effectual protection which the Government can extend to inferior holders is to define and record their rights, and to limit the demand of the Taluqdár as against such persons, during the currency of the settlement, to the amount fixed by the Government as the basis of its own demand.' Wherever the zamíndárí right is clearly established, and the fact of the zamíndár's having held a lease under the Taluqdár within the period of limitation, the Financial Commissioner considers that he is bound, not merely by the common law and usage of the country, but also by the terms of the letter above quoted, to admit the claim to a subsettlement."

To an unsophisticated mind, this doctrine seems unimpeachable enough, but it was objected to by the Taluqdárs, who, to a certain extent, succeeded in converting Mr. Davies himself to their views. One of the stipulations on which they had agreed to the extension of the period of limitation for under-proprietary claims to twelve years has already been mentioned. But there was another, or rather, two others, viz. that only such subordinate interests should be recorded as were held of right, and not by favour or for service, and that *temporary leases be not confounded with under-tenancies carrying a complete right of property.* This latter sentence is the important one for our present purpose. The leases held from Taluqdárs by under-proprietors during the Nawábí were almost always "temporary," often for one year only, and Mr. Davies, though holding that "a *pakka* lease held by under-proprietors does constitute a tenancy carrying a complete right of property," and that the holder of such a lease during the Nawábí for a single year, would be entitled, political restrictions apart, to a subsettlement, yet thought it highly probable that by the italicised stipulation the Taluqdárs intended to protect themselves against this construction, and were therefore entitled under the agreement to resist its application, except as regards such leases as were in force in 1855.

Mr. Davies "confessed that he had hitherto construed the word 'temporary' as the converse of *pakka*." Now almost as many volumes might be written on the meanings of, and the distinctions between, the words *pakka* or *pukhta*, and *kachchha* or *khám*, as concerning the terms "objective" and "subjective." Let it suffice, however, to state here the definition given by Captain Macandrew, which was adopted by Mr. Davies, and has since met with general acceptance. According to this definition, a village is said to be *pakka* when the zamíndár (or the lessee) is entitled to the profit, or liable to the loss, that may accrue according as the collections exceed or fall short of the sum which he has bound himself to pay as the rental for the year. It is said to be *khám* when there is no such title to profit or liability to loss, the rents being collected directly by the landlord or his agents, and no account of collections being rendered to a zamíndár or lessee. A village may be *pakka* even if the person who has engaged for it at a fixed sum be put out of rent-collecting possession altogether, as is the case where a third party, commonly called a *jamoghdár*, is put in to make the collections, or even when the landlord makes them himself, so long as this is done with the consent of the zamíndár or lessee, and an account of the collections rendered to him. The point upon which the distinction turns is the existence or non-existence of the right to profit and the correlative liability to loss on the part of the person who has engaged for the lease, whether he be an under-proprietor (*zamíndár* or *qábiz darmiyání*), or a mere farmer (*thekadár* or *mustájir*).

Bearing this analysis in mind, it is not easy to understand how Mr. Davies can have " construed the word ' temporary ' as the converse of *pakka*." There is only one possible converse to *pakka* as above defined, and that is *kachchha*, and it is of course clear that a *pakka* lease may be, and in ninety-nine cases out of a hundred actually was, ' temporary.' Every lease, indeed, so long as it lasts, is *pakka*, and only ceases to be so on being cancelled. Such a thing as a *kachchha* lease is a contradiction in terms. But whatever the process by which Mr. Davies arrived at the distinction, the principle by which he had been guided was, in his own words, that " though the mere holding of a temporary lease was not sufficient proof of intermediate proprietorship, yet that if this main point of zamíndári tenure were clearly proved, the holding of a temporary lease under the Taluqdár within the twelve years *would* qualify an under-proprietor for a decree of subsettlement, but would not so qualify a mere *thekadár*, or farmer, without any under-proprietary right." He still held that, " as a matter of law, settlement officers were bound to decree subsettlements wherever persons proved to be under-proprietors could show that they had held a village *pakka* from the Taluqdár during the period of limitation. But as the question was complicated by the conditions under which the Taluqdárs had agreed to the extension of the period of limitation, he requested, in his letter to the Chief Commissioner dated the 10th of June 1865, that his 'views should be authoritatively affirmed or corrected.'" Mr. Wingfield's opinion was that there was a well-marked distinction between the right to subsettlement founded on usage and prescription, and claims based on mere temporary casual leases"; and that "some continuance of possession, not by any means necessarily uninterrupted, of a *bonâ fide* lease, giving the management of the village lands, is necessary to establish the *pukhtadári* right (*i.e.* the right to hold *pakka*), and a title to a subsettlement." He also felt himself in a position to state, "as the interpreter of the sentiments of the Taluqdárs," that their object in making the stipulation against the confusion of temporary leases with "under-tenancies conveying a complete right of property" *was* to protect themselves against claims to subsettlement of the kind which Mr. Davies thought himself legally bound to decree.

In reply to this letter, the Financial Commissioner took up a more decided position, and, though regretting that the ambiguous stipulation aforesaid had been made, as susceptible of misconstruction, thought that he had in his letter of the 10th of June attached undue weight to it, and that its terms were not infringed by a subsettlement, if the under-proprietors had contracted for the revenue for any one year during the period of limitation.

Apart from the legal effect of this questionable stipulation, the point in issue between Mr. Wingfield and Mr. Davies was briefly this—Had zamíndárs whose villages had been incorporated in a taluqa a right to engage for the revenue of them under native rule?

Mr. Davies maintained the affirmative. According to Mr. Wingfield, they sometimes had the right, and sometimes not, according to the circumstances under which the incorporation of the village with the taluqa took place.

Captain Macandrew maintained the still more extreme view that the zamíndárs of a village included in a taluqa had *no* right to engage for the revenue of it, and that their *sir* and *nánkár* lands were the measure of their rights. This position, however, seems sufficiently disposed of by Mr. Carnegy, whose opinion here, as in the case of occupancy rights, coincided with that of the Chief Commissioner. "In this class of unpurchased tenures," he wrote, "it was very far from the impression of the former proprietors that it was a matter contingent solely on the will and pleasure of the Taluqdár to hold *pakka* or *khám* at his option; on the contrary, they believed that in all justice they had the most undeniable right themselves to hold *pakka* under the Taluqdár, to the extent, and I know many instances in which the right was exercised, that they could even withdraw their village altogether from a taluqa, and themselves engage for it direct with Government, or include it in the rent-roll, on similar terms, of some other estate. In such cases as these, how is it possible to say that the rights of the sub-proprietors under the native rule amounted to no more than the profits of their *sir* and *nánkár*? and on what principle of justice could we now confine their sub-proprietary interests to these perquisites alone?"

Apart from the ambiguous proviso by which the Taluqdárs had guarded themselves, and which had been accepted by the Governor-General, apparently without a clear apprehension of the use which might be made of it, there would seem to be little doubt that Mr. Davies was correct in his contention that proprietors of land had an inherent right to engage for the revenue of that land, which was not abrogated merely by its incorporation in a taluqa. If they parted with their proprietary right to a Taluqdár by *bonâ fide* sale, then of course the right to engage for the revenue was transferred from them to him. Or if their proprietary right had been forcibly effaced beyond the period of limitation, it could not be recognised by our courts, and the right to engage perished with it. But fraudulent and fictitious sale deeds, such as were many of the *bainámas* produced in the settlement courts, should have been treated as worthless; and where a village was voluntarily, and without even any pretence of purchase, put into a taluqa for the sake of the Taluqdár's protection, justice, of course, demanded that when the protection ceased, the village proprietors should be released from a connection which they wished to put an end to, and which, owing to altered circumstances, was no longer in any way advantageous to them. *Cessante causâ cessat et effectus.* This course, however, being barred by the *sannads*, the next best thing would have been to give the zamíndárs a subsettlement under the Taluqdár, allowing the latter a small percentage on the revenue as málikána, whether the right of engaging had been exercised by the proprietors during the period of limitation or not. This course, again, was limited by the proviso on which the Taluqdárs had consented to the extension of the period of limitation, viz. that under-proprietors should not be decreed anything more than the best terms they had actually enjoyed in any year since the incorporation of their village in the taluqa, and within the period of limitation. All under-proprietors who had not held *pakka* within that period were thus debarred from a subsettlement. But in the case of those who had held *pakka*, even for a single year, the right was kept alive, and should have been decreed. It was at this stage of the eliminative process that the stipulation regarding temporary leases came into play, and that the dispute as to its meaning became important.

It is much to be regretted that the Taluqdárs were ever asked for their assent to the extension of the period of limitation, and that any stipulations at all on the subject were allowed. For their assent was wholly unnecessary. Our pledges to them provided that "whatever holders of subordinate rights might be under them should be preserved in their former right," and there was no limitation of these rights to those actually exercised in 1855. Mr. Wingfield, indeed, had attempted so to limit them in his "Record of Rights" Circular, but that was a mere instruction to settlement officers, having no legal force, and containing no pledge or promise to anybody. It was therefore perfectly open to the Government of India, and was indeed its bounden duty, to prescribe a proper and reasonable period of limitation for the assertion of subordinate rights, and the Taluqdárs should not have been allowed, nor, had they not been given false notions of their own importance and position, is it in the least probable that they would have claimed, any voice whatever in the matter. About the right of under-proprietors to engage for the revenue of their lands, there seems, apart from the complications with which it was injudiciously hampered, to be no reasonable doubt. "The truth is," as Mr. Davies puts it, that "there was neither settlement nor subsettlement in the Nawábí. As proprietor, a zamíndár had a right to contract for the revenue of his village, but he might decline without loss of proprietorship. In the Nawábí the contract was not sought after, now it is. We cannot deprive a proprietor of the right of contracting for the revenue without breach of the conditions of the *sannads*. This privilege is inherent in the proprietorship of land in India. The Taluqdár has now obtained the right to pay to Government the revenue of all villages in his taluqa; but as the rights of the under-proprietors are reserved, that which they formerly enjoyed, of contracting for the revenue of their own villages, remains to them."

Rights, in short, do not cease to be rights because in certain states of society their assertion is not always profitable. Land may have been worthless until the construction of a railway in its neighbourhood turns it into a valuable property. But the right of the owner before the construction of the railway only differs from his right after it has been constructed in being more valuable.

During the Nawábí, villages were usually included in taluqas either by purchase, with which, when *bonâ fide*, we have here no concern; or by violence and against the will of the village proprietors, in which case the incorporation was simple robbery; or with the consent of the village proprietors, yielded for the sake of the protection against Government officials and other landholders which the Taluqdár was able to afford. In this latter case the incorporation was intended to be temporary, and terminable at the will of either party, and it was, in fact, based on a fair, give-and-take, bilateral contract, in which protection and assistance on one side were exchanged for submission and services, and generally a money payment, on the other. The arrangement when voluntarily entered into by both parties, though necessitated by a vicious and disorganized state of society, was not, in itself, morally objectionable. But the Government of India, by confirming in perpetuity to Taluqdárs the superior right in all villages for which they happened to have been permitted to engage at the second summary settlement, turned a bilateral into a unilateral contract. The protection afforded by the Taluqdár was the correlative of the services and payments which he received from the village proprietors, and when that protection ceased to be afforded, the payments, as well as the services, should also have been discontinued. The duty, however, of the Taluqdár to afford protection seems to have been altogether ignored, and was rendered unnecessary and impossible by the introduction of a settled system of Government, while the dependence and payments on the part of the village proprietors were continued and enforced.

In most taluqas there is a considerable proportion of villages of which the Taluqdár was, during the Nawábí, the real and sole proprietor, and that in these he was rightly maintained as such, no one disputes. But in very many of the villages in which subsettlements were claimed, the Taluqdár's tenure under native rule had been, at best, that of a mere farmer, and was, not unfrequently, something very much worse. This farming, or other still less respectable tenure, was by our policy and proclamations converted into a superior proprietorship, and all, therefore, that could be awarded to the zamíndárs was an under-proprietary right. The fact that we had put it out of our power to do them complete justice was surely an additional reason, if any were needed, for doing them such justice as we could.

It is but fair, however, to note that no less an authority than Sir William Muir agreed with Mr. Wingfield in thinking that the fact of under-proprietors having held *pakka* from the Taluqdár within the period of limitation was not in itself enough to entitle them to a subsettlement of any other lands than those in their own cultivating possession as *sír* or *nánkár*. To obtain the subsettlement of a whole village, he thought it was necessary that they should show that " the title has been kept alive over the whole area claimed, within the term of limitation." Such evidence was to be found in the exercise of such incidents of proprietorship as management of the cultivating arrangements, breakage of waste, control over the jungle, and enjoyment of manorial dues and perquisites. Mr. Muir also suggested that under-proprietary villages in which the right to subsettlement was proved might be divided into three classes, and the Taluqdár's share in the profits adjusted accordingly. In the first class of such villages, where the Taluqdár had hardly interfered at all, and the lease had been held continuously by the zamíndárs, he proposed that the *malikána* allowance should be fixed at 5 per cent. on the revenue; in the second class, where the zamíndárs were occasionally excluded, at 15 per cent.; in the third, where they were frequently excluded, and their interest in the property weakened by this or other causes, at 25 per cent.

The tenant and under-proprietary right questions having been thus exhaustingly, if not exhaustively, discussed in minutes and memoranda, were next to pass through a phase of demi-official correspondence between Sir John Lawrence and Mr. Wingfield, conducted through the medium of Mr. Grey. The Governor-General desired to secure some degree of fixity of tenure to all cultivators of old standing, but his sympathies were more especially enlisted on behalf of ex-proprietors or their descendants, whose proprietary rights had been obliterated, but who remained in possession, as tenants, of the fields of which they had formerly been owners. This class, he thought, and, no doubt, rightly thought, had a stronger claim to protection than the mass of cultivators whose condition was not embittered by memories of ancient ownership. The object which he insisted on was that such cultivators should be " recognised and recorded as possessing a right of occupancy in their hereditary fields, and entitled to hold at the most favourable rates of rent prevailing among other classes of cultivators in the vicinity," whether they were forcibly dispossessed of their former proprietary right, or voluntarily parted with it, unless, in the latter case, it was stipulated or implied, as a part of the transaction, that their right to retain their cultivating holdings was annihilated. If the Taluqdárs would assent to this, the question of tenant-right, " so far as the late proceedings and the present settlement are concerned," was to be considered closed. Sir John Lawrence, however, had extremely exaggerated notions of the proportion of Oudh tenantry whom such a measure would protect. He thought that it would "not, probably, be found to comprise more than 15 or 20 per cent. of the whole number of cultivators." Two per cent. would probably be an excessive estimate.

These views were conveyed by Mr. Grey to the Chief Commissioner. The latter wished to see the question finally disposed of by the simple expedient of cancelling all circulars or orders which in any way recognised a right of preferential or any other occupancy on the part of non-proprietary cultivators, and confining the jurisdiction of the revenue (rent) courts to suits brought by such tenants for breach of contract by the landlord, or for ouster in the middle of the agricultural year. The admission of even such suits as these to a hearing was, of course, to confer upon the ryot a right which he had no power, during the later years, at any rate, of the Nawábí, to enforce, and might therefore, on Mr. Wingfield's principles, have been deemed an infringement of the *sannads* as he interpreted them. Practice is, happily, sometimes more benevolent than theory. Mr. Wingfield, however, agreed to waive his own ideal solution of the difficulty so far as to consent to propose to the Taluqdárs to concede a right of occupancy, at a rent less by two annas in the rupee than that of ordinary cultivators, to ex-proprietary tenants or their descendants. But he was only prepared to do this on the following conditions :—

(1.) That the Taluqdárs might be assured that no other occupancy rights "arising from prescription and not from special contract," should be recognised, and that the proposed arrangement, if carried out, should be "held to dispose finally of the tenant question in Oudh";

(2.) That the protected class should include only ex-proprietors who had been forcibly dispossessed, or their descendants, and not those who had "alienated their rights";

(3.) That each case was to be decided on its merits, "after judicial inquiry," by a European officer.

The Governor-General would not agree to any promises which might seem in any way to waive the right of Government to interfere for the protection of oppressed cultivators, which would, he considered, be a breach of the conditions under which Lord Canning granted the *sannads*. And in this particular, both Mr. Grey and Mr. Wingfield practically agreed with him. They differed, indeed, in thinking that the right to interfere should not be expressly reserved, on the ground that such express reservation would be likely to "make the Taluqdárs suspicious," but their language as to the existence of the right leaves nothing to be desired.

"Inasmuch," wrote Mr. Grey, "as the *sannads* clearly stipulate for a proper and considerate treatment of their ryots by the Taluqdárs, nothing that may be said now could be held to prevent the interference by Government at a future time, by legislation or otherwise, if the relations between the ryots and their landlords should at any time become so unsatisfactory as to demand the intervention of Government. This is so obvious that, perhaps, it may not be thought necessary to express such a reservation."

Similarly, Mr. Wingfield:—

"The condition in the *sannads*, that the Taluqdárs shall promote the agricultural prosperity of their estates, would alone furnish the Government with warrant for stepping in to prevent oppression of the cultivators, for they cannot be oppressed without agricultural deterioration. But interference would be justified on the broad grounds of good government. The Taluqdárs will see this clear enough."

In other words, all that it was proposed to abandon was the intention of according fixity of tenure to non-proprietary cultivators on the ground of any *right*, prescriptive or otherwise, on their part. The competence of Government to confer fixity of tenure on every cultivator in Oudh, if it should ever become, or be perceived to be, necessary, as a matter of public policy, to do so, could be in no way affected by any engagements which had been, or which might be, made with the Taluqdárs. Of course no such engagement ever was made, and had it been made, it would have been invalid, for the simple reason that no Government can bind its successors, or itself, by promises to any class of its subjects, not to do what may at any time be found requisite for the welfare of the nation as a whole.

To Mr. Wingfield's proposals, including the cancellation of the existing revenue circulars regarding occupancy and rent rates, the Governor-General assented, but insisted that all ex-proprietors should be protected who had retained possession of the fields they formerly owned in their ancestral villages, in whatever way they might have parted with or been deprived of their proprietary rights.

To these conditions Mr. Wingfield endeavoured to induce the Taluqdárs to agree. He reduced the Governor-General's terms to writing, and made them over to the two Mahárájas, Sir Mán Singh of Mahdona, and Sir Dirgbigai Singh of Balrámpur, for communication to all other Taluqdárs then in Lucknow. This was on the 10th of March 1866, and on the 14th *id.*, some fifty of the leading Taluqdárs waited on Mr. Wingfield with their written reply. This was, in substance, a flat refusal to accept the terms proposed. It seems scarcely possible that they can have understood what those terms really were, for "we look in vain," they said, "to see what compensation we are to get in lieu of the perpetual loss, year by year, of *one-eighth part of our recognised and customary income.*" They can hardly have supposed that what the Governor-General desired was a general reduction of rents all round by two annas in the rupee. Yet the words underlined seem incapable of bearing any other construction. What Sir John Lawrence supposed himself to be seeking was a reduction by that amount, or one-eighth, of the rents payable by, at the most, 20 per cent. of the cultivating body, which would have lowered the income of the Taluqdárs not by one-eighth, but by one-fortieth. And they must have been aware that the proportion of tenants whom the proposed arrangement would protect certainly did not amount to 5 per cent. of the whole. Either, therefore, they wholly misunderstood the terms offered to them, or else they multiplied by at least twenty the effect it would have had upon their incomes. If, they continued, Mr. Wingfield, who was on the point of retiring from the service, would stay six months longer in Oudh, then, indeed, they "might do something." But as it was, they had "now no expectation of gaining any advantage in this matter." At a final discussion on the 15th of March, they declined to "give up one cowry on plea of proprietorship." Thus this attempt at a compromise ended in failure.

Mr. Wingfield gave over charge of his office to Mr. Strachey a day or two afterwards. From Cawnpore, on the 19th of March, he wrote his report of the breakdown of the negotiations, and with a Parthian arrow fired from Karáchi in the shape of a memorandum dated the 22nd of April, finally disappeared from the stage of Oudh politics, which he had dominated so completely for nearly seven years, and where he cannot be denied the merit of having left an enduring mark. He had espoused the interests, real or supposed, of a small but influential class with a fervour which, though doubtless sincere, blinded him in a great measure to the rights and the welfare of the great mass of the agricultural population, the high-caste yeomanry and the low-caste cultivators. He had endeavoured, not altogether without success, to commit the Government of India to declarations which should render it impossible hereafter to modify his policy without incurring the charge of breach of faith; and had fostered on the part of the Taluqdárs a sense of their own importance and of the magnitude of their claims which has become a serious obstacle to anything like even-handed revenue legislation for the province. It would, however, be absurd to deny that he conducted the affairs of his clients, the territorial aristocracy of Oudh, with great ability and unfailing energy and persistence, and that by his singular mastery of details, combined with argumentative power, he practically gained his object of establishing their ascendancy in the teeth of the prepossessions of the Governor-General and of a majority of the Council.

In a "Note on Tenant-Right in Oudh," dated the 14th of May 1866, the new Chief Commissioner, Mr. Strachey, recommended that Government should accept the result of the late inquiry, and declare that there were no rights of occupancy which could be maintained against the will of the landlord ; that all orders recognising any such right should be cancelled : that no further inquiry into other than proprietary rights should be made by settlement officers ; that claims to an occupancy right by non-proprietary cultivators should be heard only in the civil courts ; that " the jurisdiction of the summary suit courts in respect of suits brought by tenants-at-will should be confined to complaints of illegal distraint, breach of contract, exaction, or ouster in the middle of the agricultural year "; that previous rules should be revised so as to be brought into conformity with orders based on the above proposals; *but*, lastly, that " nothing in these orders shall affect the position hitherto held by former proprietors, or their descendants, who, although they may have lost their proprietary rights, still retain possession, as cultivators, of the land which they formerly held as proprietors. In respect of this class, the Government reserves, for further consideration, the determination of the measures which shall be taken."

Mr. Strachey urged that the Government was getting itself into an awkward position, and the sooner it got out of it the better; that his proposals afforded, if not a satisfactory, at least a not undignified solution of the difficulty; and that he was confident that the Taluqdárs would agree to terms on behalf of ex-proprietors which the Government would consider fair; but, failing such assent, he thought that public opinion would support the Government in legislation for the purpose of protecting ex-proprietors. He thus converted the question at issue from one of the interpretation of our pledges to the Taluqdárs to that of how much public opinion would stand in the way of contravening, or what he supposed to be contravening, those pledges. Mr. Davies assented to these proposals, but urged that a clause should be inserted in the declaration, providing that nothing which it contained was to be " understood as lessening the obligation devolving on the Taluqdárs, under the conditions of their *sunnuds*, to promote the agricultural prosperity of their estates."

Mr. Strachey followed up his suggestions for a disposal of the tenant-right question by proposing sundry rules regarding subsettlements and other under-proprietary rights. The most important of these rules was that which laid down the conditions on which alone a subsettlement could be decreed. These conditions were—(1) proof of under-proprietary right in the lands of which subsettlement was claimed; (2) proof that such right had been kept alive, within the period of limitation, over the whole area claimed; (3) proof that the claimant, or the person from whom he had inherited, had, " by virtue of his under-proprietary right, and not merely through privilege granted on account of service or by favour of the Taluqdár, held such land under contract (*pakka*), with some degree of continuousness, since the village came into the taluqa."

The phrase " some degree of continuousness," of course, required definition, and was to be interpreted as follows :—

(1.) " If the village was included in the taluqa before the 13th of February 1836, the lease must have been held for not less than twelve years between that date and the annexation of the province.

(2.) " If the village was included in the taluqa after the 13th of February 1836, but before the 13th of February 1844, the lease must have been held for not less than one year more than half the period between the time at which the village was so included and the annexation of the province.

(3.) " The lease must in all cases have been held for not less than seven years during the term of limitation, unless the village was included for the first time in the taluqa after the 13th of February 1844, in which case the village must have been held for not less than one year more than half of the period between the time at which the village was so included and the annexation of the province."

It was further provided that if both Taluqdár and under-proprietor had been for any period dispossessed of the village and lease respectively, the term of such dispossession should not count against the latter. Also, that nothing in these rules was to apply to the case of villages which had been included in a taluqa after the 13th of February 1844, and in which no lease had been held for any period under the Taluqdár. It will, perhaps, be remembered that, in May 1864, Mr. Wingfield had entered into an agreement with the Taluqdárs by which the latter consented to the establishment of a twelve-years' period of limitation for under-proprietary claims, on the condition that "where villages have been annexed to the taluqa within twelve years, the persons who were in full proprietary possession will not be entitled to recover the equivalent of their former rights, viz. a sub-settlement at 5 per cent. upon the Government demand, but only to the most favourable terms they had enjoyed in any one year since the incorporation of their lands with the taluqa." From the wording of this agreement it, of course, resulted that if a village had been forcibly seized by a Taluqdár in, say, 1853, and the zamíndárs entirely crushed or driven out, so that they had exercised no rights whatever in the village from the time of their dispossession up to annexation in 1856, they had no claim to any rights at settlement. For the only rights that could be claimed were such as had been held in subordination to the Taluqdár, and by the supposition they had held no such rights, though they had been independent owners of the village, and forcibly dispossessed of their property within three years before annexation. This result, however, was too much for the Government of India to swallow undiluted, [though Mr. Wingfield thought, and no doubt correctly, that it was " in entire accordance with the pledges given by Government "], and it was finally agreed that zamíndárs in such cases should be allowed a subsettlement at the Government demand, *plus* 25 per cent. as a rent-charge to the Taluqdár. Thus the loss which the zamíndárs had suffered by robbery of the worst type was halved instead of being wholly redressed. The Oudh settlement, in some of its aspects, has certainly been a forcible illustration of Shakespeare's aphorism,

"Some sins do bear their privilege on earth,"

and the deputation of Taluqdárs who congratulated and were congratulated by Lord Lytton in the autumn of 1876 on the passing of the Oudh Land Revenue Act, did not speak without reason when they assured him that "the land and all its complex relations are viewed in Oudh in quite a different light from those in other parts of the country, and our ideas of social economy and political connection"—whatever that may mean, perhaps political justice—"have little in common with those of other provinces."

It is time, however, to return from this digression to Mr. Strachey's proposed rules, of which the most obvious feature is that they require the existence of a right to be proved by its exercise from seven to twelve times instead of once, as is the ordinary maxim of law. This somewhat anomalous principle, moreover, was given retrospective effect, and all cases in which claims to under-proprietary rights had been already decreed otherwise than in accordance with these and sundry other rules—excepting cases disposed of by arbitration or compromise—were to be open to revision. The share of the gross rental payable by the under-proprietor to the Taluqdar was to be calculated with reference to the former gross rental and the former payments. No subsettlement could be made if the under-proprietor's share of the profits had amounted to less than 12 per cent., but in that case the latter's *sir* and *nánkár* lands were to be preserved to him, and if the profits of such lands fell short of 10 per cent. of the gross rental, they were to be increased by the Taluqdár up to that sum. If the profits of an under-proprietor entitled to subsettlement exceeded 12 per cent., but fell short of 25 per cent. of the gross rental, they were to be increased to 25 per cent., the sacrifice being equally shared by the Taluqdár in the shape of reduced profits, and the Government in that of a lower revenue demand. .

In return for this disposal—so favourable to them—of the subsettlement question, the Taluqdárs signified their consent to a concession of the right of occupancy proposed by Mr. Strachey on behalf of ex-proprietary tenants, who had been, either by themselves, or by the persons from whom they claimed, in possession as proprietors in any village or estate within thirty years prior to annexation.

Such persons were to have a right of occupancy in the lands which they held or cultivated on the 24th of August 1866, provided those lands had not come into their possession for the first time since the 13th of February 1856.* The rent payable by such tenants was to be two annas in the rupee less than the rent usually paid for similar land by tenants not having a right of occupancy, and of the same class or caste, and was not liable to be enhanced more than once in five years. Tenants, also, who had improved their holdings were not to be liable to ejectment, nor was their rent to be enhanced, for thirty years after the execution of the improvements, except on payment of compensation.

Why the limit of thirty years was fixed is not clear. The original phrase employed was "unexhausted improvements," which was obviously much more fair. The imposition of a thirty-years limit merely postpones for that period the landlord's power of appropriating the fruits of another's labour. As long as the improvements have any appreciable value, so long should the tenant, if ejected, be deemed entitled to compensation for them. "Considering," as Mr. Strachey wrote, "that, as a general rule, all improvements are made by the tenants," it is surely desirable that they should have some inducement for making improvements likely to endure longer than thirty years.

Such, in substance, was "the Oudh Compromise" which was embodied in Act XXVI. of 1866, and Act XIX. of 1868, the former pleasantly called the Subsettlement Act, as having for its object the prevention of subsettlements, and the latter the Oudh Rent Act. In return for curtailments of, and restrictions on, subsettlement, by which they, as a body, gained very largely, the Taluqdárs consented to the recognition of rights of occupancy, of the value above indicated, on the part of what may be, at a liberal estimate, 1 per

---

* The possession of this right was made incompatible with the retention of any under-proprietary right whatever, *e.g.* a man who had been decreed half-a-dozen trees in under-proprietary right could not acquire a right of occupancy in the same village or estate.

cent. of their tenantry, and yielded a very limited right to compensation for improvements. It is probable that both concessions together have not reduced their incomes by $\frac{1}{2}$ per cent., say eight annas in every hundred rupees. Assuredly they were wise in their generation, and well deserved Mr. Strachey's congratulations on "having as their chief leader and adviser a man of such remarkable intelligence as Mahárája Mán Singh." The Taluqdárs in general, and that nobleman in particular, received an assurance that their conduct was highly appreciated by the Governor-General in Council, and Mr. Strachey was warmly thanked for his services in inducing them to concur in such a satisfactory conclusion of questions of so difficult and complicated a character." Thus everybody—except, perhaps, a few thousand under-proprietors who lost control over their villages, and a few million cultivators whose fancied security of tenure was somewhat rudely disturbed—was content, and the chorus of complacency was wound up by Sir Stafford Northcote, who, as Secretary of State for India, had much pleasure in learning that this long agitated question had now been "settled in a manner which appears to be in every respect satisfactory, alike to your Excellency's Government and to the Taluqdárs."

CHAPTER VIII.

CONCLUSIONS.

NEARLY twelve years have elapsed since the edifice of the Oudh Compromise was crowned by the passing of Act XIX. of 1868, but such legislation for the province as has been effected during that period has been concerned with details rather than with principles, and has but little general interest. The main features of the system of agricultural polity have not been materially altered by Acts XVII. and XVIII. of 1876—the Oudh Land Revenue Act and the Oudh Laws Act —and the different classes of the population have been left "free to work out their several good, to go forward in the bright career before them," almost wholly unhampered by any such interference between landlord and tenant as was so earnestly deprecated by the organ of the Taluqdárs.

In the preceding chapters it has been attempted to give a general idea of the actual condition and mutual relations of the agricultural population of Oudh, and to sketch, however inadequately, the process by which that condition and those relations have been arrived at. A more difficult task remains, that of endeavouring in some degree to estimate the effects on various classes of twenty-four years of British rule, and to indicate certain practicable remedies for some of the evils from which the province at present suffers.

For the purposes of this endeavour, the rural population may be roughly divided into four classes, viz.:—

(1.) Single landowners, large and small, superior and subordinate.

(2.) Coparcenary communities, independent or under-proprietary.

(3.) Tenants without any proprietary right, including that very minute proportion to whom a right of occupancy has been decreed.

(4.) Labourers, *i.e.* persons subsisting mainly by agricultural labour for hire, whether they cultivate a small patch of land on their own account or not.

Concerning each of these four classes a few remarks will be made.

(1.) *Single landowners, large and small.*

This class includes the most prosperous portion of the agricultural community. It consists of everyone who holds land in his own right and without shareholders, from the large Taluqdár, master of several hundred thousand acres, to the petty under-proprietor who has obtained a decree for a few *bighas* of *sir* or *nánkár*. Many of the class are very wealthy; nearly all ought to be above the reach of actual want of the means of subsistence; most have the fate of a larger or smaller number of tenants in their hands.

The Taluqdárs have, of course, gained immensely, from a pecuniary and social point of view, by British rule. The very stars in their courses seem to have fought for them ever since the Mutiny. The irregular and temporary accessions to their estates to which the disorders of the Nawábí gave rise have been legalised and made permanent. Their title to the superior ownership of every village included in their *sannads* has been rendered unassailable. They have been exempted from all the risks of oppression and ill-treatment to which they were exposed at the hands of the King's officials, and, since the passing of the Oudh Land Revenue Act, are no longer liable even to confinement in the civil jail for arrears of revenue. All doubtful questions, not to speak of some about which there should have been no doubt, which arose between them and their under-proprietors have been decided in their favour.

Socially, they have been treated as the honoured favourites of the Government, instead of as its natural and, at best, its tolerated enemies. They enjoy a degree of personal liberty and consideration to which they were formerly strangers. They can come and go whither they will, may array themselves in silk, and drive their carriages in the streets of Lucknow, privileges which were never conceded to them by the Nawábs or Kings of Oudh.

Altogether, they are probably the most fortunate body of men in India. And taking them as a whole, one may gladly admit that, considering all things, they have done quite as much in return for the favours they have received as there was any reasonable ground for expecting of them. Though often culpably indifferent to the welfare of their tenantry, they are seldom actively oppressive. They are entitled to the credit, and it is no small praise, of having generally refrained from any very marked abuse of the almost unlimited powers conferred on them by our legislation. Improving landlords, or regenerators of agriculture, of course they are not; but that was not to be expected.

The smaller independent zamíndárs have also gained largely by the introduction of British rule. They have been secured in their property against all risks but such as arise from bad seasons or their own mismanagement. And the danger which they ran in the Nawábí of being crushed by the exactions of native officials and of absorption by their more powerful neighbours, was, of course, greater than in the case of a strong Taluqdár, who was generally able to protect himself against oppression. They probably live more within their incomes and are often less pushed for money than Taluqdárs, their scale of personal expenditure being less pretentious.

The same remarks apply, *mutatis mutandis*, to *sir* and *nánkár* holders, who are mostly to be found in Taluqdárí villages. Where their holdings are very minute, they, of course, are raised but little above the level of the ordinary cultivator, except, and it is a considerable exception, that they are, *pro tanto*, exempt from all fear of enhancement of rent during the term of settlement, or of eviction.

The economic evil from which the class in question chiefly suffers is indebtedness. They are probably much more deeply in debt than they were in the Nawábí, their credit being better, and the demands both of the State and of their creditors being much more irresistible. So far as their indebtedness is due to personal extravagance, there is nothing to be done but to trust to the gradual influence of education and experience of the painful results of careless lavishness. No Government can save spendthrifts from the consequences of their own folly, and no wise Government will attempt that hopeless task. But so far as it is due to our revenue arrangements, it behoves us to consider whether the latter are in fault, and if so, how they can be amended.

There is, apparently, something like a general consensus of opinion that our revenue system errs in being over-rigid and inelastic; that, by compelling payment of the same fixed sum in good and bad years alike, it is apt to drive into debt and embarrassment many who, if allowed time, could satisfy all demands without incurring any such burthen. Our theory assumes that, the assessment not being more than might be paid without difficulty on the average of a series of years, the landholder will save in good years enough to make up for the deficiencies of bad ones. But this assumption is vitiated by two facts. Firstly, where money rents prevail, as is the case over by far the greater part of the province, a landowner cannot raise rents within the year merely because the harvests of that year happen to be good. It is only in so far as he is himself a cultivator, which, in all but very diminutive estates, is but to a very slight proportional extent, that he reaps any further benefit from a plenteous harvest than that of being able to collect his rents with comparatively little difficulty or pressure on his tenants. For instance, if a settlement officer has ascertained that the full gross rental of an estate is, or ought to be, Rs. 10,000, he will probably assess the revenue of that estate at about Rs. 5,000. However good the harvests of any particular year, the landlord cannot, if cash rents prevail, realise more than Rs. 10,000.

But in a bad year, if the failure of the crops be at all general, he will not be able to realise so much, within the year at any rate. Perhaps he may not be able to collect more than Rs. 8,000, or, if he does, it will be by forcing his tenants to plunge into debt to satisfy his rent demand. It is therefore only to a very limited extent correct to say that the extra profits of good years make up for the deficiencies of bad ones.

In the second place, so far as landlords do realise larger profits in seasons of plenty or of high prices, as undoubtedly is the case in grain-rented estates, it is not true that by any means all, or even perhaps a majority of them, put by their extra profits as a fund to meet the strain of bad seasons when they come. When they find themselves with more money than usual, they, as a general rule, spend more.

Thus the assumptions on which our system rests of fixing the revenue demand for a period of thirty years, and realising the total sum assessed in thirty annual instalments, do not correspond with the actual facts of the case, and a rigid adherence to that system, as, for instance, during the scarcity, in many districts amounting to famine, of 1877-78, has sometimes undoubtedly the effect of forcing into debt men who might otherwise have kept out of it.

One remedy for this defect in our arrangements which has been often recommended of late may be stated as follows. Instead of realising the same amount every year, whatever the state of the harvest, it is proposed that the demand of, say, ten years should be regarded as a lump sum payable by instalments varying according to the seasons. Thus, if the revenue assessed on an estate be Rs. 5,000, the demand for ten years will be Rs. 50,000. If the first year of the series be a bad one, the collector will perhaps think that not more than Rs. 3,500 can be realised without driving the zamíndár, or his cultivators, or both, into debt. He will content himself, therefore, with collecting that amount, leaving Rs. 46,500 to be recovered during the remaining nine years. If the next harvest be more than usually abundant, perhaps the zamíndár may be able to pay as much as Rs. 7,000. And so on.

This scheme, if it could be carried out, would certainly have the effect of making the revenue demand buoyant and elastic enough. But it appears open to sundry grave objections. It would, to begin with, destroy the moral effect in promoting providence and foresight which the present system of a fixed annual demand certainly tends to produce. And its introduction, so long, at any rate, as the rents of cultivators are not authoritatively fixed, would almost inevitably cause great confusion in the accounts of landlord and tenant. While the rents payable by the great majority of tenants are, as at present, left to be determined by agreement between them and their landlord, there would be serious difficulty, on the one hand, in preventing the *málguzár* from realising from his tenants in bad years an amount of rent proportionately greater than the amount of revenue realised from himself; and, on the other hand, in enabling him, in good years, to realise a proportion of his rental corresponding to his own revenue payments. If, indeed, rents of all cultivators were authoritatively fixed, the matter would be greatly simplified. Until, however, that desirable consummation is attained, Oudh does not seem the most fitting field on which to try the experiment. In grain-rented lands, of course, there is a natural and self-working process of adjustment between harvests and rents, and in estates where grain-rents largely prevail, such as are to be found in some parts of the three northern districts, a revenue demand varying with the season would have a very fair chance of success. Where cash rents are the rule, the fluctuations in rental are, naturally, much more limited, the brunt of bad seasons falling more on the cultivators and less on the landlord; and in such estates a varying revenue demand would be chiefly valuable as giving Government an authoritative right to forbid the realisation from tenants of any larger proportion of rent than it itself collects of revenue. The more the revenue payer is himself in the position of a cultivator, *i.e.* the more his income tends to fluctuate with good or bad harvests, the greater would be to him the boon of an elastic revenue demand. Therefore grain-rented *maháls*, and *maháls* in which, though cash rents prevail, the landlord himself cultivates a large proportion of the land on which he pays revenue, seem the most suitable for the tentative introduction of the proposed scheme.

On the whole, it appears probable that the good effects which might result from a sliding scale of revenue collections have been a good deal over-rated, while the objections to it have been a good deal overlooked. Most of its advantages, without its drawbacks, might be attained by the simpler process of giving collectors larger discretionary power to suspend the demand whenever they consider that to satisfy it in full would cause actual distress or compel resort to the money-lender, and to worry them with fewer requisitions for reports and returns. One great, if not the greatest, cause of the growing lack of independence on the part of Anglo-Indian officials is the yearly increasing certainty that the utterance of any objection to carry out orders, or the expression of any opinion unpopular with their superiors, will be met by an immediate demand for a detailed report, accompanied probably by a tabular statement, as to the grounds of the objection or the opinion. So much energy is expended in showing why things should or should not be done, that little is left for doing them, and almost as much time is spent by a district officer in recording or defending his administrative achievements as in their actual performance. The result is too often little but acres of statistics, which, even if trustworthy, are apt to be wholly uninstructive.

The conclusion of the whole matter, as regards single landholders, large and small, appears to be this, that, except in occasional cases of over-assessment, the only economic evil from which they suffer with which we can in any way deal is indebtedness; and that the only remedy which, at present, at least, we can advantageously apply is to give the collector a more unfettered discretion as to suspensions, and, in a few rare cases, as to remissions of the land revenue.

2. *Coparcenary communities, independent and under-proprietary.*

The sorrows of these village brotherhoods have always, and naturally, attracted more attention than the less romantic troubles of mere cultivators. It may be that we, like Sordello, have—

> ". . . unconsciously contrived forget
> The whole, to dwell on the points,"

and thought, like him, that we—

> ". . . . . . . might assuage
> The signal horrors easier than engage
> With a dim, vulgar, vast, unobvious grief
> Not to be fancied off, or gained relief
> In brilliant fits, cured by a happy quirk,
> But by dim, vulgar, vast, unobvious work
> To correspond."

But their woes, though more picturesque, are none the less sternly real, and it is to be feared that the sympathy and attention which their interesting nature has excited have done little to alleviate the sufferings of those who have to bear them.

The condition of the village brotherhoods, though it may be theoretically better, is probably practically worse than it was during the Nawábí. It is true that under native rule they had few rights which they could legally enforce, and certain such rights we have given them. But our general principle of maintaining the *status quo* in name has really altered it to their disadvantage. The native officials and the Taluqdárs often exercised powers unlimited by any law properly so-called, and the village communities were not seldom the victims of unscrupulous aggression. But the fact that they could frequently resist the Chakladár and the baron with some chance of success preserved them in most cases from extreme oppression. There were doubtless instances not a few of hardship and tyranny and torture very much worse than any which could be found now, but our system of giving ourselves and the Taluqdárs powers which, though theoretically less, are practically and in the long run more stringent than those which the native Government and the Taluqdárs previously exercised, seems to have reduced the coparcenary brotherhoods to a dead level of poverty and discomfort. The possibility of successful resistance saved them at least from the crushing sense of being in the vice of an irresistible necessity. A state of chronic warfare with an enemy who, though bound by no rules, is not invincible is, to people of the habits and character of the Oudh yeomanry, less oppressive and disheartening than hopeless subjection to a power which, however well-meaning and observant of the laws of war, is at once exacting and irresistible. Our system makes it comparatively easy for them to default, but also renders the penalty of default, when it does come, far more crushing. "The bankruptcy court of the jungle" is a thing of the past. When we annexed the country, we found it in a state of anarchy and solution which, after considerable modifications, at first favourable, but after the Mutiny generally adverse to the interests of the zamíndárs, we proceeded to crystallise. In this process we have raised the depths and depressed the heights, while the general level of comfort among the coparcenary bodies is, it is to be feared, lower than it was. When a rigid system of law is imposed on an anarchic country, the gain or loss of the conflicting elements in that country will be in proportion to their capacity or incapacity of adapting themselves to the new conditions, their ability or inability to comprehend and utilise the altered situation. Without forming any extravagant estimate of the mental calibre of the Oudh Taluqdárs, it may be safely asserted that they possess a larger measure of this adaptive faculty than belongs to the village communities, and the loss of the latter has been the gain of the former.

In addition to the burthen of indebtedness, which is probably still heavier and more general among coparcenaries than among single landholders, is the evil of internal dissensions, arising mainly from disputes about shares of land and division of profits. Where the community is numerous, the shares are often exceedingly small, and the profits in proportion.

These are evils which it is only to a very limited extent in the power of Government to mitigate. Reduction of revenue can have but a very insignificant effect in relieving the poverty of a crowded coparcenary body. If, for instance, the revenue demand on a village held by such a body be Rs. 1,000, and there are twenty-five sharers, the reduction of the revenue by one-half would only give them, on an average, Rs. 20 each, a sum which would not make a very appreciable difference in their condition, would not suffice to raise them from discomfort to comfort. All that can be done for them, except where their assessment may be proved by experience to be excessive, is to suspend the demand when seasons are bad, and to facilitate and cheapen partitions. Partitions, it may be here observed for the benefit of the uninitiated, are of two kinds, "perfect," which terminates all joint responsibility for the revenue, and "imperfect," which leaves that responsibility in the last resort unimpaired. Generally speaking, it may be said that imperfect has less tendency than perfect partition to disintegrate the structure of the community, and to weaken the feeling of brotherhood and solidarity. It is, therefore, only desirable to carry out the latter where enmity between co-sharers is very inveterate indeed. All that was practicable in this way has perhaps been done already by the provisions relating to partition of the Oudh Land Revenue Act.

One other object there is to be kept in view in the case of subsettled Taluqdárí villages, and that is the dissolution, wherever it may become possible, of the tie which binds them to the Taluqdár. This cannot be done without the consent of the latter—which would seldom or never be accorded—except in case of sale. Where this occurs, the opportunity should be seized to assert a right of pre-emption on behalf of the State, and then make the settlement direct with the zamíndárs, no longer under-proprietors, recovering the purchase-money from them by instalments spread over a long series of years. This remedy can only be partial, but where we cannot do all we would, we must try to be content to do what we can. The experiment would at any rate be worth trying when it happens that a portion of a taluqa, containing subsettled villages in which marked antagonism exists between the superior and subordinate holders, comes to be sold in satisfaction of decrees against the Taluqdár. The under-proprietors of Oudh, as a body, have suffered many things at the hands of our administration. But we can at least address to them, though with truer meaning, the words of Richard of Gloucester to his brother's injured widow—

"We cannot make you what amends we would,
Therefore accept such kindness as we can."

(3.) *Tenants without any proprietary right.*

Here is the field which is still open to us if we have a sincere desire to elevate the condition of the rural masses. Something like six millions of cultivators, men, women, and children, are material sufficient for the widest philanthropy to operate on. The evils which chiefly afflict this "dim common population" are poverty and ignorance, both of a more intense type than prevails among the peasant proprietors and under-proprietors. Of their mode of life some account has been attempted in Chapter II. Here let it suffice to say that they are often under-fed, generally under-clothed, and have, as a rule, scarcely anything that they can call their own beyond a pair of lean little oxen, half-a-dozen pots and pans, a few rude agricultural implements, and, perhaps, a little silver jewellery. Are they ever to rise above their present condition? That is the biggest question which the future of Oudh has to solve.

If they ever do so rise, it will have to be by their own exertions. No Government can hope to do for them what they can, and, there is every reason to believe, will do for themselves, if only the ordinary motives to exertion are allowed free play. That free play is not allowed at present, owing to the tenure under which they cultivate their fields. The one great boon which we can bestow upon them is perfect security of tenure, at a rent either fixed in perpetuity, or, at least, not liable to be enhanced by the caprice or greed of an interested individual. The most essential of all conditions to the growth of industry and foresight is simply this, that to each man be assured, with the utmost attainable certainty, the fruits of his own labour. In no agricultural community where the land is tilled mainly by petty cultivators can this condition be realised without fixity of tenure. This is a service which it is, beyond dispute, in the power of our Government to perform. But it has not been performed while, as in Oudh, hundreds of thousands of cultivators are always liable to ejectment for no better cause than the *sic volo sic jubeo* of their landlord, be he the Taluqdár of half a district, or the zamíndár of a fraction of a village. For it must be remembered that it is perhaps in small even more than in large properties that the cultivator is in need of protection. "A poor man that oppresseth the poor is like a sweeping rain which leaveth no food." Whether or no the power of eviction is very frequently exercised may, perhaps, be a disputed question, though 38,636 notices of ejectment were issued in 1877, and the average of the three years 1875–1877 was over 30,000; but the power is always there. The Oudh peasant who has no recorded rights has no twelve-years' rule to fall back upon. His tenure depends altogether on the will of the proprietor of the soil which he happens to cultivate, and if it is the profit or the caprice of that proprietor to eject him, ejected he must be. It does not need much reflection to perceive the reality of the hindrance which this obstacle must oppose to habits of continuous industry and exertion, and to all efforts at improvement which rise beyond the mere routine of agriculture. The natural hindrances in a country great part of whose harvests are dependent on an uncertain rainfall are sufficiently serious to relieve us from all necessity of creating artificial ones. Vast sums have been, and are likely to be, expended in India in famine relief. Would it not be well to devote more attention to the duty which lies nearest to our hands, a duty which it is beyond question incumbent upon every state to discharge, that of affording security to the cultivator where he is too helpless to take his own part, rather than expend our energies in the attempt to secure dense populations against famine by expedients which, however indispensable they may be, and, so long as the land laws remain unaltered, are likely to continue, cannot but tend to weaken habits of independent self-reliance? The necessity for abnormal efforts such as these is nearly always the result of a long course of previous neglect of the commonplace every-day duties steady performance of which would have rendered the application of more heroic remedies superfluous. Let the peasantry of Oudh, or of any part of India, enjoy for thirty years security of tenure at a fixed rent, without the power to sublet or mortgage their holdings, and it is hardly too much to predict that the necessity for famine relief will disappear. Speculation on final causes is always somewhat hazardous, but if such a conjecture may be ventured, perhaps the final cause of the famines by which India has of late years been afflicted is to inculcate the necessity of a return to a normal and healthy system of agricultural tenure. In proportion as life conforms more nearly to rational principles does the sphere of casual acts of benevolence and good nature contract *Si nous voulions être toujours sages, rarement aurions nous besoin d'être vertueux.*

This question of land tenure is more important to the welfare of the cultivator in particular and the Empire in general than irrigation, roads, railways, improved agricultural methods, or any other thing whatsoever. The State cannot hope to do as much *for* the people, as it may reasonably count on being able to do *through* them. And not only will what the people can do for themselves if they get fair play, and if the ordinary motives to exertion are allowed to operate, be far greater in amount than anything that can possibly be done for them, but it will be more intrinsically valuable, inasmuch as it will not only improve their material condition, but will also tend to raise their character as human beings.

There is, as has been already observed, no question in Oudh of the relative merits of *grande* and *petite culture*, for the sufficient reason that the former cannot be said to exist. There are very large proprietors, but no large farmers. A farm of five hundred acres in the hands of one man is almost, if not altogether, unknown. Wealthy zamíndárs, indeed, and large lessees occasionally cultivate considerable areas with their own ploughs. These, however, are not in one plot, but consist of scattered patches in perhaps twenty or thirty villages, tilled in methods which in no way differ from those employed by the petty tenant of a dozen acres. Given, then, *petite culture*, the problem before us is to make the best of it. The agricultural system of Oudh is, speaking broadly, a system of large estates divided into very small farms, occupied by tenants-at-will, cultivating with their own stock, and without any security of tenure. Under such conditions *petite culture* never has succeeded, and it may be safely prophesied that it never will succeed. For the one great strong point of *petite culture* by peasant proprietors or by rent-paying cultivators secure of their tenure, is the ardour of individual industry with which it inspires the cultivator. It is this that has enabled it to triumph over all the superior advantages of capital and machinery possessed by large farmers. But that ardour of individual industry cannot exist where there is not perfect security that it shall enjoy the fruits of its own labour. This truth has been at last, though inadequately, recognised in Ireland; it is surely time that it began to be recognised in Oudh.

Advocates of the Taluqdárí system seem to have imagined that if they could but create a class of large landed proprietors at the top, and a mass of tenants-at-will at the bottom, with only the smallest possible number of peasant proprietors and privileged tenants between them, the virtues such as they are, of the English agricultural polity would, in some mysterious way, be the result. They seem to have serenely ignored the fact that there is no class of capitalist farmers in Oudh, and no large farms; that the agricultural classes, instead of being, as in England, one-sixth of the population, are more than two-thirds, *i.e.* seventy, instead of seventeen, per cent.; and lastly, that there is no commerce or manufactures capable of finding employment for the agriculturists whose divorce from the soil they looked forward to with so much equanimity. There is only one profession which evicted peasants are likely to embrace, and that is, theft in its various branches, dacoity and highway robbery for Bráhmans and Rájpúts, petty larceny for low-caste men.

No position, consistent with a settled government, can well be conceived less likely to encourage industry and a desire to make the most of the soil than that of the tenant-at-will. If he improves his land by high cultivation, he exposes himself at once to the risk of a demand for enhanced rent,

This demand can be enforced by a notice of ejectment, which no length of occupancy, no regularity in paying his rent, can give him any legal grounds for successfully contesting. It is true that if he builds an irrigation well, or digs a tank, or constructs an embankment, he cannot be ejected for thirty years without payment of compensation, nor can his rent be enhanced. But, to say nothing of the frequent unwillingness of landlords to allow him to do anything of the kind, the tendency towards making such improvements is in itself so weak as to be very effectually discouraged by the prospect of having to prove a title to compensation in a rent court. Why, moreover, should the limit of thirty years be fixed? As already remarked, the phrase in the original draft of the Rent Act was "unexhausted improvements," and as long as the well, tank, or other work, possesses any appreciable value, so long should the constructor, or his heirs, be deemed entitled to compensation if deprived of it by ejectment. Yet this provision, such and so limited as it is, is the only security which a tenant-at-will, *i.e.* ninety-five out of every hundred Oudh cultivators, at present possesses against capricious eviction.

There is no need to prove, nor is it here asserted, that the majority, or even a large minority, of Oudh landlords habitually abuse the power of ejectment which was—provisionally, as I believe—entrusted to them by the Rent Act of 1868. The mere fact of such a power residing in the will of any individual landlord, however benevolent or enlightened, is quite sufficient materially to check the spirit of improvement on the part of those over whom he is at liberty to exercise it. It is idle to expect men to work without motive, and from the influence of the strongest of all motives to exertion the tenant-at-will is wholly excluded. It is to the cultivator, not to the owner of the soil, that, in Oudh, at any rate, we must look for improvements. Of such improvements as are made at present, by far the greater part are made by tenants. If an illustration be asked for of the extent to which the improvement of the country depends upon the actual cultivators, and how small a part the large landlords play in it, it may be found in the Oudh Revenue Report for 1864–65, where we read that in the Sultánpur district, which is largely Taluqdárí, between 1861 and 1864 there were 7,947 common wells dug, of which 6,476 were dug by cultivators. Out of 1,172 masonry wells built during the same period, 913 were built by cultivators. "In the late drought the disproportion was still greater, the Taluqdárs contributing only three wells out of several thousands." Landholders do often contribute something in the shape of materials, but it is " quite certain that the agriculture of the country is carried on by bullocks, irrigation, manure, and labour, all provided by the ryots, and that the interposition of the large landholders is confined to assessing and collecting the rents." We have heard a great deal of the necessity of creating a feeling of security in the minds of landlords. Would it not be well to try the novel experiment of creating a similar feeling in the minds of tenants?

There is no denying that the condition of the ordinary tenant, cultivating, say, five acres of land with a single plough, and paying a rent of, perhaps, thirty or five-and-thirty rupees, and with a wife and three or four children, not to speak of aged and helpless relatives, to support, is unsatisfactory. And so long as he remains a tenant-at-will, there seems little chance of its amelioration. The most obviously needful preliminary to such amelioration is an increase of the produce which he grows, and, as a necessary condition precedent to this, the prevention, not so much of the increase of rent, as of the liability of rent to increase. As long as the cultivator is aware that if he enlarges the out-turn of his holding by careful tillage, or by the construction of improvements, he is liable to have the whole or a part of the increment taken from him in the form of enhanced rent; as long as he knows that he is liable to eviction at the caprice of an individual who is pretty certain to exercise his power of ejectment if crossed in any way by any inconvenient manifestation of independence, so long will he be shut out from the influence of the strongest motive to improvement, the certainty that he will enjoy the fruits of his own labour.

Mere fixity of tenure will not suffice to make the position of those who are now tenants-at-will what it ought to be.

But it is the indispensable condition without which no appreciable improvement can be looked for. Arguments against interference between landlord and tenant derived from experience of capitalist farming in England, and from the theories regarding the rights of private property which find acceptance there, have, it need hardly be said, no application to the state of things which exists in Oudh, or, perhaps, in any part of India. It is only rent paid by capitalists that is regulated by the capacity of the soil alone. In India the helplessness of the cultivator is one of the chief factors in determining its amount. Competition rent and wages, in the mouths of the well-to-do, usually mean rent or wages determined by free competition of one cultivator or labourer against another, for the benefit of a landlord or a capitalist employer; not a competition on something like equal terms between capital and associated labour. Strictly speaking, the rent paid by the Indian ryot is not economic rent at all. This is recognised by Act XIX. of 1868, which defines rent simply as "the money or portion of the produce of land, payable on account of the use or occupation of land, or on account of the use of water for irrigation." And yet the assumptions on which the Act is based are such as to apply only to economic rent, of which the theory may be said to be that it is limited by the necessity of leaving a sufficient margin of profit to the agriculturist to prevent him from withdrawing his capital to other employments. Rent paid by Indian ryots is not so limited, for there is, speaking broadly, no other employment save field labour to which these hereditary cultivators can turn. One in a thousand may obtain domestic service, but what is he among so many? A tenant who, rather than submit to a demand for enhanced rent, relinquishes his holding and migrates to another village can rarely get, at the most, more than a field or two of arable land to begin with. He has to break up waste soil for himself, which is probably of inferior quality, and for the first year will most likely yield no return. Rather than do this, he will often submit to enhancement to an extent which encroaches on his small capital until the chance of a bad season, or an outbreak of cattle disease, leaves him without the means of cultivation, and he sinks to the level of a day labourer on a precarious income of from three-halfpence to twopence farthing, or, at most, in harvest-time, threepence a day ; or, for an advance of a few rupees, becomes the bond slave of some cultivator better off than himself, whose plough he and his children after him will be henceforth destined to guide. Even if he had the promptitude and decision of character to relinquish his holding at once on the first demand for enhanced rent, and seek better terms elsewhere, he would still be but putting off the evil day, and, sooner or later, he or his children would have to " go through the sad probation all again," and betake themselves once more to unfamiliar fields. Even if, warned by bitter experience, he should induce the owner of the waste which he broke up to give him a perpetual lease, the chances are that the latter, or his successor, would under the confiscation sections (52 and 53) of the Oudh Revenue Act, be able to resume the grant should it ever become worth resuming.

The material condition of rural Oudh cannot improve without an increase in the amount of produce raised, which can only result from the application of more industry and capital to the soil. The experience of twenty years has shown that large landlords will not thus apply capital to any considerable extent, and the industry is not theirs to apply. Even if they did lay out capital in improvements, by far the greater part of the returns would only benefit themselves in the form of increased rent, without doing any good to the cultivator. It is to the actual cultivators themselves that we must look to work out their own economic salvation by the amelioration of the soil. If the capital in their hands increases, we may safely trust to their applying it to the land, provided that the investment be made a perfectly secure one. What is wanted is, in the words of Mr. Caird, " *a sounder system of land tenure, and thereby the substitution of an improving for an exhausting agriculture.*"

The increase of capital must depend, according to Mr. Mill's analysis, on (1) the amount from which saving can be made ; (2) strength of the dispositions which prompt to saving.

Now, in Oudh, as regards ordinary cultivators, both these are at a minimum. The surplus of the produce of their labour, after supplying themselves with the barest necessaries of life and paying their rent, is on an average of years, extremely small, and in bad seasons, not unfrequently a minus quantity. And motives for applying the surplus, when it exists, to the improvement of the soil, are extremely weak. The small farmer knows well enough that if he makes his land capable of paying an enhanced rent, that enhancement is pretty sure to take place. Why, then, should he improve his land ? The result is that the few small farmers who have a little spare cash do not apply it to the soil, but lend it to their poorer neighbours—who, as likely as not, expend it in marriage festivities—at 24 or 36 per cent. interest, which undoubtedly, as far as they are concerned, is a more profitable investment.

The stock assertion that tenant-right is "opposed to the principles of political economy" is at present, perhaps, hardly in need of refutation. Political economy, so far as it is a science, rests, partly on physical laws, partly on certain assumptions as to the motives which govern human conduct, and its fundamental assumption is that every individual desires to accumulate wealth. That measure or policy is most in accordance with the dictates of political economy which, by giving the freest scope and fullest play to the ordinary motives to accumulation, holds out the strongest encouragement to productive industry. And that measure or policy is directly opposed to economic principles which, by weakening or hampering those motives, checks the productive and accumulative tendencies. The first set of characteristics belongs to any system of land tenure under which the actual cultivator enjoys the secure possession of his fields at a moderate fixed rent; the latter, to any system under which he enjoys no such security; and a system which exposes the tenant to the double risk of capricious ejectment from his land, and to a demand for enhanced rent if his industry should increase the margin out of which rent can be paid, is in the highest degree discouraging to the productive impulse, and therefore deserving of the most severe and summary condemnation upon all principles of political economy in any reasonable sense of the term.

That is an exceedingly narrow and, consequently, mistaken conception of political economy which regards it as merely the theory of *laisser-faire*. That this conception of it should be so common as it is, is probably due to the fact that the science—if one's Positivist friends will allow one to call it so—came into contact when it first arose with sundry restrictive and cumbrous regulations, such as the mercantile system, the corn laws, and others, over which it has now happily triumphed by opposing to them the principles of free trade, an important branch of the still wider law of the " freedom of each, limited only by the equal freedom of all." Political economy has positive resources as well as negative, though it is doubtless true that the most important services which it has hitherto performed have been wrought by demonstrating the injurious results of many kinds of interference on the part of the State in the private concerns of individuals. The attacks of Comte and his disciples have contributed much towards establishing economic theories on a sound footing, by drawing attention to the radical distinction between those so-called laws which have no other basis than positive morality and existing social arrangements, and those real laws of nature which are beyond the control of human will. The absence of a clear perception of this distinction, a confusion of the transient and arbitrary with the permanent and unalterable, has done more, perhaps, than anything else to bring political economy into undeserved discredit.

The general sense of mankind in every age and country, except perhaps in England during the last century and a half or thereabouts, has always regarded the possession of land as carrying with it very different duties and responsibilities from those involved by the possession of merchandise; and the argument that a landlord is as much entitled to " market rates " for his land as a shopkeeper to the *bázár* price of his goods, is merely a misleading analogy. There are moral relations between the owner of the soil and those who cultivate it which differ *toto cœlo* from the mere " cash-payment " which suffices for the " sole nexus " between seller and buyer. As a writer in the "Academy" has well remarked, "the tendency of the law of advancing society has been in the direction of increased legal protection to tenant farmers. The history of the law of tenure is in fact the history of successive interpositions of courts of justice to give security to the cultivators of the soil, who originally were regarded as the servants or serfs of the landlord, and as holding their farms at his will." Landed property is to a great extent "out of the ordinary region of commercial contract, to which the maxim of *laisser-faire* applies. A landlord runs no risk of being driven out of the field by competition like an ordinary trader."

It is true that there is always, even in India, a *primâ facie* presumption in favour of *laisser-faire*; but the presumption is much less strong than in any country of Western Europe. In India, where civilisation, in the modern sense of the term, is still an exotic, the secret of growing which is at present almost confined to its foreign rulers, the duty of the Government is considerably wider than in a country of which the civilisation is indigenous, and has been worked out by itself from within. Mere tranquillity, simple preservation of the peace, will not suffice to bring about progress unless the germs of growth which every society has in itself are carefully fostered. It is not enough to leave the capacity for improvement alone; it must be judiciously nurtured. The task of the Government of India is, on the one hand, so to mould outward circumstances, and on the other so to tutor the intelligence of the people, that the two may act and react on each other until between them they generate a force sufficient to lift the masses out of the ever-deepening pit of stagnation in which centuries of immobility have left them. The first indispensable condition of success in this attempt is, by maintaining order and tranquillity, to secure a medium in which the real work of enlightenment and education may be done, and without such a medium that work could no more be performed than certain experiments could be carried on without the previous exhaustion of the atmosphere by an air-pump. But the maintenance of a medium alone will not suffice for the success of an experiment. In other words, the people of India will not be regenerated by mere preservation of the peace, by *laisser-faire* and unrestricted competition. The germ of growth which is to be found, so far as the rural masses are concerned, in the capacity for improved agriculture and a higher standard of living, must be preserved from the blighting influences of rack-renting and competition, and fostered by the maintenance of perfect security of tenure, of the certainty of enjoyment by the labourer of the fruits of his toil. It may be that at some distant period the day will come when Indian agricultural industry shall be able to take care of itself, and when the keen air of competition shall be but a healthy tonic, and not, as at present, a withering blast. But if the advent of that time is prematurely anticipated, and acted on as if it were already here, it may be safely predicted that it will never come at all.

The train of ideas which we have introduced—individual right, as opposed to family or tribal custom, contract as opposed to status—has already vastly changed, and seems certain, if unchecked, entirely to alter, and that ruinously for the worse, the conditions of agricultural life. And the change is one over which it is impossible, at present, to feel enthusiastic, and which, if, as it has been, and is being, prematurely accelerated, will not and cannot come to good.

We all know what is to be urged in its favour. This breaking up of old ties, it is said, is a necessary step in the path of progress. The earliest state of historic man is corporate life, the life of the family and the tribe. From this he has emerged in Europe, and is emerging in India, to the stage of individualism, in which everything seems to indicate that his next step will be towards corporate life again, but a corporate life, this time, of a grander and larger type, which shall find room for and include individuality; in a word, towards a system, chiefly, at first, at least, industrial, of conscious and voluntary association. Individualism is a necessary step in the progress towards a higher mode of association, towards the co-ordination of the individual with the collective life.

Now few, probably, will deny the justice and truth, on a

large scale and in the long run, of such considerations as these. But it is surely difficult not to feel that they look, so to speak, far over the heads of the actual facts around us. The terms of the formula are too vast to admit of its being a safe guide for our practice. The periods of time which are required to render it a trustworthy clue to the interpretation of history are centuries, not years, or even decades. The state of social conditions prevailing in rural Hindústán at the present day probably resembles that which existed in England a few years after the Norman conquest more nearly than any which has succeeded it in our own history. The results which it has taken England, roughly speaking, eight centuries to reach, Oudh is not likely to go very far towards attaining in twenty, or in two hundred years, even supposing the results themselves to be much more undeniably satisfactory and desirable than they actually are. In truth, these large generalisations are apt to lend themselves to the formation of most dangerous rules for the guidance of our political practice. The principle of natural selection, as exemplified in history, is a grand and imposing spectacle, but it is not for us to identify ourselves too closely with the destruction of weaker by more vigorous types. Natural laws can take very good care of themselves, and the true function of the rulers of mankind is rather to temper and soften their working, to infuse, so far as may be, an element of kindly human pity into the vast unconsciousness and impersonality of these tremendous agents, than to throw their influence, such as it is, into the descending scale, and to attempt the wholly superfluous task of assisting a chemical movement by mechanical means. "Wholesale moral arrangements," as Oliver Holmes happily remarks, "are so different from retail," and all consciously devised human efforts may be regarded as retail, in contradistinction to the illimitable and ultimately irresistible march of Nature. Nor is this in any way to advocate a blind resistance to natural processes; rather is it to urge the duty of clearly apprehending the character and tendency of those processes, that so we may follow their movements, and succour the unfortunates who have been crushed beneath the mighty wheels of the irreversible engine. We can never break the laws of nature; to attempt it is but to break ourselves against them; but we may do something, at least, to alleviate, if not to avert, the ruin of those whom these laws have overwhelmed. Progress, we have been told on high authority, is a "march from status to contract," and it is probably impossible, still more probably undesirable, to reverse or materially alter this tendency. But it is both possible and desirable to make the change less bitter and ruinous, to make it even beneficial, to those whose lives, hitherto based on custom, are being broken up and overwhelmed by the subversive agency of contract.

Wherever the operation of the principle of *laisser-faire*, or unrestricted competition, does not suffice to secure a fairly approximate coincidence of actual with economic rent, a case is made out for legislative interference. The rents paid by Oudh cultivators leave them little or no profit after supplying themselves with the barest necessaries of life. There is thus no source from which they can accumulate capital, and so long as the rent demand remains unlimited, and ready to swallow up a part if not the whole of the increased produce which would result from better agriculture, it may be safely asserted that such increased produce will not come into existence at all. The land, as has been well observed, "reflects like a mirror the motives at work upon it," and as long as the predatory impulse of the landlord is allowed to swamp the productive impulse of the tenant, so long will the increase of wealth, if not altogether checked, be confined within very much narrower limits, both of extension and intension, than it would attain if the productive impulses had free play.

The great evil of rural Oudh is, as has been already observed, the insufficiency of the produce of the soil to maintain the population in comfort, after defraying their rent and the cost of cultivation. While this is so, of what use is it for Government to devote its energy and its resources to anything but direct action on the sources of the evil? While the millions suffer from chronic hunger, it would be as easy to make a pyramid stand upon its apex as to regenerate them by ornamental legislation, or by anything but putting them beyond the ceaseless pressure of physical want. While the one thing greatly needful is left undone, mortuary statistics, and crop statements, and wholly uncalled-for alluvion and diluvion reassessments, and all the similar inventions on which the energy and patience of district officers are at present expended, can be little better than so many pretentious futilities.

At least fifty per cent., probably far more, of the population of Oudh are too poor to be able to send their children to school, or to have any desire to do so. Their life is a narrow round of small but grinding vicissitudes, the pressure of which is not to be relieved by such instruction as our schools can impart. "Education," to quote Mr. Mill, " is not compatible with extreme poverty. It is impossible effectually to teach an indigent population." Population and subsistence are always running an endless race, and the material well-being of any community depends, *cæteris paribus*, on the extent to which it can succeed in handicapping population. It is, of course, a physical impossibility for population actually to *outrun* subsistence, but it may press on it so closely as to leave no margin upon which men may pause a breathing while, no interval of ease which they can devote to any higher aim than the provision for merely physical needs. Human welfare is mainly dependent on the possession and good use of such a margin. To use it well is as important as to possess it, but it must be possessed before it can be used at all.

The soil of Oudh, densely crowded though it be, is quite capable of supporting a considerably larger population in far greater comfort than the existing population enjoys. Small as the great majority of cultivating holdings are, they are quite sufficient, if tilled with the industry which is at present almost the monopoly of a few special castes, to yield a return which, supposing the rent demand to be limited to its present amount, would put their occupants beyond the reach of actual want of food or clothing. It should never be forgotten that what is needed is not the breaking up of fresh soils, but the better and more careful cultivation of the land already under tillage. The area available for grazing is already far too scanty in at least nine districts out of twelve, and the pastures of the three northern districts are by no means too extensive for the great herds of cattle which are driven up to them from the south. It is therefore far from desirable, except in small occasional tracts of peculiarly circumstanced country, that cultivation should be extended. The increased produce which is needed for the adequate support of the people must be derived from an increased intensity of industry, not from an extension of its area. If, as is probable, the fixation of rents all over Oudh should have a tendency to confine cultivation to lands already under the plough, and to hinder the further breaking up of waste, this result would be in itself a very strong argument in favour of such a measure, not, as has been sometimes urged, an objection to it. The best, if not the only hope of saving the breed of cattle from still further deterioration is to keep the existing grazing grounds undiminished.

The dependence of the Government of India for so large a portion of its income upon the land naturally disinclines it to interfere with the power of the landlord to increase the rents out of which he pays his revenue. But, if the condition of the rent-payer is not to go on from bad to worse, this reluctance must be overcome, and the fact recognised that rents have increased and are increasing, and that the increase ought to be checked. In some few instances a fixation of rents might necessitate modifications of the revenue demand. But these would probably be very few, and if any landlord chose to complain of breach of faith, though such a complaint would, considering the circumstances and history of Oudh, be without foundation, his mouth would be effectually stopped by an offer, which it is practically certain would not be accepted, to take his estate off his hands at a fair valuation.

But the value of land, even to the landlord, would not, if Irish precedents may be trusted, be ultimately reduced by the establishment of a sound system of tenure. Mr. O'Connor Morris, in the "Fortnightly Review" for September 1876, assures us that the value of land in Ulster, in the time of Cromwell, was but one-third of what it was in Leinster, one-half of what it was in Munster, and about equal to that of Connaught. It is now nearly equal to that of Leinster, and much greater than in Munster or Connaught, having thus increased nearly three times as fast as in the former, and five or six times as fast as in the two latter provinces. The causes, apart from Protestantism and the growth of manufactures, to which this rise in the value of landed property in Ulster is attributed by Mr. Morris are the comparative soundness of the prevailing tenure, and the fact that the peasantry were not kept in such a state of serfdom as in the south and west of the island.

It is not uncommon to hear people defend the introduction of rules framed in the interests of landlordism, and the exclusion of rules opposed to those interests, on the ground that such introduction or exclusion is "a legitimate consequence of the Taluqdárí system." But, as a matter of fact, this is no argument at all. Inasmuch as no form of land policy produces, to adapt a passage from the sixth book of Mr. Mill's "Logic," "all possible beneficial effects, but all are attended with more or fewer inconveniences; and since these cannot usually be combated by means drawn from the very causes which produce them; it would often be a much stronger recommendation of some practical arrangement, that it does not follow from what is called the general principle of the policy than that it does." The sweeping measures in favour of a landed aristocracy which succeeded our reoccupation of Oudh are in themselves a sufficient ground for refraining from further minor arrangements of the same tendency, and for introducing qualifying measures to prevent the humbler landed interests from being altogether dwarfed and blighted by the shadow of a widely spreading landlordism.

Two of the most necessary qualities, and at the same time the most difficult of combined attainment, in any society are, manliness of individual character, and the habit of obedience to the law of the community. They cannot be combined if the law, directly or indirectly, requires the sacrifice of manliness, and the result of that requirement will be widely different, but equally pernicious, according to the characters of those brought under its influence. Those who are manly in excess, *i.e.* turbulent, will learn the habit of evading and defying law until they become practically outlaws; while those who are naturally deficient in manliness will become mean and slavish subservients of an authority which they do not in their hearts respect or recognise as just. This is exactly what our land policy in Oudh tends to bring about. By putting under-proprietors and tenants in a position in which subservience and self-abasement before their landlord is their best chance of escaping oppression, we tend to disgust all nobler spirits with our laws and ourselves, while we put a heavy premium on mean servility for those whose natural tendency is in that direction. Law should enlist on its side the best, not the most contemptible tendencies of human nature. "What is honour?" asks Wordsworth. And he answers that it is "the finest sense of justice which the human mind can frame." We may feel sure that a system which divorces honour from justice will not be likely to make those whom it affects either honourable or just.

Much as every reasonable reformer must wish to conciliate all classes, and to avoid arousing class irritation, it is still needful clearly to recognise that the pecuniary interest of the rent-payer and the rent-receiver are not, and never can be, identical. It is an inseparable feature of all social evolution that antagonisms such as these are constantly brought into clearer and clearer relief, and the issues more and more sharply defined. From a purely abstract point of view, the soil of a country belongs by natural right, if there be such a thing as natural right at all, to the whole people who inhabit that country, and that portion of the people who are allowed by the community to occupy the soil should be permitted to do so only as tenants of the State, and subject to such conditions as it imposes. Of these conditions, the two most indispensable would seem to be the payment of a tax as return for the privilege of occupation, and cultivation by the actual holder. Such is the true Hindú theory of land tenure, which was adopted, though with many divergences from it in practice, by the Mughals, and no more unexceptionable source of public income could well be conceived than a land tax based on these principles. To have

allowed individuals to acquire rights of property in the soil
other than rights of cultivating occupancy under the State,
has perhaps been one of the greatest misfortunes which have
befallen the societies of Western Europe. It was a mistake
from which India, in theory at least, remained to a great
extent free, until, in an evil hour, we committed her to its
theoretical as well as its practical adoption. By this, of
course, it is not intended that we found the country everywhere in the hands of occupancy tenants of the State, and
subverted their rights in favour of a class of absolute landlords created by ourselves. We did something not very
unlike this in Bengal, but in Oudh no one would think of
denying the existence of a class of landlords whose rights
it was impossible to ignore. But the native Government
always asserted, and, in an exceedingly feeble and spasmodic
way, sometimes actually exercised, its right to interfere
between landlords and tenants in order to preserve the latter
from extortion and oppression. So recently as at the beginning
of the present century, S'ádat Ali did a great deal more than
this, and asserted by actual exercise the right of the ruling
power to abolish any privileges assumed by middlemen which
it deemed injurious to the welfare of the actual cultivators
of the soil. Our right thus to interpose has fortunately
never been abdicated, but has been allowed to fall into abeyance by disuse. The evils of any system of absolute proprietorship exercised by individuals over land which they do
not themselves cultivate may be disguised and modified by
the benevolence and unselfishness of particular landlords;
but every such system is in itself radically vicious, and,
where carried out in all its bad integrity, means the exploitation of the industrious poor by the idle rich, the appropriation
of the fruits of labour by indolence, the interception of the
just dues, and far more than the just dues, of the State by
landlords who, in England, give next to no direct return for
them, and in India—from an abstract, not an historical,
point of view—are little better than absurdly over-paid taxgatherers. Underlying all agrarian struggles and controversies is the fundamental antagonism of the landlord to the
actual occupiers and tillers of the soil, whether these be

farmers and labourers, or small labouring farmers. This warfare, which, at home, has been the evil outcome of the abnormal history of English land, might have been put an end to in India by clearly recognising and formulating the ancient doctrine of the country, that the State is the sole landlord, and that though the rights of middlemen, where of long and clearly defined standing, must in justice be maintained, they should be confined to the limits which they have actually reached, and not permitted to extend themselves indefinitely in the future by absorbing a continually increasing share of the produce of the soil. It is true that in Oudh departures from and abuses of the original theory of tenure had, at the period of annexation, become so general and inveterate as to make the blunder of mistaking them for the theory itself more excusable than in, perhaps, any other part of India. But the fact remains that the direct tendency of our rule has been to saddle the province with the burthen of something not unlike our own unique English system, which our enormous trade and manufactures have with difficulty enabled us to bear, and which, even with these advantages, seems on the point of breaking down. The benefits conferred by strong rule and settled Government should indeed be great to compensate such an overwhelming injury as this, if it were final and irreparable.

Final and irreparable, however, it is not. There is still room to remedy the mischief which has been wrought, by allowing the right, or rather the duty, of the State to interfere when needful for the protection of the cultivator to remain thus long in abeyance.

And here it will probably be objected that any such interference would be a breach of faith towards Taluqdárs. That this objection is baseless seems to me to be demonstrated by a study of the controversies extending over the ten years from 1858 to 1868, of which in the preceding chapter I have endeavoured to give an impartial, though certainly not an indifferentist, account. Here, however, it may be repeated that the objection is sufficiently answered by the already quoted third paragraph of Schedule I. of Act I. of 1869:—

"This right (the right of the Taluqdárs to engage for the

revenue of their taluqas) is conceded subject to any measure which the Government may think proper to take for the purpose of protecting the inferior zamíndárs and village occupants from extortion, and of upholding their rights in the soil in subordination to the Taluqdárs."

To this there appear to be only two objections which a Taluqdár could take, viz. (1) that "village occupants" does not include mere cultivators; (2) that the rights to be upheld were rights existing at the time the reservation was made, not rights subsequently created.

Now whether or no Lord Canning, when he penned the words in question, was thinking only of zamíndárs and of rights already existing, the plain meaning of protecting village occupants from extortion includes the protection of the resident cultivators of a village from rack-renting; and experience has sufficiently shown, what should never have been considered doubtful, that without a legally recognised tenant-right cultivators cannot be effectually protected from rack-renting.

If anything further were needed to complete the case in favour of interference, it might be found in Sir C. Wingfield's letter to Sir W. Grey, dated the 2nd of March 1866, of which the following passage bears directly on the point in question :—

"The condition in the sannads that the Taluqdárs shall promote the agricultural prosperity of their estates would alone furnish the Government with warrant for stepping in to prevent oppression of the cultivators, for they cannot be oppressed without agricultural deterioration. But interference would be justified on the broad grounds of good government. The Taluqdárs will see this clear enough."

What Sir Charles Wingfield has admitted, it is probable that but few advocates of the Taluqdárs will seek to deny. "The broad grounds of good government" suffice to justify, or, to speak more correctly, impose on us as a binding obligation, the protection of the cultivator from rack-renting *in esse*, and still more *in posse*. It is the liability to be rack-rented, rather than the severity of the rent actually paid, which is fatal to improvement. Even where rent is at present heavy, there is every reason to believe that, if it were fixed and made permanent, it would in a few years come to be paid with ease out of the increased produce to the growth of which the influence of the magic power of security in the mind of the cultivator would almost certainly lead. Even on grounds of "parchment," the case for interference is sufficiently made out ; but

> "What needs the bridge much broader than the flood ?
> The fairest grant is the necessity."

That necessity being sufficiently patent, no word more need, perhaps, be said here of its justification.

It has been well remarked, however, that "the arguments are never all one side in any political question, and the writer who sees absolutely no difficulty suggests to a wary reader that he is ignoring something relevant." Speaking in all seriousness and sincerity, I can see but two objections that are entitled to any weight to the establishment of universal tenant-right. That they are grave objections may be freely admitted; but they are not such as should turn the scale in favour of leaving things as they are.

The first and least weighty of them is that the measures necessary for the introduction and record of fixity of tenure would involve the creation of a special agency, which would, of course, cost money. It would probably, if the measures were to be effective, cost a good deal of money. The officers employed would need to be of the most undoubted trustworthiness, especially if, as seems most desirable, their proceedings and orders were declared final and unappealable. They would have to revise, on the spot, the rent-roll of every village in the province, and to rely as little as possible upon native subordinates. No appellate court could have anything like the same means of arriving at a sound decision on the facts as the officers on the spot; and even if they made occasional mistakes, it would be a far less evil that these should remain uncorrected, than that landlords and peasants should be alike impoverished and their minds disturbed by the grant of the dangerous power of appeal. Supervision of their proceedings could, of course, be exercised by the Commissioners of divisions.

The actual cost of such an agency can only be very rudely estimated. But suppose two officers to be appointed for each district on, say, Rs. 800 and Rs. 700 a month respectively. Each of them would probably require a couple of writers on, say Rs. 60 and Rs. 40 *per mensem*, and perhaps five *amins* on Rs. 20 a month each. Allowing a margin of Rs. 100 for contingencies, the total cost per district would be Rs. 2,000 a month or Rs. 24,000 per annum, and for the whole province Rs. 288,000 yearly, or about one-quarter of the land revenue of a good-sized district. If the work was carried on at the rate of a village a day, excluding Sundays, for thirty weeks during the year, the four and a half months from the 1st of June to the 15th of October being spent at the head-quarters of the district or in the hills, 360 villages would be disposed of yearly. Taking the average number of villages in a district to be 2,000, the work would be accomplished in between five and six years, and its total cost would be under £175,000, or less than one-eighth of the entire land revenue of the province for one year. It might, perhaps, be done more cheaply and more expeditiously, but the effectiveness of the work would be more important than the price or the rate of speed at which it was accomplished. If we call to mind the circumstances under which Oudh was annexed, and the protestations of the then Government of India that they were acting solely for the good of the province, and their assurances that the cost of all measures needed for its development should be defrayed out of its taxes before the appropriation of the surplus for imperial revenues, it can hardly be denied that the necessity for expending such a sum as this should not stand in the way of a measure of supreme importance to the welfare of something like seven-tenths of the population.

The second objection is of a more serious nature, and may be thus stated :—After a great deal of agitation and ill-feeling caused by protracted settlement operations and litigation extending over a long period of years, and only very recently concluded, the minds of the people should be allowed to settle down quietly, and to reconcile themselves to existing facts. Any further disturbance and agitation are therefore to be deprecated. Interference between landlord and tenant will merely irritate the former, without really benefiting the latter, whose fate would probably be made worse instead of better if he were forced into a position of antagonism to the owner of the soil he tills, whose generosity and good feeling, if allowed free play, would be his best protection. Landlords would consider any measure calculated to make their tenants independent of them a breach of faith, even if it were not really so, and would do all in their power to discredit it and throw difficulties in the way of its execution.

I trust I have not understated the objections which might be urged on this score, and have certainly no conscious desire to under-estimate their gravity. I freely admit that if the measure I have tried to advocate were of secondary importance, if it were a measure of which, however desirable it might be at present, the need would in time come to be less felt, and without which rural prosperity might, with reasonable likelihood, be ultimately hoped for, then the objections to it would be overwhelming. It is only because I firmly believe it to be an *articulus stantium aut cadentium rerum agrestium*, that I venture to urge so persistently its adoption in the teeth of all difficulties. The obstacles in the way of its accomplishment may be great, but they are far from insuperable; and if they were ten times as formidable as they actually are, they will still have to be faced sooner or later. The sooner, therefore, they are faced the better, for they will increase, not diminish, with lapse of time. The truth which underlies the fable of the Sibylline books is of perennially wide application, and to no class of questions does it apply more forcibly than to that now under consideration. The longer we wait the greater will be the strength of prejudice to be overcome, and the less valuable, though not the less indispensable, will be the result to be obtained. If the peasantry of Oudh are not to become cottiers of the most debased type, if they are not to be degraded by want and starvation below even their present level, they must be given security of tenure at a fixed rent. That is the cardinal point to be kept in view. That the tendency of the tenure of all unprivileged cultivators in Oudh is straight in the direction of cottierism, appears wholly undeniable. How long it may take to reach that evil goal, how long it may be before the last shreds of beneficial custom are torn away, it is impossible to predict. But this, at least, is certain, that when that goal is once reached—and we can see it clearly enough, even now, in its half-veiled nakedness—all remedial measures will be, if not altogether too late, at least vastly more difficult of execution and very much less likely to succeed than if they are applied now while it is yet time. Let us, therefore, "open our eyes, lest they be painfully opened for us."

I earnestly hope that arrangements to secure the end in view may be devised by heads so much wiser and more experienced than my own, as to render wholly superfluous any attempt on my part to propound anything like a scheme for its attainment. But after having insisted at, I fear, such wearisome length on the necessity of security of tenure and fixity of rent, it would, perhaps, be shirking the consequences to omit all suggestion as to the practical means of obtaining them. Let me endeavour, then, with all due diffidence, to state as briefly as may be what I hope some day to see done.

In the first place, it should be announced to the people of Oudh that the Government of India has become convinced that the condition of the cultivators is not what it ought to be, and has satisfied itself that the only way to prevent its passing from bad to worse is to fix rents for a term of certainly not less than thirty years, and to maintain the actual occupants in possession so long as the rents thus fixed are paid. The grounds of this opinion might be very briefly and clearly explained, and it might be pointed out that the Emperors of Delhi, the Nawábs and Kings of Oudh, and all native sovereigns throughout India, always possessed, though in modern times, at least, they rarely exercised, the power of interference for protection of the cultivator; that nothing which has occurred since the annexation of the province has, or could have, deprived the Government of the power so to interfere; and that that power it is now intended to assert, not as a right, but as a duty which has been too long neglected.

It might be added that the Government is aware that this announcement will be unwelcome to a large majority of the landholders affected by it, and regrets the fact; but believes that the incomes which they actually enjoy will not be diminished, and promises that if, in any case, the aggregate rent-roll of an estate as authoritatively fixed should be found to be less than double the Government demand, that demand shall be reduced accordingly. It would hardly need saying that, whatever the rent-roll, the revenue would in no case be enhanced during the term of settlement. The only change which would be brought about in the position of landlords would be that they would henceforth have no power of enhancing the rents authoritatively determined, or of ejecting any cultivator on any other ground than failure to pay the amount so fixed, powers which cannot, consistently with the welfare of the cultivators, be left in the hands of any individual landlord, however benevolent or enlightened, and the withdrawal of which would, therefore, convey no slur or disgrace upon anyone. In conclusion, it might be declared that while Government relies upon the loyal acceptance by landlords of the decision at which it has arrived, and upon their belief in its disinterestedness and sincere desire for the good of its subjects, it will view with extreme displeasure, and will take measures effectually to punish, all wilful attempts to deceive or throw obstacles in the way of the officers to be appointed to carry out the necessary measures. On the other hand, all landholders who co-operate cordially with those officers will be deemed to have established a claim to its special consideration and favour.

The next step would be to introduce a short Act to amend the Rent Act (XIX. of 1868) by providing that henceforth the only grounds on which a tenant shall be liable to ejectment will be failure to pay rent at the rate fixed by the officer supervising rent-rolls. Any tenant against whom a decree for arrears of rent had been passed should be liable to ejectment if the decree remained unsatisfied after one month from the date of an application by the decree holder for his dispossession, or after such further time, not exceeding six months, as the court in its discretion might allow. Thus the idle spendthrift or dishonest embezzler, whom no one wishes to protect, would remain liable to the penalty of his idleness or dishonesty; while the hard-working, straight-going cultivator would be secured from all danger of rack-renting or capricious eviction. The position of all non-proprietary cultivators would thus be assimilated to that of the few who at present hold a right of occupancy under the Rent Act, except that their rent would not be fixed at a rate less by two annas in the rupee than that generally prevailing, and would only be liable to enhancement in the event of a fresh settlement of the land revenue, instead of once in every five years. The effect which this new security of tenure would produce by stimulating its recipients to industry and improvement cannot be estimated by the use which the few who already possess it have made of their advantages, though that is not inconsiderable. For it must be remembered that the latter, with the exception of a few Musalmáns, are almost exclusively Bráhmans and Chhatris, the idlest and least improving classes of the cultivating body. The Kurmis, Muráos, and all the more industrious castes, are at present almost wholly unprotected, and would certainly turn the boon of security to far better account.

Independently of any general fixation of rents, and as a temporary measure, it might be provided that no tenant should be liable to ejectment except for failure to pay the rent previously agreed on between him and his landlord, or for refusal to agree to the payment of a fair rent in future, of which the rate, where the parties are unable to come to terms, should be decided, on the spot, by the Court, whose order should be final and unappealable.

There should, it need hardly be said, be no limitation of the right of occupancy to tenants who have held the same fields for twelve years, or for any other period. Any such rule is open to the obvious objections that it would not protect the cultivators against the very class of landlords from whom they most need protection, the tyrants and extortioners who are constantly evicting their tenants and changing their holdings; and that it would often lead landlords to evict wholesale all tenants who had not held for the prescribed period. It must once more be repeated, with an iteration which would be utterly damnable if it were not so entirely indispensable, that *absolute security of tenure, at a fixed, equitable rent, must be made the indefeasible right of every cultivator whomsoever, not treated as the privilege of a favoured few.* As a necessary condition of healthy agriculture and sound rural economy, it should be conferred on the Chamár no less than on the Bráhman, on the tenant of one year's standing, as well as on him of five hundred years'. As previously remarked, any special rights which may be derived from ancient status, high caste, or relationship to the landlord, should find recognition in a favourable rent-rate. But security of tenure at a fixed rent must not be deemed a privilege of the cultivator; its maintenance is one of the very first and most binding duties of the State. In our accurate survey, in our field maps and settlement statistics, we have facilities for attaining this great ideal such as no previous rulers of Hindústán—Hindú, Pathán, or Mughal—ever possessed. Let not the latter end of our rule in Oudh so wholly forget the beginning as to perpetuate and stereotype that degradation of the cultivators to remedy which we professedly annexed the country. The Mutiny should have been treated as an interruption of our policy, charged, indeed, with grave lessons well worthy of being laid to heart, but not as a new revelation changing its aims and objects. Let it not be said of us by the future historian that, with all the means in our hands of raising the peasantry of Oudh from the squalid poverty and debasement which for centuries past have been their lot, we ignobly suffered them to perish for mere want of an enactment that they should be saved.

The last measure requisite would be to appoint officers to carry out the revision of rent-rolls and to frame the record of rents and holdings. Rules would, of course, have to be laid down for their guidance. These would involve many points of detail, to treat of which this is not the place, but the spirit of them should be, as far as possible, in favour of maintaining existing facts. Rents, it need scarcely be said, should not be raised merely because they are light. Where a tenant holds land under a lease at a progressive rent, the amount payable in the last year of the lease, or one somewhat greater, might be taken as the rent to be paid from the date of its expiry. Where good reason is apparent for raising an inordinately low rent for the lightness of which no ground can be assigned, the increase should in no case exceed 50 per cent., and wherever it exceeds 25 per cent., the rise should be gradual and distributed over not less than five years. If any tenant declined to agree to the rent fixed by the supervisor, it should be clearly explained to him that by declining he will lose all right to be maintained in possession against the will of the landlord, except such as he may be able to establish in a civil court, whereas by agreeing to the rent determined he will be secure from all enhancement until, at any rate, the expiry of the term of settlement. If he still adheres to his refusal, the fact should be recorded, and the recusant left to his fate. Rent-free holdings would, of course, not be interfered with unless on the application of both landlord and occupant. Powers should be conferred on the supervising officers summarily to fine any person attempting to obstruct or deceive them. Such sentences should be unappealable, but it ought, of course, to be impressed on the officers on whom these powers are conferred that their exercise must be strictly confined to cases in which there is no possibility of the least shadow of doubt. The hands of the supervisors would need to be strengthened in every reasonable way, and the principle to be kept in view should be to choose good men and then trust them implicitly. So far as practicable, and except where it is manifestly absurd or unfair, the *status quo* should be adhered to.

The most difficult cases to be disposed of would probably be those of the tenants known as *shikmis*, *i.e.* sub-cultivators holding under another, who is generally a proprietary or privileged tenant. Their names are not to be found in the rent-roll, though they may have cultivated the same land for generations. It is most desirable that the principle of fixing rents should be carried out in its integrity, and therefore that *shikmi* cultivators should be included in the operations.

But if it were found by experience so difficult as to be impracticable, the record might be confined to those tenants whose holdings are recorded in the rent-roll, and *shikmis* left to the protection of a general rule that no cultivator whose rent has not been authoritatively fixed shall be ejected, except for failure to pay the rent that has been agreed on between him and the person entitled to receive it, or for refusal to pay a fair rent in future, the fairness of such rent, where disputed, to be settled by the court, and when once thus determined, not to be altered during the current term of settlement. Subletting would have to be guarded against by some such provision as that no suit brought by a recorded cultivator, as a sublessor against a sublessee, for rent of the whole or any part of his recorded holding should be entertained, unless where the sublease was in force at the time the holding was recorded. The whole subject is by no means free from difficulties, and the rules for guidance of supervisors would need to be thought out with the utmost care. Their chief characteristic should be what may be called an elaborate simplicity, *i.e.* a simplicity resulting from the careful thought and patience devoted to their elaboration.

But, assuming tenant-right to be an accomplished fact, and every cultivator in the province to be in the enjoyment of security of tenure at a rent fixed for a period not less than the current term of settlement, there remains one difficulty to be considered. It may be said that the occupancy right of the cultivator will soon pass into the hands of the money-lender, whether mahájan or zamíndár, by mortgage, sale, and the action of the civil courts. Of the reality of this danger the state of the petty proprietors of Jhánsí is sufficient proof. But the remedy is obvious and simple. All that is needed is a mere enactment that occupancy rights shall be incapable of mortgage, or of attachment or sale in execution of civil decrees. Sale accompanied by an immediate delivery of possession might, perhaps, be permitted, to meet the case of a cultivator who had expended capital on his land, and wished to abandon his holding for good, and to emigrate or pursue some other calling. But of such sale the sanction of the Collector should be an indispensable condition, and should only be accorded where he has satisfied himself that the cultivator's intention and desire to sell are *bonâ fide*, and not forced upon him by any terrorism or cajolery of the would-be purchaser. This restriction would be needed to protect the peasant from his own weakness and ignorance and from the earth-hunger of the mahájan. As long as the former has land to mortgage on which he can raise money without immediate loss of possession, so long will he, in five cases out of six, be unable to resist temptation, and will fall, an easy prey, into the meshes of the net spread for him by the money-lender. But unless he means to abandon agriculture altogether, he will hardly ever sell his holding outright. He will thus have all the advantages of a zamíndár, except that his rent will, of course, on an average, be about double the incidence of the revenue assessment on his fields, and that he will be without the dangerous privilege, which has been the ruin of so many zamíndárs, of raising money on his holding. Such a position will afford the strongest possible inducements to thrift and good husbandry, and will expose him to the minimum of danger from the wiles of his natural enemy, though, at present, indispensable associate, the mahájan. The stock objection that, without the power of mortgage, the tenant will be unable to borrow money when needed, and will have to pay a higher rate of interest on what he does borrow, is entitled to no weight whatever. His present power of borrowing, such as it is, is quite sufficient for him, and it would be, to say the least, in no way impaired by the measures proposed. It is very doubtful whether, even by mortgaging, he would be able to borrow on much more favourable terms than at present. Taluqdárs in Oudh seldom borrow at less than 18 per cent., and the poorest cultivators generally pay not more than 24 per cent. It is obvious that such a trifling difference as this would be wholly incommensurate with the risk which would be run by the tenant, were the power of mortgage conferred upon him, of the total loss of his rights. Moreover, such occupancy rights as at present exist under the Rent Act are incapable of either sale or mortgage, and no particular need of any such power appears to be felt by their holders. The power of sale might, as already remarked, be allowed, to meet exceptional cases; and it might be added to the conditions imposed upon it that the approval by the landlord of the intending purchaser should be required, the Collector being empowered to over-rule his objections if they appeared to be manifestly due to spite or any unworthy motive. But the power to mortgage should be rigorously excluded.

If to these measures were added the extension to Oudh of the provisions contained in Chapter III. of the "Dakkhan Agriculturists Relief Act," enabling the court to go into the history and merits of all suits for debt brought against cultivators, and to decree only the principal sum actually received, together with such interest as it deems reasonable; and also the exemption from sale in execution of civil decrees of houses, plough-cattle, agricultural implements, and such grain, clothes, and household utensils as the court deems indispensable for the support of the cultivator and his family, and the payment of his rent; we should then, perhaps, have done for the peasantry of the province all that legislation can reasonably be expected to do. If, in spite of all this, they still failed to rise in the social scale, if they still remained involved in debt and destitution, the fault would be theirs, not ours. It is true that—

> "The ample proposition that hope makes
> In all designs begun on earth below
> Fails in the promised largeness."

But there is, at least, strong reason for hoping that these designs, if fairly tried, would not fail; and while this is so, the mere possibility of failure is no excuse for a refusal to make the attempt to execute them. When that attempt has been honestly made, our hands will at any rate be washed clean of the heavy responsibility which attaches to us until we have done what we can to redeem the cultivators of Oudh from the slough of poverty and degradation in which they are now involved. The present Lieutenant-Governor and Chief Commissioner, in his "Oudh Revenue Administration Report for 1875," declared that he regarded 'the position of the Indian cultivator as the saddest and most difficult problem we have to solve; for all that he has to trust to against rapacity is the value of his services"; and wished that he "could devise a remedy for this state of things." The problem is indeed of the saddest and most difficult. Is it always to remain, I will not presume to say, unsolved, but even unattempted?

4. *Labourers.*

The lot of the landless agricultural labourers is one of the least enviable that can well be conceived. Those who, in addition to working for hire, cultivate small patches of land on their own account are so far better off that they can, if out of other work, employ themselves on their own fields. These, however, are probably a minority, and the greater number are dependent for the means of subsistence on the wages of their labour and on them alone.

The result of our rule, which has most markedly affected the condition of this unfortunate class, of whose whole expenditure four-fifths, perhaps, is on food, has been a marked and general rise in the price of grain. The Indian labourer, indeed, resembles Robin Ostler of the inn at Rochester, who, "poor fellow, never joyed since the price of oats rose; it was the death of him." During the Nawábí hardly any grain at all seems to have been exported from Oudh in ordinary years; and exportation, as already remarked, was legally prohibited whenever the price of wheat rose above twenty *sirs* to the rupee. The great fertility of the soil enabled it, in days when railroads were not, and roads could scarcely be said to be, to support its dense population with comparative ease. But of recent years, greater security of traffic and improved communications, combined, probably, with a fall in the value of money, have greatly raised prices in Oudh itself. Where the agricultural labourer receives his wages in grain, this rise in prices does not much affect him, except in so far as, on the one hand, it disinclines his employer to give him so much of it, and, on the other, increases the purchasing power of the very minute surplus, if any, which remains after himself and his family are fed. Generally speaking, where paid in kind, he still gets his *kachchha panseri* (or 4 lbs.) a day. If paid in cash, he gets from one anna to one anna six pie *per diem*. The latter sum would rarely purchase more than 6 lbs. of coarse grain, and in years of scarcity perhaps from 3 to 4 lbs. Thus, the tendency, and to some extent the actual effect, of our rule on the agricultural labourer has been to reduce to a still lower pitch his already lamentably low standard of living, and his condition, therefore, has been made worse rather than better by annexation and its results. For what good can the most enlightened and vigorous administration, with tranquillity never so profound, with never so many railways, roads, bridges, schools, jails, police-stations, dispensaries, and court-houses, do to the ordinary Indian coolie which can be at all commensurate with the ever-present evil of being underfed? Muflis, Chamár, or Láchár Baksh Lonya, were just as happy going along the old cart-track as they are now on the most scientifically constructed metalled road. Once or twice in a year, perhaps, they might have had to pay a pice to the ferryman who took them over the river which they now cross without payment by a bridge. Their children never by any chance go near a school. Dispensaries can do little to keep underfed bodies in a healthy condition. The *thána*, the jail, and the court-house, indeed, they may know something of; but their acquaintance with those institutions profits them but little. Comparative freedom from forced labour and from gross ill-treatment we have, to a great extent, conferred upon them, and this is probably the most real benefit for which they have to thank us. But exemption from occasional bullying and brutality is hardly adequate compensation for the gnawing discomfort of chronic hunger. The rise in the price of grain and fall in the value of money cannot, of course, be imputed to our Government as a fault. These are effects of such causes as improved communications, increased security of property, which has caused money to be circulated instead of hoarded, and import of bullion in payment of exports. But the doleful fact remains that the tendency of our rule has distinctly been in the direction of making the life of the day labourers of Oudh harder and more pinched.

No direct amelioration of their lot can be effected by the

influence of the State. It is in the power of Government, by a stroke of the pen, to limit rents, but not to raise wages. The only chance for the labourers seems to be a prior improvement in the condition of the classes who employ them, and an increased out-turn from the soil. If zamíndárs and cultivators become more well-to-do, they will have the means of paying their labourers better, and for inducement to do so, we must trust mainly to a diminution in the supply of agricultural labour arising from an increase in the demand for labour of other kinds, as, *e.g.* for railways and public works. If the great army of village drudges could thus be thinned, the services of those who remained would, it might be hoped, become more valuable and better paid. This seems a somewhat distant hope to trust to, but it is to be feared that there is no other. Any idea of instructing Indian agricultural labourers in the gospel according to Malthus, and thus persuading them to restrain their rate of multiplication, is, of course, utterly visionary. Their children do not, and cannot, go to school, and we have no way whatever of getting at such intelligence as they possess. They can only be influenced from above. So much the more urgent is the necessity of doing what we can to raise the condition of the cultivators, any considerable elevation of which can scarcely fail to effect a corresponding improvement—and an improvement to be brought about in no other way—in the condition of the class below them.

Here must end this attempt to review the condition of the four classes into which the rural population has been divided, and to suggest specifics for its improvement. But to some it may seem that the main obstacle to all schemes for amelioration has, thus far, been, if not wholly shirked, at least not looked fairly in the face. No Government, it may be said, can do anything for a country of which the day labourers, with a precarious income of from fifteen to eighteen pence a week if paid in cash, and four pounds of coarse grain a day if paid in kind, habitually marry at sixteen, and have, perhaps, half-a-dozen starveling urchins by the time they are five-and-twenty. A people whose habits are thus hopelessly anti-Malthusian, and among whom improvements in production are almost unknown, can only be kept alive, paradoxical as it may sound, by famine, slaughter, or disease. Where moral or prudential checks on multiplication have no existence, the balance between the number of mouths to be filled and the quantity of food available to fill them can only be maintained by such physical checks as epidemics and starvation. While inability to procure a minimum of the coarsest possible food continues to be the only limit to the increase of population, it will continue to be worse than useless to move the limit a little further back, for the only possible result of so doing will be to increase the number of beings whose existence can hardly fail to be a curse to themselves and others. Any addition to the numerator of that miserable vulgar fraction of life which they possess must inevitably lead to a corresponding increase of its denominator, and the fraction itself will be no larger than before. Unless their habits can be so altered as to accustom them to a higher standard of living, rather than forego which they will refrain from multiplying, we had better sit still and do nothing. If, for instance, the poorer classes could be accustomed to two meals a day of wheaten flour, instead of to one meal of coarse grain, for a sufficiently long period to make them regard these things as more indispensable than having a large number of children, they would be really benefited. But merely to enable a larger number of persons to subsist on one meal of pulse a day would be doing harm rather than good.

Thus might argue a rigid disciple of Malthus, and it must be conceded that it would not be altogether easy to answer him. Perhaps, indeed, all that could be replied is, that as, at present, all Hindús and most Musalmáns marry, and marry young, and apparently do not regulate the numbers of their children with any particular regard to their means of supporting them, an improvement of their condition would only, for a good many years at any rate, tend to increase population by diminishing the number of deaths, not by increasing the number of births. And it might be hoped that the effect of any considerable improvement in their condition would not be confined to a mere diminution of the number of deaths, but would also permanently improve the condition of those who remained alive. It may, however, be admitted that without a change of habits, no permanent amelioration need be looked for.

Now, is it possible thus to alter the habits of the people, and, if so, by what means? The answer is that the thing has been done before, and may be done again, by the adoption of measures similar to those which have elsewhere proved successful. If we turn to Mr. Mill, who, while insisting more emphatically than, perhaps, any other modern economist upon the impossibility of permanently benefiting the poorer classes except by restraining their tendency to increase, has also asserted with greater intensity of conviction the possibility of modifying that tendency, we shall find, in that portion of the second book of his great work which deals with the remedies for low wages, the following passage:—

"A sudden and very great improvement in the condition of the poor has always, through its effects on their habits of life, a chance of becoming permanent. What happened at the time of the French Revolution is an example. . . . The majority of the population being suddenly raised from misery to independence and comparative comfort, the immediate effect was that population, notwithstanding the destructive wars of the period, started forward with unexampled rapidity. . . . The succeeding generation, however, grew up with habits considerably altered. . . . For the purpose of altering the habits of the labouring people, there is needed a twofold action, directed simultaneously upon their intelligence and their poverty. An effective national education of the children of the labouring class is the first thing needful; and, coincidently with this, a system of measures which shall, as the Revolution did in France, extinguish extreme poverty for one whole generation."

To begin with the question of education:—It cannot be denied that the Government of India has at its disposal means for influencing the minds of the poorer, if not of the very poorest classes, which have hitherto been very imperfectly utilised. There are schools all over the country, attended by large numbers of children drawn from the ranks of all the agricultural classes except the lowest, and it is for the Government to decide on the nature of the works to be studied there. Hitherto the books in use have consisted mainly of childish fables, absurd mythological stories, and the barest skeleton outlines of history and geography. Would it not be well that these schoolboys, while learning to read, should at the same time learn something which might conceivably be of some practical use to them in after life? The notion of teaching political economy in village schools may seem eutopian, but it would be perfectly possible to state, in half-a-dozen pages of moderate size, the principles of population and subsistence in a form so concrete and simple as to be readily intelligible to any child capable of understanding the first four rules of arithmetic. Any child can comprehend that a field of which the produce is sufficient to support five people will not equally well support ten, even though double the amount of labour be bestowed upon it; or that five rupees divided as wages among twenty workmen will give them four annas each, while if it is divided among forty, they will get but two annas apiece. That is practically the whole theory of population and subsistence, and it is at least as likely to impress a boy's mind as the information that Stámbúl is the capital of Rúm, and, once apprehended, indefinitely better adapted to do him actual service in life than the most intimate familiarity with the exploits of Shri Krishn or Hanumán. Similarly, the great increase caused by irrigation in the fertility of the soil might be inculcated. Such sentences as, "Irrigated lands yield twice as much as unirrigated," or, "One *pakka* well will water twenty bíghas of land," might alternate in copy-books with, "Men increase faster than food can be grown to feed them," "The more mouths to feed, the less there is for each," and similar gems from Malthus. If the matter were seriously taken up, much more might be done to popularise sound notions on economical questions than would at first sight be supposed. The fundamental doctrines of political economy, all those which it especially concerns a labouring class to know, are as simple and obvious and concrete as they can possibly be; and if they were once absorbed into the minds of, say, five per cent. of the boys who attend our schools, they might be trusted gradually to filter through the various strata of native society. The agency of the vernacular press might also be utilised. When these obvious means for the economical education of the people have been tried, it will be time enough to find out others. Whether the results thus produced would be great or small, can only be tested by making the experiment; but if it be true that the economical welfare of the people depends so largely on understanding and obeying the law of population, it is surely a duty to put them, as far as possible, in the way of gaining sound notions on the subject. We cannot, at a stroke, elevate the masses into models of prudence and virtue, but we can introduce an agricultural and economical catechism into our schools, and can require vernacular newspapers to publish Government resolutions and advice. We cannot make the horse drink, but we can at least increase the chances of his doing so by leading him to the water.

In order to "extinguish extreme poverty for one whole generation," Mr. Mill proposed two measures—colonisation on a large scale, and "the devotion of all common land hereafter brought into cultivation to raising a class of small proprietors." Neither of these proposals is directly applicable to the circumstances of Oudh. Emigration could hardly be made sufficiently extensive to have any appreciable effect on the condition of those who remained behind. It is something, no doubt, to have such outlets of escape as Trinidad and Demerara open to those who can no longer carry on the struggle for existence at home. It is, in most cases, a great advantage to those who go, but these will always be too few sensibly to relieve those who stay. If emigration from Oudh were ever attempted on a large scale, the best field for locating the emigrants would probably be the more thinly peopled tracts of the Central Provinces.

Of Mr. Mill's second specific, the creation of a class of small proprietors, enough has perhaps been said already. A peasant proprietor may be defined as a peasant who either owns the land he cultivates, or holds it at a rent fixed either by law or custom and not abandoned to competition. From this definition it, of course, follows that so far as the rents of Oudh cultivators were fixed by custom, they were peasant proprietors. But they have now ceased, or are almost everywhere ceasing, to be anything of the kind. Custom, as the determining agency of rent, is, more or less rapidly, but with unmistakeable certainty, giving place to competition; and, as a consequence the great mass of ordinary cultivators are sinking into the condition of cottiers, and into all the miseries which a cottier tenure involves. What is wanted to arrest this lamentable process is a measure which shall fix their rents for at least a considerable period, the term of settlement being probably, for the present, the most appropriate. By the time that period has expired, it may be hoped that we shall have arrived at some definite conclusions as to the merits of a permanent settlement of the land revenue. If one might venture to prophesy, it would perhaps be a fairly safe prediction that it will be ultimately recognised that, while a permanent settlement which merely fixes the demand upon the landlord, leaving all, or even any considerable number of the subordinate holders at his mercy, is one of the worst schemes that could be devised, a settlement which should be *permanent all the way down*, protecting the actual cultivator as effectively as the landlord, would be the very best. If a settlement in perpetuity were deemed inexpedient, a fixation of the demands both of the State and of landlords for, say, ninety-nine years, would be almost equally beneficial. Such an extension would, probably, go far to remove the objections which would naturally be felt by landlords to the bestowal of occupancy rights upon their tenants.

Whatever the measures adopted, whether to raise the intelligence of the people, or to improve their external condition, the real and, for the present, ultimate end of such measures, viz. the elevation of the standard of comfort and the extinction of extreme poverty among the poorer classes, should never be lost sight of. All means for the attainment of this end should be adopted simultaneously, not successively. Otherwise, their effect will be frittered away, and more than counterbalanced by the stimulus they will give to population.

One word in explanation of the phrase used above—" for the present, ultimate end "—may not be superfluous, lest it should be suspected to denote forgetfulness of any higher aim than mere " barley feeding and material ease." However firmly one may believe in the uses of adversity, one must admit that there are degrees of suffering which not only render any moral or material growth impossible, but corrupt and degrade the sufferer. Of these, semi-starvation is one. " What human virtue can be expected of the man who is holding a wolf by the ears ? " All sorrow is potential force; but it can only become actual force by being assimilated with the constitution of the mind, and transmuted into intensity of soul; as heavy rain renders worthless the soil on which it lies in flood, and only strengthens and fertilises it when absorbed. Suffering which cannot be thus absorbed is worse than useless as an educational agency, and if it be not pure evil, there can be no such thing as pure evil in the universe. This, again to quote *Sordello*, is that—

" . . . . dismal brake of prickly pear
Which bristling holds Cydippe by the hair,
Lames barefoot Agathon : this felled, we'll try
The picturesque achievements by and by."

Perhaps one of the sins which most easily beset a bureaucracy of foreigners is an exaggerated faith in what may be called machinery. The assumption that any number of canals, roads, railways, and mechanical appliances can, of themselves, save India from famine, indicates a radically unsound conception of social and economical welfare and of the conditions of its attainment. All attempts to regenerate an impoverished country by mechanical means alone must of necessity be defeated by the growth of population to which their employment will, *cæteris paribus*, give rise. The most effective forces of the world are the chemical, or moral forces, and it is only when, and in so far as, the operation of these is secured, that genuine progress begins. The true mode of securing such co-operation in India, and more particularly, perhaps, in Oudh, is the protection of individual industry.

The original source of all industry was the connection, more or less certain, between labour, and the retention and enjoyment of its produce by the labourer. And, as Mr. Herbert Spencer has put it, "that function by which a thing begins to exist we may well consider its all essential function. . . . If it was by maintaining the rights of its members that society began to be, then to maintain those rights must ever be regarded as its primary duty." Mr. Spencer would, perhaps, add that this is the sole duty binding on society; and if this is not true of India, the fact is mainly owing to the wide disparity of civilisation which there exists between the rulers and the ruled. It is undeniable, however, that to afford such protection is our first duty, and that to the agricultural industry of Oudh it is, and under the existing land system must be, very imperfectly extended.

Agriculture is, of course, very much the most important business of India, and will probably always continue so to be. But there still survives, though, thanks to the competition of English machinery and capital, in a sadly blighted and frost-bitten condition, a germ of manufacturing industry, which may some day develop into something more significant than its present appearance would seem to indicate. And towards this also we have a duty to fulfil. Manufacturing industry is, indeed, sufficiently secured from external violence, but it is in grievous need of development and instruction, without which it can never attain such superiority to, or, at least, such equality with, foreign products as will enable it to relieve the heavily burthened soil to any appreciable extent. And the most obvious methods of imparting such instruction would seem to be industrial schools and State manufactures. There must be articles for the production of which Oudh possesses special facilities. Paper, glass, leather, and gold and silver work are probably among the number. Really great results might be obtained if the principle of the division of labour could once be fairly introduced among native artisans. At present it can scarcely be said to exist, in the European sense of the term. As has been well remarked by Dr. Hunter, division of labour, in the language of political economy, is a division of processes with a view to the ultimate combination of the results of each process; while, as predicable of Indian arts or industries, it amounts merely to a division of final results, attained by a combination of the intermediate processes, each workman performing all the operations requisite to the production of a single result. This, as regards Indian manufactures, may be somewhat over-stated, but it does point to a cardinal defect which might well be remedied by the teaching of industrial schools. Such a change would, in fact, amount to the elevation of native industry from the first stage of division of labour, in which one man makes boots, another hats, and a third coats, to the second and more effective stage in which each of the several processes necessary for the production of boot, hat, or coat, is the work of a separate individual.

To resume:—The first and most crying need of Indian industry is protection, security; and the second is instruction, enlightenment. Agriculture is mainly in need of the former, arts and manufactures of the latter. The two branches of labour, rural and urban, are mutually interdependent, and one can scarcely flourish without the other. For the present, at least, the need of security for the cultivator is the most urgent of the wants of Oudh, and the rulers of the province might well adopt as their motto some such paraphrase of the Comtist watchword as this :—

Réorganiser, sans oppression ni féodalité, par la culte systématique de l'industrie individuelle.

It has been tacitly assumed throughout this chapter that reason will ere long reassert her reign in the counsels of the State, that the blood and treasure of the Empire will no more be poured out upon the barren hills of Afghánistan, and that our energy and resources will be concentrated on their rightful object, the improvement of the condition of the people of India. But if the "wild and dream-like trade of blood and guile" which has led our armies to Kábul, and seems but too likely to lead them to the Hindú Kúsh, be persisted in much longer, the catastrophe in which such a course must surely end cannot be long delayed. When "old mismanagements, taxations new" have produced their inevitable harvest of misery and disaffection, we shall find, too late, that, by wasting our strength in fighting a chimera, and attempting to subjugate a race of savage mountaineers, whose single virtue is their passsionate love of freedom and independence, for fear that they should voluntarily submit themselves to Russian supremacy, we have thrown away the noblest opportunity a nation ever possessed of regenerating and elevating some two hundred millions of people.

"The gods be good unto us!" cried Sicinius, when misfortune, born of folly, was hard at hand. "No," replied Menenius, "in such a case the gods will not be good unto us."

RECENT WORKS ON

AFGHANISTAN, AND THE CENTRAL ASIAN QUESTION, &c.

Selected from W. H. ALLEN & CO.'s Catalogue.

HERAT: The Granary and Garden of Central Asia. With an Index and a Map. By Colonel G. B. MALLESON, C.S.I., Author of "History of the Indian Mutiny." 8vo. 8s.

"Colonel Malleson's book on Herat is full of valuable information, and deserves the fullest attention of everyone interested in Central Asian politics."—*Professor Vambery to "The Times."*

THE AFGHAN WAR. Gough's Action at Futtehabad. By the Rev. C. SWINNERTON, Bengal Chaplain, Chaplain in the Field with the First Division, Peshawur Valley Field Force. Crown 8vo., with Frontispiece and Plans, 5s.

"A spirited and accurate account of the action, compiled from descriptions furnished by the officers who were actually engaged."—*Broad Arrow.*

CENTRAL ASIAN PORTRAITS: The Celebrities of the Khanates and the Neighbouring States. By DEMETRIUS CHARLES BOULGER, M.R.A.S., Author of "England and Russia in Central Asia." Crown 8vo. 7s. 6d.

"This is a volume as interesting as it is useful, and which ought to be studied by everyone who wishes to judge accurately of the momentous Central Asian Question."—*Whitehall Review.*

ENGLAND AND RUSSIA IN CENTRAL ASIA. By DEMETRIUS CHARLES BOULGER, M.R.A.S., Author of "The Life of Yakoob Beg, of Kashgar." With Appendices and two Maps, one Map being the latest Russian Official Map of Central Asia. Two vols. 8vo. 36s.

"Mr. Boulger's volumes contain an immense amount of valuable information in regard to what is known as the Central Asian Question."—*Pall Mall Gazette.*

NARRATIVE OF A JOURNEY THROUGH THE PROVINCE OF KHORASSAN AND ON THE N.W. FRONTIER OF AFGHANISTAN IN 1875. By Colonel C. M. MACGREGOR, C.S.I., C.I.E., Bengal Staff Corps. Two vols. 8vo. With Map and numerous Illustrations. 30s.

"Exceedingly interesting, and must prove of great practical value to intending travellers in Persia. We close with regret such an entertaining book of travel; one written in a simple, unpretentious style, and yet replete with useful information."—*Army and Navy Gazette.*

MOOHUMMUDAN LAW OF INHERITANCE,
and Rights and Relations affecting it. Sunni Doctrine. Comprising together with much collateral information, the substance, greatly expanded, of the Author's "Chart of Family Inheritance." By ALMARIC RUMSEY, of Lincoln's Inn, Barrister-at-Law, Professor of Indian Jurisprudence at King's College, London. Author of "A Chart of Hindu Family Inheritance," &c. 8vo. 12s.

THE KABUL INSURRECTION OF 1841–42.
(Revised and corrected from Lieut. Eyre's original Manuscript.) By Major-General Sir VINCENT EYRE, K.C.S.I., C.B. Edited by Colonel G. B. Malleson, C.S.I. Crown 8vo. With Map and Illustrations. 9s.

"The republication of this volume is well justified both by the stirring nature of its contents, and the bearing which it has on recent events."—*Daily News.*

A HISTORY OF AFGHANISTAN; from the Earliest Period to the outbreak of the War of 1878. By Colonel G. B. MALLESON, C.S.I. Author of "Historical Sketch of the Native States of India," "History of the Indian Mutiny," &c. Second Edition. 8vo. With Map. 18s.

"At the present time there could be no more seasonable publication. The book deserves to be thoughtfully and extensively read by everybody who desires to probe to the pith of the Indian Frontier question."—*Daily Telegraph.*

THE PUS'HTO MANUAL (the Language of the Afghans). Comprising a concise Grammar, Exercises and Dialogues, Familiar Phrases, Proverbs, and Vocabulary. By Major H. G. RAVERTY, Bo. N.I. (Retired). Author of the "Pushto Grammar," "Dictionary," &c. Fcap. 5s.

"This book shows all the painstaking care for which Major Raverty has long been famous, and it can be used with confidence by any one wishing to learn the language of the Afghans."—*Homeward Mail.*

A TEXT-BOOK of INDIAN HISTORY, with Geographical Notes, Genealogical Tables, Examination Questions, and Chronological, Biographical, Geographical, and General Indexes. By the Rev. G. U. POPE, D.D. Small 4to. 12s.

February, 1880.

BOOKS, &c.,

ISSUED BY

MESSRS. WM. H. ALLEN & Co.,

𝕻𝖚𝖇𝖑𝖎𝖘𝖍𝖊𝖗𝖘 & 𝕷𝖎𝖙𝖊𝖗𝖆𝖗𝖞 𝕬𝖌𝖊𝖓𝖙𝖘 𝖙𝖔 𝖙𝖍𝖊 𝕴𝖓𝖉𝖎𝖆 𝕺𝖋𝖋𝖎𝖈𝖊,

COMPRISING

MISCELLANEOUS PUBLICATIONS IN GENERAL LITERATURE. DICTIONARIES, GRAMMARS, AND TEXT BOOKS IN EASTERN LANGUAGES. MILITARY WORKS, INCLUDING THOSE ISSUED BY THE GOVERNMENT. INDIAN AND MILITARY LAW. MAPS OF INDIA, &c.

In January and July of each year is published in 8vo., price 10s. 6d.,

THE INDIA LIST, CIVIL & MILITARY.

BY PERMISSION OF THE SECRETARY OF STATE FOR INDIA IN COUNCIL.

CONTENTS.

CIVIL.—Gradation Lists of Civil Service, Bengal, Madras and Bombay. Civil Annuitants. Legislative Council, Ecclesiastical Establishments, Educational, Public Works, Judicial, Marine, Medical, Land Revenue, Political, Postal, Police, Customs and Salt, Forest, Registration and Railway and Telegraph Departments, Law Courts, Surveys, &c., &c.

MILITARY.—Gradation List of the General and Field Officers (British and Local) of the three Presidencies, Staff Corps, Adjutants-General's and Quartermasters-General's Offices, Army Commissariat Departments, British Troops Serving in India (including Royal Artillery, Royal Engineers, Cavalry, Infantry, and Medical Department), List of Native Regiments, Commander-in-Chief and Staff, Garrison Instruction Staff, Indian Medical Department, Ordnance Departments, Punjab Frontier Force, Military Departments of the three Presidencies, Veterinary Departments, Tables showing the Distribution of the Army in India, Lists of Retired Officers of the three Presidencies.

HOME.—Departments of the Office of the Secretary of State, Coopers Hill College, List of Selected Candidates for the Civil and Forest Services, Indian Troop Service.

MISCELLANEOUS.—Orders of the Bath, Star of India, and St. Michael and St. George. Order of Precedence in India. Regulations for Admission to Civil Service. Regulations for Admission of Chaplains. Civil Leave Code and Supplements. Civil Service Pension Code—relating to the Covenanted and Uncovenanted Services. Rules for the Indian Medical Service. Furlough and Retirement Regulations of the Indian Army. Family Pension Fund. Staff Corps Regulations. Salaries of Staff Officers. Regulations for Promotion. English Furlough Pay.

WM. H. ALLEN & Co.,

Works issued from the India Office, and Sold by Wm. H. ALLEN & Co.

Tree and Serpent Worship;

Or, Illustrations of Mythology and Art in India in the First and Fourth Centuries after Christ, from the Sculptures of the Buddhist Topes at Sanchi and Amravati. Prepared at the India Museum, under the authority of the Secretary of State for India in Council. Second edition, Revised, Corrected, and in great part Re-written. By JAMES FERGUSSON, Esq., F.R.S., F.R.A.S. Super-royal 4to. 100 plates and 31 engravings, pp. 270. Price £5 5s.

Illustrations of Ancient Buildings in Kashmir.

Prepared at the Indian Museum under the authority of the Secretary of State for India in Council. From Photographs, Plans, and Drawings taken by Order of the Government of India. By HENRY HARDY COLE, LIEUT. R.E., Superintendent Archæological Survey of India, North-West Provinces. In One vol.; half-bound, Quarto. Fifty-eight plates. £3 10s.

The Illustrations in this work have been produced in Carbon from the original negatives, and are therefore permanent.

Pharmacopœia of India.

Prepared under the Authority of the Secretary of State for India. By EDWARD JOHN WARING, M.D. Assisted by a Committee appointed for the Purpose. 8vo. 6s.

The Stupa of Bharhut. A Buddhist Monument.

Ornamented with numerous Sculptures illustrative of Buddhist Legend and History in the Third Century B.C. By ALEXANDER CUNNINGHAM, C.S.I., C.I.E., Major-General, Royal Engineers (Bengal Retired); Director-General Archæological Survey of India. 4to. Fifty-seven Plates. Cloth gilt. £3 3s.

Archæological Survey of Western India.

Report of the First Season's Operations in the Belgam and Kaladgi Districts. January to May, 1874. Prepared at the India Museum and Published under the Authority of the Secretary of State for India in Council. By JAMES BURGESS, Author of the "Rock Temples of Elephanta," &c., &c., and Editor of "The Indian Antiquary." Half-bound. Quarto. 58 Plates and Woodcuts. £2 2s.

Archæological Survey of Western India. Vol. II.

Report on the Antiquities of Káthiáwád and Kachh, being the result of the Second Season's Operations of the Archæological Survey of Western India. 1874–75. By JAMES BURGESS, F.R.G.S , M.R.A.S., &c., Archæological Surveyor and Reporter to Government, Western India. 1876. Half-bound. Quarto. Seventy-four Plates and Woodcuts. £3 3s.

Archæolo ical Survey of Western India. Vol. III.

Report on the Antiquities in the Bidar and Aurungabad Districts in the Territory of H.H. the Nizam of Haidarabad, being the result of the Third Season's Operations of the Archæological Survey of Western India. 1875–1876. By JAMES BURGESS, F.R.G.S., M.R.A.S., Membre de la Societé Asiatique, &c., Archæological Surveyor and Reporter to Government, Western India. Half-bound. Quarto. Sixty-six Plates and Woodcuts. £2 2s.

Adam W. (late of Calcutta) Theories of History.
An Inquiry into the Theories of History,—Chance,—Law,—Will. With Special Reference to the Principle of Positive Philosophy. By WILLIAM ADAM. 8vo. 15s.

Akbar. An Eastern Romance.
By Dr. P. A. S. VAN LIMBURG-BROUWER. Translated from the Dutch by M. M. With Notes and Introductory Life of the Emperor Akbar, by CLEMENTS R. MARKHAM, C.B., **F.R.S.** Crown 8vo. 10s. 6d.

Allen's Series.
1.—World We Live In. 2s.
2.—Earth's History. 2s.
3.—Geography of India. (See page 9.) 2s.
4.—2000 Examination Questions in Physical Geography. 2s.
5.—Hall's Trigonometry. (See page 10.) 2s.
6.—Wollaston's Elementary Indian Reader. 1s. (See page 29.)
7.—Ansted's Elements of Physiography. 1s. 4d.

Anderson (P.) The English in Western India.
8vo. 14s.

Andrew (W. P.) India and Her Neighbours,
With Two Maps. 8vo. 15s.

Ansted (D. T.) Physical Geography.
By Professor D. T. ANSTED, M.A., F.R.S., &c. Fifth Edition. Post 8vo., with Illustrative Maps. 7s.
CONTENTS:—PART I.—INTRODUCTION.—The Earth as a Planet.—Physical Forces.—The Succession of Rocks. PART II.—EARTH.—Land.—Mountains.—Hills and Valleys.—Plateaux and Low Plains. PART III.—WATER.—The Ocean.—Rivers.—Lakes and Waterfalls.—The Phenomena of Ice.—Springs PART IV.—AIR.—The Atmosphere. Winds and Storms.—Dew, Clouds, and Rain.—Climate and Weather. PART V.—FIRE.—Volcanoes and Volcanic Phenomena.—Earthquakes. PART VI.—LIFE.—The Distribution of Plants in the different Countries of the Earth.—The Distribution of Animals on the Earth.—The Distribution of Plants and Animals in Time.—Effects of Human Agency on Inanimate Nature.

"The Book is both valuable and comprehensive, and deserves a wide circulation."—*Observer.*

Ansted (D. T.) Elements of Physiography.
For the use of Science Schools. Fcap. 8vo. 1s. 4d.

Ansted (D. T.) The World We Live In.
Or First Lessons in Physical Geography. For the use of Schools and Students. By D. T. ANSTED, M.A., F.R.S., &c. Fcap. 2s. 25th Thousand, with Illustrations.

Ansted (D. T.) The Earth's History.
Or, First Lessons in Geology. For the use of Schools and Students. By D. T. ANSTED. Third Thousand. Fcap. 2s.

Ansted (D. T.)
Two Thousand Examination Questions in Physical Geography. pp. 180. Price 2s.

Ansted (D. T.) and Latham (R. G.) Channel Islands. Jersey, Guernsey, Alderney, Sark, &c.
THE CHANNEL ISLANDS. Containing: PART I.—Physical Geography. PART II.—Natural History. PART III.—Civil History. PART IV.—Economics and Trade. By DAVID THOMAS ANSTED, M.A., F.R.S., and ROBERT GORDON LATHAM, M.A., M.D., F.R.S. New and Cheaper Edition in one handsome 8vo. Volume, with 72 Illustrations on Wood by Vizetelly, Loudon, Nicholls, and Hart; with Map. 8vo. 16s.

"This is a really valuable work. A book which will long remain the standard authority on the subject. No one who has been to the Channel Islands, or who purposes going there will be insensible of its value."—*Saturday Review.*

"It is the produce of many hands and every hand a good one."

Ansted (D. T.) Water, and Water Supply.
Chiefly with reference to the British Islands. Part I.— Surface Waters. 8vo. With Maps. 18s.

Archer (Capt. J. H. Laurence) Commentaries on the
Punjaub Campaign—1848-49, including some additions to the History of the Second Sikh War, from original sources. By Capt. J. H. LAWRENCE-ARCHER, Bengal H. P. Crown 8vo. 8s.

Aynsley (Mrs.) Our Visit to Hindustan, Kashmir, and Ladakh.
By Mrs. J. C. MURRAY AYNSLEY. 8vo. 14s.

Bernay (Dr. A. J.) Students' Chemistry.
Being the Seventh Edition of Household Chemistry, or the Science of Home Life. By ALBERT J. BERNAYS, PH. DR. F.C.S., Prof. of Chemistry and Practical Chemistry at St. Thomas' Hospital, Medical, and Surgical College. Crown 8vo. 5s. 6p.

Binning (R. M.) Travels in Persia, &c.
2 vols. 8vo. 16s.

Blanchard (S.) Yesterday and To-day in India.
By SIDNEY LAMAN BLANCHARD. Post 8vo. 6s.

    CONTENTS.—Outward Bound.—The Old Times and the New.—Domestic Life.—Houses and Bungalows.—Indian Servants.—The Great Shoe Question.—The Garrison Hack.—The Long Bow in India.—Mrs. Dulcimer's Shipwreck.—A Traveller's Tale, told in a Dark Bungalow.—Punch in India.—Anglo-Indian Literature.—Christmas in India.—The Seasons in Calcutta.—Farmers in Muslin.—Homeward Bound.—India as it Is.

Blenkinsopp (Rev. E. L.) Doctrine of Development in the Bible and in the Church. By REV. E. L. BLENKINSOPP, M.A., Rector of Springthorp. 2nd edition. 12mo. 6s.

Boileau (Major-General J. T.)
A New and Complete Set of Traverse Tables, showing the Differences of Latitude and the Departures to every Minute of the Quadrant and to Five Places of Decimals. Together with a Table of the lengths of each Degree of Latitude and corresponding Degree of Longitude from the Equator to the Poles; with other Tables useful to the Surveyor and Engineer. Fourth Edition, thoroughly revised and corrected by the Author. Royal 8vo. 12s. London, 1876.

Boulger (D. C.) Central Asian Portraits; or the Celebrities of the Khanates and the Neighbouring States. By DEMETRIUS CHARLES BOULGER, M.R.A.S. Crown 8vo. 7s. 6d.

Boulger (D. C.) The Life of Yakoob Beg, Athalik Ghazi and Badaulet, Ameer of Kashgar. By DEMETRIUS CHARLES BOULGER, M.R.A.S. 8vo. With Map and Appendix. 16s.

Boulger (D. C.) England and Russia in Central Asia. With Appendices and Two Maps, one being the latest Russian Official Map of Central Asia. 2 vols. 8vo. 36s.

Bowring (Sir J.) Flowery Scroll.
A Chinese Novel. Translated and Illustrated with Notes by SIR J. BOWRING, late H.B.M. Plenipo. China. Post 8vo. 10s. 6d.

Boyd (R. Nelson). Coal Mines Inspection: Its History and Results. 8vo. 11s.

Bradshaw (John) The Poetical Works of John Milton, with Notes, explanatory and philological. By JOHN BRADSHAW, LL.D., Inspector of Schools, Madras. 2 vols., post 8vo. 12s. 6d.

Brandis' Forest Flora of North-Western and Central India. By DR. BRANDIS, Inspector General of Forests to the Government of India. Text and Plates. £2 18s.

Briggs (Gen. J.) India and Europe Compared. Post 8vo. 7s.

Bright (W.) Red Book for Sergeants. By W. BRIGHT, Colour-Sergeant, 37th Middlesex R.V. Fcap. interleaved. 1s.

Browne (J. W.) Hardware; How to Buy it for Foreign Markets. 8vo. 10s. 6d.

Buckle (the late Capt. E.) Bengal Artillery. A Memoir of the Services of the Bengal Artillery from the formation of the Corps. By the late CAPT. E. BUCKLE, Assist.-Adjut. Gen. Ben. Art. Edit. by SIR J. W. KAYE. 8vo. Lond. 1852. 10s.

Burke (P.) Celebrated Naval and Military Trials. By PETER BURKE, Serjeant-at-Law. Author of "Celebrated Trials connected with the Aristocracy." Post 8vo. 10s. 6d.

Christmas (Rev. H.) Republic of Fools (The). Being the History of the People of Abdera in Thrace, from the German of C. M. Von Wieland. By Rev. HENRY CHRISTMAS, M.A., F.R.S. 2 Vols. crown 8vo. 12s.

Christmas (Rev. H.) Sin: Its Causes and Consequences. An attempt to Investigate the Origin, Nature, Extent and Results of Moral Evil. A Series of Lent Lectures. By the REV. HENRY CHRISTMAS, M.A., F.R.S. Post 8vo. 5s.

Cochrane, (John) Hindu Law. 20s. (See page 12.)

Collette (C. H.) Henry VIII. An Historical Sketch as affecting the Reformation in England. By CHARLES HASTINGS COLLETTE. Post 8vo. 6s.

Collette (C. H.) The Roman Breviary.
A Critical and Historical Review, with Copious Classified Extracts. By CHARLES HASTINGS COLLETTE. 2nd Edition. Revised and enlarged. 8vo. 5s.

Cooper's Hill College. Calendar of the Royal Indian Engineering College, Cooper's Hill. Published by authority in January each year. 6s.

CONTENTS.—Staff of the College; Prospectus for the Year; Table of Marks; Syllabus of Course of Study; Leave and Pension Rules of Indian Service; Class and Prize Lists; Past Students serving in India; Entrance Examination Papers, &c.

Cruise of H.M.S. "Galatea,"
Captain H.R.H. the Duke of Edinburgh, K.G., in 1867—1868. By the REV. JOHN MILNER, B.A., Chaplain; and OSWALD W. BRIERLY. Illustrated by a Photograph of H.R.H. the Duke of Edinburgh; and by Chromo-Lithographs and Graphotypes from Sketches taken on the spot by O. W. BRIERLY. 8vo. 16s.

Danvers (Fred. Chas.) On Coal.
With Reference to Screening, Transport, &c. 8vo. 10s. 6d.

Daumas (E.) Horses of the Sahara, and the Manners of the Desert. By E. DAUMAS, General of the Division Commanding at Bordeaux, Senator, &c., &c. With Commentaries by the Emir Abd-el-Kadir (Authorized Edition). 8vo. 6s.

"We have rarely read a work giving a more picturesque and, at the same time, practical account of the manners and customs of a people, than this book on the Arabs and their horses."—*Edinburgh Courant.*

Doran (Dr. J.) "Their Majesties Servants":
Annals of the English Stage. Actors, Authors, and Audiences. From Thomas Betterton to Edmund Kean. By Dr. DORAN, F.S.A., Author of "Table Traits," "Lives of the Queens of England of the House of Hanover." &c. Post 8vo. 6s.

"Every page of the work is barbed with wit, and will make its way point foremost. . . . . . provides entertainment for the most diverse tastes."—*Daily News.*

Drury (Col. H.) The Useful Plants of India,
With Notices of their chief value in Commerce, Medicine, and the Arts. By COLONEL HEBER DRURY. Second Edition, with Additions and Corrections. Royal 8vo. 16s.

Edwards' (H. S.) The Russians At Home and the Russians Abroad. Sketches, Unpolitical and Political, of Russian Life under Alexander II. By H. SUTHERLAND EDWARDS. 2 vols., Crown 8vo. 21s.

Eyre, Major-General (Sir V.), K.C.S.I., C.B. The Kabul Insurrection of 1841–42. Revised and corrected from Lieut. Eyre's Original Manuscript. Edited by Colonel G. B. MALLESON, C.S.I. Crown 8vo., with Map and Illustrations. 9s.

Fearon (A.) Kenneth Trelawny. By ALEC FEARON. Author of "Touch not the Nettle." 2 vols. Crown 8vo. 21s.

Forbes (Dr. Duncan) History of Chess. From the time of the Early Invention of the Game in India, till the period of its establishment in Western and Central Europe. By DUNCAN FORBES, LL.D. 8vo. 7s. 6d.

Gazetteers of India.
Thornton, 4 vols., 8vo. £2 16s.
„ 8vo. 21s.
„ (N.W.P., &c.) 2 vols., 8vo. 25s.

Gazetteer of Southern India. With the Tenasserim Provinces and Singapore. Compiled from original and authentic sources. Accompanied by an Atlas, including plans of all the principal towns and cantonments. Royal 8vo. with 4to. Atlas. £3 3s.

Geography of India. Comprising an account of British India, and the various states enclosed and adjoining. Fcap. pp. 250. 2s.

Geological Papers on Western India. Including Cutch, Scinde, and the south-east coast of Arabia. To which is added a Summary of the Geology of India generally. Edited for the Government by HENRY J. CARTER, Assistant Surgeon, Bombay Army. Royal 8vo. with folio Atlas of maps and plates; half-bound. £2 2s.

Glyn (A. C.) History of Civilization in the Fifth Century. Translated by permission from the French of A. Frederic Ozanam, late Professor of Foreign Literature to the Faculty of Letters at Paris. By ASHBY C. GLYN, B.A., of the Inner Temple, Barrister-at-Law. 2 vols., post 8vo. £1 1s.

Goldstucker (Prof. Theodore), The late. The Literary Remains of. With a Memoir. 2 vols. 8vo. 21s.

Grady (S. G.) Mohamedan Law of Inheritance & Contract. 8vo. 14s. (See page 11.)

Grady (S.G.) Institutes of Menu. 8vo. 12s. (See page 11.)

Greene (F. V.) The Russian Army and its Campaigns in Turkey in 1857–1858. By F. V. GREENE, First Lieutenant in the Corps of Engineers, U.S. Army, and lately Military Attaché to the United States Legation at St. Petersburg. 8vo. With Atlas. 32s.

Griffith (Ralph T. H.) Birth of the War God. A Poem. By KALIDASA. Translated from the Sanscrit into English Verse. By RALPH T. H. GRIFFITH. 8vo. 5s.

Hall (E. H.) Lands of Plenty, for Health, Sport, and Profit. British North America. A Book for all Travellers and Settlers. By E. HEPPLE HALL, F.S.S. Crown 8vo., with Maps. 6s.

Hall's Trigonometry. The Elements of Plane and Spherical Trigonometry. With an Appendix, containing the solution of the Problems in Nautical Astronomy. For the use of Schools. By the REV. T. G. HALL, M.A., Professor of Mathematics in King's College, London. 12mo. 2s.

Hamilton's Hedaya. A new edition, with the obsolete passages omitted, and a copious Index added by S. G. Grady. 8vo. £1 15s. (See page 11.)

Handbook of Reference to the Maps of India. Giving the Lat. and Long. of places of note. 18mo. 3s. 6d.
*** This will be found a valuable Companion to Messrs. Allen & Co.'s Maps of India.

Harcourt (Maj. A. F. P.) Down by the Drawle. By MAJOR A. F. P. HARCOURT, Bengal Staff Corps, author of "Kooloo, Lahoul, and Spiti," "The Shakespeare Argosy," &c. 2 Vols. crown 8vo. 21s.

Hough (Lieut.-Col. W.) Precedents in Military Law. 8vo. cloth. 25s.

Hughes (Rev. T. P.) Notes on Muhammadanism.
Second Edition, Revised and Enlarged. Fcap. 8vo. 6s.

Hutton (J.) Thugs and Dacoits of India.
A Popular Account of the Thugs and Dacoits, the Hereditary Garotters and Gang Robbers of India. By JAMES HUTTON. Post 8vo. 5s.

India Directory (The).
For the Guidance of Commanders of Steamers and Sailing Vessels. Founded upon the Work of the late CAPTAIN JAMES HORSBURGH, F.R.S.

PART I.—The East Indies, and Interjacent Ports of Africa and South America. Revised, Extended, and Illustrated with Charts of Winds, Currents, Passages, Variation, and Tides. By COMMANDER ALFRED DUNDAS TAYLOR, F.R.G.S., Superintendent of Marine Surveys to the Government of India. £1 18s.

PART II.—The China Sea, with the Ports of Java, Australia and Japan and the Indian Archipelago Harbours, as well as those of New Zealand. Illustrated with Charts of the Winds, Currents, Passages, &c. By the same. (*In preparation.*)

Indian and Military Law.

Mahommedan Law of Inheritance, &c. A Manual of the Mahommedan Law of Inheritance and Contract; comprising the Doctrine of the Soonee and Sheea Schools, and based upon the text of Sir H. W. MACNAGHTEN's Principles and Precedents, together with the Decisions of the Privy Council and High Courts of the Presidencies in India. For the use of Schools and Students. By STANDISH GROVE GRADY, Barrister-at-Law, Reader of Hindoo, Mahommedan, and Indian Law to the Inns of Court. 8vo. 14s.

Hedaya, or Guide, a Commentary on the Mussulman Laws, translated by order of the Governor-General and Council of Bengal. By CHARLES HAMILTON. Second Edition, with Preface and Index by STANDISH GROVE GRADY. 8vo. £1 15s.

Institutes of Menu in English. The Institutes of Hindu Law or the Ordinances of Menu, according to Gloss of Culluca. Comprising the Indian System of Duties, Religious and Civil, verbally translated from the Original, with a Preface by SIR WILLIAM JONES, and collated with the Sanscrit Text by GRAVES CHAMNEY HAUGHTON, M.A., F.R.S., Professor of Hindu Literature in the East India College. New edition, with Preface and Index by STANDISH G. GRADY, Barrister-at-Law, and Reader of Hindu, Mahommedan, and Indian Law to the Inns of Court. 8vo., cloth. 12s.

Indian Code of Criminal Procedure. Being Act X of 1872, Passed by the Governor-General of India in Council on the 25th of April, 1872. 8vo. 12s.

Indian Code of Civil Procedure. In the form of Questions and Answers, with Explanatory and Illustrative Notes. By ANGELO J. LEWIS, Barrister-at-law. 12mo. 12s. 6d.

Indian Penal Code. In the Form of Questions and Answers. With Explanatory and Illustrative Notes. By ANGELO J. LEWIS, Barrister-at-Law. Post 8vo. 7s. 6d.

Hindu Law. Principally with reference to such portions of it as concern the Administration of Justice in the Courts in India. By SIR THOMAS STRANGE, late Chief Justice of Madras. 2 vols. Royal 8vo., 1830. 24s.

Hindu Law. Defence of the Daya Bhaga. Notice of the Case on Prosoono Coomar Tajore's Will. Judgment of the Judicial Committee of the Privy Council. Examination of such Judgment. By JOHN COCHRANE, Barrister-at-Law. Royal 8vo. 20s.

Law and Customs of Hindu Castes, within the Dekhan Provinces subject to the Presidency of Bombay, chiefly affecting Civil Suits. By ARTHUR STEELE. Royal 8vo. £1 1s.

Chart of Hindu Inheritance. With an Explanatory Treatise, By ALMARIC RUMSEY. 8vo. 6s. 6d.

Manual of Military Law. For all ranks of the Army, Militia and Volunteer Services. By Colonel J. K. PIPON, Assist. Adjutant General at Head Quarters, & J. F. COLLIER, Esq., of the Inner Temple, Barrister-at-Law. Third and Revised Edition. Pocket size. 5s.

Precedents in Military Law; including the Practice of Courts-Martial; the Mode of Conducting Trials; the Duties of Officers at Military Courts of Inquests, Courts of Inquiry, Courts of Requests, &c., &c. The following are a portion of the Contents:—
1. Military Law. 2. Martial Law. 3. Courts-Martial. 4. Courts of Inquiry. 5. Courts of Inquest. 6. Courts of Request. 7. Forms of Courts-Martial. 8. Precedents of Military Law. 9. Trials of Arson to Rape (Alphabetically arranged.) 10. Rebellious. 11. Riots. 12. Miscellaneous. By Lieut.-Col. W. HOUGH, late Deputy Judge-Advocate-General, Bengal Army, and Author of several Works on Courts-Martial. One thick 8vo. vol. 25s.

The Practice of Courts Martial. By HOUGH & LONG. Thick 8vo. London, 1825. 26s.

Indian Criminal Law and Procedure,
Including the Procedure in the High Courts, as well as that in the Courts not established by Royal Charter; with Forms of Charges and Notes on Evidence, illustrated by a large number of English Cases, and Cases decided in the High Courts of

India; and an APPENDIX of selected Acts passed by the Legislative Council relating to Criminal matters. By M. H. STARLING, ESQ., LL.B. & F. B. CONSTABLE, M.A. Third edition. 8vo. £2 2s.

Indian Infanticide.
Its Origin, Progress, and Suppression. By JOHN CAVE-BROWN, M.A. 8vo. 5s.

Jackson (Lt.-Col. B.) Military Surveying, &c. 8vo. 14s. (See page 20).

Jackson (Lowis D'A.) Hydraulic Manual and Working Tables, Hydraulic and Indian Meteorological Statistics. Published under the patronage of the Right Honourable the Secretary of State for India. By LOWIS D'A. JACKSON. 8vo. 28s.

Jackson (Lowis D'A.) Canal and Culvert Tables. Based on the Formula of Kutter, under a Modified Classification, with Explanatory Text and Examples. By LOWIS D'A. JACKSON, A.M.I.C.E., author of "Hydraulic Manual and Statistics," &c. Roy. 8vo. 28s.

Jerrold (Blanchard) at Home in Paris.
2 Vols. Post 8vo. 10s.

Joyner (Mrs.) Cyprus: Historical and Descriptive. Adapted from the German of Herr FRANZ VON LÖHER. With much additional matter. By Mrs. A. BATSON JOYNER. Crown 8vo. With 2 Maps. 10s. 6d.

Kaye (Sir J. W.) The Sepoy War in India.
A History of the Sepoy War in India, 1857—1858. By Sir JOHN WILLIAM KAYE, Author of "The History of the War in Affghanistan." Vol. I., 8vo. 18s. Vol. II. £1. Vol. III. £1.
 CONTENTS OF VOL. I.:—BOOK I.—INTRODUCTORY.—The Conquest of the Punjab and Pegu.—The " Right of Lapse."—The Annexation of Oude.—Progress of Englishism. BOOK II.—The SEPOY ARMY: ITS RISE, PROGRESS, AND DECLINE.—Early History of the Native Army.—Deteriorating Influences.—The Sindh Mutinies.—The Punjaub Mutinies. Discipline of the Bengal Army. BOOK III.—THE OUTBREAK OF THE MUTINY.—Lord Canning and his Council.—The Oude Administration and the Persian War.—The Rising of the Storm.—The First Mutiny.—Progress of Mutiny.—Excitement in Upper India —Bursting of the Storm.—APPENDIX.
 CONTENTS OF VOL. II.:—BOOK IV.—THE RISING IN THE

North-west.—The Delhi History.—The Outbreak at Meerut.—The Seizure of Delhi.—Calcutta in May.—Last Days of General Anson.—The March upon Delhi. Book V.—Progress of Rebellion in Upper India—Benares and Allahabad.—Cawnpore.—The March to Cawnpore.—Re-occupation of Cawnpore. Book VI.—The Punjab and Delhi.—First Conflicts in the Punjab.—Peshawur and Rawul Pinder.—Progress of Events in the Punjab.—Delhi.—First Weeks of the Siege.—Progress of the Siege.—The Last Succours from the Punjab.

Contents of Vol. III.:—Book VII.—Bengal, Behar, and the North-west Provinces.—At the Seat of Government.—The Insurrection in Behar.—The Siege of Arrah.—Behar and Bengal. Book VIII.—Mutiny and Rebellion in the North-west Provinces.—Agra in May.—Insurrection in the Districts.—Bearing of the Native Chiefs.—Agra in June, July, August and September. Book IX.—Lucknow and Delhi.—Rebellion in Oude.—Revolt in the Districts.—Lucknow in June and July.—The siege and Capture of Delhi.

Kaye (Sir J. W.) History of the War in Afghanistan.
New edition. 3 Vols. Crown 8vo. £1. 6s.

Kaye (Sir J. W.) H. St. G. Tucker's Life and Correspondence.
8vo. 10s.

Kaye (Sir J. W.) Memorials of Indian Governments.
By H. St. George Tucker. 8vo. 10s.

Keatinge (Mrs.) English Homes in India.
By Mrs. Keatinge. Part I.—The Three Loves. Part II.—The Wrong Turning. Two vols., Post 8vo. 16s.

Keene (H. G.) Mogul Empire.
From the death of Aurungzeb to the overthrow of the Mahratta Power, by Henry George Keene, B.C.S. Second edition. With Map. 8vo. 10s. 6d.
This Work fills up a blank between the ending of Elphinstone's and the commencement of Thornton's Histories.

Keene (H. G.) Administration in India.
Post 8vo. 5s.

Keene (H. G.) Peepul Leaves.
Poems written in India. Post 8vo. 5s.

Keene (H. G.). The Turks in India.
Historical Chapters on the Administration of Hindostan by the Chugtai Tartar, Babar, and his Descendants. 12s. 6d.

Latham (Dr. R. G.) Russian and Turk,
From a Geographical, Ethnological, and Historical Point of View. 8vo. 18s.

Laurie (Col. W. F. B.) Our Burmese Wars and Relations with Burma. With a Summary of Events from 1826 to 1879, including a Sketch of King Theebau's Progress. With various Local, Statistical, and Commercial Information. By Colonel W. F. B. Laurie, Author of "Rangoon," "Narrative of the Second Burmese War," &c. 8vo. With Plans and Map. 16s.

Lee (F. G.) The Church under Queen Elizabeth.
An Historical Sketch. By the Rev. F. G. Lee, D.D. Two Vols., Crown 8vo. 21s.

Lee (F. G.) The Words from the Cross: Seven Sermons for Lent, Passion-Tide, and Holy Week. By the Rev. F. G. Lee, D.D. Third edition revised. Fcap. 3s. 6d.

Lee (Dr. W. N.) Drain of Silver to the East.
Post 8vo. 8s.

Lewin (T. H.) Wild Races of the South Eastern Frontier of India. Including an Account of the Loshai Country. By Capt. T. H. Lewin, Dep. Comm. of Hill Tracts. Post 8vo. 10s. 6d.

Lewis (A. J.) Indian Penal Code
In the Form of Questions and Answers. With Explanatory and Illustrative Notes. By Angelo J. Lewis. Post 8vo. 7s. 6d.

Lewis (A. J.) Indian Code of Civil Procedure.
In the Form of Questions and Answers. With Explanatory and Illustrative Notes. By Angelo J. Lewis. Post 8vo. 12s. 6d.

Leyden and Erskine's Baber.
Memoirs of Zehir-ed-Din Muhammed Baber, Emperor of Hindustan, written by himself in the Jaghatai Turki, and translated partly by the late John Leyden, Esq., M.D., and partly by William Erskine, Esq., with Notes and a Geographical and Historical Introduction, together with a Map of the Countries between the Oxus and Jaxartes, and a Memoir regarding its construction. By Charles Waddington, of the East India Company's Engineers. 4to. Lond. 1826. £1 5s.

Liancourt's and Pincott's Primitive and Universal Laws of the Formation and development of language; a Rational and Inductive System founded on the Natural Basis of Onomatops. 8vo. 12s. 6d.

Lockwood (Ed.) Natural History, Sport and Travel.
By EDWARD LOCKWOOD, Bengal Civil Service. late Magistrate of Moughyr. Crown 8vo. With numerous Illustrations. 9s.

Lovell (Vice-Adm.) Personal Narrative of Events from 1799 to 1815. With Anecdotes. By the late Vice-Adm. WM. STANHOPE LOVELL, R.N., K H. Second edition. Crown 8vo. 4s.

McBean (S.) England, Egypt, Palestine & India by Railway. Popularly Explained. Crown 8vo., with a coloured Map. 4s.

MacGregor (Col. C. M.) Narrative of a Journey through the Province of Khorassan and on the N. W. Frontier of Afghanistan in 1875. By Colonel C. M. MACGREGOR, C.S.I., C.I.E., Bengal Staff Corps. 2 vols. 8vo. With map and numerous illustrations. 30s.

Malleson (Col. G. B.) Final French Struggles in India and on the Indian Seas. Including an Account of the Capture of the Isles of France and Bourbon, and Sketches of the most eminent Foreign Adventurers in India up to the period of that Capture. With an Appendix containing an Account of the Expedition from India to Egypt in 1801. By Colonel G. B. MALLESON, C.S.I. Crown 8vo. 10s. 6d.

Malleson (Col. G. B.) History of the Indian Mutiny, 1857-1858, commencing from the close of the Second Volume of Sir John Kaye's History of the Sepoy War. Vol. I. 8vo. With Map. 20s.

CONTENTS. BOOK VII.—Calcutta in May and June.—William Tayler and Vincent Eyre.—How Bihar and Calcutta were saved. BOOK VIII.—Mr. Colvin and Agra.—Jhansi and Bandalkhand.—Colonel Durand and Holkar.—Sir George Lawrence and Rajputana.—Brigadier Polwhele's great battle and its results.—Bareli, Rohilkhand, and Farakhabad. BOOK IX.—The relation of the annexation of Oudh to the Mutiny.—Sir Henry Lawrence and the Mutiny in Oudh.—The siege of Lakhnao.—The first relief of Lakhnao.

VOL. II.—Including the Storming of Delhi, the Relief of Lucknow, the Two Battles of Cawnpore, the Campaign in Rohilkhand, and the movements of the several Columns in the N.W. Provinces, the Azimgurh District, and on the Eastern and South-Eastern Frontiers. 8vo. With 4 Plans. 20s.

VOL. III.—In the Press.

Malleson (Col. G. B.) History of Afghanistan, from the Earliest Period to the Outbreak of the War of 1878. 8vo. 2nd Edition. With Map. 18s.

Malleson (Col. G. B.) Herat: The Garden and Granary of Central Asia. With Map and Index. 8vo. 8s.

Manning (Mrs.) Ancient and Mediæval India.
Being the History, Religion, Laws, Caste, Manners and Customs, Language, Literature, Poetry, Philosophy, Astronomy, Algebra, Medicine, Architecture, Manufactures, Commerce, &c., of the Hindus, taken from their writings. Amongst the works consulted and gleaned from may be named the Rig Veda, Sama Veda, Yajur Veda, Sathapatha Brahmana, Bhagavat Gita, The Puranas, Code of Manu, Code of Yajnavalkya, Mitakshara, Daya Bhaga, Mahabharata, Atriya, Charaka, Susruta, Ramayana, Raghu Vansa, Bhattikavya, Sakuntala, Vikramorvasi, Malati and Madhava, Mudra Rakshasa, Ratnavali, Kumara Sambhava, Prabodha, Chandrodaya, Megha Duta, Gita Govinda, Panchatantra, Hitopadesa, Katha Sarit Sagara, Ketala, Panchavinsati, Dasa Kumara Charita, &c. By Mrs. MANNING, with Illustrations. 2 vols., 8vo. 30s.

Mayhew (Edward) Illustrated Horse Doctor.
Being an Accurate and Detailed Account, accompanied by more than 400 Pictorial Representations, characteristic of the various Diseases to which the Equine Race are subjected; together with the latest Mode of Treatment, and all the requisite Prescriptions written in Plain English. By EDWARD MAYHEW, M.R.C.V.S. 8vo. 18s. 6d.

CONTENTS.—The Brain and Nervous System.—The Eyes.—The Mouth.—The Nostrils.—The Throat.—The Chest and its contents.—The Stomach, Liver, &c.—The Abdomen.—The Urinary Organs.—The Skin.—Specific Diseases.—Limbs.—The Feet.—Injuries.—Operations.

"The book contains nearly 600 pages of valuable matter, which reflects great credit on its author, and, owing to its practical details, the result of deep scientific research, deserves a place in the library of medical, veterinary, and non-professional readers."—*Field.*

"The book furnishes at once the bane and the antidote, as the drawings show the horse not only suffering from every kind of disease, but in the different stages of it, while the alphabetical summary at the end gives the cause, symptoms and treatment of each."—*Illustrated London News.*

Mayhew (Edward) Illustrated Horse Management.
Containing descriptive remarks upon Anatomy, Medicine, Shoeing, Teeth, Food, Vices, Stables; likewise a plain account

of the situation, nature, and value of the various points; together with comments on grooms, dealers, breeders, breakers, and trainers; Embellished with more than 400 engravings from original designs made expressly for this work. By E. MAYHEW. A new Edition, revised and improved by J. J. LUPTON, M.R.C.V.S. 8vo. 12s.

CONTENTS.—The body of the horse anatomically considered. PHYSIC.—The mode of administering it, and minor operations. SHOEING.—Its origin, its uses, and its varieties. THE TEETH. —Their natural growth, and the abuses to which they are liable. FOOD.—The fittest time for feeding, and the kind of food which the horse naturally consumes. The evils which are occasioned by modern stables. The faults inseparable from stables. The so-called "incapacitating vices," which are the results of injury or of disease. Stables as they should be. GROOMS.—Their prejudices, their injuries, and their duties. POINTS.—Their relative importance and where to look for their development. BREEDING.—Its inconsistencies and its disappointments. BREAKING AND TRAINING.—Their errors and their results.

Mayhew (Henry) German Life and Manners.
As seen in Saxony. With an account of Town Life—Village Life—Fashionable Life—Married Life—School and University Life, &c. Illustrated with Songs and Pictures of the Student Customs at the University of Jena. By HENRY MAYHEW, 2 vols., 8vo., with numerous illustrations. 18s.

A Popular Edition of the above. With illustrations. Cr. 8vo. 7s.
"Full of original thought and observation, and may be studied with profit by both German and English—especially by the German."*Athenæum.*

McCosh (J.) Advice to Officers in India.
By JOHN McCOSH, M.D. Post 8vo. 8s.

Meadow (T.) Notes on China.
Desultory Notes on the Government and People of China and on the Chinese Language. By T. T. MEADOWS. 8vo. 9s.

Military Works—chiefly issued by the Government.
Field Exercises and Evolutions of Infantry. Pocket edition, 1s.
Queen's Regulations and Orders for the Army. Corrected to 1874. 8vo. 3s. 6d. Interleaved, 5s. 6d. Pocket Edition, 1s.
Musketry Regulations, as used at Hythe. 1s.
Dress Regulations for the Army. 1875. 1s. 6d.

Infantry Sword Exercise. 1875. 6d.

Infantry Bugle Sounds. 6d.

Handbook of Battalion Drill. By Lieut. H. C. SLACK. 2s; or with Company Drill, 2s. 6d.

Handbook of Brigade Drill. By Lieut. H. C. SLACK. 3s.

Red Book for Sergeants. By WILLIAM BRIGHT, Colour-Sergeant, 37th Middlesex R.V. 1s.

Handbook of Company Drill; also of Skirmishing, Battalion, and Shelter Trench Drill. By Lieut. CHARLES SLACK. 1s.

Elementary and Battalion Drill. Condensed and Illustrated, together with duties of Company Officers, Markers, &c., in Battalion. By Captain MALTON. 2s. 6d.

Cavalry Regulations. For the Instruction, Formations, and Movements of Cavalry. Royal 8vo. 4s. 6d.

Cavalry Sword, Carbine, Pistol and Lance Exercises, together with Field Gun Drill. Pocket Edition. 1s.

Manual of Artillery Exercises. 1873. 8vo. 5s.

Manual of Field Artillery Exercises. 1877. 3s.

Standing Orders for Royal Artillery. 8vo, 3s.

Principles and Practice of Modern Artillery. By Lt.-Col. C. H. OWEN, R.A. 8vo. Illustrated. 15s.

Artillerist's Manual and British Soldiers' Compendium. By Major F. A. GRIFFITHS. 11th Edition. 5s.

Compendium of Artillery Exercises—Smooth Bore, Field, and Garrison Artillery for Reserve Forces. By Captain J. M. McKenzie. 3s. 6d.

Principles of Gunnery. By JOHN T. HYDE, M.A., late Professor of Fortification and Artillery, Royal Indian Military College, Addiscombe. Second edition, revised and enlarged. With many Plates and Cuts, and Photograph of Armstrong Gun. Royal 8vo. 14s.

Notes on Gunnery. By Captain Goodeve. Revised Edition. 1s.

Text Book of the Construction and Manufacture of Rifled Ordnance in the British Service. By STONEY & JONES. Second Edition. Paper, 3s. 6d., Cloth, 4s. 6d.

Handbooks of the 9, 16, and 64-Pounder R. M. L. Converted Guns. 6d. each.

Handbook of the 9 and 10-inch R. M. L. Guns. 6d. each.

Handbook of 40-Pounder B. L. Gun. 6d.

Handbooks of 9-inch Rifle Muzzle Loading Guns of 12 tons, and the 10-inch gun of 18 tons. 6d. each.

Treatise on Fortification and Artillery. By Major HECTOR STRAITH. Revised and re-arranged by THOMAS COOK, R.N., by JOHN T. HYDE, M.A. 7th Edition. Royal 8vo. Illustrated and Four Hundred Plans, Cuts, &c. £2 2s.

Military Surveying and Field Sketching. The Various Methods of Contouring, Levelling, Sketching without Instruments, Scale of Shade, Examples in Military Drawing, &c., &c., &c. As at present taught in the Military Colleges. By Major W. H. RICHARDS, 55th Regiment, Chief Garrison Instructor in India, Late Instructor in Military Surveying, Royal Military College, Sandhurst. Second Edition, Revised and Corrected. 12s.

Treatise on Military Surveying; including Sketching in the Field, Plan-Drawing, Levelling, Military Reconnaissance, &c. By Lieut.-Col. BASIL JACKSON, late of the Royal Staff Corps. The Fifth Edition. 8vo. Illustrated by Plans, &c. 14s.

Instruction in Military Engineering. Vol. 1., Part III. 4s.

Elementary Principles of Fortification. A Text-Book for Military Examinations. By J. T. HYDE, M.A. Royal 8vo. With numerous Plans and Illustrations. 10s. 6d.

Military Train Manual. 1s.

The Sappers' Manual. Compiled for the use of Engineer Volunteer Corps. By Col. W. A. FRANKLAND, R.E. With numerous Illustrations. 2s.

Ammunition. A descriptive treatise on the different Projectiles Charges, Fuzes, Rockets, &c., at present in use for Land and Sea Service, and on other war stores manufactured in the Royal Laboratory. 6s.

Hand-book on the Manufacture and Proof of Gunpowder, as carried on at the Royal Gunpowder Factory, Waltham Abbey. 5s.

Regulations for the Training of Troops for service in the Field and for the conduct of Peace Manœuvres. 2s.

Hand-book Dictionary for the Militia and Volunteer Services, Containing a variety of useful information, Alphabetically arranged. Pocket size, 3s. 6d.; by post, 3s. 8d.

Gymnastic Exercises, System of Fencing, and Exercises for the Regulation Clubs. In one volume. Crown 8vo. 1877. 2s.

Army Equipment. Prepared at the Topographical and Statistical Department, War Office. By Col. Sir HENRY JAMES, R.E., F.R.S., &c., Director.

    PART. 1.—*Cavalry.* Compiled by Lieut. H. M. HOZIER, 2nd Life Guards. Royal 8vo. 4s.
    PART 4.—*Military Train.* Compiled by Lieut. H. M. HOZIER, 2nd Life Guards. Royal 8vo. 2s. 6d.
    PART 5.—*Infantry.* Compiled by Capt. F. MARTIN PETRIE. Royal 8vo. With Plates. 5s.

PART 6.—*Commissariat.* Compiled by Lieut. H. M. HOZIER, 2nd Life Guards. Royal 8vo. 1s. 6d.
PART 7.—*Hospital Service.* Compiled by Capt. MARTIN PETRIE. Royal 8vo. With Plates. 5s.

Text-Book on the Theory and Motion of Projectiles; the History, Manufacture, and Explosive Force of Gunpowder; the History of Small Arms. For Officers sent to School of Musketry. 1s. 6d.

Notes on Ammunition. 4th Edition. 1877. 2s. 6d.

Regulations and Instructions for Encampments. 6d.

Rules for the Conduct of the War Game. 2s.

Medical Regulations for the Army, Instructions for the Army, Comprising duties of Officers, Attendants, and Nurses, &c. 1s. 6d.

Purveyors' Regulations and Instructions, for Guidance of Officers of Purveyors' Department of the Army. 3s.

Priced Vocabulary of Stores used in Her Majesty's Service. 4s.

Transport of Sick and Wounded Troops. By DR. LONGMORE. 5s.

Precedents in Military Law. By LT-COL. W. HOUGH. 8vo. 25s.

The Practice of Courts-Martial, by HOUGH & LONG. 8vo. 26s.

Manual of Military Law. For all ranks of the Army, Militia, and Volunteer Services. By Colonel J. K. PIPON, and J. F. COLLIER, Esq. Third and Revised Edition. Pocket size. 5s.

Regulations applicable to the European Officer in India. Containing Staff Corps Rules, Staff Salaries, Commands, Furlough and Retirement Regulations, &c. By GEORGE E. COCHRANE, late Assistant Military Secretary, India Office. 1 vol., post 8vo. 7s. 6d.

Reserve Force; Guide to Examinations, for the use of Captains and Subalterns of Infantry, Militia, and Rifle Volunteers, and for Serjeants of Volunteers. By Capt. G. H. GREAVES. 2nd edit. 2s.

The Military Encyclopædia; referring exclusively to the Military Sciences, Memoirs of distinguished Soldiers, and the Narratives of Remarkable Battles. By J. H. STOCQUELER. 8vo. 12s.

The Operations of War Explained and Illustrated. By Col. HAMLEY. New Edition Revised, with Plates. Royal 8vo. 30s.

Lessons of War. As taught by the Great Masters and Others; Selected and Arranged from the various operations in War. By FRANCE JAMES SOADY, Lieut.-Col., R.A. Royal 8vo. 21s.

The Soldiers' Pocket Book for Field Service. By Col. SIR GARNET J. WOLSELEY. 2nd Edition. Revised and Enlarged. 4s. 6d.

The Surgeon's Pocket Book, an Essay on the best Treatment of Wounded in War. By, Surgeon Major J. H. PORTER. 7s. 6d.

A Precis of Modern Tactics. By COLONEL HOME. 8vo. 8s. 6d.
Armed Strength of Austria. By Capt. COOKE. 2 pts. £1 2s.
Armed Strength of Denmark. 3s.
Armed Strength of Russia. Translated from the German. 7s.
Armed Strength of Sweden and Norway. 3s. 6d.
Armed Strength of Italy. 5s. 6d.
Armed Strength of Germany. Part I. 8s. 6d.
The Franco-German War of 1870—71. By CAPT. C. H. CLARKE. Vol. I. £1 6s. Sixth Section. 5s. Seventh Section 6s. Eighth Section. 3s. Ninth Section. 4s. 6d. Tenth Section. 6s. Eleventh Section. 5s. 3d. Twelfth Section. 4s. 6d.
The Campaign of 1866 in Germany. Royal 8vo. With Atlas, 21s.
Celebrated Naval and Military Trials By PETER BURKE. Post 8vo., cloth. 10s. 6d.
Military Sketches. By SIR LASCELLES WRAXALL. Post 8vo. 6s.
Military Life of the Duke of Wellington. By JACKSON and SCOTT. 2 Vols. 8vo. Maps, Plans, &c. 12s.
Single Stick Exercise of the Aldershot Gymnasium. 6d.
Treatise on Military Carriages, and other Manufactures of the Royal Carriage Department. 5s.
Steppe Campaign Lectures. 2s.
Manual of Instructions for Army Surgeons. 1s
Regulations for Army Hospital Corps. 9d.
Manual of Instructions for Non-Commissioned Officers, Army Hospital Corps. 2s.
Handbook for Military Artificers. 3s.
Instructions for the use of Auxiliary Cavalry. 2s. 6d.
Equipment Regulations for the Army. 5s. 6d.
Statute Law relating to the Army. 1s. 3d.
Regulations for Commissariat and Ordnance Department 2s.
Regulations for the Commissariat Department. 1s. 6d.
Regulations for the Ordnance Department. 1s. 6d.
Artillerist's Handbook of Reference for the use of the Royal and Reserve Artillery, by WILL and DALTON. 5s.
An Essay on the Principles and Construction of Military Bridges, by SIR HOWARD DOUGLAS. 1853. 15s.

Mill's History of British India,
With Notes and Continuation. By H. H. WILSON. 9 vols. cr. 8vo. £2 10s.

Morgan's (Lady) Memoirs.
Autobiography, Diaries and Correspondence. 2 Vols. 8vo., with Portraits. 18s.

Morrison (Rev. R.) View of China,
For Philological Purposes. Containing a Sketch of Chinese Chronology, Geography, Government, Religion, and Customs. Designed for the use of Persons who study the Chinese Language. By Rev. R. MORRISON. 4to. Macao, 1817. 6s.

Muller's (Max) Rig-Veda-Sanhita.
The Sacred Hymns of the Brahmins; together with the Commentary of Sayanacharya. Published under the Patronage of the Right Honourable the Secretary of State for India in Council. 6 vols., 4to. £2 10s. per volume.

Mysteries of the Vatican;
Or Crimes of the Papacy. From the German of DR. THEODORE GREISENGER. 2 Vols. post 8vo. 21s.

Nirgis and Bismillah.
NIRGIS; a Tale of the Indian Mutiny, from the Diary of a Slave Girl: and BISMILLAH; or, Happy Days in Cashmere. By HAFIZ ALLARD. Post 8vo. 10s. 6d.

Notes on the North Western Provinces of India.
By a District Officer. 2nd Edition. Post 8vo., cloth. 5s.
    CONTENTS.—Area and Population.—Soils.—Crops.—Irrigation.—Rent.—Rates.—Land Tenures.

Osborne (Mrs. W.) Pilgrimage to Mecca (A).
By the Nawab Sikandar Begum of Bhopal. Translated from the Original Urdu. By Mrs. WILLOUGHBY OSBORNE. Followed by a Sketch of the History of Bhopal. By COL. WILLOUGHBY-OSBORNE, C.B. With Photographs, and dedicated, by permission, to HER MAJESTY, QUEEN VICTORIA. Post 8vo. £1. 1s.
This is a highly important book, not only for its literary merit, and the information it contains, but also from the fact of its being the first work written by an Indian lady, and that lady a Queen.

Owen (Sidney) India on the Eve of the British Conquest.
A Historical Sketch. By SIDNEY OWEN, M.A. Reader in Indian Law and History in the University of Oxford. Formerly Professor of History in the Elphinstone College, Bombay. Post 8vo. 8s.

Oxenham (Rev. H. N.) Catholic Eschatology and Universalism. An Essay on the Doctrine of Future Retribution. Second Edition, revised and enlarged. Crown 8vo. 7s. 6d.

Oxenham (Rev. H. N.) Catholic Doctrine of the Atonement. An Historical Inquiry into its Development in the Church, with an Introduction on the Principle of Theological Development. By H. NUTCOMBE OXENHAM, M.A. 2nd Edit. 8vo. 10s. 6d.

"It is one of the ablest and probably one of the most charmingly written treatises on the subject which exists in our language."—*Times.*

Oxenham (H. N.) The First Age of Christianity and the Church. By John Ignatius Döllinger, D.D., Professor of Ecclesiastical History in the University of Munich, &c., &c. Translated from the German by Henry Nutcombe Oxenham, M.A., late Scholar of Baliol College, Oxford. Third Edition. 2 vols. Crown 8vo. 18s.

Ozanam's (A. F.) Civilisation in the Fifth Century. From the French. By The Hon. A. C. GLYN. 2 Vols., post 8vo. 21s.

Pebody (Charles) Authors at Work. Francis Jeffrey—Sir Walter Scott—Robert Burns—Charles Lamb—R. B. Sheridan—Sydney Smith—Macaulay—Byron Wordsworth—Tom Moore—Sir James Mackintosh. Post 8vo. 10s. 6d.

Pelly (Sir Lewis). The Miracle Play of Hasan and Husain. Collected from Oral Tradition by Colonel Sir LEWIS PELLY, K.C.B., K.C.S.I., formerly serving in Persia as Secretary of Legation, and Political Resident in the Persian Gulf. Revised, with Explanatory Notes, by ARTHUR N. WOLLASTON, H.M. Indian (Home) Service, Translator of Anwar-i-Suhaili, &c. 2 Vols. royal 8vo. 32s.

Pipon and Collier's Manual of Military Law. By Colonel J. K. PIPON, and J. F. COLLIER, Esq., of the Inner Temple, Barrister-at-Law. 5s.

Pollock (Field Marshal Sir George) Life & Correspondence. By C. R. Low. 8vo. With portrait. 18s.

Pope (G. U.) Text-book of Indian History; with Geographical Notes, Genealogical Tables, Examination Questions, and Chronological, Biographical, Geographical, and General Indexes. For the use of Schools, Colleges, and Private Students. By the Rev. G. U. POPE, D.D., Principal of Bishop

Cotton's Grammar School and College, Bangalore; Fellow of the Madras University. Third Edition, thoroughly revised. Fcap. 4to. 12s.

Practice of Courts Martial.
By Hough & Long. 8vo. London. 1825. 26s.

Prichard's Chronicles of Budgepore, &c.
Or Sketches of Life in Upper India. 2 Vols., Foolscap 8vo. 12s.

Prinsep (H. T.) Historical Results.
Deducible from Recent Discoveries in Affghanistan. By H. T. Prinsep. 8vo. Lond. 1844. 15s.

Prinsep (H. T.) Tibet, Tartary, and Mongolia.
By Henry T. Prinsep, Esq. Second edition. Post 8vo. 5s.

Prinsep (H. T.) Political and Military Transactions in India.
2 Vols. 8vo. London, 1825. 18s.

Raverty (Major H. G.) The Pus'hto Manual; comprising a Condensed Grammar, with Idiomatic Phrases, Exercises and Dialogues, and Vocabulary. By Major H. G. Raverty, Bombay Army, Retired List. Fcap. 5s.

Richards (Major W. H.) Military Surveying, &c.
12s. (See page 20.)

Sanderson (G. P.) Thirteen Years among the Wild Beasts of India; their Haunts and Habits, from Personal Observation; with an account of the Modes of Capturing and Taming Wild Elephants. By G. P. Sanderson, Officer in Charge of the Government Elephant Keddahs at Mysore. With 21 full page Illustrations and three Maps. Second Edition. Fcp. 4to. £1 5s.

Sewell (R.) Analytical History of India.
From the earliest times to the Abolition of the East India Company in 1858. By Robert Sewell, Madras Civil Service. Post 8vo. 8s.

*** The object of this work is to supply the want which has been felt by students for a condensed outline of Indian History which would serve at once to recall the memory and guide the eye, while at the same time it has been attempted to render it interesting to the general reader by preserving a medium between a bare analysis and a complete history.

Sherer (J. W.) Who is Mary?
A Cabinet Novel, in one volume. By J. W. Sherer, Esq., C.S.I. 10s. 6d.

Simpson (H. T.) Archæologia Adelensis; or a History of the Parish of Adel, in the West Riding of Yorkshire. Being an attempt to delineate its Past and Present Associations, Archæological, Topographical, and Scriptural. By HENRY TRAILL SIMPSON, M.A., late Rector of Adel. With numerous etchings by W. LLOYD FERGUSON. Roy. 8vo. 21s.

Starling (M. H.) Indian Criminal Law and Procedure.
Third edition. 8vo. £2 2s. See page 12.

Steele (A.) Law and Customs of Hindu Castes.
BY ARTHUR STEELE. Royal 8vo. £1. 1s. (See page 12.)

Stent (G. C.) Entombed Alive,
And other Songs and Ballads. (From the Chinese.) By GEORGE CARTER STENT, M.R.A.S., of the Chinese Imperial Maritime Customs Service, author of "Chinese and English Vocabulary," "Chinese and English Pocket Dictionary," "The Jade Chaplet," &c. Crown 8vo. With four Illustrations. 9s.

Strange's (Sir T.) Hindu Law.
2 Vols. Royal 8vo. 1830. 24s. (See page 12.)

Thomson's Lunar and Horary Tables.
For New and Concise Methods of Performing the Calculations necessary for ascertaining the Longitude by Lunar Observations, or Chronometers; with directions for acquiring a knowledge of the Principal Fixed Stars and finding the Latitude of them. By DAVID THOMSON. Sixty-fifth edit. Royal 8vo. 10s.

Thornton's History of India.
The History of the British Empire in India, by Edward Thornton, Esq. Containing a Copious Glossary of Indian Terms, and a Complete Chronological Index of Events, to aid the Aspirant for Public Examinations. Third edition. 1 vol. 8vo. With Map. 12s.

*** *The Library Edition of the above in 6 volumes, 8vo., may be had, price £2. 8s.*

Thornton's Gazetteer of India.
Compiled chiefly from the records at the India Office. By EDWARD THORNTON. 1 vol., 8vo., pp. 1015. With Map. 21s.

*** *The chief objects in view in compiling this Gazetteer are:—*
1st. To fix the relative position of the various cities, towns, and villages with as much precision as possible, and to exhibit with the greatest practicable brevity all that is known respecting them; and
2ndly. To note the various countries, provinces, or territorial divisions, and

to describe the physical characteristics of each, together with their statistical, social, and political circumstances.

To these are added minute descriptions of the principal rivers and chains of mountains; thus presenting to the reader, within a brief compass, a mass of information which cannot otherwise be obtained, except from a multiplicity of volumes and manuscript records.

The Library Edition.
4 vols., 8vo. Notes, Marginal References, and Map. £2 16s.

Thornton (E.) Gazetteer of the Punjaub, Affghanistan, &c.
Gazetteer of the Countries adjacent to India, on the northwest, including Scinde, Affghanistan, Beloochistan, the Punjaub, and the neighbouring States. By EDWARD THORNTON, Esq. 2 vols. 8vo. £1 5s.

Thornton (T.) East India Calculator.
By T. THORNTON. 8vo. London, 1823. 10s.

Thornton (T.) History of the Punjaub,
And of the Rise, Progress, and Present Condition of the Sikhs. By T. THORNTON. 2 Vols. Post 8vo. 8s.

Tilley (H. A.) Japan, the Amoor and the Pacific.
With notices of other Places, comprised in a Voyage of Circumnavigation in the Imperial Russian Corvette *Rynda*, in 1858—1860. By HENRY A. TILLEY. Eight Illustrations. 8vo. 16s.

Tod (Col. Jas.) Travels in Western India.
Embracing a visit to the Sacred Mounts of the Jains, and the most Celebrated Shrines of Hindu Faith between Rajpootana and the Indus, with an account of the Ancient City of Nehrwalla. By the late Lieut.-Col. JAMES TOD, Illustrations. Royal 4to. £3 3s.
⁎ *This is a companion volume to Colonel Tod's Rajasthan.*

Trimen (Capt. R.) Regiments of the British Army,
Chronologically arranged. Showing their History, Services, Uniform, &c. By Captain R. TRIMEN, late 35th Regiment. 8vo. 10s. 6d.

Trotter (L. J.) History of India.
The History of the British Empire in India, from the Appointment of Lord Hardinge to the Death of Lord Canning (1844 to 1862). By Captain LIONEL JAMES TROTTER, late Bengal Fusiliers. 2 vols. 8vo. 16s. each.

Trotter (L. J.) Warren Hastings, a Biography.
By Captain LIONEL JAMES TROTTER, Bengal H. P., author of a "History of India," "Studies in Biography," &c. Crown 8vo. 9s.

Turkish Cookery Book (The).
A Collection of Receipts from the best Turkish Authorities. Done into English by FARABI EFENDI. 12mo. Cloth. 3s. 6d.

Vambery (A.) Sketches of Central Asia.
Additional Chapters on My Travels and Adventures, and of the Ethnology of Central Asia. By Armenius Vambery. 8vo. 16s.
"A valuable guide on almost untrodden ground."--*Athenæum.*

Waring (E. J.) Pharmacopœia of India.
By EDWARD JOHN WARING, M.D., &c. 8vo. 6s. (See page 2.)

Watson (M.) Money.
By JULES TARDIEU. Translated from the French by MARGARET WATSON. Crown 8vo. 7s. 6d.

Watson (Dr. J. Forbes) Textile Manufactures and Costumes
of the People of India. As originally prepared under the Authority of the Secretary of State for India in Council. By J. FORBES WATSON, M.A., M.D., F.R.A.S., Reporter on the Products of India. Folio, half-morocco. With numerous Coloured Photographs. £3. 5s.

This work—by affording a key to the Fashions of the People, and to the Cotton, Silk, and Wool Textiles in actual use in India—is of special interest to Manufacturers, Merchants, and Agents; as also to the Student and lover of ornamental art.

Watson (Dr. J. F.) and J. W. Kaye, Races and Tribes of
Hindostan. The People of India. A series of Photographic Illustrations of the Races and Tribes of Hindustan. Prepared under the Authority of the Government of India, by J. FORBES WATSON, and JOHN WILLIAM KAYE. The Work contains about 450 Photographs on mounts, in Eight Volumes, super royal 4to. £2. 5s. per volume.

Webb (Dr. A.) Pathologia Indica.
Based upon Morbid Specimens from all parts of the Indian Empire. By ALLAN WEBB, B.M.S. Second Edit. 8vo. 14s.

Wellesley's Despatches.
The Despatches, Minutes, and Correspondence of the Marquis Wellesley, K.G., during his Administration in India. 5 vols. 8vo. With Portrait, Map, &c. £6. 10s.

This work should be perused by all who proceed to India in the Civil Services.

Wellington in India.
Military History of the Duke of Wellington in India. 1s.

Wilberforce (Edward) Social Life in Munich.
By EDWARD WILBERFORCE, Second Edition. Post 8vo. 6s.
"A very able volume. Mr. Wilberforce is a very pleasant and agreeable writer whose opinion is worth hearing on the subject of modern art which enters largely into the matter of his discourse."—*Saturday Review*

Wilberforce (E.) Franz Schubert.
A Musical Biography, from the German of Dr. Heinrich Kreisle von Hellborn. By EDWARD WILBERFORCE, Esq., Author of "Social Life in Munich." Post 8vo. 6s.

Wilk's South of India.
3 vols. 4to. £5. 5s.

Wilkins (W. N.) Visual Art; or Nature through the Healthy Eye.
With some remarks on Originality and Free Trade, Artistic Copyright, and Durability. By WM. NOY WILKINS, Author of "Art Impressions of Dresden," &c. 8vo. 6s.

Williams (F.) Lives of the English Cardinals.
The Lives of the English Cardinals, from Nicholas Breakspeare (Pope Adrien IV.) to Thomas Wolsey, Cardinal Legate. With Historical Notices of the Papal Court. By FOLKESTONE WILLIAMS. 2 vols., 8vo. 14s.

Williams (F.) Life, &c., of Bishop Atterbury.
The Memoir and Correspondence of Francis Atterbury, Bishop of Rochester, with his distinguished contemporaries. Compiled chiefly from the Atterbury and Stuart Papers. By FOLKESTONE WILLIAMS, Author of "Lives of the English Cardinals," &c., 2 vols. 8vo. 14s.

Williams (Monier) Indian Wisdom.
Or Examples of the Religious, Philosophical and Ethical Doctrines of the Hindus. With a brief History of the Chief Departments of Sanscrit Literature, and some account of the Past and Present Condition of India, Moral and Intellectual. By MONIER WILLIAMS, M.A., Boden Professor of Sanscrit in in the University of Oxford. Third Edition. 8vo. 15s.

Wilson (H. H.) Glossary of Judicial and Revenue Terms, and of useful Words occurring in Official Documents relating to the Administration of the Government of British India. From the Arabic, Persian, Hindustani, Sanskrit, Hindi, Bengali, Uriya, Marathi, Guzarathi, Telugu, Karnata, Tamil, Malayalam, and other Languages. Compiled and published under the authority of the Hon. the Court of Directors of the E. I. Company. 4to., cloth. £1 10s.

Wollaston (Arthur N.) Anwari Suhaili, or Lights of Canopus
Commonly known as Kalilah and Damnah, being an adaptation of the Fables of Bidpai. Translated from the Persian. Royal 8vo., 42s.: also in royal 4to., with illuminated borders, designed specially for the work, cloth, extra gilt. £3 13s. 6d.

Wollaston (Arthur N.) Elementary Indian Reader.
Designed for the use of Students in the Anglo-Vernacular Schools in India. Fcap. 1s.

Woolrych (Serjeant W. H.)
Lives of Eminent Serjeants-at-Law of the English Bar. By Humphry W. Woolrych, Serjeant-at-Law. 2 vols. 8vo. 30s.

Wraxall (Sir L., Bart.) Caroline Matilda.
Queen of Denmark, Sister of George 3rd. From Family and State Papers. By Sir Lascelles Wraxall, Bart. 3 vols., 8vo. 18s.

Wraxall (Sir L., ar) Military Sketches.
By Sir Lascelles Wraxall, Bart. Post 8vo. 6s.
"The book is clever and entertaining from first to last."—*Athenæum.*

Wraxall (Sir L., Bart.) Scraps & Sketches, Gathered Together.
By Sir Lascelles Wraxall, Bart. 2 vols., Post 8vo. 12s.

Young (J. R.) Course of Mathematics.
A Course of Elementary Mathematics for the use of candidates for admission into either of the Military Colleges; of applicants for appointments in the Home or Indian Civil Services; and of mathematical students generally. By Professor J. R. Young. In one closely-printed volume. 8vo., pp. 648. 12s.

"In the work before us he has digested a complete Elementary Course, by aid of his long experience as a teacher and writer; and he has produced a very useful book. Mr. Young has not allowed his own taste to rule the distribution, but has adjusted his parts with the skill of a veteran."—*Athenæum.*

A SELECTION FROM

MESSRS. ALLEN'S CATALOGUE

OF BOOKS IN THE EASTERN LANGUAGES, &c.

HINDUSTANI, HINDI, &c.

[*Dr. Forbes's Works are used as Class Books in the Colleges and Schools in India.*]

Forbes's Hindustani-English Dictionary in the Persian Character, with the Hindi words in Nagari also; and an English Hindustani Dictionary in the English Character; both in one volume. By Duncan Forbes, LL.D. Royal 8vo. 42s.

Forbes's Hindustani-English and English Hindustani Dictionary, in the English Character. Royal 8vo. 36s.

Forbes's Smaller Dictionary, Hindustani and English, in the English Character. 12s.

Forbes's Hindustani Grammar, with Specimens of Writing in the Persian and Nagari Characters, Reading Lessons, and Vocabulary. 8vo. 10s. 6d.

Forbes's Hindustani Manual, containing a Compendious Grammar, Exercises for Translation, Dialogues, and Vocabulary, in the Roman Character. New Edition, entirely revised. By J. T. Platts. 18mo. 3s. 6d.

Forbes's Bagh o Bahar, in the Persian Character, with a complete Vocabulary. Royal 8vo. 12s. 6d.

Forbes's Bagh o Bahar in English, with Explanatory Notes, illustrative of Eastern Character. 8vo. 8s.

Forbes's Bagh o Bahar, with Vocaby. English Character. 5s.

Forbes's Tota Kahani; or, "Tales of a Parrot," in the Persian Character, with a complete Vocabulary. Royal 8vo. 8s.

Forbes's Baital Pachisi; or, "Twenty-five Tales of a Demon," in the Nagari Character, with a complete Vocabulary. Royal 8vo. 9s.

Forbes's Ikhwanu s Safa; or, "Brothers of Purity," in the Persian Character. Royal 8vo. 12s. 6d.

[*For the higher standard for military officers' examinations.*]

Forbes's Oriental Penmanship; a Guide to Writing Hindustani in the Persian Character. 4to. 8s.

Platts' Grammar of the Urdu or Hindustani-Language. 8vo. 12s.

Eastwick (Edward B.) The Bagh-o-Bahar—literally translated into English, with copious explanatory notes. 8vo. 10s. 6d.

Small's (Rev. G.) Tota Kahani; or, "Tales of a Parrot." Translated into English. 8vo. 8s.

Platts' J. T., Baital Pachisi; translated into English. 8vo. 8s.

Platts' Ikhwanu S Safa; translated into English. 8vo. 10s. 6d.

Hindustani Selections, with a Vocabulary of the Words. By JAMES R. BALLANTYNE. Second Edition. 1845. 5s.

Singhasan Battisi. Translated into Hindi from the Sanscrit. A New Edition. Revised, Corrected, and Accompanied with Copious Notes. By SYED ABDOOLAH. Royal 8vo. 12s. 6d.

Robertson's Hindustani Vocabulary. 3s. 6d.

Akhlaki Hindi, translated into Urdu, with an Introduction and Notes. By SYED ABDOOLAH. Royal 8vo. 12s. 6d.

Sakuntala. Translated into Hindi from the Bengali recension of the Sanskrit. Critically edited, with grammatical, idiomatical, and exegetical notes, by FREDERIC PINCOTT. 4to. 12s. 6d.

SANSCRIT.

Haughton's Sanscrit and Bengali Dictionary, in the Bengali Character, with Index, serving as a reversed dictionary. 4to. 30s.

Williams's English-Sanscrit Dictionary. 4to., cloth. £3. 3s.

Williams's Sanskrit-English Dictionary. 4to. £4 14s. 6d.

Wilkin's (Sir Charles) Sanscrit Grammar. 4to. 15s.

Williams's (Monier) Sanscrit Grammar. 8vo. 15s.

Williams's (Monier) Sanscrit Manual; to which is added, a Vocabulary, by A. E. GOUGH. 18mo. 7s. 6d.

Gough's (A. E.) Key to the Exercises in Williams's Sanscrit Manual. 18mo. 4s.

Williams's (Monier) Sakuntala, with Literal English Translation of all the Metrical Passages, Schemes of the Metres, and copious Critical and Explanatory Notes. Royal 8vo. 21s.

Williams's (Monier) Sakuntala. Translated into English Prose and Verse. Fourth Edition. 8s.

Williams's (Monier) Vikramorvasi. The Text. 8vo. 5s.

Cowell's (E B.) Translation of the Vikramorvasi. 8vo. 3s. 6d.

Thompson's (J. C.) Bhagavat Gita. Sanscrit Text. 5s.
Haughton's Menu, with English Translation. 2 vols. 4to. 24s.
Johnson's Hitopadesa, with Vocabulary. 15s.
Hitopadesa, Sanscrit, with Bengali and English Trans. 10s. 6d.
Johnson's Hitopadesa, English Translation of the. 4to. 5s.
Wilson's Megha Duta, with Translation into English Verse, Notes, Illustrations, and a Vocabulary. Royal 8vo. 6s.

PERSIAN.

Richardson's Persian, Arabic, and English Dictionary. Edition of 1852. By F. JOHNSON. 4to. £4.

Forbes's Persian Grammar, Reading Lessons, and Vocabulary. Royal 8vo. 12s. 6d.

Ibraheem's Persian Grammar, Dialogues, &c. Royal 8vo. 12s. 6d.

Gulistan. Carefully collated with the original MS., with a full Vocabulary. By JOHN PLATTS, late Inspector of Schools, Central Provinces, India. Royal 8vo. 12s. 6d.

Gulistan. Translated from a revised Text, with Copious Notes. By JOHN PLATTS. 8vo. 12s. 6d.

Ouseley's Anwari Soheili. 4to. 42s.

Wollaston's (Arthur N.) Translation of the Anvari Soheili. Royal 8vo. £2 2s.

Keene's (Rev. H. G.) First Book of The Anwari Soheili. Persian Text. 8vo. 5s.

Ouseley's (Col.) Akhlaki Mushini. Persian Text. 8vo. 5s.

Keene's (Rev. H. G.) Akhlaki Mushini. Translated into English. 8vo. 3s. 6d.

Clarke's (Captain H. Wilberforce, R.E.) The Persian Manual. A Pocket Companion.
    PART I.—A CONCISE GRAMMAR OF THE LANGUAGE, with Exercises on its more Prominent Peculiarities, together with a Selection of Useful Phrases, Dialogues, and Subjects for Translation into Persian.
    PART II.—A VOCABULARY OF USEFUL WORDS, ENGLISH AND PERSIAN, showing at the same time the difference of idiom between the two Languages. 18mo. 7s. 6d.

A Translation of Robinson Crusoe into the Persian Language. Roman Character. Edited by T. W. H. TOLBORT, Bengal Civil Service. Cr. 8vo. 7s.

BENGALI.

Haughton's Bengali, Sanscrit, and English Dictionary, adapted for Students in either language; to which is added an Index, serving as a reversed dictionary. 4to. 30s.

Forbes's Bengali Grammar, with Phrases and dialogues. Royal 8vo. 12s. 6d.

Forbes's Bengali Reader, with a Translation and Vocabulary Royal 8vo. 12s. 6d.

Nabo Nari. 12mo. 7s.

ARABIC.

Richardson's Arabic, Persian and English Dictionary. Edition of 1852. By F. Johnson. 4to., cloth. £4.

Forbes's Arabic Grammar, intended more especially for the use of young men preparing for the East India Civil Service, and also for the use of self instructing students in general. Royal 8vo., cloth. 18s.

Palmer's Arabic Grammar. 8vo. 18s.

Forbes's Arabic Reading Lessons, consisting of Easy Extracts from the best Authors, with Vocabulary. Royal 8vo., cloth. 15s.

Matthew's Translation of the Mishkat-ul-Masābih. 2 vols in 1. By the Rev. T. P. Hughes, Missionary to the Afghans at Peshawur. (*In the press.*)

TELOOGOO.

Brown's Dictionary, reversed; with a Dictionary of the Mixed Dialects used in Teloogoo. 3 vols. in 2, royal 8vo. £5.

Campbell's Dictionary. Royal 8vo. 30s.

Brown's Reader. 8vo. 2 vols. 14s.

Brown's Dialogues, Teloogoo and English. 8vo. 5s. 6d.

Pancha Tantra. 8s.

Percival's English-Teloogoo Dictionary. 10s. 6d.

TAMIL.

Rottler's Dictionary, Tamil and English. 4to. 42s.

Babington's Grammar (High Dialect). 4to. 12s.

Percival's Tamil Dictionary. 2 vols. 10s. 6d.

GUZRATTEE.

Mavor's Spelling, Guzrattee and English. 7s, 6d.
Shapuaji Edalji's Dictionary, Guzrattee and English. 21s.

MAHRATTA.

Molesworth's Dictionary, Mahratta and English. 4to. 42s.
Molesworth's Dictionary, English and Mahratta. 4to. 42s.
Stevenson's Grammar. 8vo., cloth. 17s. 6d.
Esop's Fables. 12mo. 2s. 6d.
Fifth Reading Book. 7s.

MALAY.

Marsden's Grammar. 4to. £1 1s.

CHINESE.

Morrison's Dictionary. 6 vols. 4to. £10.
Marshman's—Clavis Sinica, a Chinese Grammar. 4to. £2 2s.
Morrison's View of China, for Philological purposes; containing a Sketch of Chinese Chronology, Geography, Government, Religion and Customs, designed for those who study the Chinese language. 4to. 6s.

MISCELLANEOUS.

Reeve's English-Carnatica and Carnatica-English Dictionary. 2 vols. (Very slightly damaged). £8.
Collett's Malayalam Reader. 8vo. 12s. 6d.
Esop's Fables in Carnatica. 8vo. bound. 12s. 6d.
A Turkish Manual, comprising a Condensed Grammar with Idiomatic Phrases, Exercises and Dialogues, and Vocabulary. By Captain C. F. MACKENZIE, late of H.M.'s Consular Service. 6s.

A CHRONOLOGICAL AND HISTORICAL

CHART OF INDIA,

Price, fully tinted, mounted on roller or in case, 20s. size, about 40 in. by 50 in.

Showing, at one view, all the principal nations, governments, and empires which have existed in that country from the earliest times to the suppression of the Great Mutiny, A.D. 1858, with the date of each historical event according to the *various eras used in India.*

BY

ARTHUR ALLEN DURTNALL,

Of the High Court of Justice in England.

By this Chart, any person, however ignorant of the subject, may, by an hour's attention, obtain a clear view of the broad lines of Indian History, and of the evolutions which have resulted in the dominion of Her Majesty as EMPRESS OF INDIA. It will be found invaluable for EDUCATIONAL PURPOSES, especially in Colleges and Schools, where an Indian career is in contemplation. It will also be found of PERMANENT UTILITY in all Libraries and Offices as a work of ready reference for the connection of events and dates. Besides the History of India, it includes the contemporaneous histories of AFGHANISTAN, CENTRAL ASIA, and EUROPE.

A RELIEVO MAP OF INDIA.

BY

HENRY F. BRION.

In Frame, 21s.

A map of this kind brings before us such a picture of the surface of a given country as no ordinary map could ever do. To the mind's eye of the average Englishman, India consists of 'the plains' and 'the hills,' chiefly of the former, the hills being limited to the Himalayas and the Nilgiris. The new map will at least enable him to correct his notions of Indian geography. It combines the usual features of a good plain map of the country on a scale of 150 miles to the inch, with a faithful representation of all the uneven surfaces, modelled on a scale thirty-two times the horizontal one; thus bringing out into clear relief the comparative heights and outlines of all the hill-ranges, and showing broad tracts of uneven ground, of intermingled hill and valley, which a common map of the same size would hardly indicate, except to a very practised eye. The plains of Upper India are reduced to their true proportions; the Central Provinces, Malwa, and Western Bengal reveal their actual ruggedness at a glance; and Southern India, from the Vindhyas to Cape Comorin, proclaims its real height above the sea-level. To the historical as well as the geographical student such a map is an obvious and important aid in tracing the course of past campaigns, in realising the conditions under which successive races carried their arms or settlements through the Peninsula, and in comprehending the difference of race, climate, and physical surroundings which make up our Indian Empire. Set in a neat frame of maplewood, the map seems to attract the eye like a prettily-coloured picture, and its price, a guinea, should place it within the reach of all who care to combine the useful with the ornamental."—*Home News.*

MAPS OF INDIA, etc.

Messrs. Allen & Co.'s Maps of India were revised and much improved during 1876, with especial reference to the existing Administrative Divisions, Railways, &c.

District Map of India; corrected to 1876:
  Divided into Collectorates with the Telegraphs and Railways from Government surveys. On six sheets—size, 5ft. 6in. high; 5ft. 8in. wide, £2; in a case, £2 12s. 6d.; or, rollers, varn., £3 3s.

A General Map of India; corrected to 1876:
  Compiled chiefly from surveys executed by order of the Government of India. On six sheets—size, 5 ft. 3 in. wide; 5 ft. 4 in. high, £2; or, on cloth, in case, £2 12s. 6d.; or, rollers, varn., £3 3s.

Map of India; corrected to 1876;
  From the most recent Authorities. On two sheets—size, 2 ft. 10in. wide; 3 ft. 3 in. high, 16s.; or, on cloth, in a case, £1 1s.

Map of the Routes in India; corrected to 1874;
  With Tables of Distances between the principal Towns and Military Stations On one sheet—size, 2 ft. 3 in. wide; 2 ft. 9 in. high, 9s.; or, on cloth, in a case, 12s.

Map of the Western Provinces of Hindoostan,
  The Punjab, Cabool, Scinde, Bhawulpore, &c., including all the States between Candahar and Allahabad. On four sheets—size, 4 ft. 4in. wide; 4 ft. 2 in. high, 30s.; or, in case, £2; rollers, varnished, £2 10s.

Map of India and China, Burmah, Siam, the Malay Peninsula, and the Empire of Anam. On two sheets—size, 4 ft. 3 in. wide; 3 ft. 4 in. high, 16s.; or, on cloth, in a case, £1 5s.

Map of the Steam Communication and Overland Routes between England, India, China, and Australia. In a case, 14s.; on rollers, and varnished, 18s.

Map of China,
  From the most Authentic Sources of Information. One large sheet—size, 2 ft. 7 in. wide; 2 ft. 2 in. high, 6s.; or, on cloth, in case, 8s.

Map of the World;
  On Mercator's Projection, showing the Tracts of the Early Navigators, the Currents of the Ocean, the Principal Lines of great Circle Sailing, and the most recent discoveries. On four sheets—size, 6ft. 2 in. wide; 4 ft. 3 in. high, £2; on cloth, in a case, £2 10s; or, with rollers, and varnished, £3.

Handbook of Reference to the Maps of India.
  Giving the Latitude and Longitude of places of note. 18mo. 3s. 6d.

Russian Official Map of Central Asia. Compiled in accordance with the Discoveries and Surveys of Russian Staff Officers up to the close of the year 1877. In 2 Sheets. 10s. 6d., or in cloth case, 11s.

THE ROYAL KALENDAR,

AND

COURT & CITY REGISTER

FOR

England, Ireland, Scotland, and the Colonies

FOR THE YEAR

1880.

CONTAINING A CORRECT LIST OF THE TWENTY-FIRST IMPERIAL PARLIAMENT, SUMMONED TO MEET FOR THEIR FIRST SESSION—MARCH 5TH, 1874.

House of Peers—House of Commons—Sovereigns and Rulers of States of Europe—Orders of Knighthood—Science and Art Department—Queen's Household—Government Offices—Mint—Customs—Inland Revenue—Post Office—Foreign Ministers and Consuls—Queen's Consuls Abroad—Naval Department—Navy List—Army Department—Army List—Law Courts—Police—Ecclesiastical Department—Clergy List—Foundation Schools—Literary Institutions—City of London—Banks—Railway Companies—Hospital and Institutions—Charities—Miscellaneous Institutions—Scotland, Ireland, India, and the Colonies; and other useful information.

Price with Index, 7s.; without Index, 5s.

Published on the arrival of every Mail from India. Subscription 26s. per annum, post free, specimen copy, 6d.

ALLEN'S INDIAN MAIL,

AND

Official Gazette

FROM

INDIA, CHINA, AND ALL PARTS OF THE EAST.

ALLEN'S INDIAN MAIL contains the fullest and most authentic Reports of all important Occurrences in the Countries to which it is devoted, compiled chiefly from private and exclusive sources. It has been pronounced by the Press in general to be *indispensable* to all who have Friends or Relatives in the East, as affording the only *correct* information regarding the Services, Movements of Troops, Shipping, and all events of Domestic and individual interest.

The subjoined list of the usual Contents will show the importance and variety of the information concentrated in ALLEN'S INDIAN MAIL.

Summary and Review of Eastern News.

Precis of Public Intelligence	Shipping—Arrival of Ships
Selections from the Indian Press	,, ,, Passengers
Movements of Troops	,, Departure of Ships
The Government Gazette	,, ,, Passengers
Courts Martial	Commercial—State of the Markets
Domestic Intelligence—Births	,, Indian Securities
,, ,, Marriages	,, Freights
,, ,, Deaths	&c. &c. &c.

Home Intelligence relating to India, &c.

Original Articles	Arrival reported in England
Miscellaneous Information	Departures ,, ,,
Appointments, List of Furloughs, Extensions, &c.	Shipping—Arrival of Ships
,, Civil	,, ,, Passengers
,, Military	,, Departure of Ships
,, Ecclesiastical and	,, ,, Passengers
,, Marine	,, Vessel spoken with
	&c. &c. &c.

Review of Works on the East.—And Notices of all affairs connected with India and the Services.

Each year an INDEX is furnished, to enable Subscribers to bind up the Volume which forms a complete

ASIATIC ANNUAL REGISTER AND LIBRARY OF REFERENCE.

LONDON: WM. H. ALLEN & Co., 13, WATERLOO PLACE, S.W.

(PUBLISHERS TO THE INDIA OFFICE),

To whom Communications for the Editor, and Advertisements are requested to be addressed.

MESSRS. WM. H. ALLEN & Co.'s
LIST OF FORTHCOMING WORKS.

RUSSIAN CAMPAIGNS AGAINST THE TURKOMANS,
From 1869 to the present time. By C. MARVIN. With Maps, Plans, and Portraits.

THE AFGHAN WAR. GOUGH'S ACTION AT FUTTEHABAD.
By the Rev. C. SWINNERTON, Bengal Chaplain, in the Field with the First Division, Peshawur Valley Field Force.

HISTORY OF THE INDIAN MUTINY, 1857–1858,
Commencing from the close of the Second Volume of Sir John Kaye's History of the Sepoy War. By Colonel G. B. MALLESON, C.S.I. Vol. III.

SKETCHES FROM NIPAL.
By Dr. OLDFIELD.

DESERT LIFE:
Recollections of an Expedition in the Soudan. By B. SOLYMOS.

A PLEASURE TRIP TO INDIA,
During the Visit of H.R.H. the Prince of Wales, and afterwards to Ceylon. By M. E. CORBET.

A CHART OF FAMILY INHERITANCE, ACCORDING TO ORTHODOX MOOHUMMADAN LAW,
With an Explanatory Treatise. By ALMARIC RUMSEY, of Lincoln's Inn, Barrister-at-Law, Professor of Indian Jurisprudence at King's College, London.

THE ARABIC MANUAL,
A Compendium of Classical and Colloquial Arabic. By Prof. E. H. PALMER.

www.ingramcontent.com/pod-product-compliance
Lightning Source LLC
Chambersburg PA
CBHW030425300426
44112CB00009B/853